# HANDBOOK FOR MIDDLE SCHOOL TEACHING

# HANDBOOK FOR MIDDLE SCHOOL TEACHING

**Paul George**

**Gordon Lawrence**

UNIVERSITY OF FLORIDA

**Scott, Foresman and Company**
Glenview, Illinois    London

*Library of Congress Cataloging in Publication Data*

GEORGE, PAUL S.
  Handbook for middle school teaching.

  (Goodyear series in education)
  Includes bibliographical references.
  1. High school teaching.  2. Middle schools.
I. Lawrence, Gordon, 1930–  II. Title.
III. Series
LB1623.G4      373.11'02      81-18234
ISBN  0-673-16024-6          AACR2

ISBN:  0-673-16024-6

15–RRC–9493

TO OUR FAMILIES:

Reisa,
Andy,
Evan,
 and
Cherie,
Karen,
Mark

# CONTENTS

**In most books you can skip the introduction.
Not so with this book.**
The introduction tells you how this book is
different and why, and how to use it.

# Introduction

## WHAT KIND OF BOOK IS THIS?

Teachers, particularly first year teachers, often tell us about a gap they feel between education theory and classroom realities. In their teacher-preparation programs they developed great expectations about teaching and about their own capacities to be good teachers. Then, unfortunately, the realities of classroom life dashed their hopes and dimmed the picture they had. The theory they had studied was inadequate for real teaching responsibilities.

The gap teachers tell about comes largely from an inadequate notion of learning found in many teacher education programs: spectator-learning. Lecturing and using books, films, and demonstrations presume that students learn as spectators. These approaches teach *about* teaching; they present concepts abstracted from teaching behavior. They offer the abstractions as theory to guide future behavior. They do not typically offer participant-learning, the concrete experiencing of teaching behavior.

We have designed this book for participant-learning. Each chapter contains a sequence of activities and readings that reflect our notion of participant-learning. First in the sequence are several questions that highlight the theme of the chapter, some introductory comments or an orientation activity that is meant to offer participant-understanding of what the chapter contains, as well as a statement of the general objectives.

Next you approach some aspect of teaching in a new way, analyze your action using resources given in the chapter, and then move through this cycle again to try out the new skill and strengthen it. Readings, which cover more than half of the pages of the book, are part of the action-reflection cycle. They offer information, new ways of thinking about teaching, and guidelines for action.

The procedures in each chapter give you some options in planning your own learning sequence to fit your learning style and your teaching situation. Most chapters include some activities that require access to a school and opportunities to observe or talk with students. These activities are designated by a schoolhouse. We urge readers to undertake as many of those activities as they can. Each chapter closes with the next steps you might take in skill development and with a bibliography. The emphasis throughout is on your participation-learning, not just on the storing up of knowledge for some future use.

## IS THIS BOOK FOR YOU?

As with all books, this one can be used by anyone who is interested in the topics listed in the contents. Its fullest use, however, will be enjoyed by those who answer yes to all four of these questions:

1. Are you teaching, or expect to teach ten- to fourteen-year-old students?
2. Do you have access to a group of students and do you have the opportunity to introduce new material and procedures with the group?
3. Do you have *time* to work with the students in trying out new teaching skills?
4. Do you have a small group of peers (two, three, or four) with whom you can cooperatively work through this book, planning, analyzing, giving and receiving feedback and support?

The book is designed to guide the practicum portion of preservice teacher education and to be used as a resource for inservice teachers who want to improve their professional skills. As a resource book or handbook, it can be pulled off the shelf to be used in solving teaching problems as they arise. While the chapters are presented in a sequence that satisfies the authors, you need not follow them in the order in which they are presented.

The focus of the book is on teaching in the middle grades—whether these grades are housed in an elementary school, a K-8 or K-12 school, a junior high or a middle school. We believe the teaching skills and procedures appropriate for ten- to fourteen-year-old students do not depend upon grade arrangements but upon basic characteristics of the age group. We have not attempted to deal with all competencies needed for middle level teaching. This is not a comprehensive, general introduction to methods of teaching. It is a guidebook to be used in developing teaching strategies distinctively important for working with ten- to fourteen-year-old students. Our selection of topics is based on many hundreds of hours spent working with teachers in middle grades. We have seen many teachers use the concepts, skills, and procedures that we have written about. It is the students, teachers, and administrators who have shown us what should be included.

The teachers we know have crowded curriculums, cramped schedules, too many things calling for their attention hour by hour. They are hard pressed to find the time for one more set of prescriptions on how to change their teaching. Teachers, please be alerted to our intentions: if it serves you as we intend, this book will not add to your load by asking you to juggle still more teaching tasks. Rather, this book is designed to help you organize teaching in a more comprehensive way freeing your time and energy for student needs and your own needs that have not been met. Our aim for you is more efficiency, a greater sense of accomplishment, more receiving and not just giving, and more support for you in your daily work.

## HOW IS THE BOOK DESIGNED TO BE USED?

The procedures described below call upon users to assume extensive responsibilities for managing their own learning experiences and evaluations. The responsibility is more substantial than is typically found in preservice teacher education programs. We have seen the learner-management system work well in several university settings, so we are confident about the procedures we have written. The book may also be used in an instructor-managed program in which the instructor assigns tasks to learners, monitors and assists their activities, and evaluates student work. Each chapter has been written to accommodate either approach, or a combination of both. Similarly, when used by teachers in service, both self-management and supervisor management are served by the design.

We favor the self-management approach. We believe that when instructors design, plan, and conduct learning experiences for teacher candidates, without the latter's involvement in those processes, the candidates tend to distrust their own judgments and rely heavily on those in authority. We believe that when supervisors take the authority role in managing inservice education, when they diagnose and prescribe for teachers and rate teacher performances, teachers tend to be discouraged from taking initiative and responsibility for continuing their own professional development.

Instructors and supervisors who want to consider the self-management approach should turn to the Appendix, "Learner-Managed Professional Development," and read the introductory pages there. The appendix includes complete guidelines for using each chapter with a learner-management process. Each chapter can also be used just as it reads, but we suggest that the instructor review the activities to see which are feasible in the instruction program.

Finally, we want to emphasize that the purpose of this book is to provide a framework for an individual plan for professional growth, but not to provide the total plan. It can be used as the basis of a formal plan arranged between you and your supervisor or instructor, or it can guide you informally in the development of specific skills. Once you have used the book as described, you will recognize in it a pattern of procedures for continuing your professional development beyond the content of the book.

As you use the book, we sincerely invite you to send us your reactions and suggestions. The ideas we have gathered here have been distilled and developed through the experiences of many teachers. We would value your help in refining them further.

*Paul George*
*Gordon Lawrence*
COLLEGE OF EDUCATION
UNIVERSITY OF FLORIDA
GAINESVILLE, FL  32611

# MATERIALS FOR REPRODUCING

# PART ONE

# The Students

Educators who work with ten- to fourteen-year olds are emphatic: this age group has special characteristics! Teachers readily admit the unique nature of their charges, and school administrators say that the students are the basis for the special features of the school.

In this section we invite you to explore the developmental characteristics of students between the ages of ten and fifteen. This period of life encompasses the transition from childhood to adolescence, a passage increasingly recognized for its significance in the lives of all Americans. Read about, observe, and interact with your students.

We hope that when you have completed this section of the text, you will have a deeper understanding of boys and girls of this age group. The four chapters of the section deal with their intellectual, physical, social, and emotional development and with the practical things teachers can do to enhance this development. These learning experiences are intended to assist you in tailoring your professional efforts more closely to the characteristics of your clients, the students.

# CHAPTER ONE

# CHILDHOOD INTO ADOLESCENCE

Think back for a few minutes to when you were twelve and thirteen years old . . . (If you can, plan to spend fifteen minutes or so reading this page, with enough pauses to let your memory work on these questions.)

- What do you recall about yourself at that time—what occupied your energies, your thoughts, your emotions?
- Describe your physical self at that age—how did you feel about yourself physically?
- What do you remember about your social relationships—with girls and boys of your own age and with adults?
- What activities did you value most? What school-related activities did you value most and least?
- How many of your seventh and eighth grade teachers do you remember as having been important to you? What distinguished those teachers from the ones who were not important to you?

Most likely you answered the last question, in effect, that the important teacher(s) understood your motives, interests, preoccupations, and developmental needs. We strongly believe that an understanding of how children emerge into adolescents is fundamental to successful teaching in the middle grades. These chapters are designed to show what the world is like in the experience of middle level students.

Donald Eichhorn (1966) introduced the term *transescence* to represent the stage of development that begins prior to the onset of puberty and extends through early adolescence. A transescent, then, is a young person in transition from childhood into adolescence. We find the term helpful even though it feels awkward when first encountered. It conveys an important message: Young people to whom it refers share a pattern of development probably as distinctive as those to whom the terms *adolescents* or *infants* are applied. This is a developmental group that educators and others need to differentiate from the younger and older groups.

Chapter One has been designed to describe transescents "in the round," that is, to convey a feeling for the thinking, growing, feeling, changing transescent. It sketches with broad strokes what life is like for them and highlights the characteristics that distinguish them from younger and older groups. It will help you see how the physical, intellectual, social, and emotional processes of development in transescents are facets of a whole pattern that is not really divisible. Finally, Chapter One will help you identify ways in which a school does and does not serve some basic developmental needs of students.

## ACTIVITY 1
### Read two autobiographical sketches.

Here are two brief essays written by adults looking back on their transescent years. Do they reflect some of your own experiences?

## Autobiography of a Transescent Boy

(What) were we doing in that progressive school? One moment we were locked away, just the boys, with our science teacher whose legendary ways and white coat made him the only one in the world to answer our questions about the universe and about sex. We had access to a little red question box which was safeguarded by a delicate but trustworthy silver lock. Anyone could write a question, deposit it unsigned, and find out whatever he wanted to know about boys and girls together—about sex. Come to think of it, it *was* a progressive school, even though the sexes were segregated during these juicy question and answer sessions . . .

The one question which I remember and how it stayed with me and how I couldn't wait to make an empirical test of it because Mr. M. said, I won't answer this, find out on your own, was: Is it normal for your heart to kind of flutter or beat unevenly (I think those were the words that someone had written) when you urinate? The problem was that it never was resolved. Was it or was it not normal? Some of the boys agreed it happened, although no one dared to speak about how foolish they looked pulling up their shirts to examine their stomachs, which meant, of course, taking their minds off their business. Some boys were so fat they actually could not discern what in fact their heart was doing during micturation. (We were learning words then that far surpassed wee-wee and tinkle.) But most important, a thought had been born, namely, that on the inside of the body extraordinary connections, some rather delicious, but most rather terrifying were becoming evident. If your heart fluttered when you urinated, then when you, oh no, that was too much to think about.

(In) gym class . . . we used to play . . . the game of bombardment. It was a game of rudimentary rules, merciless and cruel, and manifestly adolescent. Two teams of equal number are parted forever by the half-court lines on a basketball floor. Three hard rubber balls the size of soccer balls are thrown into the middle. When you get one the object is to throw it at someone on the other side. If you hit him he's out of the game and the winner is the team that has even one player left (alive). But always you must throw hard because should your heave be caught,

EXCERPTED BY PERMISSION FROM T.J. Cottle "The Connections of Adolescence," in *Daedalus*, Vol. 100, No. 4 (Fall 1971), pp. 1177-1190.

you, the thrower, go out of the game. I remember that unbelievable thud of the ball slamming against a guy's chest and his catching it. Raw courage.

Often it did go right down to the battle of the giants, those mammoth gladiators exploding perhaps three balls at a time, or did they take away some balls as the number of people diminished? I can't remember. During it all, the rest of us, who, I am certain, were glad to be eliminated, stood along the sidelines, some not paying attention, others screaming boyish words, rooting, and thanking God Himself that he had escaped unharmed for that one day.

I was stricken with fear during bombardment. I feared for my face, for my hands and genitals and gut. It was my back and buttocks, I prayed, that would take the punishment. I could not, however, face up to this torture, I mean literally advance head on into this salvo of cruelty and aggression. But I never told a single human being of my fright. Not one single person knew my terror, so I believed. There was nothing here of any supreme consequence, no sense of humanity or morality, no notions about proper educational ideology or appropriate conduct. I was not really discovering, but encountering the deeply internal and ultimately public display of my body, of my movement, more sexual than ever before, in social space and social time. I simply didn't want to get hurt, but I did feel strongly that if I could just bonk a few guys with that hard ball, maybe even sink one of their lungs when they caught my throw, and be able to get off without retribution, I'd be in good shape. I would be a better man for it. I would, perhaps, be a man.

Gym class, aggression, and bodies presented something else too. We used to play basketball a lot, and the obvious way to differentiate teams was by one team taking off their shirts. It was known as the skins against the shirts. "All right, your team is the skins. C'mon, Cottle, get those shirts and sweaters and underwear off." Why was it so embarrassing, this exposure of skin and the display of our chests and backs? Some of us had acne and that was humiliating, but I think that more than anything, it was that physically we simply were not up to the ideal stature and the ideal posture, size, and strength. The ideal was evidently present in all of our minds. Partly it was an athelete here or some great guy in the high school "above us" there, but in the main it was my father's body that I had indelibly internalized as the medical model, as the model specimen against which all future assessments and evaluations of anatomy would be made. The only part of us at age twelve which showed sufficient development was the legs, and for those whose legs were thin or whose ankles were excessively fat, or whose budding, truly incongruous leg hair was already unsightly and growing uglier by the day, there was no escape if they couldn't procure long sweat pants from the gym equipment office in the basement of the school.

As skins and shirts we played each other in basketball, expending muscular energy, expending competitive energy, for sports offered the perfect way to find out who were the best, the elite, and ultimately, who was the single heroic one. Half-dressed as we were, we might check out this ostensibly random rate of maturation, for on a jump ball, or a throw-in after an out-of-bounds play, or best of all, in the struggle of bodies for the rebound, one could get a glimpse of hair under the arms and all varieties of relative muscular development, and be able to gauge the flow of manly sweat. When the gymnasium smelled, you knew men had been in there. The girls knew it too. And you were proud to sniff, like a dog, at your very own crevices and corners, and know that you had contributed to that aroma of masculinity, that ineluctable ambience of maleness. How many millions of jokes were made about athletic supporters!

Intelligence or appearing smart was an aspect of maturation and public imagery more difficult to assess. How does one describe it? To hit a home run or score a bushel of points, even in a "choose-up" game, was an unequivocal event. It tallied up at once to fame and fortune in the going currency of adolescence. Publicly and privately it felt good. It *was* good.

Not so with intelligence. Being bright earned an equivocal acceptance, for one could always draw a dangerously thin line between brilliance and pomposity, verbal aptitude and conceit, literary acumen and snottiness. Everyone, of course, was supposed to read and abide by what they used to call the "dictionary habit." But one was not supposed to read more than what had been assigned, and certainly not use those convoluted words the dictionary seemed to treasure. One could joke about big words, like Parkie, who used to parade his favorite mouthful and spell out for us: a-n-t-i-d-i-s-e-s-t-a-b-l-i-s-h-m-e-n-t-a-r-i-a-n-i-s-m. That was safe because no one could really use that word no matter what it meant. But once in the seventh grade, we heard a kid utter the word "perfidious." He actually had the temerity to flip that word at the rest of us right in the middle of a sentence, right in the middle of English class. "Perfidious" just flew out of his mouth as naturally as anything. Two periods later on the hard dirt of the East Field we almost killed him.

Only naturally did the intelligent and informed ones seek out each other and band together as a surreptitious subculture concocting a collective ideology that would make the others even more angry and envious. While there were many talents and activities that formed the basis of groupings then, the intelligence factor, in its way, seemed to be the most special and salient. After all, this was school and the major activity, though no one dared confess it, was learning, which meant that we all valued the "smarties," despite the fact that our culture forbid us to publicly proclaim our admiration for those people. In their homes after school or on weekends when we examined the contents of their rooms and just how much of their parents' property they got to use, we could let a bit of our awe spill forth. And when we went home and made those inevitable comparisons and pledges to read at least one book a week, some of our true feelings about learning would at last break through.

By Monday morning in school, our conversations were back to the clothes and the girls and the sports. But those glimpses into the recently discovered private worlds of our friends, symbolized as they were by the artifacts of knowledge, never left us. They possessed something unique, the intelligent ones, an access perhaps to different realms with absolutely marvelous temporal and spatial parameters. They actually cared about and for years, perhaps forever, *remembered* the substance and the facts of school and books. They were able to recall for us in the eighth grade, moments and data of the sixth grade, and as they sat proudly beneath the afterglow of their magical enunciations, the rest of us angrily slumped in our chairs and muttered words like "genius" and "photographic memory."

         . . .

We laughed all the time, of course, if something else, or better, if someone else were strange. We laughed at the "sound" of words like puberty and vagina, too. I know that has not changed. And we laughed at styles of appearance and voice, and, best of all, tangible deformity drove us into hysterics. Knowing it was dreadful of us, we nonetheless could rarely contain ourselves if we caught a buddy's eyes in class or while riding a bus. Someone would be overly fat, or tall, or dressed differently, or have long hair, or slip on a stair, or ask a bus driver in "broken" English for the location of a street, and we would look and listen intently and then, blam, we would be busting with the pains of laughter, the tears rolling down our cheeks, and grappling to catch some inner strand or throw a switch that might bring us back to normalcy. If one of us got a glare or caught a few words from an old lady there would be instantaneous composure and fright, but then, as soon as our eyes would meet across the muddied aisle of the bus, we were at it again, this time even worse than before.

Other kids, other adults often seemed strange to us, and thereby funny. There were invariably funny last names and funny fantasies about Italian or Japanese or German families. Or Russia; Russia and Russian in those days meant quite a bit. Nausea or a bitter taste in one's mouth was often described as a feeling of having had the entire Russian army tramp through your mouth and one guy left a gym shoe . . . But the funny thing was that when I played with a kid after school in his house and a relative of his would speak with an accent, he would giggle with me almost to let me know that his uncle or grandmother sounded just as silly to him as they must have sounded to me. And yet, both of us knew this to be a different kind of differentness. Both of us just seemed to know that here was a case of a young person simultaneously honoring his family as well as the ethics and savagery of his peer group.

         . . .

Perhaps it is the word "connection" that describes so many of the dreams and fantasies we had then—that I had then. Like, I couldn't quite tell how I was connected to my sister, or for that matter how other relatives were connected to us in those imagined layers of kinship closeness and distantness. Moreover, I couldn't sort out exactly how my connection with parents was to proceed from this point on, as my discovery of sexuality, or what we presently call "heterosexual relationships," cast a rather cumbersome veil on what I might now be able to say or be in front of my parents.

At last the recollections of that age come storming back. I have found a key. We double-dated once, four of us, on a Saturday afternoon. Before entering the State and Lake Theater I purchased a bag of red pistachio nuts from the Morrow Nut House. Nut house indeed. Then, during the movies, I nibbled and cracked the nuts between my teeth, so that, when we emerged in the late afternoon light under the billion light bulb marquee, my lips and fingers were rouged with red. And everybody, I mean everybody in the world thought I had been necking my head off in the theater when in truth the best I could do in those two and a half hours of darkness was twice accidentally on purpose brush Susie L. in the left breast. So I was unable to connect with her, but significantly, I had added to my resources something that could not be shared with parents and would thereby make, I imagined, our family connections weaker by several important units.

When I left for camp, at age twelve, I cried. Though I tried as best I could with all my inner strength, I just couldn't hold back the tears. All of this despite my constant recognition of the public disgrace I had become . . .

Well, anyway, I cried at this my first real trip away from home, and my parents bought me a pair of sunglasses which at the very time I knew to be an exquisitely sensitive solution. For suddenly I had become a celebrity, protected by a hideout which bespoke the reservation and extreme reluctance I was feeling. It was remarkable how those glasses practically transformed my inner despair into public exhibition. I walked around that enormous train station wondering whether someone might mistake me for a famous something or other, and kept thinking about the time we had seen Elizabeth Taylor in that very same station . . .

Something snapped in me on that first trip to camp. Simultaneously, I had thoughts of not caring whether I would be seen as a boy or a man, and thoughts of knowing that a certain engine of my childhood, however small, however insignificant, had just been shut off. For good. Does anyone understand this? Does anyone else preserve similar memories? Would anyone else appeal to such a metaphor? But do you know that on that train, in a matter literally of seconds, I was scanning the other boys, my new summer friends to be, eyes cleared of all clues of sadness, glasses in pocket, and attempting to figure out scientifically on the basis of body types and ease of muscular motion, what kid in that noisy, boy-filled Denver Zephyr coach car was going to turn out to be a better athelete than I? So quickly had my thoughts turned from separation to competition and anxiety that even I was bewildered. It was as though work had now begun; I had serious sizing up to do if I was to survive the next few months.

I picked out one guy, a big kid from Des Moines with the even bigger nickname of "Buster," as the guy who would inevitably wreck that summer . . . (My) fantasies assured me that this was the kid, of all the kids in the world, who would put me to shame in baseball, basketball, and football. He would do it. Oh my God. I recognized with horror as he wrote on a postcard that he was left-handed like I. And so, in a stroke of unfortunate luck, he had not only supplanted me in status, he had robbed me of the one physical characteristic I could almost always rely on to make me unique. It was, moreover, the characteristic which connected me, of all the weird happenings, to my mother, a left-hander who had been "corrected." Southpaw, a grotesque but surely prodigious term, had actually become a rather major brace in my concept of self.

How can I ever describe the relief, the lifting of that leaden shroud, that ripple of freedom that emanated from my intestines and exploded all over my once-again adored body when I saw Buster throw a baseball for the first time. One throw only. Not even a catch in return, and I knew this boy's physical capacities like an internist totally on top of a diagnosis of a duodenal ulcer. Athlete? Buster from Des Moines was a complete "spasmo."

. . .

Height and weight told an important story. What a curse to be the shortest or the tallest of the lot. Because of the age period, one only naturally suspected that genetics had either been good to him by assuring him a projected normal height, a height equal to his dad, or had a curse upon him by leaving him five feet four in a world of giants. I'll bet we inquired about normal male heights and weights for various ages twenty times a year.

Age, too, had an incomprehensible self-assessment quality about it. The oldest and youngest in the class had to be computed at the commencement of each new academic year. "This means you'll be seventeen and six months at graduation." To be even three days older than another or share a birthday in the same month or season meant something rather vital at the time. And he or she who entered the incomparable "teen's" first was unquestionably Godly, for despite our recognition of the artificial and commercial nature of becoming a teenager, turning thirteen was still magical and surely would bring us, in time, a sweet but essential reward.

At the very least, becoming teenagers would bring us closer together in the same narrow destiny. For the most part, we never aged or traveled alone. We moved in time and space as a swarm connected by temperature and noise and the swells of motion and sensuous delight and agony, our bodies clanging together in the halls, on the street, on the stairs . . .

The utter safety of those mobs still impresses me. One could control one's freedom and degrees of dependency so easily. One could stand out from the crowd, fall back into it, shield a spindly value system, and preserve those codes of a granite morality which had grown up from nowhere to handle our spreading tendrils of sexuality. But mainly there were a billion things to talk over, with one of the most important being what to talk over with whom in order to find out if you were really going through life as it was supposed to be gone through. I mean, you knew that having pimples, though a ghastly fate, was normal, because you could see the others and maybe even surprise them once applying Acnomel, or whatever it was called, to their cheeks, forehead, and chin. But there was the morality of it all. Like, what was supposed to be happening in those houses when all the couples would assemble at 7:30 and turn off the lights and you just had to neck with her, like it or not. And you didn't know where to begin or conclude, but in the midst of accidentally-on-purpose flopping your arm down, actually rather hard, there you were, having landed on some girl's newly arrived breast.

Those were genuinely unbelievable moments. What did we say to those girls? What did they hear after that confusion and excruciating pain had subsided? How did we, like little lawyers together, arrive at the agreements that have to be agreed upon as sex unfolds? How did they ever teach us about underwear, menstruation and cramps, getting the curse, and cutting gym? And why, for that matter, did so many of us completely deny this unthinkable biological and temporal feature of the other sex? It never quite sunk in, that special event of theirs. But then again, the necessary magical words and sacred deeds, the "dirty deeds," were exchanged, and felt, and the terror undraped. Words like curse, virgin, hard on, were memorized, stored away, then dragged out and rightly applied.

. . .

Older kids were a part of it now, and even though we had assuredly grown up, some of the girls were suddenly looking beyond us with a new perspective. They were dating juniors and seniors! They were dating the school's heroes, the untouchables. They were actually going to the movies with the objects of our athletic and masculine curiosities and afterward doing heaven only knows what with them. They were bringing them to our sex soirees and introducing them to us. Small, weaker, and less important than we, the girls had "made it" before us. They had the chance of being as old as we and older than we at the same time, and there was nothing to do but exude jealousy and warn of the day when we would be the seniors dating the freshmen (and some of those sixth graders even now looked pretty good). Then, then we would let our female colleagues pine away for their college boyfriends. We would even let them write in their diaries on weekend nights as they waited for Thanksgiving and Christmas vacations and the return of those—how could we have ever considered them heroes?—guys!

## Autobiography of a Transescent Girl

Until I was 14, I lived in a small, quiet, one-industry town. My parents were well known and well liked and very sociable. For entertainment, friends mostly got together in each others' homes. In those days before World War II domestic help was readily available and inexpensive. Card parties were common. My mother and her friends didn't work outside the home. So, the message I got in many ways was *be* socially adept, *become* socially adept. Physically and socially I often felt like an outsider looking in. I remember my first date, to the freshman dance. He stood a head shorter than I! And I wondered: Which is better . . . missing my first high school dance or having the awkward feeling that I am leading my partner around the dance floor?

Being "different" during those growing up years was uncomfortable. And I was aware of physical and social differences. My nicknames were "Shorty" and "Freckles." I was taller than most of my friends, and it was hard to feel like one of the crowd among my peers. My mother was an attractive, well groomed lady of 5'2". Towering over her felt awkward, too. My body offered me no particular comfort. There was one activity that gave me a lot of satisfaction and pleasure. A swimmer since I was six, I spent many hours at the local pool during the summers.

Although I had a special girlfriend in my early school years, that girl moved away, and during the adolescent years I had no particular confidant. I joined Rainbow Girls and Campfire Girls, but my feeling was that I ought to join, ought to enjoy. It felt like somone else's agenda.

WRITTEN FOR this chapter by Cherie Lawrence.

Each birthday and Christmas a librarian aunt made sure that I had a new book to unwrap. She loved reading and books, and transmitted these feelings to me. In the evening when dinner and dishes were done I liked to settle myself in bed with some volume. For that bit of time I could be uninterrupted, quiet, and away from the lives of others. It felt warm and secure and totally mine. Reading became a very engrossing pasttime. In fact, my father often declared that I needed to get more exercise and sunshine, especially over the weekends. I remember one particular time when I satisfied both his need and mine by taking my book out on the back steps to read in the sunshine. It gave me a good feeling of oneupmanship.

Music was important to me. Everyone in my family liked popular music, but only I had an affection for the long haired stuff. My family tolerated this idiosyncrasy. I was given (as opposed to took) piano lessons for five years, and perhaps because of the stipulation that I practice an hour a day, I felt like it was being done to me. I resented my lack of power to refuse. Any pleasure that I may have taken from learning a new skill was more than offset by my anger at being coerced.

In school I pretended to study while working instead on improving my drawing of such things as the female face. When I was 13 I took lessons in oil painting. A friend and I learned how to imitate the little lady's style—her skies, her mountains, her cacti; and when people complimented me on the finished product, I felt like a fake and then somehow ungrateful to my parents who had paid for the lessons. I wanted the skills of the painter and I didn't know how to get those without being a copycat.

Music, art and books—they all made soft places in my days. And I needed those soft places to see me though the tougher spots.

I got mixed messages about sex from my parents. My father enjoyed telling jokes of all kinds. At parties in our home he was called on to share his latest. He usually saved the "dirty" ones to tell when my brother and I were out of the room, but we got bits and pieces of some stories, and there was always the overheard laughter after we had left. On the other hand, my laughter about some new sexual information brought immediate disapproval from both parents, and later during bedtime prayers I was questioned and scolded by mother. I was 6 or 7 at the time, and I learned my lesson well: It's all right for adults to laugh about sexual things, but not for children to.

Most of my sexual information came from peers or older children. In fact, my mother told me about menstruation *after* my first period. I had gone to visit a family on a ranch. They were acquaintances not friends, and I remember my embarrassment at sharing this personal event with people I barely knew. When I returned home my mother talked about menstruation with me, but I remember thinking then that all the information was coming too late to be very helpful. At that point I was so uncomfortable and self-conscious that I wasn't able to see that my own grown-up mother was feeling very awkward, too. That realization came to me much later.

I must have given very little attention to events in the adult world. But I do remember the day the New York Philharmonic program was interrupted . . . I was sitting in the living room that Sunday afternoon as usual . . . Pearl Harbor had been bombed. I sat there alone for a moment trying to comprehend or imagine the "Why?" and the "What now?" I was eleven then and could remember seeing the newspaper headlines "Hitler Invades Poland!" two years before. But this was an attack on the U.S. I felt apprehensive, even unexplainably excited. I may have asked my parents questions but I have no memory of it. My life during the war years was relatively untouched: ration cards, fewer trips in our car in order to conserve gas, letters to my soldier cousin in the Pacific, more time with my family listening to news programs. If my history or current events classes in school focused on the developments of the war, I have no recollection of that. It may have been my war, our war, but for me it felt like the grownups' war. For if I couldn't *do* much about it myself, why spend time *thinking* much about it.

My relationship with my father during those years was fairly good. I liked his humor and his easy relationships with people. His work placed some limits on the time and/or energy he had left over for his family. His own health was marginal. There was never a time when he didn't have bouts of gout. I can remember being cautioned to be quiet because he was resting, and I can also recall family meals that were tailored to his specific diet. Mother gave a good deal of herself to all of us. She was physically demonstrative and there was the unspoken expectation that this would be returned. She was more even tempered than my father, and in fact she called his bursts of temper "childish." I think he wasn't sure that he could express his feelings—especially negative ones—and my mother often carried his messages for him.

I shared many of my private hurts with my mother. Part of the time she was a good friend, but the "teacher-parent" role sometimes got in the way of close confidences. I wasn't always comfortable baring my hurts to her. I think I must have been a moody young person. I didn't have permission to "argue" or "fight" with my parents, so anger went inside. As a result, I didn't work through our differences until many years later.

## ACTIVITY 2
### Read and analyze the table, "Patterns of Transescent Development."

**A.**   While American transescents display many idiosyncrasies in their development, they also follow patterns common to nearly all their age mates. Here are twenty-three such characteristics that are supported in research literature. The statements encompass all four of the facets of development addressed in this book: physical, intellectual, social, and emotional. As you read through the table, decide which facet(s) of development is represented in each statement and place a check mark in the appropriate box(es) at the left. Most statements reflect more than one area of development, suggesting an interrelationship between the areas—which is the main message of this activity. You can compare your judgment with ours by using the key, "Four Facets of Development," which follows the table.

# Patterns of Transescent Development

| P H Y S I C A L | I N T E L L E C T U A L | S O C I A L | E M O T I O N A L | |
|---|---|---|---|---|
| ☐ | ☐ | ☐ | ☐ | 1. *Social Perspective.* They show a conspicuous increase in ability to criticize the social environment realistically and to judge moral conflicts. |
| ☐ | ☐ | ☐ | ☐ | 2. *Space-Time.* Their orientation in space and time approaches the adult level. |
| ☐ | ☐ | ☐ | ☐ | 3. *Social Discrimination.* They are beginning to be fully conscious of differences and discrimination between classes, races, and national minorities. |
| ☐ | ☐ | ☐ | ☐ | 4. *Peer Relations.* Relations with same-sex peers is a predominant feature of peer involvement. |
| ☐ | ☐ | ☐ | ☐ | 5. *Peer Groups.* They congregate in peer groups to discharge emotional tensions; thus the peer group's function seems to be chiefly expressive. |
| ☐ | ☐ | ☐ | ☐ | 6. *Conformity.* Pressure to conform to peer group norms is strong. |
| ☐ | ☐ | ☐ | ☐ | 7. *Friendships.* At grades four to six a decisive change in the relations between children occurs. These relations deepen, become more stable, and bear a more personal character than those prevailing at lower grades. They are based on mutual long-range interests and are of a more permanent nature. |
| ☐ | ☐ | ☐ | ☐ | 8. *Adult Models.* The insecurity of transescents requires daily examples of adults who exhibit confidence and faith in themselves. |
| ☐ | ☐ | ☐ | ☐ | 9. *Teasing Adults.* They delight in teasing teachers and other adults, who may be irritated if they cannot see the humor from the child's point of view. |
| ☐ | ☐ | ☐ | ☐ | 10. *Adjustment to Maturation.* How well they adjust to the maturation process depends, to a large extent, on the kinds of relationships they can achieve with both their adult and peer associates. |
| ☐ | ☐ | ☐ | ☐ | 11. *Independence.* They must gain some intellectual and emotional distance from their families. |
| ☐ | ☐ | ☐ | ☐ | 12. *Emancipation.* The process by which they move from a dependent to an independent status is related to the culture in which they are living. |
| ☐ | ☐ | ☐ | ☐ | 13. *Emotional Resilience.* At this age they are able to overcome hypochondriac anxieties, which are characteristic of the small child, and to demonstrate a considerable tolerance of pain and stress. |
| ☐ | ☐ | ☐ | ☐ | 14. *Criticism.* They are able to criticize teachers, subject matter, classmates, and also themselves. |
| ☐ | ☐ | ☐ | ☐ | 15. *Experimentation.* They like to indulge in all kinds of experimentation. |

## Patterns of Transescent Development (continued)

| P H Y S I C A L | I N T E L L E C T U A L | S O C I A L | E M O T I O N A L | |
|---|---|---|---|---|
| ☐ | ☐ | ☐ | ☐ | 16. *Broadening Conceptual World.* As they have contacts with children different from themselves, they increasingly find themselves forced to reexamine their own precepts and concepts in the light of those of others, and by so doing, gradually rid themselves of cognitive egocentrism. |
| ☐ | ☐ | ☐ | ☐ | 17. *Reasoning.* They are capable of applying concrete operational reasoning to wide fields of knowledge and experience. |
| ☐ | ☐ | ☐ | ☐ | 18. *Erotic Interest.* Erotic alertness and curiosity are typical of transescent girls; curiosity is typical of boys. Preadolescent heterosexual experimenting stops at puberty. |
| ☐ | ☐ | ☐ | ☐ | 19. *Physical Strength.* There is a conspicuous increase in muscle strength and activity potential. |
| ☐ | ☐ | ☐ | ☐ | 20. *Physical Endurance.* They are able to bear considerable physical stress and to withstand fatigue. |
| ☐ | ☐ | ☐ | ☐ | 21. *Physical Testing.* Many exercises and competitions that appear to be sport activities are ways in which transescents satisfy their curiosity and test the limits of their power and range of body functions. |
| ☐ | ☐ | ☐ | ☐ | 22. *Physical Self-consciousness.* Boys and girls entering puberty are preoccupied with their physical selves—appearance, sex characteristics, "growing pains"—and continually wonder whether their physical features and experiences are "normal." |
| ☐ | ☐ | ☐ | ☐ | 23. *Richness of Activity.* During transescence the brain has reached its adult size and weight, health is optimal, and the activity of these youngsters is greater and richer than it ever has been and ever will be during their lives. |

The substance of the table was taken from two books: Reuven Kohen-Raz, *The Child from Nine to Thirteen.* Chicago: Aldine-Atherton, 1971; and D. H. Eichhorn, *The Middle School.* New York: The Center for Applied Research in Education, Inc., 1966.

## KEY—FOUR FACETS OF DEVELOPMENT

*(The Authors' Responses to Activity 2 A)*

| | PHYSICAL | INTELLECTUAL | SOCIAL | EMOTIONAL |
|---|---|---|---|---|
| 1 | | X | X | X |
| 2 | X | X | | |
| 3 | | X | X | |
| 4 | X | | X | X |
| 5 | | | X | X |
| 6 | | X | X | X |
| 7 | | | X | X |
| 8 | | | X | X |
| 9 | | X | X | |
| 10 | X | X | X | X |
| 11 | | X | X | X |
| 12 | | | X | X |

| | PHYSICAL | INTELLECTUAL | SOCIAL | EMOTIONAL |
|---|---|---|---|---|
| 13 | | | | X |
| 14 | | X | X | X |
| 15 | X | X | X | X |
| 16 | | X | X | X |
| 17 | | X | | |
| 18 | X | X | X | X |
| 19 | X | | | |
| 20 | X | | | |
| 21 | X | X | X | X |
| 22 | X | | X | X |
| 23 | X | X | | |

**B.**   The writers of the two autobiographical sketches certainly were experiencing many of the developmental transitions suggested in the twenty-three statements. How true are these statements for the boy and girl described in the essays? Go back through the two essays and mark in the margins the numeral of any of the twenty-three characteristics you think is reflected in each paragraph. If you also number each paragraph (1 through 26 for the boy, and 1 through 12 for the girl) you can compare your judgment with ours.

## PATTERNS OF TRANSESCENT DEVELOPMENT
*(The Authors' Responses to Activity 2 B)*

*"Autobiography of a Transescent Boy"*

| Paragraph | Statement | Paragraph | Statement | Paragraph | Statement |
|-----------|-----------|-----------|-----------|-----------|-----------|
| 1 | 18 | 10 | 16 | 19 | 10 |
| 2 | 22 | 11 | 2 | 20 | — |
| 3 | 20 | 12 | 9 | 21 | 22 |
| 4 | — | 13 | 3,1,17 | 22 | 22 |
| 5 | 13 | 14 | 12 | 23 | — |
| 6 | 22 | 15 | 10 | 24 | 5,1 |
| 7 | 21,4 | 16 | — | 25 | 15 |
| 8 | — | 17 | 8 | 26 | 10 |
| 9 | 14,6 | 18 | 11,21 | | |

*"Autobiography of a Transescent Girl"*

| Paragraph | Statement | Paragraph | Statement |
|-----------|-----------|-----------|-----------|
| 1 | 10,22,3 | 7 | 11 |
| 2 | 22,6,21 | 8 | 18 |
| 3 | 4,5,6 | 9 | 10,14,22 |
| 4 | 11,9 | 10 | 1 |
| 5 | 12,14 | 11 | 8 |
| 6 | 1,14 | 12 | 13 |

**C.** How well can you recollect your own early adolescent experiences? How did they differ from the two you read? Write an autobiographical sketch of your own experiences at ages ten through fourteen. Don't be concerned about literary style; simple phrases, incomplete sentences will serve the purpose. Use the readings and analysis done so far in the chapter to jog your memory and to suggest categories of things to write about. Save your notes.

 *

## ACTIVITY 3
**Students write autobiographies.**

If you are now teaching transescents, or have access to someone else's class, this activity may be feasible for you. It is designed to be helpful both to you and the students. Transescents are curious about the experiences of their peers and your group of students may be

---

*Note that this activity and subsequent activities with the schoolhouse insignia require access to a school to observe or talk with students.

interested in sharing with each other the kinds of recollections that appear in the two autobiographies. Here is a suggestion for structuring the activity.

**A.**  See whether students are interested in writing autobiographies. You may want to read aloud two or three autobiographies that some students have written in advance for this purpose. The writers probably should remain anonymous.

**B.**  Prepare and hand out to each student a ditto sheet worded in the following fashion.

### A THIRTEEN-YEAR-OLD (or whatever year) LOOKS BACK

*(Don't put your name on the paper, just write boy or girl)*

1. Some things I remember very clearly from my childhood: (Allow enough space under each item for students to write a response)

2. In some ways I haven't changed much since then:

3. In some ways I've changed a lot:

4. There are some things I like about growing up:

5. There are some things I liked about being a child:

6. Some things really embarrass me:

7. I worry about some things:

8. I have a few things to say about (write about any or all of these):

   My parent(s)          My teacher(s)          Boys and girls
   My friend(s)          Other adults

Either in a handout or on the chalkboard, give the students these instructions:

   a.  After all papers are collected, I will ask you to form groups of five to discuss what has been written.
   b.  Five of the papers will come to your group.
   c.  Each person read one paper silently.
   d.  As you read, circle the numbers of the responses that were similar to your own.
   e.  Taking turns, each person read one paper aloud for your group.
   f.  Each group choose a recorder to note the number of the responses that people thought were similar to their own.
   g.  Each group will then talk about the ways the autobiographies are alike.
   h.  Recorders will report their notes to the teacher, who will summarize them on the board.
   i.  The whole class will then discuss the summary.

If you wish to structure this student activity differently, feel free to do so.

**C.** Make an analysis of the student responses and summarize your analysis on paper. Compare your summary with your own autobiographical sketch, noting similarities and differences. Share your summaries with a colleague who is also doing these activities.

## ACTIVITY 4
**Read and analyze the following reading, "Basic Needs of Young Adolescents."**

As you read and after you have finished reading, use the table, "School Responsiveness to Student Needs," to help you organize your thoughts. The table, which follows the reading, lists 12 categories of basic needs of young adolescents. Take 12 blank sheets of paper and divide each into three columns, with each column headed as shown in the table. Using one sheet for each need (e.g., 1. *A need to be needed*), write in the first column a definition of that need as you extract it from the reading. Then fill in the other columns as indicated. Make your notes complete enough so that your meaning can be understood by a colleague, and share your analysis with one or more colleagues.

## Basic Needs of Young Adolescents

In her insightful book, *Beyond Customs*, Charity James (1974) describes twelve personal needs of young adolescent students. The set of needs she identifies is refreshingly different from those offered by behavioral scientists. She speaks as a teacher to other teachers, as one who has long observed with care and affection the lives of children. Her set includes these:

- A need to be needed.
- A need to need.
- A need to move inward.
- A need to affect the outer world.
- A need for intensity.
- A need for routine.
- A need for myth and legend.
- A need for fact.
- A need for physical activity.
- A need for stillness.
- A need for separateness.
- A need for belonging.

In the paragraphs that follow, we employ her concepts to convey some of our concerns about changing schools to be more sensitive to the needs of students. Needs are stated as six pairs of opposites, or polarities. As opposites they suggest rhythms in the lives of young people and they highlight the teacher's need to understand and accommodate the ebb and flow of needs in students.

Charity James does not regard her list as finished. Nor does she imply that these needs are peculiar to early and middle adolescents. However, she does believe they have a special significance in children of that age. We agree that the twelve concepts characterize special needs of transescents, and we could go another step and propose these as a basis for rethinking the schooling processes of the middle grades.

## A NEED TO BE NEEDED

In the early years of American public schooling, children attended school for a few hours a day, a few months in the year. Their other hours and days were filled with the tasks of farm or village life. Before they reached school age they had responsibilities in the economic fabric of the community. They had a very real sense of being participants and producers in the culture. That experience they received at home, so they did not need it in the school room. A need to be needed was being met in the larger world, and the fact that classroom life was very different, treating them only as consumers of educational products, perhaps made little difference in their sense of identity as members of the society.

Today children spend a much greater proportion of their time in school, but the pattern of schooling has not changed. They are still consumers of educational products, conceived and developed for them by others. The situation outside of school has changed radically over the years. Most transescent youngsters do not work and do not have other forms of involvement readily available to them. As mere spectators of the adult culture, they are not needed for any function except to be consumers of food, entertainment, or schooling.

Deferring the satisfaction of the need to be needed until high school graduation runs the risk of denying them the self-esteem that comes with being a contributing member of the society. Junior high and middle schools have a special challenge to find ways for students to become participants in activities they regard as benefiting the culture. There is ample evidence that when schools sponsor that kind of participation by students, it has a dramatic effect on their attitude toward learning, their sense of personal worth, their sense of responsibility to the culture, and their school achievement, to name only a few outcomes.

## A NEED TO NEED

We have all had the experience of being part of a work team that has a variety of tasks to do. The tasks somehow get divided among the team members, often according to people's strengths and interests. Members come to recognize that the product of the teamwork is greater than they could have accomplished by themselves individually, and they find value in the mutual interdependence of team effort. In this kind of collaborative work they find a new kind of personal identity, without having to submerge their identities, to merely conform, as they are as often pressed to do today. When needing other people is thought of in this way, it is not at all incompatible with the goal of self-reliance.

Unfortunately, the typical pattern in schools encourages neither self-reliance nor teamwork in learning. When school authorities decide what shall be learned and school authorities decide what is good work and what is bad, and school authorities decide who shall be rewarded and who shall not, then the student is not encouraged to rely on his or her own judgment, which, of course, is at the heart of self-reliance. Nor does this pattern deal with the need to need in a healthy way; a student who is expected to master essentially the same curriculum, independently of other students, has little reason to draw upon the resources of other students in a collaborative way. This pattern of schooling promotes dependency on the teacher, but not the kind of community participation that is a fundamental need of children.

A need to need has another meaning as well. Feeling the pull of a need to know something or to master some skill is a vital need of young people. Not many of us "hunger and thirst" for knowledge, but we do value the stimulation of feeling impelled into a learning activity by the sense of our own lack and the satisfaction of solving the problem or attaining the target we were after. This is, in effect, the satisfaction of being one's own diagnostician, prescription writer, and problem solver. Transescents need that experience as they move toward adult responsibilities, but they are denied it if their learning needs are defined only by someone else's diagnosis and their learning tasks structured only by someone else's prescription.

## A NEED TO MOVE INWARDS

When transescents have an opportunity to choose freely the subjects of inquiry in school, they often choose to study aspects of human behavior, such as emotions, the effects of technology on people, the causes of war, the workings of human groups and speculation about life in the future. All of these are means of better understanding human nature, and ultimately, one's own inner nature. Through elementary school, the child's attention seems to be naturally focused on the world outside. The middle school child is ready to turn attention inward to the processes operating inside.

American teachers who have attempted to respond to this need to move inward have had mixed results. Why some succeeded and others failed is not clear. The explanation that makes the most sense to us is that the unsuccessful programs may have made the study of human behavior too abstract, too formal and impersonal, so that it no longer seemed connected to the lives of students.

## A NEED TO AFFECT THE OUTER WORLD

In the transescent period, children enter into a new relationship with the material environment. As many of them develop the capacity for abstract thought, they realize that their environments are not just given facts, but have been powerfully influenced by the people that live in them. For the first time they see clearly a gap between social realities and the ideals they are now able to envision. They do not passively observe this gap; rather, they feel a strong need to close it, to bring their efforts into the work of making the material world more nearly fit their image of what it might become.

If transescents' needs to affect the outer world are not honored by the adult community, if they cannot obtain some power they regard as significant, the natural consequence is a retreat into apathy or a grasping for power in some destructive way.

The challenge to the school is to provide children with opportunities to work with materials, animate and inanimate, to experience the consequences of their work and in that way to see more realistically their own strengths and possibilities. When children merely read and talk about the world's materials and do not have first hand experience with them, their relationship to the substantive world is likely to be shallow and verbal. James expresses it this way: "It seems particularly important to help this age range to sustain dialogues with plants, animals, and inanimate nature. This is one reason why I became so concerned to find art teaching often reduced to 'skills' teaching when the attitude to materials should be sensitive and exploratory, even reverent . . ." (p.28).

James also believes that young people feel a greater need to affect their physical world than the social world, such as operating a school government. Students want to be consulted, but they seem not to feel the need to take up the responsibilities of decision making about school policy. But with the physical environment, they want to know that it will respond to their initiatives, and thus confirm to them their own personal connection with reality.

## A NEED FOR INTENSITY

Probably people of all ages need to experience intensity, but in transescents this need has a special significance. If they do not find constructive ways of experiencing intensity, they may fill the void with a pursuit of excitement, seeking various means to get high or to court danger.

One way that schools can help with the need for intensity is to provide conditions in which students can take psychic risks, to stretch themselves in a supportive environment: "to risk failure at a project on which one has set one's heart; to risk personal expression of powerful feelings in a number of media; for boys to try out roles they may see as effeminate, such as working in dance improvisation, sewing, or cooking; for girls to become involved enough in their inventions or designs to stop pretending to be more sophisticated and less intelligent than they are . . . ." (p.32).

The arts are especially important in transescence, whether for individual expression or shared activities such as drama and choral music. James reminds us that "the intensity of shared creation is one of the great experiences of youth." The school program can provide for the experiencing of intensity in ways other than producing something. James mentions the intensity of listening or looking, sensitivity exercises, the experience of quiet, and field experiences such as outward-bound programs, exploring trips, and camping.

Violence, heavy drinking, drug abuse, reckless driving, all remind us that youth's need for intensity will be expressed in one form or another. Can the schools pick up the challenge?

## A NEED FOR ROUTINE

Routine is one thing schools have a lot of, but there is ample evidence that it is not the kind that serves students' needs well. Routine, in the sense of drill or practice, is essential to the development of all skills. Routine means having an atmosphere that encourages steady, determined effort toward a goal. The reason that routine in schools is often counter-productive is that children are put to work at tasks not of their own choosing; they have no sense of being partners in the choice of goals or of means to attain the goals.

Transescents have a need for routine not only to help them understand the rhythm of skill development, but also for psychological and aesthetic reasons. They need the security and privacy that routine gives them. And finally, when students have identified their own need for routine it takes on an aspect of ritual, an aesthetic value creating "a beauty of order in time and space."

## A NEED FOR MYTH AND LEGEND

Myths, whether essentially factual or largely fanciful, are important to the health of a culture and to the development of individuals. People can learn indirectly through myths what they cannot learn through conscious analysis. Myths play out fundamental human issues in ways that young people can understand.

The efforts of Afro-Americans and Mexican-Americans to restore a continuity with the past is a process that all young people might benefit from. It is the myths of a culture that provide the continuity.

At the beginning of transescence, children are moving into an understanding of space and time that will allow them to grasp the historical significance of myths and legends. James sees this age as a prime time for studying the myths about creation, about the uniqueness of each person's journey through life and the inevitability of death. She notes that the bards and storytellers of our heritage were often less heavy handed than we are in dealing with matters of creation, life, love, and death. In the schools, myths can be dramatized and set to music and dance. Some children may be inspired to create their own myths, including myths of the future, such as science fiction.

## A NEED FOR FACT

A need for fact is a need to find out for one's self. It is a need to develop skill in looking for evidence, a need to distinguish between opinion and evidence, a need to attend to details and not be satisfied with thin generalities and empty verbalisms. This is a developmental need in the sense that a neglect of it during transescence impairs the adult's capacity to think and act effectively.

School emphasis upon right and wrong answers tends to thwart the need for fact. The remedy is to keep the factfinding process as concrete and personal as possible. When students have experience with concrete data, and the quest for evidence, they can move into formal cognitive operations.

## A NEED FOR PHYSICAL ACTIVITY

Any adult who has been in a junior high or middle school even briefly is aware of the restless energy of transescents. It is a very concrete evidence of their need for physical activity—a need that isn't being met by typical school programs and classroom patterns.

Today's teachers have inherited a long-standing traditional belief that students should sit still at desks for their own good—hour after hour. The tradition arose from the erroneous view that the mind is released for thinking when the body is disciplined, preferably by self-control but by teacher control if necessary. Of course, it is the whole organism that gives or withholds attention, gets distracted, is *mind*ful or not of the business at hand. The challenge for teachers is to break with the traditional pattern and invent ways to structure learning tasks so that physical activity is possible, and better yet, is an integral part of the intellectual objective.

The many reasons why transescents need physical activity, and some suggestions for teachers, are subjects of the chapter on physical development.

## A NEED FOR STILLNESS

Stillness, as the polarity to physical activity, means muscular relaxation and lowered brain rhythms. The process of quiet centering provides the young person with a way of getting in touch with himself or herself that is not possible through active outward movement. Whether schools incorporate some of the processes stemming from Eastern mysticism or rely on some traditional Western forms—such as the quiet, personal arts and nature study—students need opportunities to experience deeper relaxation that does not depend on dulling the senses with loud music or drugs.

## A NEED FOR SEPARATENESS

Separateness means both privacy and retreat from group involvement. The transescent's need for privacy is more likely to be honored outside of school than inside. The possibility of privacy in the school depends on the uses of space and time. When students move from one classroom to another with five minutes in the hall between them; when students have time for privacy only by getting formal permission to leave the classroom; and when washrooms and PE facilities do not offer some sheltering from the gaze of other students, then the school is not honoring the need for privacy. There are indeed practical difficulties in having school spaces that permit privacy, but many schools have overcome the problems by analyzing school policy to determine whether it has been formed more on the basis of administrative convenience than by careful consideration of time and space design in relation to student needs.

The opportunity to retreat from involvement with other people also depends upon the uses of space and time. Are there quiet corners or lawns where one can be alone, and is there time to go there? Can a student get some alone time in a classroom or media center without having to pretend to be studying?

## A NEED FOR BELONGING

James uses the term "belonging" to mean belonging *with*, not belonging *to*—students sharing, participating, and collaborating with their peers and with significant adults as well. Despite their intensive participation in peer groups, students understand very little of the workings of groups, and their own sense of belonging may be limited by their lack of understanding. Finding satisfaction in group membership depends upon having an understanding of how groups work, how peer pressure operates and upon having some skills of effective group participation. To honor the student's need for belonging and to sponsor the development of group membership skills, a school faculty must work against the traditional pattern of having each student do separate work only. That is a difficult task, but a very rewarding one. Teachers we know who have broken through to the group pattern could not be persuaded to go back.

## School Responsiveness to Student Needs

*(See instructions given in Activity 4)*

| Basic Needs of Early Adolescents (James, *Beyond Customs*) | What the School Now Does to Meet This Need (For all or most students, not just a few) | School Changes Needed to Meet This Need More Fully |
|---|---|---|
| 1.  The Need to Be Needed | | |
| 2.  The Need to Need | | |
| 3.  The Need to Move Inward | | |
| 4.  The Need to Affect the Outer World | | |
| 5.  The Need for Intensity | | |
| 6.  The Need for Routine | | |
| 7.  The Need for Myth and Legend | | |
| 8.  The Need for Fact | | |
| 9.  The Need for Physical Activity | | |
| 10.  The Need for Stillness | | |
| 11.  The Need for Separateness | | |
| 12.  The Need for Belonging | | |

## NEXT STEPS

1. If you want to pursue one or more of your ideas for change in your school (Activity 4), we suggest you read relevant parts of Charity James' book, *Beyond Customs*, as a starter. Then use appropriate chapters in this book to develop your plan of action further.

2. Did the student autobiographies suggest to you any units of study you might develop or curriculum changes the school might undertake? You may want to examine some resources on human development prepared for middle level students.

3. Did the use of this chapter suggest to you any changes you might make in your self-assessment of competencies you need to develop?

4. Examine the NSSE yearbook, *Toward Adolescence: The Middle School Years*. It has chapters that review the study of early adolescence from many viewpoints and that can be good resources for you as you use this book.

## REFERENCES

COTTLE, THOMAS J., "The Connections of Adolescence," *Daedalus* 100(4) Fall 1971.

EICHHORN, DONALD H., *The Middle School.* New York: The Center for Research in Education, Inc., 1966.

JAMES, CHARITY, *Beyond Customs.* New York: Agathon Press, Inc., 1974.

JOHNSON, MAURITZ, (ED.), *Toward Adolescence: The Middle School Years.* Seventy-ninth Yearbook of the National Society for the Study of Education, Part I. Chicago: University of Chicago Press, 1980.

KOHEN-RAZ, REUVEN, *The Child from Nine to Thirteen.* Chicago: Aldine-Atherton, 1971.

# CHAPTER TWO

# PHYSICAL DEVELOPMENT: TEN TO FOURTEEN

"... I feel so hairy!"

"... And what I hate is the rope climb ... everybody watching and some monster kid on the other team going up twice as fast as me."

"I'm hungry."

"She had her first period two *years* ago!"

"... But who will I dance with? The boys I know don't even come up to my chin."

"I *am* sitting still."

"There's this lump. What I'm worried about is this lump down inside my left boob ... my other one doesn't have it."

"Oh, no! It shows my pimples. The picture shows my pimples!"

"I'm still hungry!"

When transescents talk about their changing bodies they most often complain. When they find satisfaction in their new strength or changing appearance they are not so likely to talk about it. But the talk, and the nonverbal messages as well, give a hint of the profound impact that physical development is having on their lives. Not surprisingly, students are preoccupied with their physical selves in school as well as out, and that physical side of students is there for teachers to understand and deal with every day.

Too often activities for transescent students do not go according to plan. One common reason for difficulty is that the plans do not give adequate attention to the physical side of the students, their stage of physical development. Some activities, being primarily cognitive, expect something physically from the students that might be unreasonable to expect, such as sitting *still* for thirty minutes.

This chapter is designed to help you (a) to understand the basic physical development processes of transescent students; (b) to identify how a school may or may not be responsive to students' physical needs. In the chapter you will also learn how to make objective observations of your students to see whether changes you make really have a constructive effect on student behavior.

This chapter emphasizes observation of students. The first activity guides you in observing several transescents informally. Then, after you read what the human development experts have to say about physical development, we introduce you to some systematic observation techniques.

## ACTIVITY 1
### Observe specific student behavior.

Find some situation where you can observe transescents and make notes about their behavior without disturbing their natural patterns of activity. Consider these: a school library/media center, lunchroom, classroom, and informal groups gathered to talk outside the school building or in someone's home. Select two or three different situations to observe for fifteen minutes each or longer. The object of the observation is to adopt the anthropologist's viewpoint, to watch and record the physical behavior. What do the bodies do? What are the patterns of hand, arm, trunk, and leg movement? How much of the time are they still and how long are the periods of stillness? Describe the bodies. Watch and record the behavior of two or three students, but no more, at one time.

Organize your notes and write out what conclusions or generalizations you can make about the physical traits of the set of students you observed. Save the notes and comments to share with colleagues and to include in your portfolio.

## ACTIVITY 2
### Read what experts say and analyze your observations.

Read "Physical Development Patterns of the Transescent," then go back over your notes and see if your observations are consistent with the generalizations in the reading. Can the findings of the scientists account for some of the behaviors you observed? Can you relate other experiences of yours to their findings?

## Physical Development Patterns of the Transescent

Body changes that occur at puberty are more dramatic than at any stage of life except fetal development and during the first two years. But, as Tanner reminds us, the baby is "not the fascinated, charmed, or horrified spectator that watches the developments, or lack of developments," that the adolescent is of himself or herself (Tanner, 1971, p.907). Considering the magnitude of the drama, one wonders how the adolescents manage to think about anything but the physical self—their skin, sex organs, hair, stomach and other internal workings, and so on—and that of their peers.

What are the facts of transescent physical development, the developmental events that have the greatest bearing on life in schools? Below is a selection of key generalizations, drawn mainly from the monumental work of Tanner (1962, 1971).

1. Muscle size and strength increase, but much more for boys than girls, making boys capable of doing heavier work and running faster and longer. This greater male muscle growth is regarded as an evolutionary adaptation of primitive

primate man, suiting him to the tasks of dominating, fighting, and foraging for food. That the muscle structures are better suited to primitive life than to twentieth century urban living may account for some of the aggressive play and roughness of middle school and junior high boys.

*Implications for Schools:* Provide regular and frequent opportunities for energy to be channeled into constructive action: projects that involve physical activity; physical games and exercises (not in P.E.); and classroom rules and procedures that allow students to move about quietly and to work in postures that seem strange to adults. Students will stay on track better under these conditions, especially if they know the opportunities for movement can be curtailed if they abuse them.

2. The sequence of adolescent changes has remained constant for as long as such events have been recorded. In general, girls develop two years ahead of boys, but individual children differ considerably in the timing of puberty. One boy may have completed the adolescent growth cycle while another boy the same chronological age will not have started. The ages of greatest variability in maturation of girls are 11, 12, and 13; for boys the ages are 13, 14, and 15.

*Implications for Schools:* Any school should examine policies or activities that ignore variability in maturation, as when students are grouped for physical education by chronological age, or when the school supports pairing off for dates. "Boys who are advanced in development are likely to dominate their contemporaries in athletic achievement and sexual interest alike. Conversely, the late developer is the one who all too often loses out in the rough and tumble of the adolescent world; and he may begin to wonder whether he will ever develop his body properly or be as well endowed sexually as those others he has seen developing around him" (Tanner 1971, p.917). Students must have adequate information about human development and its variabilities. Late developing boys not only need assurance that their turn will come, in full measure, but they also need school activities that minimize detrimental comparisons of relative size, strength, and sexual-social attractiveness.

3. While the sequence of adolescent development remains constant, the age of puberty's onset has been changing for both boys and girls. The average transescent girl today has her first menstrual period shortly before her thirteenth birthday, one year earlier than the average in her mother's day and nearly two years earlier than for the average of her grandmother's generation. Today in the United States the peak velocity in growth and height occurs for girls, on the average, at age 12.0, for boys at age 14.0.

*Implications for Schools:* This earlier onset of puberty, along with some indications of earlier social maturation, has been a key reason for shifting from a seven-nine junior high school organization to a five-eight or six-eight middle school organization.

4. The growth spurt in muscle occurs at the same time and rate as the spurt in skeletal growth, because the same hormones are responsible for both. There is a popular notion that the fatigue and listlessness often seen in adolescents occur

because the body frame grows faster than the muscle strength and heart capacity. Scientific data give little support to this notion. On the contrary, "power, athletic skill, and the physical endurance all increase progressively and rapidly throughout adolescence. It is certainly not true that the changes accompanying adolescence enfeeble, even temporarily. If the adolescent becomes weak and easily exhausted, it is for psychological reasons and not physiological ones" (Einstein 1979).

*Implications for Schools:* Because student lassitude is not primarily physical, the teacher should examine the classroom emotional climate and instructional procedures for clues to the problem. In dealing with physical needs, the evidence clearly points to variety and change of pace as vital ingredients in helping students maintain their interest and concentration and avoid fatigue. Time for a "seventh-inning stretch," a break for relaxation; and a classroom structure that permits students to move about are needed for release of physical energies. Learning activities that engage the whole body are more difficult for some teachers to plan and manage than is seatwork, but active activities (it is curious that we need to use redundancy to make the point) are clearly better suited to the transescent. A researcher at Syracuse University, Harry Morgan, has found that transescents who have a particularly strong need for physical activity can show dramatic gains in achievement, self-image, and self-management when placed in a classroom that combines opportunities for physical movement with a business-like, self-paced pattern of instruction.

5. Relative freedom from illness is typical of this age group, but the diet and sleeping habits of many transescents are poor. These habits may be the major physical reasons for symptoms of fatigue. One dietician has estimated that only ten percent of children in this group have an adequate diet (Biehler 1971, p.129).

*Implications for Schools:* Teacher comments to students about their eating and sleeping habits are not likely to have much impact on them. However, students do respond to concrete experience that demonstrates the consequences of their behavior. Such experience needs to be provided in the curriculum. Health (body chemistry, nutrition, diet, hygiene, human development, sexuality, etc.) *can* be taught in ways that engage and change student behaviors and attitudes.

6. The adolescent growth spurt occurs at a different tempo for various body parts. Legs generally reach their peak of growth first. Hands, feet, and head are the first structures to reach adult size, while shoulder width is last. This sequence of growth and the temporary disproportion of body parts often make transescents feel ungainly and awkward. Some have difficulty with body coordination. They bump furniture. They spill and drop objects. How much of the awkwardness is due to uneven growth of structures and how much comes from feelings about oneself is not clear; but both the awkwardness and the feeling of awkwardness are facts the educator must cope with.

*Implications for Schools:* Girls especially need reassurance that the disproportion of feet and hands to the rest of the body is temporary, so too the difficulty with coordination. Moving school furniture and other objects to minimize the effects of awkward movements is a good precaution. Discomfort with their changing bodies may prompt students to try a variety of sitting positions. They need some latitude for experimenting in that regard. Attention to traffic patterns in rooms and hallways can usually suggest changes that will give students more comfortable spaces for moving and sitting. Some teachers have successfully rearranged their classrooms for easy physical movement and traffic flow by putting the teacher's desk in the middle of the room with space around it for movement. Student desks, tables, chairs, and resources are distributed around the walls of the room, some clustered for group work and some separated for individual work.

7. Some girls will move through the whole adolescent cycle, from the onset of puberty to full physical maturity, in 18 months. For others the cycle will take 6 years. Both patterns are normal. Whether the cycle is short or long seems to be independent of whether puberty begins early or late. A girl's first menstrual period may occur six months after her first breast change is evident, or it may occur five and one-half years after. Again, both patterns are normal.

*Implications for Schools:* Girls need factual information and an opportunity to talk about their apprehensions.

8. The first signs of puberty differ in children, causing some confusion among children and parents as well. In some girls "the acceleration in height is the first sign of puberty; this is never so in boys. A small boy whose genitalia are just beginning to develop can be unequivocally reassured that an acceleration in height is soon to take place, but a girl in the corresponding situation may already have had her height spurt (Tanner 1971, p.920).

Transescent girls and boys are entitled to have teachers who understand the changes they are going through and the traumas associated with the changes. Girls and boys need time to adjust to their new bodies, and they need comfortable living-spaces, both physical and psychic, in which to work out their adjustments.

# ACTIVITY 3
**Consider what schools can do in response to transescent physical development.**

The table, "Ten Basic Facts of Transescent Physical Development," contains ten statements that are summary/generalizations of the information in the previous reading. We have included the list to help you think of what can be done in the school and classroom to accommodate students' physical traits and needs. The right side of the table is for you to use to write in your ideas of what students need in the school setting that corresponds to each of the ten developmental facts. When you have compiled your list, you can compare yours with ours, which follows the table. Discuss your list and ours with a colleague.

## TABLE 1
## Ten Basic Facts of Transescent Physical Development and What Schools Can Do to Help

| Characteristics of Transescent Physical Development | What Students Need in the School and Classroom to Accommodate Their Physical Development |
|---|---|
| 1. Aggressive play and roughness among boys increase because of physiological changes at puberty. | |
| 2. Rapid muscular growth is accompanied by the discharge of restless energy. | |
| 3. A combination of physical changes, plus a preoccupation with the changing body and awakening sexual interests, make concentration on studies difficult for the student; attention span is often short. | |
| 4. Girls in general move through puberty two years ahead of boys. | |
| 5. Individual children differ greatly in the onset of puberty and also in the timing of all the events in the adolescent cycle. | |

## TABLE 1
## Ten Basic Facts of Transescent Physical Development and What Schools Can Do to Help (continued)

| Characteristics of Transescent Physical Development | What Students Need in the School and Classroom to Accommodate Their Physical Development |
|---|---|
| 6. Transescent students frequently show fatigue, for psychological reasons or because of poor health habits, not because of physiological changes. | |
| 7. Desire for food increases, but the majority of American young people have improper diets. | |
| 8. During transescence, body parts grow at different tempos resulting in temporary disproportion and a feeling of awkwardness. Some students have trouble with coordination. | |
| 9. Transescents have little knowledge of the facts of human development and have a strong desire to understand what is happening to their bodies. | |
| 10. Transescents are very self-conscious about their bodies. | |

## TABLE 1
## The Authors' View: Ten Basic Facts of Transescent Physical Development and What Schools Can Do to Help

| Characteristics of Transescent Physical Development | What Students Need in the School and Classroom to Accommodate Their Physical Development |
|---|---|
| 1. Aggressive play and roughness among boys increase because of physiological changes at puberty. | 1. Physical games and exercises, some competitive and some noncompetitive (such as body building activities with equipment); lesson plans that include physical activity, some vigorous. |
| 2. Rapid muscular growth is accompanied by the discharge of restless energy. | 2. Seventh-inning stretch; opportunities and places for movement in the classroom; physical education or vigorous activity every day. |
| 3. A combination of physical changes, plus a preoccupation with the changing body and awakening sexual interests, make concentration on studies difficult for the student; attention span is often short. | 3. Opportunities for students to choose short-duration activities (student choice, not only teacher prescription); change of focus of activities several times in a class period. |
| 4. Girls in general move through puberty two years ahead of boys. | 4. School activities should minimize any detrimental comparisons of relative size and sexual-social development and attractiveness (such as dating games, dances, and beauty contests). |
| 5. Individual children differ greatly in the onset of puberty and also in the timing of all the events the adolescent cycle. | 5. Activities such as dating games, dances, and beauty contests should be avoided as should compulsory competitive athletics in which a few early developers are likely to dominate; late developers need facts and assurance that their time will come; students should have choices of P.E. activities. |
| 6. Transescent students frequently show fatigue, for psychological reasons or because of poor health habits, not because of physiological changes. | 6. Students need frequent change of pace, variety, exercise breaks, and regular opportunities for physical movement in the classroom. |
| 7. Desire for food increases, but the majority of American young people have improper diets. | 7. They need a health curriculum that is very personal. |

**TABLE 1**
## The Authors' View: Ten Basic Facts of Transescent Physical Development and What Schools Can Do to Help (continued)

| | |
|---|---|
| 8. During transescence, body parts grow at different tempos resulting in temporary disproportion and a feeling of awkwardness. Some students have trouble with coordination. | 8. Facts and reassurance are needed; teachers should study traffic patterns in classrooms and halls, then adjust objects to minimize students' bumping, spilling, and dropping objects; emphasize polishing existing physical skills, not acquisition of new ones. |
| 9. Transescents have little knowledge of the facts of human development and have a strong desire to understand what is happening to their bodies. | 9. Students need facts and opportunities to ask questions anonymously to get straight answers. |
| 10. Transescents are very self-conscious about their bodies. | 10. Students need opportunities for privacy; they need P.E. activities that are sensitive to some students' reluctance to expose their bodies. |

## ACTIVITY 4
### Analyze classroom action.

Now it is time to analyze a classroom and decide what changes could be made in lesson plans, instructional techniques, or classroom structure to better accommodate students' physical needs. To help you gather data for analyzing a classroom, we have constructed the Student Physical Activity Record, included at the end of the chapter. Its purpose is to give the teacher a picture of student physical behavior as it is related to various instructional activities. The SPAR is first used to identify patterns of student behavior: How long is the attention span for X activity? How widespread is restlessness toward the end of the period? How frequently are students distracted from their tasks? And so on.

To train yourself and any observation partner(s) in the use of the instrument, follow the guidelines of "How to Use the Student Physical Activity Record."

Use the instrument a second time after you have analyzed students' physical needs and have made appropriate classroom changes. Comparing "before" and "after" observations gives you evidence of the effect of your changes on student behavior. Share outcomes with your observation partner.

After you have collected your observation data, use it along with our list and yours written in Activity 3 to plan three or four specific changes you would make in a classroom to better accommodate students' physical development. Write out in detail your proposed changes and prepare to ask for feedback about them from your colleagues.

If some students remain restless and distractable after you have made what changes you can, consider what social and psychological factors may be involved. Two other chapters may help you identify the problems: Social and Emotional Development: Ten to Fourteen, and Helping Students Take Responsibility. If you need assistance beyond that, we suggest the book, *The Aggressive Child*, by Fritz Redl and David Wineman. They make the point that restlessness is a natural response to anxiety or nervousness. Children's fidgeting may be a way of protecting themselves from the fact that they feel a lack of control. For some students, fidgeting can quickly escalate into aggression if they feel out of control and believe that the teacher will not or cannot stop them. Your school psychologist or counselor should be able to help with students you believe have that kind of anxiety.

## How to Use the Student Physical Activity Record

Systematic observation instruments, such as this one, are shorthand methods of recording important information about people's activities; in this case, students in a classroom. With this instrument, an observer can watch students in action and record activities in nine categories. Any student action can be coded in one of the categories. When an observation period is complete, the total number of tallies in each category will show the frequency with which that action occurred.

The purpose of this instrument (and of others introduced in other chapters of the book) is to provide the teacher-as-learner with information that can be used in analyzing classroom processes, planning for improvement, and measuring progress. It is not an evaluation instrument. The observer does not judge the value of what he or she observes, but, like a movie camera, records and reports what occurs. Because the observer records objectively and does not evaluate the data, teachers have found the process easy and comfortable to use.

To use the Student Physical Activity Record as part of this chapter follow these steps (Form 1):

1. Discuss the observation form with your observation partner(s). You will want to assure yourselves that the nine categories of student behaviors have the same meaning to each of you.

2. Practice using the instrument, with two or more observing the same events at the same time. One way to practice and check the agreement between observers is to select three students to watch in a classroom, observe each of them in sequence, and make a tally in one of the nine categories every five seconds (or start at a slower rate if you need to). That is, watch Student A for a moment, select the category most descriptive of his/her behavior at that moment and record it in Column A with a tally mark. With a rhythm of making a mark every five seconds, go on to Student B. Make a tally mark in Column B for that student, five seconds later Student C, and five seconds later Student A again. Continue for ten minutes. Then total the tallies for each student and compare totals with your fellow observer. Agreement of 85 percent or better is possible and should be sought (a

tally every five seconds would add up to 120 tallies in ten minutes; if two observers agree on more than 100 of those tallies, they have approximately 85 percent agreement).

3. Now you are ready for data collection to begin. First you want to know what is the typical pattern of student activity in a classroom. You will need three or more samples of activity. Each should be of fifteen minutes duration or longer, with each sample taken at different times on different days, but taken of the same group of students. For example, suppose you have a class that meets for forty-five minutes each day. We suggest that you use one of these sampling schedules:

(a) first day: 15-minute sample—first 1/3 of period
    second day: 15-minute sample—second 1/3 of period
    third day: 15-minute sample—third 1/3 of period

or (b) first day: 5-minute sample each of first 1/3, second 1/3, and third
        1/3 of period
    second day: repeat first-day procedures
    third day: same

You must decide which sampling schedule will most likely give a representative picture of the classroom. The patterns of students' physical movements will differ according to the instructional events in progress at the time: starting a new topic; discussion session; individual seatwork just starting, five minutes later, fifteen minutes later; small group project work; taking a test; listening to a speaker, etc. The object of collecting the data is to obtain a "before" picture that you can compare with one or more "after" pictures. If your purpose is to reduce student restlessness, for example, by providing opportunities for more task-related movement around the room or scheduling "seventh-inning stretches," you will need your *before* and *after* samples of behavior to be *taken during similar instructional events*, e.g., test-taking *before* compared with test-taking *after*. At the bottom of the observation sheet the observer must record, for each observation cycle (column), the instructional situation being observed; for example, "small group work, using maps, in progress five minutes, students familiar with tasks;" or "in pairs, students quizzing each other on spelling words, just started." You may have the observer record the physical activity of all the class or part of it. If you have five or six students whose restless or disruptive behavior you want to give special attention to, the observer can follow the recording procedure described in Step 2. If you want a profile of a larger number of students or the whole class, the observation process will differ, and you use Form 2:

A. Select a sequence, a path for the eye, from one student to another, from one end of the room to the other. In this kind of tallying, you do *not* use the columns for individual students. Column A is used for tallies until you have gone once around the room; then you begin Column B.

B. Watch the first student for a moment, decide which of the nine categories best describes his/her behavior at that moment and make a tally mark in

Column A opposite that category number. Go to the next student and make a tally in Column A for that person and continue until all students have been recorded once in Column A. Then begin the rounds again, this time using Column B. The third round goes in Column C, and so on.

C. When each new column is started, describe the instructional event in the space provided at the bottom of the observation sheet.

D. Add up the tally marks in each cell and write in the sum. Also sum each row.

4. Analyze the "before" data your observer(s) has collected. There are no objective standards for the nine categories; you must decide for yourself what is a desirable profile and what needs to be changed. Obviously, Category 5 is the most desirable, and Category 4 is preferable to other movement categories. But what ideal pattern you work toward is up to you. Identify the physical activity patterns you most want to affect, then plan and implement the changes you believe will affect them. When you think the changes have occurred, enough to be observable, proceed with Step 5.

5. With another observer, plan an *after* observation schedule so that samples are taken that will represent the various instructional situations observed in your *before* data. When the samples have been collected, add the tallies cell by cell and by rows and compare the totals with the appropriate *before* totals.

6. Of course, you can repeat the sequence ( Steps 4 and 5) if you are not satisfied with the changes observed in student behavior. When you have accomplished your objective, place the *before* and satisfactory *after* profiles in your portfolio along with a description of the changes you made in classroom procedure that brought about the changed behavior profile.

Introducing you to the observation instrument has a purpose beyond the objectives of this chapter. We hope it will be more than a one-shot training device, that it will become part of your regular way of getting feedback about the effectiveness of your teaching. Short attention span and restlessness are signals of a mismatch between the student and the learning situation. Good teachers are alert to signals like those whether their radar is an instinctive, intuitive process or a learned technique such as systematic observation. We also hope the nine categories will become part of your way of viewing the classroom, of distinguishing between the varieties of student behaviors and giving pinpoint attention to the ones that need it.

We see no reason for you to carry all the burden of making changes in your classroom; using tools such as observation instruments, students can become helpers or partners in the process. Some of them will be eager to be investigators in this kind of action research, just as they are willing to help manage changes in group behavior. As trained observers some of them may be a bit weak on accuracy and objectivity, but the main benefit for them is their increased sense of responsibility for classroom behavior.

# FORM 1
## Student Physical Activity Record

|   | A | B | C | D | E | F | Total |   |
|---|---|---|---|---|---|---|-------|---|
| 1 | ☐ | ☐ | ☐ | ☐ | ☐ | ☐ | ☐ | 1. *Disruptive, Hostile:* Grabbing, hitting, pushing, kicking, pulling |
| 2 | ☐ | ☐ | ☐ | ☐ | ☐ | ☐ | ☐ | 2. *Disruptive, Nonhostile:* Intentional poking, teasing, bothering, annoying, manipulating, horseplay |
| 3 | ☐ | ☐ | ☐ | ☐ | ☐ | ☐ | ☐ | 3. *Movement That Disrupts Others Unintentionally:* Walking about clumsily, making noise, bumping |
| 4 | ☐ | ☐ | ☐ | ☐ | ☐ | ☐ | ☐ | 4. *Movement (Off-Task) That Does Not Disrupt Others:* Taking a break, walking about quietly, releasing tension (e.g., stretching, yawning) |
| 5 | ☐ | ☐ | ☐ | ☐ | ☐ | ☐ | ☐ | 5. *Involved in Work, Definitely and Completely:* Seatwork with interest, helping, responding, on-task; task-related movement |
| 6 | ☐ | ☐ | ☐ | ☐ | ☐ | ☐ | ☐ | 6. *Probably Involved in Work:* Some restlessness and distractability may be present |
| 7 | ☐ | ☐ | ☐ | ☐ | ☐ | ☐ | ☐ | 7. *Passive and Submissive On-Task:* Quietly doing assigned work without much interest |
| 8 | ☐ | ☐ | ☐ | ☐ | ☐ | ☐ | ☐ | 8. *Disrupted, Passive, Off-Task:* Looking around, slumping, doodling, sleeping |
| 9 | ☐ | ☐ | ☐ | ☐ | ☐ | ☐ | ☐ | 9. *Restless Off-Task:* Fidgeting, wiggling, showing physical tension |

A  B  C  D  E  F

◄——— *Write Students' Names Here*

## FORM 2
### Student Physical Activity Record

|   | A | B | C | D | E | F | Total |
|---|---|---|---|---|---|---|-------|
| 1 | ☐ | ☐ | ☐ | ☐ | ☐ | ☐ | ☐ |
| 2 | ☐ | ☐ | ☐ | ☐ | ☐ | ☐ | ☐ |
| 3 | ☐ | ☐ | ☐ | ☐ | ☐ | ☐ | ☐ |
| 4 | ☐ | ☐ | ☐ | ☐ | ☐ | ☐ | ☐ |
| 5 | ☐ | ☐ | ☐ | ☐ | ☐ | ☐ | ☐ |
| 6 | ☐ | ☐ | ☐ | ☐ | ☐ | ☐ | ☐ |
| 7 | ☐ | ☐ | ☐ | ☐ | ☐ | ☐ | ☐ |
| 8 | ☐ | ☐ | ☐ | ☐ | ☐ | ☐ | ☐ |
| 9 | ☐ | ☐ | ☐ | ☐ | ☐ | ☐ | ☐ |

1. *Disruptive, Hostile:*
   Grabbing, hitting, pushing, kicking, pulling

2. *Disruptive, Nonhostile:*
   Intentional poking, teasing, bothering, annoying, manipulating, horseplay

3. *Movement That Disrupts Others Unintentionally:*
   Walking about clumsily, making noise, bumping

4. *Movement (Off-Task) That Does Not Disrupt Others:*
   Taking a break, walking about quietly, releasing tension (e.g., stretching, yawning)

5. *Involved in Work, Definitely and Completely:*
   Seatwork with interest, helping, responding, on-task; task-related movement

6. *Probably Involved in Work:*
   Some restlessness and distractability may be present

7. *Passive and Submissive On-Task:*
   Quietly doing assigned work without much interest

8. *Disrupted, Passive, Off-Task:*
   Looking around, slumping, doodling, sleeping

9. *Restless Off-Task:*
   Fidgeting, wiggling, showing physical tension

*Column Total*

← *Instructional Situation Observed*

## NEXT STEPS

Students in middle grades generally get information about their physical development through a health education unit of study included somewhere in the school curriculum. How is that information provided to students in your school district? The district coordinator for health education can tell you how and perhaps can loan you the curriculum materials that students use. The material may be helpful to you in responding to students' questions or concerns about their bodies. J.M. Tanner's work, noted earlier in the chapter, is another useful source for further study.

Physical games and movement education should not be left to one small fraction of the school day, to be managed only by the physical education teacher. Students' capacities to think and to sustain attention in quiet, mental work depends upon regular and frequent opportunities to do something physical. Besides having stretch breaks and other simple means of releasing physical tension, you can lead students in some simple physical games and movements that require little or no equipment. Two books on games and fitness that we like are *Everybody's a Winner* by Tom Schneider (Little, Brown and Co., 1976) and *The New Games Book*, edited by Andrew Fluegelman (Dolphin Books/Doubleday and Co., 1976). Perhaps the P.E. teacher has some suggestions for you.

You have analyzed a classroom to improve the physical environment for students. What about other areas of the school? Can you identify any conditions that cause physical tensions to escalate? Emotional outbursts are often a signal of too much physical tension. Where do you see signs of tension? Is the school schedule a possible cause? The sequence of classes or activities? Is the passing time from class to class a source of tension? Ask the students to analyze their school day to identify sources of tension. Discuss your findings with other teachers and consider what steps can be taken to make improvements.

Opportunities to be physically active in their studies can be found for students in almost any area of the curriculum. Teachers at Griffin Middle School in Smyrna, Georgia, borrowed fifty sphygmomanometers for a unit on blood circulation. Students took each other's blood pressure and learned that about one-fifth of them needed medical attention for hypertension. Their interest carried over into related activities, and students later coordinated a community blood drive. What opportunities for active studies can you identify in your area of teaching?

## REFERENCES

BIEHLER, R. F. *Psychology Applied to Teaching.* Boston: Houghton Mifflin Co., 1971.

EINSTEIN, ELIZABETH. "Classroom Dynamos: Making Room for the Active Minority Student," *Human Behavior* 8(4), April 1979.

FLUEGELMAN, ANDREW, ED. *The New Games Book.* New York: Dolphin Books/Doubleday and Co., 1976.

REDL, FRITZ AND DAVID WINEMAN. *The Aggressive Child.* Glencoe, Ill.: Free Press, 1957.

SCHNEIDER, TOM. *Everybody's a Winner.* Boston: Little, Brown and Co., 1976.

SOMMERS, B. B. *Puberty and Adolescence.* New York: Oxford University Press, 1978.

TANNER, J. M. "Sequence, Tempo and Individual Variation in the Growth and Development of Boys and Girls Aged 12 to 16," *Daedalus* 100(4) Fall 1971.

TANNER, J. M. *Growth at Adolescence,* 2nd Edition. Oxford: Blackwell Scientific Publications, 1962.

# CHAPTER THREE

# INTELLECTUAL DEVELOPMENT: TEN TO FOURTEEN

If you were to ask middle school students a question about moral standards, could you predict what sorts of answers they would give? To the question, "Why should people do everything they can to save another person's life?", eight students gave these answers:

- Because they love 'em a lot or they are their best friend or they feel sorry for the person.

- Because it tells you in the Bible to help your brother and stuff like that.

- Sometimes they want to be a hero or something.

- If you just let somebody die you won't have any friends.

- You can't replace somebody else's life; if you can save it you should.

- A human has a soul and a right to live.

- Because they might be in the same situation some time and would want someone to do something for them.

- To keep the generations going.

Do you see any pattern in the responses? Can you see a basic difference between the set of responses on the left and those on the right? Researchers and teachers who have studied intellectual development can see a fundamental difference: the pattern represented in the left column they would label *concrete operational thinking*; those on the right represent abstract thinking or, more properly, *formal operational thinking*. The responses on the left suggest that the speakers' thinking processes are bounded by their own concrete experience. They find it difficult, if not impossible, to view things from outside themselves, to stand in someone else's shoes, to take an abstract view of humanity—which is the viewpoint the responses on the right take.

Why is this difference important to teachers? Students in these two stages of mental development approach their studies—their whole world, for that matter—in basically different ways. Moreover, all of the eight speakers are in the same grade. Any teacher of early adolescents must deal with students who are very different in mental maturation, even though they may be in the same range of age and intelligence.

## EMPHASIS ON DEVELOPMENT, NOT ACHIEVEMENT

The pattern of instruction that is most common in today's schools does not offer the teacher much opportunity to witness the intellectual development of students. Achievement, yes, but not development. The instruction process emphasizes learning of specific information or skills, so the teacher is most aware of the student's progress in attaining those objectives. Development, on the other hand, has to do with the general structures, the cognitive equipment of action and thinking which the student brings to the learning tasks. Of course, cognitive structures are changed by learning, but that aspect of learning is not given emphasis.

Teachers try to design learning tasks to match the student's stage of intellectual development, knowing that when the match is missing, the learning falters. We are convinced that teachers want to give more attention to intellectual development so they can more adequately guide student learning; we have designed this chapter to help with that process. Assuming that users of the chapter have some knowledge of human development, we have concentrated on the practical tasks of converting that knowledge into classroom skills.

The chapter has five objectives:

1. to highlight the key features of intellectual development of transescents
2. to provide practice in identifying stages of cognitive development of individual students
3. to help you identify the range of cognitive development of one group of students
4. to guide you in planning activities suitable for the developmental range of that group
5. to guide you in evaluating existing plans to see how well they match the students' levels of development

## ACTIVITY 1
### Gather samples of students' reasoning.

This activity is designed to give you a feel for the range of intellectual development to be found in any classroom among ten- to fourteen-year-old students.

**A.**   Select a classroom group of twenty or more students and arrange time—about five minutes—for them to respond to a question.

**B.**   Give each student a three-by-five inch card or piece of paper. Read the following from the chalkboard: "Why should people generally do everything they can to keep from breaking the law?" Ask the students to write their names on one side of the paper and their own best answer to the question, in one or two sentences, on the other side. Give them time to respond and then collect the cards.

**C.**  Use your own judgment to sort the cards into three piles: "Probably *concrete* reasoning," "Probably *between* concrete and abstract reasoning," and "Probably *abstract* reasoning." Don't look at students' names as you sort the cards. After you have sorted all the cards, mark on the back of each card a *C*, a *B*, or an *A*, according to its pile, to designate them as concrete, between, and abstract. Don't be concerned if you find the sorting task frustrating or if you are not clear about the fit between your sets of responses and ours. The next two activities are designed to help you recognize the clues students give about their stage of mental development.

**D.**  Compare the responses in your three groups of cards with the three lists of responses that follow. Record your analysis of and personal reactions to the pattern of student responses. Then put your statements and the cards in your portfolio for future reference.

## Comparison List for Intellectual Development

Sample answers of middle school students given to the question: "Why should people generally do everything they can to keep from breaking the law?"

**Concrete**

- So they won't get in trouble and get put in jail.
- Because if people keep on stealing there's going to be more people mad at you.
- Because laws were made for people to obey for their own good.

**Mixed; Between Concrete and Abstract**

- So you'll have more peace and less trouble.
- So taxes and stuff won't be so high. Because taxes go up whenever crime rates go up.
- Because it's usually infringing upon other people's privileges.

**Abstract**

- Because you are taking away someone else's right when you disobey the law.
- Because if everybody broke the law there wouldn't be any Constitution— there wouldn't be any school.
- Because if nobody obeyed the law, nothing would work right. People need laws so they can live together.

---

The student responses shown here, as well as those in the orientation to this chapter, were obtained in the research of Sharon Hiett. See her dissertation, "Moral Judgment of Disruptive and Non-Disruptive Students and Their Teachers," University of Florida, 1977.

## ACTIVITY 2
**Read and test yourself on mental development processes.**

**A.**   Read "Mental Development Processes in Transescence," which follows. Make notes on the key facts of the reading by using the "Notation Sheet: Six Dimensions of Intellectual Development," which follows the reading. The recommended manner for using the notation form will become clear as you read. After completing the notation sheet, compare your notes with ours, which are on a copy of the same form.

**B.**   You may check your grasp of the main ideas in the reading by using the self-quiz that follows the notation sheet.

## Mental Development Processes in Transescence

The changes in intellectual structures at transescence are not easy for teachers and parents to see, but specialists in human development who study the cognitive changes generally regard them as vital processes that must become the business of those who educate children. Functional intelligence is not fixed at birth or any other age, and it is profoundly influenced by individual experience, especially the experience that comes under the influence of significant persons in a child's life.

Research on cognitive development indicates that many Americans never develop their reasoning ability beyond a dependence upon concrete experience and so the larger world of ideas is not available to them. Researchers believe that the early adolescent years, eleven through sixteen, are watershed years in which young people are forming life-long dispositions about how to use—and whether to even try using—the mental capacities that their neural development makes possible in those years (Kohlberg and Gilligan, 1971; Epstein, 1978). How powerful an influence is exerted by the school experience is purely speculation. We take the view that it matters whether teachers and the curriculum ignore, impede, or actively support the cognitive development of students (as distinguished from their achievement—a point emphasized earlier in the chapter).

What are the main cognitive development processes of transescents? For a comprehensive answer you can refer to any of the several authoritative books on the subject listed at the end of the chapter. A brief summary of the main themes will serve our purposes here. We have identified six themes or dimensions of development which can be regarded as continuums stretching from childhood into adolescence, including development:

1.  from concrete into abstract thinking;
2.  from an egocentric into a sociocentric perspective;
3.  from a limited into a broad perspective of time and space;

4. from a simplistic into a complex view of human motivation;
5. from reliance on slogans toward the construction of a personal ideology; and
6. development of a capacity for forming concepts that stretches from lower order into complex, higher order conceptualizing.

Keep in mind as we discuss these dimensions of development that they are *potentials* made possible by biological changes, potentials that need nurturing. No child is guaranteed passage along the developmental paths, but only a few are structurally incapable of making the trip.

### 1. From Concrete into Abstract Thinking

The transition from concrete operational thinking to formal operations, so extensively documented by Jean Piaget and others, is a facet of transescent development that most readers are acquainted with. Unfortunately, the acquaintance is not transformed readily into teaching practices and curriculum plans, for a variety of reasons. We have attempted here to present the ideas of concrete and formal operations in a manner that will help teachers put to use the power in Piaget's insights.

*Concrete* and *formal* are terms that refer to structures that emerge to manage thinking. A general structure that continues over an extended period of time, usually several years, is called a *stage*. The order in which the structures emerge is always the same, but the timing varies from person to person. A child does not obtain a new structure by being taught. It is not a skill given him by the culture. Rather, it is invented afresh in the experience of each child. As children perceive more and more of the world, their system for managing their intellectual life must change progressively to handle the new demands. New structures evolve from the previous ones.

**Concrete operational thinking.**    The structure capable of managing concrete operational thinking emerges around age seven. *Operational* means that the child can perform mental operations on objects and events. In the pre-operational stage the child could think only in one direction at a time, take only one point of view. For example, when shown two balls of clay of equal size and then one ball is flattened to a pancake shape, they cannot see that the quantity of clay has stayed the same. They can attend either to the lowered height of the lump of clay or to the increased diameter, but not to both at once to see that the change in one direction is balanced by the change in the other direction. In Piaget's terminology, attending to two directions or viewpoints at once is operational thinking. Operational thinking is reversible or can go in a zig-zag pattern as well, as is indicated in the solving of this problem: "Your friend Bill here has a friend you don't know named John. You are shorter than Bill, and Bill is shorter than John. Who is tallest?" Answering this question requires a change in point of view and direction of thinking at least three times without losing sight of the matter that started the thought process. Children in the pre-operational stage cannot answer the question because they do not know John.

While "operations" represents the major new capability of children in the concrete operations stage, "concrete" represents the major limitation of their thinking; i.e., it is tied to concrete, personal experience. They cannot deal with hypothetical situations. For example, if three girls at the concrete stage, all of them the same height, were asked this question, they could not answer it: "*Suppose* Jean were shorter than Pat, and Jan were shorter than Jean, who would be the shortest?" The question is hypothetical, suppositional, and goes beyond the concrete reality of the child ("But we're all the same height!"). Concrete operational thinking depends upon (a) the presence of concrete objects; (b) reasoning that is not required to violate what the senses tell one about concrete reality; and/or (c) concrete, personal experiences one has had in the past (memories) that one can call upon for present problem solving. If Jean, Pat, and Jan were asked to act out their hypothetical heights, by two of them stooping to make themselves shorter, then the concrete image would probably give them the answer to the puzzle quickly.

Children in the stage of concrete operational thinking are capable of a rich and wide-ranging intellectual life. They can learn a great deal of the heritage of their culture. But the extent and quality of the learning is strictly limited to the soundness of the concepts they form. If they learn concepts that are essentially empty words, empty of any concrete content from personal experience, their thinking eventually leads to dead ends with no turnarounds.

Consider, for example, the concepts of city, state, and country. These words are used often in the early grades, but many middle school students show confusion when the relationships between city, county, state, and country are considered in geography or government studies. Apparently they learned labels but not the sense of territory or jurisdiction that the label is meant to represent. One gets clues of the child's confusion, such as this set of questions from a twelve-year-old on an automobile trip from Atlanta to Miami: "Are we out of Atlanta yet? We are? Then we're in Florida, right?" Much of the heritage of the culture is stored in the form of abstractions such as these concepts. But abstractions presented to children *as abstractions*, without connection to concrete experience, are barriers to further learning.

Even more tragically, these empty abstractions may delay or prevent the development of formal operational thinking. When children find that logical operations are more frustrating than they are satisfying, they are more likely to shy away from careful reasoning and rely on whim or someone else's decision.

**Formal operations—abstract thinking.**   Junior high/middle school students range across the substages of concrete and formal operational thinking, with some still in the pre-operational stage. Concrete operational thinking is usually evident in children around age seven, but it does not arrive fully developed. "The development, differentiation, and perfection of concrete operational thought continues throughout middle childhood and seems to reach its peak during preadolescence" (Kohen-Raz 1971, pp. 54-55). When the transition from concrete to formal operational thinking occurs, one is able to reason beyond personal experience and perform logical operations about the possible and not just the actual. Formal operational thinkers are capable of comparing and combining ideas and relationships and reaching conclusions quite independent of concrete experience. They can take a conditional viewpoint: "Suppose that . . . ," "if . . . then," and "it depends on . . . ." They don't get boxed into either/or positions—for example, they may argue that neither choice in a true-false test item is a good choice.

Formal operational thinking is thinking about thinking, performing operations on previous operations, and forming abstract concepts from abstractions rather than from concrete experience. It is classifying classifications, combining combinations, and relating relationships. When the formal stage is fully developed, typically in the high school years or beyond, thinking progresses to the mode of the scientist—systematic consideration of all logical possibilities.

The common expression "from concrete to abstract thinking," used at the beginning of this section, needs some clarification. Youngsters in the stage of concrete operational thinking are quite capable of performing abstracting operations and using abstractions in sequences of *concrete* operational reasoning. For example, they can abstract properties of various foods, assign them into food groups according to the abstract properties, and then think through various issues of diet and health using the abstract concepts. However, as they perform these mental operations, the concrete base is always present in the process. When the transition is made to formal operations, the base no longer always needs to be concrete.

**The timing of formal operations development.**    Because the ages of six to ten are usually assigned to the stage of concrete operational thought, and age eleven is reported as the beginning of formal operational thought, teachers of transescents have been misled into expecting their students to be capable of formal operations. This is a serious misconception. There is no doubt that a large majority of ten- to fourteen-year-old students operate at the level of concrete thinking and need further development of the structures of concrete thought before they will reach formal operations. Some children clearly attain the capacity for concrete logical operations at age five, while others do not reach that point until eight or nine. But this capacity is attained by all children eventually (Kohlberg 1966). Formal operational thinking, in contrast, does not develop in all people. Some experiments suggest that perhaps one-third of American adults never fully achieve formal operational reasoning (Kohlberg and Gilligan 1971, p.1065).

Teachers of transescents can expect their students to range in intellectual development from pre-operational thinking to fully developed formal reasoning. A small proportion of students is likely to be at either end of the continuum. The socio-economic background of students is likely to influence the distribution along the continuum. One generalization about transescents that can be made with assurance is that the majority of them are concrete thinkers or are in transition—perfecting concrete operations and moving into formal operations, with some of their thinking in one stage and some in the other. Those who teach transescents, however, have the obviously large responsibility of providing intellectual support and challenge to all students along the continuum described above.

**Implications for teachers.**   What happens when a teacher or a textbook author expects a level of reasoning of which the student is not capable? What happens when abstractions beyond the child's range of concrete experience form the substance of a lesson? Some students stew in their frustration and quit trying. Some no doubt find a way to get the "right answer" without understanding the problem or the solution. Probably a large number of students treat this abstraction as one more piece of adult "reality" they *should not* really understand until they are initiated, at some vague point in the future, into the mysteries of adulthood.

There is nothing in cognitive development theory or in brain development studies to suggest that this mismatch of thinking task to the child's level of reasoning is in any way constructive. One does *not* promote development into formal operational thinking by expecting formal operations from a child who is not developmentally able to perform these tasks (Epstein 1978, 1979). On the contrary, a much more supportable assumption is that the only power teachers have to open the door to formal operational thinking is by guiding students through the perfecting of concrete operations.

## 2. From an Egocentric into a Sociocentric Perspective

Young children are the center of their universe. Everything has meaning only in relation to their own needs and interests. Movement away from egocentrism is called decentering and is a process that extends throughout childhood. Keep in mind that it is only one of the six dimensions, one partial way of characterizing the total process of intellectual development. All of the other five dimensions of development described in this essay can be regarded as a form of decentering. But we use the term here in a more limited way to mean the progression of thinking that leads the child toward a sociocentric view of the world, toward a sense of community and one's own community membership. We include in this dimension the development of moral reasoning.

Egocentrism, not to be confused with egotism or selfishness, is a term used to describe the perception and conviction held by children that their point of view is the only one. Young children often assume that everything literally disappears when they close their eyes. As children progress through concrete and formal operational stages of thinking, they gradually lose their egocentrism. In concrete thinking, children have progressed far enough to see various social roles that touch their lives: teacher, policeman, merchant, etc. If one asks about education, they will speak about personal experiences in the school, and will have difficulty with abstractions such as school programs, or discipline policy. Similarly a discussion

---

*For examples of activities that help students perfect concrete operations see the books by Ginsburg and Opper, Sigel and Hooper, and Taba listed among the References.

about law is personalized to the level of policeman, judge, and criminal. Why have laws? "So people don't steal and kill" (Adelson 1971, p.1016).

Adelson summarizes the concrete stage social perspective in this way:

> . . . at the threshold of adolescence the youngster gives few signs of community. Unable to imagine social reality in the abstract, he enters adolescence with only the weakest sense of social institutions, of their structure and functions, and of . . . such ideas as authority, rights, liberty, equity, interests, representation, and so on.

Social interaction is the principal factor that liberates a person from egocentrism, particularly social interaction with peers. "In the course of his contacts (and, especially, his conflicts and arguments) with other children, the child increasingly finds himself forced to re-examine his own precepts and concepts in the light of those of others, and by so doing, gradually rids himself of cognitive egocentrism" (Flavell 1963, p.279).

Interaction with others makes it possible for transescents to learn other points of view, whether or not they can rationalize or tolerate them. At this stage, the need for law and order to regulate improper points of view and behaviors becomes very evident to transescents. Their orientation toward law, as reported in the research of Adelson and his colleagues (Adelson, Green, and O'Neil 1969), illustrates the transition from concrete to abstract thinking. In answer to the question, "What is the purpose of laws?" some responses representative of four age groups were as follows:

> *An eleven-year-old:* "Well, so everybody won't fight and they have certain laws so they won't go around breaking windows and stuff and getting away with it."
>
> *A thirteen-year-old:* "To keep the people from doing things they're not supposed to, like killing people and . . . if you're in the city, like speeding in the car and things like that."
>
> *A fifteen-year-old:* "To help keep us safe and free."
>
> *An eighteen-year-old:* "Well, the main purpose would be just to set up a standard of behavior for people, for society living together so that they can live peacefully and in harmony with each other."

When the 120 answers to this question were coded by the researchers as either *concrete* or *abstract* (with the abstract code being used "generously"), percentages obtained by age groups were

### *Concrete and Abstract Views of Law*

| View of law | Age | | | |
|---|---|---|---|---|
| | 11 | 13 | 15 | 18 |
| Concrete | .72 | .69 | .19 | .07 |
| Abstract | .28 | .31 | .81 | .93 |

When the same student responses were coded as representing a view of law as *restrictive* or as *beneficial*, these percentages were obtained:

*Restrictive and Beneficial Views of Law*

| View of law | Age | | | |
|---|---|---|---|---|
| | 11 | 13 | 15 | 18 |
| Restrictive | .76 | .73 | .31 | .17 |
| Restrictive & beneficial | .10 | .17 | .27 | .21 |
| Beneficial | .14 | .10 | .42 | .62 |

In both classifications, a sharp shift can be seen between ages thirteen and fifteen. The researchers interpreted these and other data from their interviews as indicating that before age fourteen or fifteen students probably cannot grasp the needs of the total community. Their egocentrism has not yet given way to a wider view of social order and they think of law only as affecting *individual* behavior—and that in a restricting way. An authoritarian view of social order dominates transescents' thinking about social relationships until about age fifteen. They are preocccupied with human misbehavior and have little understanding of or faith in self-control as a factor in social restraint. They accept authoritarianism as a necessary fact of life and do not grasp the idea of individual and minority rights. They see laws as fixed and settled, not as social agreements subject to amendment. On an authoritarianism scale devised in this research, 85 percent of transescents scored high on the index, while only 17 percent of high school seniors scored in the high range (Adelson 1971, pp. 1026-1027).

The research of the Adelson group showed major shifts away from egocentrism occurring between ages thirteen and fifteen, with some important social concept changes apparent between ages eleven and thirteen. This research on social reasoning and that of Kohlberg concerning stages of moral development have similar findings as to the timing of the development of sociocentric perspective. Kohlberg's findings (Kohlberg and Gilligan 1971, pp. 1066-1068) suggest that two-thirds to three-fourths of ten- to fourteen-year-olds are in moral development Stages 2, 3 or 4. The three stages can be described as follows:

Stage 2. Good and bad are interpreted by the child in terms of physical consequences for misbehavior and of the physical power of those in authority. The child sees a social system or social order only in terms of rules by which he can satisfy his needs and occasionally those of others. This stage (and Stage 1) are considered preconventional moral thinking.

Stage 3. Good behavior is that which pleases important persons—family, peer group, and beyond. Conforming to be a good girl or good boy is valuable for its own sake. Standards are derived from what the child regards as normal, majority behavior. This stage and Stage 4 are considered conventional behavior.

Stage 4. Right behavior is doing one's duty, following fixed rules, showing respect for authority and maintaining the social order—which is a given fact of life, worth maintaining for its own sake.

The descriptions given by Adelson of social views of eleven- and thirteen-year-olds seem to fit Kohlberg's Stages 2, 3, and 4 quite well. Kohlberg's work shows that children in his Stage 2 are in the development stage of concrete operational thinking, while Stages 3 and 4 of moral development correspond to the beginning of formal operational thinking. Postconventional moral judgment, Kohlberg's Stages 5 and 6, has developed in about one-tenth of adolescents by age fifteen (p.1071). The kind of social perspective shown by Adelson's eighteen-year-olds is reflective of the beginning of postconventional moral judgment.

**Implications for teachers.** Just as higher levels of reasoning are genetically available to many more people than actually develop them, so too are higher levels of social thought and moral judgment. Moreover, Kohlberg's work shows that not everyone who attains formal operational thinking then develops post-conventional moral judgment. This record of underdeveloped potential stands as a challenge to teachers.

Helping students develop social responsibility is one of the oldest goals of American education. The farther a child has moved from an egocentric toward a sociocentric perspective, the greater the capacity for being socially responsible. Movement along that continuum depends upon many factors, one of which is the influence of teachers.

At least three basic implications for teachers can be drawn from what is known about the development of social reasoning.

1. School curriculums in junior high and middle schools almost invariably assume that students are capable of formal operational thought; they are not designed to develop it (Kohlberg and Gilligan 1971, pp. 1066-1068). This is true not only of traditional curriculums, but it is also evident in most of the "new social studies," "new science," and "new math" curriculums developed in the 1960s and 1970s. The traditional curriculum materials assume that students can handle abstractions that have for them no concrete, personal roots (this is particularly true of social studies textbooks); and the new curriculums emphasize problem solving, much of which cannot be accomplished except at the level of formal operational thinking. We recommend a careful review of curriculum materials to classify them according to their requirements of formal reasoning ability and sociocentric perspective.

2. The only way that children can develop social responsibility is by having social responsibilities to carry out. The common pattern of schools is that of persons in authority assigning learning tasks to students. This procedure delegates to the students themselves relatively little social responsibility. Insofar as the classroom can become a learning *community*, with responsibilities delegated to students, to that extent students can have concrete experiences in the management of a social system. Through such experiences students can begin to conceive of government as a process, not just a remote abstraction; they can conceive of laws (and rules like classroom rules) as social agreements—experiments to be tested and which are subject to change. They can be helped to see the intricate network of interrelationships that underlie any social system, and they can be helped to

stretch their capacities for moral judgments in an atmosphere that supplies constructive feedback. In the give and take with peers, students can be helped to recognize and test their own assumptions, to recognize the social consequences of their own desires and impulses. The chapters on social and emotional development of transescents, and on the teacher as advisor, contain guidelines for starting a classroom learning community.

3. Whether they wish it or not, teachers are authority models for students and teachers strongly influence the development of the sociocentric perspective, enhancing it or retarding it. Teachers can help students outgrow their authoritarian views of leadership by modeling a wider set of leadership roles. We emphasize the teacher as model because talk *about* social values is empty unless behavior is consistent with the talk.

### 3. Development of Time and Space Perspective

Young children are egocentric in space and time as well as in other ways. They are occupied with what is immediately present. As they manipulate objects and move about, judging sizes, shapes, movements, distances, and durations, they gradually extend their sense of space and time. That process is a vital part of intellectual development. In Piaget's terms, intelligence involves transcending the limits of the immediate surroundings and expanding one's relationships in space and time.

Moreover, intelligence cannot grow in the child without the development of sensory perception, and perceptual development depends upon the integration of intellectual experience and sensory habits (Kohen-Raz 1971, pp. 83-85). Without doubt, school activities that involve physical manipulation and call for space and time judgments have intellectual value beyond the more obvious skills they promote.

Children enter transescence "locked into the present," according to Adelson (1971, p.1017). At that age they show little sense of history, and rarely try to explain present events in terms of the past. When attempting to imagine the future, they can project only direct extensions of a present event or condition. The differences in responses between thirteen- and fifteen-year-olds in the Adelson study suggest that the time perspective begins to stretch distinctly at the latter age. Realization that personal histories affect present behavior is one important development. Another is the realization that the future depends, to some extent, on choices made today. Future perspective, a more powerful imagining of the future, was far more visible in these transescents than was the historical perspective. The researchers concluded that the sense of history in most of their subjects, including the eighteen-year-olds, was undeveloped.

**Implications for teachers.**   Earlier we spoke about the need of students to get physically involved in problem solving—manipulating, constructing, reconstructing, experimenting, etc.—to obtain a concrete base for abstract concepts. Here we see another reason for physical activity and concrete objects: to influence the development of time and space perspective. History, geography, geometry, and other forms of mathematics, and some science subjects depend upon time and space perspective. Generally, curriculum writers assume that the child has already developed the necessary cognitive structures or that they are developed somehow outside of, or incidental to, the curriculum. The student's sense of perspective, duration, sequence, consequence, and other *fundamental* relationships in time and space are not given direct attention by the curriculum in the middle grades.

If students' historical perspective lags behind their interest in imagining the future, perhaps a history curriculum that centers upon planning for alternative futures—that is, solving tangible social problems in anticipation of future consequences—could offer students a way to draw upon history as a resource in planning and problem solving.

## 4. Understanding Human Motivation

The fourth continuum or dimension of development is the path toward recognizing the complexities of human motivation. Young children do not conceive of motive or intention being different from a person's act. In one of Piaget's experiments, children were told two stories and asked to judge the "naughtiness" of children in the episodes. In the first, a boy attempting to get cookies from the shelf without his mother's permission, accidentally knocked a cup off the shelf and broke it. In the second story, a boy, when called to supper, opened the door to the dining room and accidentally hit and smashed a tray full of cups that were on a chair behind the door. When asked to say which boy was naughtier and why, children under ten often chose the second boy—because he caused more damage. Older children, judging the intentions of the two boys, quite consistently said the first boy was naughtier (Piaget 1948).

Motivations of people do enter into the thinking of transescents, but not deeply. They do not look for, nor expect to find, complex reasons for behavior. When a thirteen-year-old encounters hostility from someone, it is likely to be explained superficially: "He doesn't like me," or "He sure gets angry easily." A person cheats because "He's a cheater." A person acts selfishly because "He's selfish." An act of kindness or generosity is explained: "He likes me." Categories of thinking about behaviors are good or bad, black or white.

As with other aspects of cognitive maturation in the social dimension of the transescent's life, fifteen seems to be the age at which change in thinking is most evident. We turn again to Adelson's research (1971, p.1019):

> Consider the following: after a series of questions on crime and punishment, we introduced the problem of recidivism. Most people who go to jail seem to end up there again. Why? A hard question, certainly, and penetrating answers are hard to come by at any age. Yet there are clear differences in the quality of psychological inference between adolescents in the early and middle periods. The twelve- and thirteen-year-olds say such things as: "Well, they don't know anything, and you have to teach them a lesson," or "Well, it is in his mind that he has to do it and keep doing it over again," or "Well, their conscience might tell them to do this or something." At fifteen a deeper sense of motive is apparent. One youngster says that "going to jail produces a grudge against others," another suggests that they "become bitter, or feel mocked," a third speculates that they brood and thus "establish themself as being a criminal."

What is the process transescents go through in deepening their understanding of human motivation? Students of cognitive development offer this description: as children are helped to reflect on their own experiences, particularly their interactions with others, they come to see that their behavior is influenced by many forces, present and past. When they see that their own actions have complex explanations, they can begin to imagine that other people have complex motivations as well. By being helped to "take the point of view of the other," through role-playing or less structured means, they gradually are able to attribute to others motives they recognize in themselves. Very likely their ability to analyze the motives in a situation will develop first for situations in which they are only spectators, not involved participants.

The black-white, good-bad pattern of thought will break down and be seen as inadequate first in regard to their own behavior. Two categories will not be enough to deal with their conception of their own behavior. Even after they see that other people's behavior is too complex for either-or categories, they may turn back to the simplistic explanation when their own security is threatened.

Transescents probably have an intuitive or unconscious notion of other people's motives long before they can bring it into consciousness. They know that their success in social interactions depends upon how well they "read" the inclinations, moods, and feelings of other people. So one could say that it is natural for people to seek deeper understanding of human motivations as a means of becoming more successful in interactions with others. When we see people in whom this natural process seems to be cut off, we wonder how deep and painful the wounds must be that caused them to turn away from the quest for a fuller understanding of the human situation. If the schools are to encourage this quest for deeper understanding, they must provide a variety of learning situations beyond the stereotyped "please-the-teacher" motivation—a rich variety that reflects the complexity of motivations outside the classroom.

**Implications for teachers.**    Transescents' capacities to see complexity in human motivations develop more slowly than does their ability to perform formal mental operations on physical data. This is a developmental fact, so far as researchers are able to determine. We choose to treat this fact *not* as a signal for teachers of transescents to expect less of their students and "let nature take its course," but as a sign to encourage individual intellectual growth through the challenge of a stimulating environment. This is the true meaning of "nature's course."

A number of educators have demonstrated that students in the middle grades *can* be helped substantially to increase their grasp of human complexity.* Role-

---

*For example, see the descriptions of research in Part 5 of L. Raths and others, *Teaching for Thinking: Theory and Application* (Columbus, Ohio: C. E. Merrill Books, Inc., 1967); R. Fox, R. Lippitt and J. Lohman, *Teaching Social Science Material in the Elementary School* (Cooperative Research Project No. E-011, U. S. Office of Education, 1964); L. Kohlberg and E. Turiel, Eds., *Recent Research in Moral Development* (New York: Holt, Rinehart and Winston, 1972); F. Shaftel and G. Shaftel, *Role-Playing in the Curriculum* (New Jersey: Prentice-Hall, Inc., 1982); and R. Fox, R. Lippitt, R. Schmuck and E. VanEgmond, *Understanding Classroom Social Relations and Learning* (Chicago: Science Research Associates, 1966).

playing, discussions of moral dilemmas, value clarification strategies, classroom group problem solving, facilitative teaching approaches, and simulation games are all good techniques for helping students develop a deeper understanding of motivations. Examples and sources of materials for these techniques are given in another section of this chapter. Contained in each of the techniques is a basic process: causing the students to *confront* some issue or difficulty in themselves or in interpersonal relations. The confrontation reveals people's feelings, perceptions, and ideas—which are indicators of motives and which make up the raw materials students need to expand their capacities for understanding the motivations of others.

### 5. From Slogans toward a Personal Ideology

The young child who asks "Why?" is following an urge just as basic as that of the philosopher who asks the same question. The view of cognitive development that we favor includes the assumption that a child's life does *not* begin in a state of disorganization and gradually work toward organization; rather, we favor the view that the human organism is *always* organized at some level of complexity. Living matter is by definition organized and seeks to sustain itself by reorganizing as needed, when new circumstances require it. A primary motivating force in the child is to stay organized—to maintain a stable relationship with the environment. Asking "Why?" is an expression of that urge.

Young children settle for simple explanations—"God makes the thunder," "Good people always tell the truth"—because simple explanations satisfy their need for keeping an organized view of the world. As their cognitive capacity increases and their horizons widen, simple explanations and slogans are no longer adequate, and they progress to a more complex set of explanations, a more complex organization of experiences. This idea of progressive reorganization is basic to an understanding of the transescent's development from *reliance on slogans* toward the construction of a *personal ideology*.

During transescence a new capacity emerges: the disposition to examine the logic and consistency of one's existing beliefs, of one's set of explanations and assumptions that guide behavior. The timing of the arrival of this new capacity is about the same as the other developmental changes described in previous sections. The interdependence among them is evident. While a personal ideology, even a roughly organized one, cannot be formed until a transescent has mastered some skills of the formal operations stage, the process of testing one's beliefs begins before that.

In eleven-year-olds, typically, beliefs are loosely held and one belief can be quickly dropped or neglected when a more appealing slogan seems to replace it or when personal interests contradict it. Children this age will vigorously support "freedom of speech" one minute and join in stifling dissent moments later. Some thirteen-year-olds will have begun to see contradictions or instability in their beliefs, but consistency and stability will not come until the children realize that principles have a life of their own beyond specific cases. They must be able to see the connection between the specific case and the underlying principle or generalization. When they understand, for example, that the social order stands upon accepted principles and not just upon governmental power to punish specific wrongdoers, transescents have made the breakthrough that permits the construction of a personal ideology.

**Implications for teachers.**   Young transescents are capable of abstracting principles of conduct from the concrete problems they encounter. As they test the principles in new situations, they are laying the foundation for the development of a personal ideology. Their teachers need to test themselves with some pointed questions: When my students settle for simplistic or contradictory explanations, do I challenge them to examine their inconsistencies? Do I sometimes ask them to accept "principles" that are more likely empty slogans? Do thoughtful discussions of real problems happen in my classroom—discussions from which students can abstract *for themselves* some principles of conduct? When value conflicts emerge in a discussion, do I lead students into examining the sources of conflict more closely? Or do I let the class settle for the quick exit, "Well, everybody is entitled to his own opinion?"

### 6. A Growing Capacity for Forming Concepts

"What's that?" "What's this?" Young children want to know the names of things, and parents or teachers usually supply answers. Children think they are learning names; what they are not aware of is the mental process in which they are engaged: forming concepts or refining concepts already formed. At an amazingly early age they can use names such as *ball, cup,* or *dog* to refer not just to specific objects, but also to categories of objects. They can talk about a ball without one specific ball being present. They have formed concepts and can use the name of a concept as an abstraction in their thinking and talking.

In later childhood they can understand the inclusion of *ball, cup,* or *dog* within the more abstract categories of *sphere, container,* and *mammal.* These second-order concepts, as they are called, can be grasped by children whose thinking has advanced to the concrete operations stage. In that stage, the child can mentally perform operations on concrete objects, such as various ball-like objects, and can identify the properties that make up the concept *sphere.* The abstraction, *sphere,* has meaning because it is a shorthand term that simplifies and organizes the child's concrete experience. Unfortunately, children can memorize and use the name *sphere* in isolation from their other experiences; and in isolation it performs no simplifying or organizing function. The teacher often has a problem in determining whether a child has learned a specific concept or merely the empty label.

Beyond second-order concepts are still higher-order concepts. Can you distinguish a basic difference between these two lists of terms?

| | |
|---|---|
| sphere | ecology |
| evergreens | freedom |
| media | government |
| defendant | molecule |

The terms on the left are second-order concepts; they are one step removed, or one level of abstraction, from something concrete. Each of the terms on the right refers to a concept that is an abstraction from other abstractions. Each is a short-hand term referring to a set of abstractions, a set of second-order concepts, rather than to a set of concrete things. For example, *air pollution* is one second-order concept that might be used in helping students work toward an understanding of the concept *ecology*. However, many such second-order concepts must be seen in relationship to each other if the concept *ecology* is to emerge in the students' thinking.

The ability to form higher-order concepts, such as *ecology*, is one of the signs that a person has entered the stage of formal operational thinking. Many students in middle grades cannot be expected to form higher-order concepts. Many of them may use the term *ecology*, but its use will not imply a grasp of the concept unless the student can explain it in terms of the relationships of second-order concepts, such as *food chain, conservation of matter, recycling,* etc. Transescents are much more likely to use *ecology* as a second-order concept: "It means you should try to protect the environment from pollution."

Nearly all transescents have the mental structure, the mental *capacity*, to form second-order concepts, whether or not the capacity is well used. They not only are able to use second-order concepts, but they can be aware of the *process* by which things are manipulated to produce concepts.

**Implications for teachers.**   We share the view of many other teachers and writers that the schools generally have failed to give adequate attention to concept formation. The failure shows up in at least four ways:

1. Recitation and testing processes mostly measure whether or not a child can *name* a concept but not whether he has formed a full and accurate concept.

2. The sequence that teachers most often use to introduce a new concept to students is not well-suited to concrete thinkers:

> "Today we are going to talk about . . . ; here's how it is defined . . . ; there are some examples of it . . . ; see if you can use it in a sentence . . ."

This sequence first presents the abstract term and its abstract definition. The examples which follow may or may not touch on the student's prior experience, and the use of the term in a sentence may be quite artificial for some. For the concrete thinker, the instruction sequence makes more sense if it begins with a concrete experience or the need to recollect a prior experience and examine it in a new way. Inductively, concrete thinkers move from the concrete experience into an abstracting process that leads them to invent the new concept for themselves and then they are finally ready to be told the conventional name of the new concept. At that point they can use the term with meaning, a meaning which they themselves have infused into the term.°

---

°One effective and widely applicable method of teaching concepts, called the Concept Attainment Model and based on the work of Jerome Bruner, is carefully described in Marsha Weil and Bruce Joyce, *Information Processing Models of Teaching* (Englewood Cliffs, New Jersey: Prentice-Hall, Inc., 1978).

3. Teachers typically are expected to "cover the materials," which often means presenting too many concepts too rapidly for good comprehension. Because concepts that are learned superficially are likely to be forgotten, we urge a deeper development of fewer concepts.

4. A new concept takes on functional meaning for students only when they bring it into their action systems, in mental or physical activity. Moreover, they need to initiate the activity and not just respond to the teacher's or textbook writer's initiatives.

These, then, are the six continua of intellectual development. The remaining activities in the chapter offer means of making practical use of these ideas. To check your grasp of the ideas, use the self-quiz and the answer key that follows it.

## Notation Sheet:
## Six Dimensions of Intellectual Development

**For each of the six categories, fill in the key developments under the ages at which they typically happen.**

| Age 7 | Age 10 | Age 13 | Age 16 |
|---|---|---|---|

### 1. From Concrete into Formal Operational Reasoning

Concrete logic appears | Can begin to think hypothetically (If . . . then; suppose that . . . )

→ Concrete ──────────────────────────────── → Formal ──→

Concrete base is needed for abstract reasoning | Can begin to consider any logical possibility

### 2. From Egocentric into a Sociocentric Perspective

→ Egocentric ──────────────────────────────── → Sociocentric →

### 3. Development of a Time and Space Perspective

→ Limited ──────────────────────────────── → Broad ──→

### 4. Understanding of Human Motivation

→ Simple ──────────────────────────────── → Complex ──→

### 5. From Slogans toward a Personal Ideology

→ Slogans ──────────────────────────────── → Ideology ──→

### 6. A Growing Capacity for Forming Concepts

→ Concrete ──────────────────────────────── → Higher-Order →

## Self-Quiz on Reading

Record a true or false response to each item.
Check your responses with the key which follows the quiz.

_____ 1. All normal humans eventually move through preoperational and concrete operational thinking into the stage of formal operational thinking.

_____ 2. One of Piaget's main ideas is that teachers should know the cognitive stage a child is in so the child then can be taught more readily the process of thinking at the next stage.

_____ 3. A child in the concrete operations stage, pouring water from a tall slender jar into a short, squat jar, should be able to tell that the amount of water did not change in that activity.

_____ 4. Concrete operational thinking cannot include reasoning that violates what the senses tell about concrete reality.

_____ 5. Children in the concrete operational stage are quite capable of performing abstracting operations and using abstractions in concrete reasoning.

_____ 6. Prior to formal operational thought, a child cannot formally categorize complex objects.

_____ 7. A child may be at the formal operations stage in mathematical concepts and in the stage of concrete operations in historical concepts, simultaneously.

_____ 8. A child may operate at the concrete stage in some language arts reasoning tasks and at the formal stage in other tasks within the same discipline.

_____ 9. After a child is biologically ready to begin formal operational thinking, approximately age eleven, a teacher can help promote the transition by posing questions that require formal operations in the solving of them.

_____ 10. In the stage of concrete operations the child not only can understand the social roles of the policeman, farmer, and printer, but also can explain them by using such concepts as law, agriculture, and communications.

_____ 11. An authoritarian view of social order dominates transescents' thinking until about fifteen, although some hold that view into adulthood.

_____ 12. Kohlberg's work shows that not everyone who attains formal operational reasoning also develops postconventional moral judgment.

_____ 13. Many of the new national curriculum efforts of the past ten years differ from traditional curriculums in that the former do not assume that students have attained formal operational thinking; rather, they are designed to promote the transition from concrete to formal reasoning.

_____ 14. Most thirteen-year-olds show little grasp of a historical perspective and rarely try to explain present events in terms of the past.

_____ 15. By age thirteen, transescents generally are beginning to show a distinct interest in the more complex reasons for people's behavior.

_____ 16. A personal ideology, even a roughly organized one, cannot be formed until the transescent has mastered some skills of the formal operations stage.

## Self-Quiz on Reading (continued)

_____ 17. Young transescents are capable of abstracting principles of conduct from the concrete problems they encounter.

_____ 18. Concrete operational reasoning is capable of deliberate construction of a new concept.

_____ 19. The ability to form higher-order concepts, such as the concept "logic," is one of the signs of formal operational thinking.

_____ 20. Nearly all transescents have the mental structure to form second-order concepts.

**ANSWER KEY**

_Self-Quiz on Reading_

| Item | Answer | Item | Answer | Item | Answer | Item | Answer |
|------|--------|------|--------|------|--------|------|--------|
| 1 | F | 6 | F | 11 | T | 16 | T |
| 2 | F | 7 | T | 12 | T | 17 | T |
| 3 | T | 8 | T | 13 | F | 18 | T |
| 4 | T | 9 | F | 14 | T | 19 | T |
| 5 | T | 10 | F | 15 | F | 20 | T |

## The Authors' View: Six Dimensions of Intellectual Development

| Age 7 | Age 10 | Age 13 | Age 16 |
|-------|--------|--------|--------|
| 1. From Concrete into Formal Operational Reasoning | | | |
| Concrete logic appears | Can begin to think hypothetically (If . . . then; suppose that . . . ) | | |
| | Concrete base is needed for abstract reasoning | | Can begin to consider any logical possibility |
| 2. From Egocentric into a Sociocentric Perspective | | | |
| Self-centered view of rules | | Authoritarian view of social order | |
| | Conforming to please important persons | | Can see needs of the total community |
| 3. Development of a Time and Space Perspective | | | |
| Oriented to here and now | | Realizes that personal histories affect present behavior | |
| | Can imagine future only as extension of the present | | Some future perspective but little historical perspective |

## The Authors' View: Six Dimensions of Intellectual Development (continued)

| Age 7 | Age 10 | Age 13 | Age 16 |
|---|---|---|---|
| **4. Understanding of Human Motivation** | | | |
| Motive isn't separable from one's actions | | Does not look for complex reasons for behavior | |
| | Wants rewards or penalties based on motive, not just on overt act | | Begins to see people's viewpoints and motives |
| **5. From Slogans toward a Personal Ideology** | | | |
| Simple explanations and rules are accepted | | Can abstract principles of conduct from concrete situations | |
| | Beliefs are loosely held, often contradictory | | Can begin to seek consistency of beliefs |
| **6. A Growing Capacity for Forming Concepts** | | | |
| Has a large stock of concrete concepts | | Some can begin to form higher-order concepts | |
| | Can form and use second-order concepts | | Can develop and use a stock of higher-order concepts |

## ACTIVITY 3
### Collect and analyze data about students.

**A.**   In light of what you have read in Activity 2, re-examine the students' cards from Activity 1. Select two cards that have responses which you believe represent concrete thinking and two that may show formal operational thinking. Some eleven-year-olds are still pre-operational thinkers. If you have some students you believe are in that stage, you may want to select two of them to interview along with the others.

**B.**   Arrange to interview each of the students individually in a place where he or she will not be distracted. The following "Interview Tasks for Identifying Stages of Reasoning" contains instructions for the interviews. Your purpose in the interviews is to use the prepared materials and questions to obtain responses that will reveal thought patterns reflecting the stages of reasoning. Keeping an accurate and detailed record of what the students say and do is essential to the analysis. For that reason, we suggest that you conduct the interviews with a peer partner so that one of you can observe and take notes.

**C.** After the interviews, discuss the notes with your partner. Do you agree on what, if any, evidence shows formal operational reasoning? On the basis of this sample, can you estimate what proportion of the total class is in the formal reasoning stage of intellectual development? Do some of the textbooks and other materials used by the students presume that they can reason formally? The latter question is one you can answer definitively in Activity 4.

## Interview Tasks for Identifying Stages of Reasoning

*Interview Task I: Unequal Weights Problem*

Materials needed:

- a separate card or sheet for recording each student's responses
- a jar of colored water, with a lid
- two clear drinking glasses
- two weights of exactly equal size but markedly unequal in weight, neither of which will float (e.g., two identical containers filled with materials of different weights)
- two rubber bands.

This is a test of the conquest of logic over perception. The student must be able to ignore the weight of the objects as a false clue and focus attention on the size as the determining factor in displacement among nonfloating objects. The ability to put aside irrelevant information is a hallmark of formal operational thinking.

*Procedure:* Present the student with the weights; let him/her hold them. Fill the two tumblers one-half full of colored water.

1. Ask the student if both tumblers contain the same amount of water. Correct them until they satisfy the student.
2. Ask the student to place a rubber band at the water level of one tumbler.
3. Ask: "If I put this lighter weight in this glass, will the water stay the same, rise higher, or fall lower?" Place the lighter weight in the tumbler.
4. Say: "Now, if I were to put this other weight in the other glass, what would happen to the water level? Put the rubber band where it would be."
5. Say: "Now, that is where the water would be with the heavy weight in it." Wait for agreement or reaction.
6. Record the student's responses to 3, 4, and 5. You may then put the heavy weight in the tumbler and talk to the student about the results.

---

ADAPTED FROM "Discussions on Piaget: Leader's Guide." Cedar Falls, Iowa: Project BASIC Inquiry, Cedar Rapids Public Schools, 1974, p. 41.

*Interview Task II: Skateboard Episode*

1. Say: "I have a short story to tell you, and after I tell it I am going to ask you a question about it. Ready?"

    "On his way home from school, John walked past several stores. He saw a new skateboard in one of the store windows. The idea of buying the skateboard really excited him and he hurried home to ask his mother for the money to buy it. But John's mother said, "No! I don't have any money to spend on a skateboard." As John walked out of the house, he said to himself, "I don't want the skateboard anyway because I know it's not very well made and would break easily."

    "Here's the question: Was the skateboard well made? How do you know?" (Be sure the student gives a reason for his/her answer).

2. Record the student's total response.

3. After the interview is completed, analyze the student responses and decide whether they reflect concrete or formal thinking, or something in between. The concrete response would be limited mainly to the givens in the story; e.g., "No. The skateboard wasn't well made." (How do you know?) "John said so as he walked out of the house." The abstract response would show ability to infer meaning and judge the motivation implied in John's remark, e.g., "You can't tell if it was well made. John just made up an excuse because his mother wouldn't give him the money."

*Interview Task III: Testing for Pre-operational vs. Concrete Operational Thinking*

Here are four tasks you may use to distinguish pre-operational from concrete operational reasoning.

A. Obtain two clear glass jars, one tall and narrow in diameter and the other relatively short and wide in diameter. Select jars that will hold about the same volume of water. Fill the short one two-thirds full of water. Show the two jars to the student. Pour all the water from the short jar to the tall jar and ask the student, "Is there less water, more water, or the same amount of water now in this jar (pointing to the tall jar)?" Pour the water back and ask the question again, pointing to the short jar. Ask the student why and note the wording of the response. Pre-operational reasoners will attend to one dimension of the water column, probably height, and say there is more water in the tall, narrow jar. Concrete reasoners can attend to both the change in height and in diameter of the water, and can see that the volume of water has not changed.

B. A ball of clay or play-dough can be used to test the same reasoning ability, the ability to see that mass is not affected by shape. Present the clay to the student in the form of a ball. Hand it to the student and ask him or her: "Do you know what this is?" When it has been identified, put the ball on a table and flatten it. Ask: "Is there now more clay, less clay, or the same amount?" As with the jars, the demonstration can be reversed. Pre-operational reasoning will not perceive the mass as remaining the same.

C. Collect a dozen or so objects, such as wooden beads that are identical in size and shape. All but two of the beads must be identical in color as well—for example, ten red beads and two yellow. Ask the student to count the beads and tell how many of each there are. Ask what they are made of. Say: "Are they all wooden?" Establish that fact. Then ask: "Are there more red beads than yellow?" After a response, ask: "Are there more red beads or more wooden beads?" If the student says there are more red beads, you may probe a little by saying, "Are all the beads wooden?" ("Yes.") "Are there more wooden beads or more red beads?" The pre-operational response is "red beads."

D. Two pieces of yarn of equal length (about twelve inches) may also be used. With the student watching, ask if they are the same length. Get an affirmative reply, even if it means cutting one to make them even. While the student watches, crumple one piece into a loose ball. Ask: "Are the two pieces still the same length?" Pre-operational reasoning will perceive the crumpled one as now shorter. The task may be repeated, with the student handling the yarn. Pre-operational thinkers will persist in that response.

Students age ten or eleven who are still pre-operational in their reasoning are maturing very slowly intellectually. Their environment somehow has deprived them of opportunities to find satisfaction in reasoning. Their progress in school will continue to be slow and frustrating to all unless they can be helped in intellectual development. The best way we know of to promote their development is by helping them operate concretely on problems that are real and important to them. Mental tasks of the kind described above are present in dozens of events in each student's life every day. Pulling the tasks out and giving them attention is the teacher's responsibility. Please note that the examples of reasoning tasks given above do not include a teacher's statement as to which student answers are "right" or "wrong." Avoid giving a judgment on the quality of student responses. The teacher's role is to question, to stimulate thinking, not to approve or disapprove of the student for producing whatever level of reasoning the student is capable of giving at that time.

# ACTIVITY 4
## Analyze curriculum materials.

Many instructional materials for transescents are prepared with the assumption that the students are already capable of formal operational reasoning, or there is the assumption that the students already have a concrete base of experience onto which the authors can superimpose a new abstraction. The object of this activity is for you to examine some student textbook or other instructional materials to see whether these assumptions underlie the materials.

**A.** Select the materials to be analyzed, preferably something you know the students will be encountering in the next few days or weeks.

**B.**    From the material select several second- or third-level abstractions that the authors use *without any concrete introduction.*

**C.**    In a brief conversation with three or four students, ask them to tell you what each abstraction means: "Tell me what you know about _____." If you prefer, ask the whole class and record their responses on tape. One teacher we know, starting a unit of study on computers, tape-recorded students' comments about computers. He reproduced their statements verbatim on a ditto and used the statements as items of a true-false pretest. Student responses on the quiz indicated their basis of solid understanding, as well as their misconceptions. He concluded that the existing instructional material could not be used until he first helped the students build a base of concrete experience about computers.

**D.**    Analyze your students' responses and decide whether the instructional material needs to be supplemented as in the example above. Record the responses and your analysis for your portfolio.

**E.**    Briefly review other instructional materials your students would typically use. For your portfolio, record your judgments of how adequately the materials treat concrete experience as a beginning point for learning new abstractions.

**F.**    Select a textbook that requires reasoning in answering questions, such as questions at the end of a chapter. Analyze several of the questions to see whether the reasoning sequence begins with concrete experience. Do some questions ask students to reason from abstraction to abstraction, to generalize from generalizations, to relate relationships or to hypothesize about events that have no basis in their concrete experience? How can you improve the questions to make them more concrete for students? Record the book's questions and your decisions in your portfolio.


## ACTIVITY 5
**Plan a learning sequence that leads students from concrete experience into abstract reasoning.**

Throughout the reading section of Activity 2, we stressed the importance of transescent students beginning a learning sequence with concrete experience. Planning a lesson or unit that leads students from a concrete base into abstract reasoning is the objective of this activity.

When teachers introduce new concepts to young children, they usually remember to relate the new material to the children's prior experience. Teachers in middle grades, pressed to "cover the curriculum," are tempted to forget that the vast majority of their students are concrete thinkers, bound in reasoning processes to their personal experiences. Since all reasoning depends upon abstractions, the middle grade teacher must be concerned about the quality of student abstractions—whether they are empty words, distorted images, or solidly and correctly grounded in concrete experience. The planning sequence that follows should be a regularly used pattern. Use it now to plan a lesson (for your own students, or for another teacher, or for hypothetical students).

## Leading Students from Concrete Experience into Abstract Reasoning

A. First decide what concept or principle is to be learned.

1. *As I introduce the new concept to the students, I must first consider what is in their prior concrete experience to which they can tie this new abstraction.* If you identify some prior experience common to all the students, test its concreteness before you continue with your plan.

2. *Can I be fairly sure that their prior experience in this regard is really concrete or is it merely verbal and superficial?* For example, a teacher wanting to introduce the concept of *credit* thought that most students would have some prior acquaintance with credit cards to serve as a concrete base. But when he asked students to tell about credit cards and what they were for, he learned that most of the students used the term *credit* to mean delay of payment. Because their prior exposure to the word *credit* might be more misleading than helpful, the teacher decided *not* to rely on students' prior experiences in finance, and decided instead to set up a classroom simulation of the banking process. As the students worked through the process, the phenomenon of credit was invented out of necessity. The teacher *then* provided the label *credit* for what they had concretely experienced. If your plan needs some concrete event that all the students can experience together, go on to the next question.

3. *What new concrete experience can be planned for the students that will lead them to need the new concept as an organizer of their experience?* The new concrete event can be something inside the classroom or outside, managed by the teacher, by individual students or groups. For example, a teacher can introduce the mathematical concept of probability by having students in pairs flip pennies and keep a tally of the frequency (another concept contained in the activity) of heads and tails. As another example, a middle school teacher we know uses television programs to introduce the concept of character development or character depth and how an author accomplishes it in a story. Students begin by recalling the television characters they "get to know well." Then students agree to watch specific upcoming programs to see "how the author does it" and, after two or three cycles of viewing and discussing, the students have evolved a functional definition or character development that they can use in their own writing, reading, and viewing.

B. When you have the concept and the begnning concrete experience clearly in mind, decide on the steps the students are likely to need in arriving at the abstract concept. Here are some suggested steps, adapted from the work of Taba (1967), that you may find useful. We can again use the example of flipping pennies.

1. *Collecting and organizing data.* In working toward the concept of *probability* by using pennies, the first step is to have a dozen or so pairs of students flip pennies and record the number of heads and tails in, say,

twenty flips. Thus data are collected, organized into two tallies by each recorder, and organized again when the tallies of all the pairs of students are added into one tally. The purpose for the groups of data, and the names associated with each group, must be clear to each student.

2. *Interpreting, inferring, and generalizing.* If the grand tally of flips does not produce exactly 50 percent heads and 50 percent tails, students will wonder why and speculate about reasons. They are interpreting the data. Inferences follow naturally: "Probably our results mean that most groups would come out about the same but maybe not exactly." And they generalize: "On the average, the results would be 50-50." At this point, they have the basic substance of a concept and are ready to have a name for it—*probability.*

3. *Using the concept to explain and predict.* The students don't really own the concept until they can use it to explain new phenomena and predict consequences. If the students studying probability put twenty black marbles and twenty white marbles in a box, mix them up and draw out ten without looking, they should be able to explain what is happening and predict the probability of drawing the same number of whites and blacks. If twenty yellow marbles are added, the students should be able to explain the new conditions and predict the frequency of each color in the sample drawn from the box.

C. Record your plan for your portfolio. Ask a colleague for feedback.

D. If you have students of your own, guide them through the steps you have planned. Record some of the dialogue with students that illustrates their movement through the steps of data collecting and organizing, interpreting, inferring, generalizing, explaining, and predicting. Also record your reactions to the process.

E. If you have prepared the lesson for another teacher to lead, follow up on the outcomes as in D. above.

## ACTIVITY 6
### Plan and implement "thinking time" strategies.

If you are committed, as we are, to helping students develop their reasoning ability, then you will be interested in what research has revealed about classroom conditions that promote reasoning. One major research finding is that the *pace* of classroom dialogue, i.e., the pace of questions and answers in recitation or discussion, dramatically affects students' reasoning.

The directions and information that follow will show you how to examine and perhaps change the pace of classroom dialogue. This activity involves observation in a classroom, your own or someone else's.

## TIME TO THINK

**A.** Analyze the pace of dialogue in the classroom. After asking a question of students, how long does the teacher wait for an answer? If you are analyzing your own teaching pace, ask a colleague or one or two of your students to make some tallies in your class during a question-answer session.

Here are the instructions for the observer. Listen for the length of the pauses between teacher talk and student talk. Use a sheet of lined paper and make notes in columns down the paper, moving down to a new line each time there is a change in speaker. When the teacher starts speaking, write a "T." When the teacher stops speaking, waiting for a student to answer, immediately start counting seconds: one-thousand one, one-thousand two, etc. At the instant the student starts to speak, stop counting and write down beside the "T" how many seconds the pause was. If the teacher breaks the silence instead of a student, write a "T" on the second line and record the length of the next pause. When a student is answering, write an "S" on the next line. Immediately after the student stops talking, start counting the pause until the next speaker. Record the pause time, record a "T" or an "S" for the next speaker, then record the length of the next pause, and so on. After getting comfortable with the recording process, record about five minutes of dialogue. Give the record of pauses to the person you observed. Here is a sample record with explanations:

T-1 (One second elapses between the time teacher stops speaking and student responds.)

S-2 (Two seconds elapse between student's answer and teacher's next question.)

T-2 (Teacher pauses two seconds after speaking. Then teacher speaks again, e.g., rephrasing the question.)

T-3 (Teacher waits three seconds before a student responds.)

S-0 (Teacher replies in less that one second after student speaks; for example, "Good. That's right!")

**B.** Examine your pausing patterns. Research shows that the average teacher waits just one second after asking a question and then either asks it again, rephrases it, calls on another student, or supplies the answer for the students. The average pause after the student talks and before the teacher talks again is less than one second. How does your pattern compare?

Research evidence is very clear: student talk shifts strikingly from memory responses and blind guesses over toward reasoning responses when the teacher pauses three seconds to five seconds before and after the student speaks. When "wait time" is increased to three seconds, student behavior changes significantly in a number of ways, including these (Rowe 1973):

- speculative and propositional thinking increase ("if . . . then," "suppose that . . . ")
- students ask more relevant questions and volunteer more relevant comments
- responsibility for the dialogue shifts more to the students
- students talk and listen to each other more regarding the learning event

- student responses become longer and more confident
- there is less failure to respond
- contributions by "slow" students increase
- disruptive behavior decreases

Only two or three teachers in 100 naturally maintain a pausing pattern of three seconds before and after a student speaks. But that pattern can be learned and maintained by most teachers.

**C.**   Practice increasing your wait time. If transescent students are not available to you, practice with any age group. Begin by having some concrete experience for students and then conduct dialogue about the experience. Find some means to remind yourself to count silently to three seconds before and after a student speaks. Ask an observer to repeat the procedure described in Section A above. The pace of instruction is based on strong habit, so do not expect instant success. Keep trying, and keep in mind three facts: (1) Three to five seconds is the criterion; less time does not bring about the change you want. (2) Give most attention to the length of your pauses that come *after* a student speaks. You alone control that pause, while you and the students share control of the earlier pause. Of course, it helps to encourage them to take time to think: "Really think about this one." (3) Avoid phrases that shut off thinking prematurely: "Yes—but," and clipped evaluative statements, such as "Good," "Right," "OK," "Fine."

**D.**   File in your portfolio the observation sheets that record your achievement of criterion wait time (the pause after student talk). Also include notations of any changes in student thinking behavior you have observed.

**E.**   Time for students to think can be provided in another simple way. When you have an inquiry-type question for students, you can say: "Here's a question I'd like each of you to think carefully about. Take a piece of scratch paper and write out your answer. Then I'll call on some of you to tell us your answers." This process makes it easier also to involve students who don't usually volunteer or even answer when called on. Use this process occasionally—don't wear it out. Record the reactions to your initial uses of this process and put them in your portfolio.

## ACTIVITY 7
**Read about reflective thinking and implement a plan for students.**

The emphasis in this chapter has been on helping students expand their intellectual life from the concrete base of their personal experience. For the final activity, we have drawn upon the ideas of John Dewey, whose book, *How We Think*, is a classic description of thinking processes. We have selected Dewey's concept of reflective thinking as a useful way of synthesizing the key ideas of this chapter. The objectives of this activity are: to understand reflective thinking, to be aware of it when it happens in students, and to be able to stimulate it by appropriate teaching strategies.

## PROMOTING REFLECTIVE THINKING

The paragraphs below present John Dewey's ideas, freely interpreted (Dewey, 1916). Read them and then complete the activities described.

All thinking is a response to a difficulty, a disturbance, that interrupts the habitual way of behaving. Habits direct behavior until they are blocked in some way, then the blockage prompts thinking. For example, the process of driving a car is habitual; one's mind can be miles away while "one's habits drive the car." But if something out of the ordinary registers on the driver's senses, thinking is immediately brought into the here and now. Habit may need to be disengaged.

When the need for thinking arises, to deal with something that habit can't handle, there are four kinds of thinking that can come into action. The least mature kind is *panic thinking.* When the thinking process is really uncomfortable or when one is afraid to pause long enough to make a considered judgment, one grabs the first solution that comes to mind—to push the difficulty away as quickly as possible. Doubt is hardly endured at all. This is panic thinking. It hasn't much assurance of offering good solutions. And if one doesn't pay much attention to the consequences of the decision, its value is not understood anyway.

When a person can pause to consider more than one way of dealing with a difficulty, *pat-answer thinking* commonly occurs. In this case, thinking calls to mind several rules or preconceived solutions to such difficulties and selections are made from them. The ideas that come to mind are treated as fixed and are not subject to analysis. Thinking stays outside the facts and ideas being used. Custom and tradition dominate: "What was it my mother (or teacher or other authority) said to do in cases like this?" How well the rule or idea fits the difficulty is not examined; the fit is assumed on authority.

*Reflective thinking,* the third type is fundamentally different from the two kinds of thinking already described. Rules and facts are no longer fixed. Reflective thinking inspects their adequacy and value in the new situation. Solutions that emerge in reflective thinking may or may not be sanctioned by authorities and by custom; that is not the test of new ideas. The test of a new idea, of a possible solution, is whether it fits the requirements of the situation that started the thinking. Reflective thinking tests ideas, both in imagination and in action, to find out the consequences of the chosen action.

Reflective thinking differs only in degree from the fourth type, *systematic inquiry.* Reflective thinking may happen without plan, but it becomes systematic when it is deliberate and disciplined.

Reflective thinking is available to people of all ages, to the "mentally retarded" as well as the "genius." Promoting reflective thinking should be the primary business of the teacher. Unfortunately, the traditional pattern of teachers has been the promoting of pat-answer thinking. The culture expects its young to receive rules, skills, facts, and ideas more or less uncritically and largely unexamined and untested by the young receivers. But when rules, behaviors, facts, and ideas enter into one's habit system through pat-answer thinking or through panic thinking, they may restrict one's ability to function well. When a child learns a behavior pattern through panic thinking, the behavior pattern is tied into his or her habit system with emotional knots that may be inaccessible to the adult self, even through the probing of reflective thinking. On the other hand, behavior patterns that are formed reflectively are tied into one's habit system with known knots that can be untied when the behavior is no longer wanted. In transescent youth, healthy behavior patterns are drawn from concrete, personal experience through the process of reflective thinking.

The main challenge for teachers is to shift lessons and students away from pat-answer thinking into reflective thinking. How is that done? The classroom atmosphere that promotes pat answers regards knowledge as given and settled; it is a commodity to be conveyed to students. In contrast, the atmosphere that stimulates reflective thinking is open, incomplete, treating knowledge as something to be constructed by each person.

Perhaps an example will be helpful here. Max Wertheimer (1959) described a class of junior high school students that was learning to find the area of a parallelogram. All the students had memorized the rule for calculating area and had applied it correctly to several cases. Sensing that they knew the rule as a pat answer and did not know its structural meaning, Wertheimer gave them this figure, which stumped most of them:

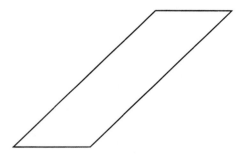

The students found that rule awkward to apply when the parallelogram was tipped on end. They had only worked problems in which the base was long and the altitude short.

Wertheimer decided to determine how students could be taught the concept through reflective thinking. He gave each student a piece of paper cut into parallelogram shape and said, "You know how to find the area of a rectangle, which has square sides. Square sides make it easy to find area in square inches. How can we find the area of this figure with slanted sides?"

Some students were quick to notice that "the problem on this end is the same as the problem on that end, only opposite." One girl asked for scissors and tape, rolled the paper into a hoop, taped the slanted ends together, cut the hoop at a right angle, and promptly calculated the square inches of the newly made rectangle. When the students understood the principle compensating for the slanted ends, the rule for calculating area was no longer a mysterious-formula-that-works-in-certain-situations-but-I-don't-know-why; it became a well-understood shortcut.

Another example of pat-answer tendencies turned into reflective thinking can be seen in one teacher's effort to help students understand the relationship of credit to inflation. Struggling with abstractions remote from their own experiences, students had learned textbook definitions but had no idea of how to apply them. When the teacher became aware of their stereotyped, inaccurate ideas about inflation and credit, he decided to set up a miniature economy in the classroom. Currency and two banks were created and students were assigned assets and a role in the economy. Through actual transactions, students soon added new concepts to their vocabularies: line of credit, commodities, interest rate, supply and demand. In this simplified economy, which gave them direct experience in the marketplace, they felt the pinch of inflation and observed some of its causes. Reflective thinking was rewarded and pat-answer thinking was not—and the rewards came through natural consequences.

One key generalization about promoting reflective thinking should be evident in these examples: it is stimulated when students have problems to solve that are linked to their own concrete experience, past or present. Another key idea is that teachers need to be alert to students' inaccurate or shallow uses of important concepts. These are the clues pointing to where reflective thinking needs to be encouraged.

*Now Try Your Hand at Promoting Reflective Thinking.*   Select a section of students' (your own students or someone else's) lessons or activities that usually requires only pat-answer thinking. Construct a new plan for the material so that reflective thinking can occur. Record your selection and your plan for your portfolio.

*If At All Possible, Implement Your Plan.*   You will need to collect evidence that students are using less pat-answer and more reflective thinking. Some evidence can be obtained in written form, as in written assignments, thought-provoking test questions, and student journals. One teacher, Gabriel Jacobs, had excellent results in encouraging reflective thinking through journal writing, and wrote a book about the experience (1970).
Classroom dialogue is the other main source of evidence. When you have structured a classroom situation to stimulate reflective thinking, tape record the dialogue.

*Analyze the Written and Taped Evidence.*   Place in your portfolio some samples of student comments and questions. Explain briefly why you regard them as a shift from pat-answer to reflective thinking. If you feel a need to confirm your analysis, obtain another person's reactions. Repeat the process until you are confident about your ability to recognize the difference between indicators of pat-answer thinking and reflective thinking, and until you have some sense of success at promoting reflective thinking.

## NEXT STEPS

In the list of references are a variety of sources that will give you ideas for extending your work on intellectual development. We particularly recommend Dewey's *How We Think* as a clear and powerful explanation of the educator's role in helping to promote reflective thinking. The Raths book contains many suggestions of activities that stimulate thinking. The October 1981 issue of *Educational Leadership* contains a dozen articles on teaching thinking skills. Most of the teaching techniques described in Joyce and Weil's *Models of Teaching* are directly useful with concrete operational thinkers. See particularly the inductive and developmental models. The Epstein references present an intriguing hypothesis of brain growth in relation to stages of mental development. The Feuerstein book introduces a dramatic achievement in the improving of intelligence in adolescents. Feuerstein's impressive work will become increasingly important.

We recommend four books that represent new kinds of resources for teachers. *Yellow Pages of Learning Resources, The Whole Universe Catalog of Science Activities,* and *My Backyard History Book* are especially well suited to active, concrete learners. They contain practical materials and suggestions for dealing with essential concepts in concrete ways. *People Types and Tiger Stripes: A Practical Guide to Learning Styles* is a book that can help you identify which students especially need concrete, hands-on and active lessons, and help you plan such lessons.

Finally, we suggest that you look at lesson ideas in teachers' journals with a critical eye. Some of them seem clearly better than others in their attention to the intellectual development of concrete learners. The journal, *Science and Children,* for example, began a new monthly feature on early adolescence in its September 1980 issue. The first article was "Early Adolescence: Active Science for Middle Schools."

## REFERENCES

ABRUSCATO, JOE, and JACK HASSARD. *The Whole Cosmos Catalog of Science Activities.* Glenview, Ill.: Scott, Foresman and Company, 1977.

ADELSON, J. "The Political Imagination of the Young Adolescent," *Daedalus* 100 (4) (Fall 1971):1013–1050.

ADELSON, J., B. GREEN, and R. O'NEIL. "Growth of the Idea of Law in Adolescence," *Developmental Psychology* 1 (1969):327–332.

DEWEY, JOHN. *Essays in Experimental Logic.* New York: Dover Publications, Inc., 1916.

———. *How We Think.* Boston: D.C. Heath and Co., 1933.

EPSTEIN, HERMAN T. "Growth Spurts During Brain Development: Implications for Education Policy and Practice," in Jeanne S. Chall and Allan F. Mirsky (Ed.), *Education and the Brain: 1978 Yearbook of the National Society for the Study of Education,* Part II (1978):343–370.

EPSTEIN, HERMAN T., and CONRAD F. TOEPFER, JR. "A Neuro-Science Basis for Reorganizing Middle Grades Education," *Educational Leadership* 36 (8) (1979):656–660.

FEUERSTEIN, REUVEN. *Instrumental Enrichment.* Baltimore, Maryland: University Park Press, 1979.

FLAVELL, J. *The Developmental Psychology of Jean Piaget.* New York: D. Van Nostrand Co., Inc., 1963.

GINSBURG, HERBERT, and SYLVIA OPPER. *Piaget's Theory of Intellectual Development*. Englewood Cliffs, N.J.: Prentice-Hall, Inc., 1969.

GRIFFIN, NANCY. "Early Adolescence: Active Science for Middle Schoolers," *Science and Children* 18(1), September 1980, 52–54.

JACOBS, GABRIEL. *When Children Think*. New York: Teachers College, 1970.

JOYCE, BRUCE, and MARSHA WEIL. *Models of Teaching*. Englewood Cliffs, N.J.: Prentice-Hall, Inc., 1972.

KOHEN-RAZ, REUVEN. *The Child from 9 to 13*. Chicago: Aldine-Adterton, Inc., 1971.

KOHLBERG, L. "Moral Education in the School," *School Review* 74 (1976):1–30.

KOHLBERG, L. and C. GILLIGAN. "The Adolescent As Philosopher: The Discovery of Self in a Postconventional World," *Daedalus* 100 (4) (Fall 1971):1050–1086.

LAWRENCE, GORDON. *People Types and Tiger Stripes: A Practical Guide to Learning Styles*, 2nd Edition. Gainesville, Florida: Center for Applications of Psychological Type, 414 SW 7th Terrace, 1982.

PIAGET, J. *The Moral Judgment of the Child*. Glencoe, Ill.: Free Press, 1948.

Project BASIC Inquiry, "Discussions on Piaget: Leader's Guide." Cedar Falls, Iowa: Cedar Falls Public Schools, 1974.

RATHS, L., S. WASSERMAN, A. JONAS, and A. ROTHSTEIN. *Teaching for Thinking*. Columbus, Ohio: C.E. Merrill Books, 1967.

ROWE, MARY BUDD. *Teaching Science as Continuous Inquiry*. New York: McGraw-Hill Book Co., 1973.

ROWLAND, THOMAS, and CARSON MCGUIRE. "The Development of Intelligent Behavior: Jean Piaget," in Glen Hass (Ed.), *Curriculum Planning: A New Approach*, Boston: Allyn and Bacon, Inc., 1977.

SHAFTEL, F., and G. SHAFTEL. *Role Playing in the Curriculum*. Englewood Cliffs, N.J.: Prentice-Hall, Inc., 1982.

SIEGLER, ROBERT S. "The Twenty Questions Game As a Forum of Problem Solving," *Child Development* 48 (2) (June 1977):395–403.

TABA, HILDA. *Teacher's Handbook for Elementary Social Studies*. Reading, Mass.: Addison-Wesley Co., 1967.

TOBIN, KENNETH G. "The Effect of Extended Teacher Wait-Time on Science Achievement," *Journal of Research in Science Teaching* 17(5), September 1980, 469–475.

WEIL, MARSHA, and BRUCE JOYCE. *Information Processing Models of Teaching*. Englewood Cliffs, N.J.: Prentice-Hall, Inc., 1978.

WEITZMAN, DAVID. *My Backyard History Book*. Boston: Little, Brown and Co., 1975.

WERTHEIMER, MAX. *Productive Thinking*. New York: Harper and Brothers, 1959.

WURMAN, RICHARD SAUL (Ed.). *Yellow Pages of Learning Resources*. Cambridge: MIT Press, 1972.

# CHAPTER FOUR

# SOCIAL AND EMOTIONAL DEVELOPMENT: TEN TO FOURTEEN

## Who Are Transescents?

Girls who play with Barbie dolls and girls who could compete in the Miss Teenage America Contest . . .

Boys who look like short playing cards turned sideways and boys who already look like grown men . . .

Girls who don't know where babies come from and those who are experimenting to find out "for sure . . ."

Boys who play with toy dump trucks and those who can operate real ones . . .

Youngsters who play with Tinker Toys and those who can dismantle, repair, and reassemble an automobile engine . . .

Those who believe their parents are the smartest people in the world and those who wonder how such stupid, old-fashioned people have survived so long . . .

Kids who can't read their own names and those whose noses seem to be always in a book . . .

Youngsters who rate the opposite sex somewhere between spinach and milk-of-magnesia and those who are "on the make . . ."

Those who munch chocolate bars and those who pop amphetamines . . .

Those who guzzle cokes and those who will soon be incurable alcoholics . . .

Those who meet the world with easy smiles and contagious laughter and those who are already being propelled by unbearable pressures toward the taking of their own lives.

These are transescents. Does your teaching or your middle school program reflect knowledge of them?

Mary F. Compton

The cynical fatalist may say, "Some lives do turn out tragically. The school can't remake society." The Pollyanna naively manages to avoid seeing the tragedy in the making. And the young teacher who comes to teach in the middle grades ill-equipped to deal with the social-emotional side of students runs the risk of being driven, by self-preservation instincts, towards one of those denying, defeatist attitudes.

---

By permission of the author. From *Middle School Journal*, 1978, 9 (3), 24.

Happily, most youngsters seem resilient enough to suffer the many knocks of growing up and still turn out sound and stable. Many adults tell of poor teachers and an unresponsive curriculum—yet, they survived. But if a school program and a faculty are responsive and attuned to the social and emotional life that its students bring to school, can it make a difference? Enough of a difference to warrant the extra personal investment required of its teachers? The massive Eight-Year Study (Aiken 1942) accumulated findings which suggest that the results are indeed worth the investment. Yet somehow the most convincing evidence and the strongest reason for hope is found in our personal knowledge of individual cases where enlightened school programs and responsive teachers made dramatic differences in the lives of students.

This chapter's emphasis is on helping you find effective and efficient ways of tuning in to the social envelope that defines each student, to the emotional pattern that each brings to school every day, and ways to use this knowledge in planning curriculum and managing your classroom. (Because social and emotional aspects of human experience are so inextricably bound together, and because "social-emotional" is an awkward phrase, throughout the chapter we generally use "social" to represent both aspects.)

Before you begin the activities, we suggest you consider your own learning style and select the sequence of activities that suits you best. If you prefer to get into action first, to gather concrete data before you analyze it and theorize about it, consider doing Activities 3 and 4 before the reading in Activity 1 and Activity 2. If you would rather get the "big picture" first (to see what specialists in human development say) and gather data afterward, follow the sequence as presented.

Whichever activity you start with, first take a simple pretest: write a list of twenty social-emotional characteristics of transescents that you regard as most important for teachers to be aware of. Save your list to compare with one you will write at the end of the chapter. Write your list now before continuing in the chapter.

## ACTIVITY 1
### Read what the specialists say.

Read "Social Development: Myths and Facts." As you read, make notes of your reactions and include any ideas you may want to try with your own students.

## Social Development: Myths and Facts

Human development specialists who study later childhood and early adolescence, or transescence, are quick to say that this is the least studied area in the human cycle. Nevertheless, in recent years the researchers and theorists have moved toward agreement on some basic facts and interpretations about the developmental experience of young people of ages ten to fourteen. They also generally agree that some commonly held assumptions about this age group are essentially false or may represent distortions of the facts.

## FIVE MYTHS

**1. Estrangement from Parents.**   A common assumption is that normal adolescents, from puberty into young adulthood, work their way through fundamental conflicts with their parents; that without clashes over essential values and life styles, the young person does not attain autonomy. Recent research seems to show that conflicts with parents typically are not so great as the myth says they are. Arguments are common, over daily matters such as dress, eating, bedtime, going out, choice of friends, etc. Arguments about these things are part of the process of the child's becoming detached and differentiated from parents. On the whole, however, adolescents do not reject the basic values of their parents, even in the process of becoming detached. The achievement of autonomy, of independent judgment and values, does not depend upon conflict with parents in any deep sense (Gallatin, 148-152).

**2. Emotional Turbulence.**   The assumed emotional upheaval in adolescence associated with sexual development and with detachment from parents is not borne out by research. Psychological turbulence is normal only for adolescents at the extremes. Transescence is not an emotionally quiet period, but it does not depart from the emotional patterns of earlier and later times in a person's life (Gallatin, 144-146; Lipsitz, 31).

**3. The Stereotype "Adolescent."**   The labels *adolescent* or *teenager* generally present an image of one typical pattern of behavior, in effect, a stereotype. The tendency of adults to react to an individual ten to fourteen years old as if he or she were typical, possessing a stock set of values and habits, is unfortunate. The *variability*—in personality, background, social development, intellectual development, etc.—is far more significant to any relationship, such as between teacher and student, than is the commonality implied in the label *adolescent*. Knowing the tendencies and patterns of adolescence is important, but these are the backdrop for the action, not the action itself.

**4. Adolescence as a Subculture.**   The cohesiveness of peer groups, the music and language of adolescents, the conforming styles of dress, the apparent ignoring of adults, and other patterns fuel the belief that adolescence is a subculture bound together by age rather than race, ethnic heritage, or occupation. This myth is supported by merchandisers because it sells products by the billions. Unfortunately, the myth has tended to promote age segregation, as in schools, and discriminatory customs or laws that discourage employment of members of this "subculture." Youth unemployment and the lack of adequate job-learning opportunities for adolescents are a national *and* local tragedy.

One does not need to assume the existence of a subculture to explain the behavior of adolescents. For example, cognitive development theory offers a likely explanation for adolescents' turning away from the adult community. Elkind (1967) notes that young adolescents, in their egocentric view of the world, commonly believe that other people are acutely aware of them and their appearance and are as critical (or admiring) of them as they are of themselves. That young people turn away from such supposed critics and turn toward peer group conformity is a logical move from that viewpoint.

**5. The Strength of Peer Relationships.**   While the peer group, as a group, exerts powerful influence on the young adolescent, friendships are not typically so strong as the myth suggests. Friendship is seldom based on intimate sharing of personal values until later adolescence. The young adolescent wants a companion whose personality will not get in the way of the enjoyment of activities important to both. If interest in the activity changes, the friendship is abandoned (Gallatin, 127).

## SOME FACTS OF TRANSESCENT SOCIAL DEVELOPMENT

Adolescence is a developmental stage triggered by endochrine glands. Throughout this stage, a person's behavior generally follows socially determined patterns which, of course, differ from culture to culture. Amid the myths about adolescence, there are some patterns, some generalizations about social development which are solid and supportable. As we reviewed the work of specialists in human development, the most striking feature that emerged was the evidence of competing forces and needs in the transescent's world. We decided that the social development process can most clearly be described in sets of competing forces that produce tensions in the young peoples' lives. Described below are a dozen such tensions.

1. The desire to be accepted by peers, to be part of the group
. . . competing with . . .
the desire to stand out as someone unique.

This tension between the need for acceptance and the need for individual achievement is probably the strongest tension in most young adolescents. Their heightened awareness of self as distinct from family and others fuels the drive for uniqueness. At the same time they feel a great pressure to accept the status in the social pecking order assigned them by the peer group system. You can predict a student's grades, for example, by knowing what clique he or she belongs to. One does not deviate far from clique norms and still remain a member (Kagan, 1102, 1105, 1107-1108).

2. The need to stake out one's own autonomous beliefs
. . . competing with . . .
the reluctance to tear down beliefs that have been stable and true for a (short) lifetime, beliefs that would be okay if they weren't tainted as hand-me-downs from one's parents.

The student who seems to waffle on value positions or hold tightly to two contradictory values is caught between these competing needs (Kagan, 1010).

3. The need to explore erotic relationships with partners of the opposite sex
    . . . competing with . . .
    the fear of rejection and inadequacy as a partner.

All the tentative maneuverings that precede dating and continue through adolescence can be seen as the product of this basic tension (Gallatin, 128-30).

4. The desire to examine seriously some adults who can be heros and models of values and lifestyles they may want to adopt
    . . . competing with . . .
    the repulsion they feel in seeing defect and taint in adults, flaws they never saw before (Kagan, 1005).

5. The need to achieve "realism"—sanguine, cool, worldly—and to throw off "childish" views—sentimental and simple—
    . . . competing with . . .
    the need to hang on to an idealism that holds hope for a good future, a better world (Adelson, 1036).

6. The security felt in parental values and neighborhood norms
    . . . competing with . . .
    the attraction of the new and varied beliefs, habits and mores encountered in the wider circle of contacts now available in the junior high or middle school.

While this tension will follow a person for many years, it is particularly acute in early adolescence for those shifting out of egocentrism into formal operation reasoning (Kagan, 1005).

7. A strong need to find support relationships among the peer group
    . . . competing with . . .
    a reluctance to break the long-standing, supporting family relationship.

The desire to avoid a break with the family appears to be much stronger than the myth suggests (Kagan, 1010).

8. The desire to accept "the promise"—the belief that success in school is a ticket to successful adulthood—and play the game as fully as possible
    . . . competing with . . .
    the desire to reject the dream as an empty promise, and to commit to what makes sense outside of school.

The transescent student can see many examples of adults who apparently have lived out "the promise," suggesting that school was the key to success. In contadiction, the student sees many nonschool or antischool rejecters of "the promise" who seem attractively successful in their distinctive alternatives: street life, anti-establishment rugged individualism, the apprentice in a craft or trade, etc. Part of the tension comes from pressure from parents who have themselves lost faith in schooling, but want their children to buy "the promise," hoping through the children to rekindle their own faith. Pressure on the same side also comes from many institutions that for political and economic reasons want to keep young people in school, the effect being to prolong childhood (Bakan, 989-991).

9. The attraction of the adult world and the desire to exercise the new powers of body and mind

. . . competing with . . .

the comfort of childhood habits and the protective cushion that adults provide for children.

Young adolescents are aware of their capacity for fertility. Girls often report that their first menstrual period was a dramatic turning point, "like growing up over night." They also begin to see in themselves other adult capacities, and that awareness pushes them toward adult ways of behaving. The tension comes from the clash with old habits, their own and adults', that tend to keep the adolescents in the secure, nonexperimenting patterns of childhood (Kagan, 1004).

10. The expectations associated with one's state of physical development

. . . competing with . . .

one's chronological age and/or social maturity or intellectual maturity.

Many young adolescents get caught in this gap. The thirteen-year-old girl, for example, who is as physically mature as a twenty-year-old may be treated as if she were twenty, while emotionally and socially she is a child. Or the boy who is slow to mature physically may feel left out or left behind. Lipsitz (24) quotes Money's terse statement that "it is very difficult for some youngsters to be caught in that no-man's land between their chronological age and their physical age, trying to keep up their social age, their academic age, their personality age, and their psychosexual age, in conformity with their chronological age" (Lipsitz, 23-25).

11. The need to turn outward to peers and the attractions of social relationships

. . . competing with . . .

the need to turn inward, to respond to a new emotionality—strong subjective moods, feelings and sensations.

Prior to adolescence, the child does not experience emotions as subjective and personal; emotional states are direct products of outside events. In saying "She hurt my feelings" or "The movie made me sad," the child sees the source of emotions as outside. In adolescence, emotions are experienced as coming from within, even when triggered by outside events. The intensive listening to music, which usually begins in early adolescence, is a sign of emotional development. According to Kohlberg and Gilligan, contemporary rock music is "explicitly a presentation of subjective mood and is listened to in that spirit." Music-social events and parties with alcohol and other drugs seem to be two ways that adolescents attempt to cope with competing pressure for the outer, social relationships and for the inner experiences, experiments with moods and sensations (Kohlberg and Gilligan, 1060-1061).

12. Contradictory emotions . . . competing with . . . each other.

"Associated with the discovery of subjective feelings and moods is the discovery of ambivalence and conflicts of feelings . . . feeling hate and love for the same person, of enjoying sadness . . ." While children cannot accept emotional contradictions, ". . . adolescents are consciously expressing such ambivalence, which is of course the stock in trade of the blues and folk-rock music beamed to them" (Kohlberg and Gilligan, 1061).

Kagan's (1007) statement offers a good summary of the twelve sets of forces described above: the young adolescent is preoccupied with resolving

- uncertainty about *sexual-social adequacy*, achieving a capacity for intimacy;
- uncertainty about *interpersonal power*, personal achievement;
- uncertainty about *acceptability* to peers;
- uncertainty about *autonomy* of belief and action, attaining individual identity and detachment from family.

## IMPLICATIONS FOR TEACHERS

The most powerful message we find in these descriptions is that transescent students have a heavy load of social and emotional concerns, a preoccupying load that surely, for most of them, must often block out their interests in any academic activities. How can social studies or math compete for students' attention? Our experience tells us that any junior high or middle school curriculum that tries to buck, bypass, or ignore the preoccupying concerns of the students cannot succeed. These concerns, of course, represent strong motives that need to be harnessed with school work and not pitted against it.

**Social Adequacy.**   What can a teacher do to harness the preoccupying motives and school tasks together? First of all, one line in the teacher's credo should be: every student needs opportunities for recognition and influence among peers—as often as possible. A sense of acceptance and power among peers is central to young adolescents' sense of self-worth, hence central to their motivation and learning. This fact has not been reflected in the typical structure of schools and classrooms. The research of Lippitt (1971) and his colleagues shows that, in most classrooms, peer acceptance and influence are very unevenly distributed among the children.

A few students have most of the positive acceptance of their peers and most of the influence, while most of the students have very little. This state of deprivation focuses the energy of most students on interpersonal status and away from academic learning challenges (page 2).

The students preoccupied with status are found to underutilize their intellectual capacities in comparison with high-status peers.

Unfortunately, teachers reinforce the pecking order. "Low-status children get far more negative feedback from the teacher than do high-status children" and, predictably, the low-status students reciprocate by directing most hostility toward the teacher. "The findings show, impressively, that the more negative the child feels toward the teacher, the less the teacher can influence him to accept learning opportunities" (Lippitt, 2).

Activities and evaluations that rank or compare students in achievement have commonly been accepted as "motivators" to students lower in rank. The ranking was thought to stimulate lower ranking students to work harder to get higher. For early adolescents, that assumption is essentially false. When pitted against the need for peer acceptance, the need to achieve usually loses. In Kagan's words,

> Regardless of the absolute ability of the top six students in any classroom the child in rank six who perceives that there are five who are more talented than he will begin to doubt his ability either to perform with excellence or to challenge the expertise of the first five . . . Hence the top 25 to 30 percent of any classroom have the easiest time maintaining motivation over the course of the school year, for they and their friends have come to an agreement about who has a better than average probability of success. The less fortunate two-thirds withdraw effort in proportion to their anticipation of less than average performance (1007-1008).

If a teacher wants to avoid ranking and comparing students, to avoid diminishing students' influence with their peers, what can be done? Johnson and Johnson's major review of research (1974) and their subsequent book offer important insights:

- Most American children perceive school as being competitive (that is, promoting ranking—winning-losing, higher-lower). The longer they are in school the more competitive they become.
- The myth that interpersonal competitive skills are important to achievement in American adult society is not supported by research. Succesful adults far more often have well-developed skills of cooperation rather than competition.
- Ambition, achievement, drive, and motivation do not depend on competitive skills or on a competitive social climate.
- Cooperative learning situations (those in which individual goals are attained by mutual effort, and the individual rewards are proportional to the quality of the group work) are superior to competitive learning situations in nearly all respects:
  —higher school achievement in problem solving;
  —high student productivity (the sum of all students' work);
  —more positive student attitudes toward school work;
  —higher student motivation for learning and thinking;
  —more positive interpersonal relationships and attitudes (mutual liking, respect for differences, friendliness, sense of responsibility and desire to win respect of others);

—more open, effective and accurate communication among students.

- Cooperative activities appear to be important for reduction of egocentrism and development of social perspective, empathy, and moral jugment.
- Competitive structure seems to be effective for:
  —drill on simple tasks;
  —speed improvement on tasks where quantity is the objective and help from others is not needed;
  —students who voluntarily choose to compare their skills with those of other students.

How does a cooperative structure get started? The Johnson and Johnson book (1975) offers many concrete suggestions, as does Stanford in *Developing Effective Classroom Groups*.

Cooperative learning techniques, such as team learning and peer tutoring, work well with transcent students, but most students must be helped to understand the roles involved. They have little or no background to legitimate collaboration. In one study the most frequent meaning students gave for "helping each other in the classroom" was "cheating." Suggestions and sources to use for starting team learning and peer tutoring are given in Activity 4 of this chapter.

The sexual side of young peoples' striving for social adequacy also needs the teacher's attention. Much of the transcent's preoccupation with sex is really a concern for understanding gender role, for finding out how to function well in the male or female roles of the culture. Within the curriculum for each student, there need to be planned opportunities to examine and discuss social conventions, standards, and behavior, including dating behavior. The school, as the main gathering place of young people, has a significant opportunity to influence the social climate of girl-boy relationships. We believe the "extracurriculum" needs much more planning and attention than it typically receives. Life in schools outside the classroom is the setting where much of the exploration in boy-girl relationships begins. That setting needs deliberate planning to provide low pressure, noncompetitive opportunities for socializing.

**Interpersonal Power and Personal Achievement.**   Ridicule and name calling, teasing and chasing, and roughplay—especially among boys—can be found every day in middle and junior high schools. In the corridors of some schools the air is literally charged with these efforts to assert power. The need to have some sense of power and achievement is very strong; if it is thwarted in finding constructive directions, it will find spiteful and hostile channels for expression. Hostility is a barometer to be watched. The more competitive the classroom norms, the more hostile the social climate outside the classroom. Teasing and rough play are part of transescence, but the climate influences them to be friendly or antagonistic.

A new capacity for self-criticism emerges in transescence. With it comes new frustrations from seeing a wider gap between one's idealized self and one's actual performance. When teachers help students to set *realistic* goals for themselves, some of the frustrations can be minimized. *All* students need to take on leadership responsbilities, to take manageable risks that will stretch their sense of power.

**Acceptance by Peers.**   Teachers can easily fall into the mistake of expecting and promoting student behavior that violates peer group norms. If the student complies with certain teacher expectations, he or she may lose face with peers. With or without student compliance, the teacher risks loss of influence with the students. To avoid clashing with informal student norms, the teacher needs to observe and collect data about them; to identify the informal leaders among the students; and to enlist their participation in support of pro-school norms and rules. Two books listed in the bibliography—Robert Fox and others, *Diagnosing Classroom Learning Environments*, and Schmuck and Schmuck, *Group Processes in the Classroom*—offer concrete steps to follow in directing and dispersing student leadership.

**Autonomy and Identity.**   Conflicts with school rules and teacher rules are natural to transescents because of their development toward autonomy. They now understand that rules are human inventions to regulate relationships; and human inventions can be changed. Teachers can keep conflicts at a minimum and keep them constructive by having rules that are fair, that are few and simple, that are formulated by group consensus, and that are administered fairly with swift and sure justice. The administration of rules also needs to leave some room for rule-breakers to save face.

Transescents expect fairness from teachers, but they may not apply the same standards of fairness to their own actions. Their sensitivity to fair treatment (for themselves) combined with the power of peer influence make the "classroom meeting" an important tool for social development. As characterized in two chapters of Glasser's *Schools Without Failure*, the classroom meeting can be managed by any teacher for a variety of purposes—academic issues, behavior problems, and open agenda. The main purpose of meetings is to bring students into the making of decisions that materially affect them.

The emotional ups and downs of transescents mostly need gentle responses from the teacher. The troubles probably will pass if the teacher does not over-react. Some of the students' emotional flares are *acting*, testing out dramatic behaviors to see what happens. Teachers we know who seem most successful with transescents give their students regular opportunities for expressive activities. Through dramatic skits, role playing, simulations, expressive writing, dance activities, and creative uses of media, these teachers channel the students' emotional energies into construcuve expressions. They see these activities as important to the self-concept and self-assertion needs of the students.

Activity 2 includes guidelines and references for most of the student activities and teaching strategies suggested above.

# ACTIVITY 2
## Plan techniques that promote social maturity.

The development of social maturity is much too complex to be reduced to a few goal statements and assigned to a set of techniques described in a few pages. If you share our conviction that teachers of transescent students must actively promote their social development, we believe you will continue to find new goals and strategies beyond the few we describe here.

What goals do you see as most important to work on now? We suggest you choose two goals from the list below and concentrate on techniques to implement them.

### Goals for Social and Emotional Development

For all students, the opportunity to:

- develop leadership skills;
- obtain influence and recognition;
- take constructuve and manageable risks in new roles;
- socialize in low pressure, noncompetitive situations;
- develop expressive skills;
- clarify personal values;
- develop realistic personal goals;
- develop skills of independent self-management;
- appreciate their own strengths and accomplishments;
- develop trust relationships;
- develop sharing skills;
- develop active listening skills;
- develop skills of giving and receiving help.

When you decide which two goals you want to pursue and develop into classroom plans, use any of the following suggestions and sources that will help you with your plans. When you have your plan(s) on paper, obtain a written reaction from one or more colleagues.

**A.** *Emphasize Cooperative Norms.*   The reading section in this chapter, "Social Development: Myths and Facts," describes the review of research made by Johnson and Johnson concerning cooperative, competitive, and individualistic goal structures in instruction. The research shows, impressively, that competitive structure is most used and least effective for all but a narrow band of objectives. Cooperative structure is least used and most widely effective. If you want to consider converting classroom activities to the most effective goal structures, or minimizing the pecking order among students, the Johnson and Johnson book, *Learning Together and Alone*, is the resource to turn to first. It includes very concrete suggestions and examples.

**B.** *Organize for Team Learning.*   Consider starting peer panels in your classroom. Most of the ideas and guidelines in Chapter 6 apply to transescent learners as well as to adult learners. Your own experiences as a peer panel member can serve you well as you decide whether team learning or partner learning makes sense for your students, and the amount of structuring they will need from you.

By the time they reach middle grades, most students have learned how to work competitively and individually, but not cooperatively. You may need to begin with simple forms of cooperation, such as the jigsaw-puzzle method that was the vehicle for research on cooperation conducted by Elliot Aronson and his colleagues (1975). The jigsaw-puzzle method proved very effective in promoting peer respect and influence, self-esteem, an attitude of sharing and helping, listening skills, and a sense of ownership in the curriculum content—all of this without sacrificing content mastery. In the jigsaw-puzzle method, the students are organized into small learning groups of equal size, five or six students each. Some printed material to be learned, such as a brief biography of a notable person, is divided into six parts and distributed—one paragraph to each team member. Thus, each learning group has the whole story but each member has no more than one-sixth of it. Each member is dependent on the others to complete the picture, and each is responsible for teaching the others. Mastery of the whole is expected from each. The several children in the room who have part one, for example, may help each other learn their parts, but then the student who has part one of the puzzle teaches that part to the other five in his or her group.

Accustomed to competing for attention or win/lose rewards, many students will try competition, but will find that it does not work in this context. After several days they should be able to use the new technique effectively. Moreover, the quicker students will often encourage and help the slower ones.

We suggest that you consider keeping friendship groups intact rather than splitting friends into separate teams—the customary "divide and conquer" strategy. The cooperative structure of this plan and the expectation of individual accountability keep friends on track and enhance the natural motivations for the school objectives.

Even when studies are individually prescribed, there are some students who work better in a helping or sharing relationship with a friend, whether the work is self-selected or drill. Students should have the chance to work together so long as their talking does not distract others or themselves from the learning tasks. Social development is enhanced and task achievement is not retarded (Damico and Watson, 1976).

**C.** *Cooperation on Mastery Tasks: Learn, Teach, and Test.*   Every curriculum includes some procedures and sets of information that should be learned to a high level of mastery. Learning theorists speak of "overlearning," mastering something so well that it becomes second nature, a ready tool to use in later learning. Basic computation skills are an example of something that should be overlearned. One technique that allows for social development as well as stimulating mastery is the "learn, teach, and test" cycle. As described by Thiagarajan (1973), the strategy begins with instructional material that is divided into short learning units, usually packets or sections in a textbook. Each student works with the material in three roles: learner, teacher, and tester. When a student (say Mary) is ready for a new unit, she seeks out someone (say Jan) who has already learned it to criterion. Jan, in the teaching role, keeps teaching until Mary meets criterion, too. Both then shift to new roles. Mary is ready for the teacher role and Jan is ready to be a tester. When Mary finds a learner for that unit, she stays with that person until the test is satisfactorily passed. Mary then is available as a tester. The tester uses a testing guide and/or scoring key and helps diagnose what the learner and teacher need to know if the criteria are not met. At each transaction the participants sign each other's record cards to signal a step completed. Thiagarajan's article gives clear guidelines for implementing the system.

**D.** *Other Ways That Students Can Be Teachers.*   Peer tutoring, in which a few advanced students work as assistant teachers, is a form of tutoring that does not necessarily help social development. Some students are usually left out of the responsible role of tutor. Ginott's (1972, p. 265) suggestion of a "resource directory" seems better suited to supporting social goals. A classroom or learning community directory of "Who Is Good in What in This Class (or L.C.)" will give anyone needing assistance a means of making contact with a student who can be a tutor. This system offers one more way that prestige and influence may be redistributed among students.

The other form of tutoring that seems to be well-suited to middle school students, a form well supported by research, is cross-age tutoring. Tutors typically learn more than tutees, and in most cases, tutees in the experiments learn more than students in control groups who are learning only with their adult teachers. Tutoring is an especially important experience for the student who has a low self-image as learner and is behind others in achievement. Such students can be encouraged to become tutors to younger students by being made aware of an asset they possess: they are expert at knowing the frustrations and other feelings of not catching on quickly. They are likely to have more patience and more insight into what blocks a younger child's learning. In many cases, it becomes a self-fulfilling prophecy.

Olders can tutor youngers within a middle or junior high school, but the best effects seem to come from tutoring elementary students. Social maturation and improved attitude toward school are often more striking gains than the academic achievement gains. Tutoring should not be undertaken without a plan that is carefully developed and monitored. Several sources listed at the end of the chapter—Melaragno, Lippitt (1975) and the National Commission on Resources for Youth—offer explicit guidelines for implementing tutoring programs. Listed also are two comprehensive reviews of research on tutoring (Devin-Sheehan and Paolitto).

**E.** *Student Government in the Middle School.*   Young people develop social responsibility and social skills by having responsibilities. Junior high and middle school students can take part in some schoolwide management decisions as well as decisions about classroom life.

The rule of thumb is that people ought to have the opportunity to participate in decisions that materially affect them. Perhaps middle schoolers should have the opportunity, but most of them are not interested in most administrative and instructional decisions. Their interest is keen, however, in issues of fairness, discipline, justice, behavior rules, and morality. In those areas of school and classroom governance, students will take an active part and can grow through their participation.

A committee of the Maryland Middle School Association studied ways that students might be involved in school governance, and its conclusions were summarized in a report. "A Design for Student Government in the Middle School," which follows, reflects the committee's work.

If you have the opportunity to explore with other faculty members the possibility of student government for your school, the Maryland report should be valuable to you. If you pursue the idea, keep notes and minutes for your portfolio.

## A Design for Student Government in the Middle School

In analyzing new programs in middle schools, members of the Maryland Middle School Association noted a general lack of attention to student government. They also recognized that where student government did exist in individual schools, it tended to be an imitation of the high school organization. The Association then appointed a committee to investigate the ways that middle schools might develop student governance. In its report the committee presented (a) a set of student objectives to guide a student government plan; (b) a statement of assumptions about student government for middle schools; and (c) a general model for student government.

The form of student government proposed by the committee integrates governance into the curriculum and the schedule of the school. It does not stand as a separate entity. Rather, it is a broad-based program involving all students and containing a strong instructional component. The Association presented the model as a general one, to be modified and adapted as needed by individual schools.

I. *Objectives of student government for the middle school*
   The student going through the middle school should be able to:
   A. Make up a list of rules of common courtesy in group meetings
      1. recognize and demonstrate respect for the rights of others
      2. know procedures that work for presenting ideas to a large group
      3. recognize commonly accepted rules of order for individuals and groups
   B. Communicate effectively with fellow students
      1. identify problems in both talking and listening
      2. identify and understand basic nonverbal communications
      3. grasp the ideas in and the feelings behind someone's statements
      4. figure out what to say back to the other person, based on all that was seen and heard
      5. be able to see how the other person thinks and feels, especially when there is disagreement
      6. know and be able to express his/her own opinions
      7. express his/her opinion before a group
   C. Communicate effectively with other groups
      1. know the relationship of a school government to other policy making groups operating in a school
      2. understand and use channels of communication operating within a school and operating on the school from the outside
      3. understand the principles and procedures of due process

ADAPTED FROM the report of the Committee on Student Government, Maryland Middle School Association, 1976.

D. Develop the skills needed to be a leader and a follower
   1. understand how groups work
      a. understand that there are different roles at work in a group
      b. understand that some roles help a group's progress, while some roles hinder it
      c. know that people's feelings can influence interaction
      d. understand how to take care of others' feelings
      e. be able to clarify and keep focused on the group's task
      f. encourage everyone to participate
   2. develop problem-solving skills
      a. recognize that there is a basic pattern in making decisions that can be used in most situations
      b. understand that these steps are:
         (1) knowing what the conflict is
         (2) brainstorming alternative sources of information on the problem
         (3) gathering and evaluating information on the choices that are open
         (4) listing the practices involved in the decision or problem
         (5) deciding which are the best choices
         (6) considering what would happen from doing each of the choices
         (7) in a group situation being able to identify means of reaching agreement
         (8) learning what she/he already believes, in order to decide which choice is best
         (9) making a decision and stating that decision in some way

E. Learn straight-thinking skills
   1. separate fact from opinion
   2. separate fact from common belief
   3. recognize loaded words
      a. the effect they can have
      b. how they can be misleading
      c. how they can be valuable
   4. recognize that statements taken out of the context in which they were written or spoken:
      a. are not necessarily valid
      b. can sway opinions
   5. recognize generalizations
      a. the effect they have
      b. how they can be valid
      c. that to be valid, a generalization must:
         (1) be based on enough facts
         (2) take into account the exceptions which do not fit the generalization
      d. how they can be misleading
      e. how to fix them by qualifying them

6. how to argue without getting personal or engaging in name-calling
7. how to avoid assigning guilt by association
8. understand the use and the misuse of authority to stress points

F.  Understand the structure of governance
1. understand patterns in the ways people govern themselves
2. analyze differences and similarities between various forms of governance
3. clarify advantages and disadvantages, strengths and weaknesses in the ways people govern themselves
4. be able to adapt their existing form of government, as the need arises

II. *Assumptions about student government for middle schools*
Student government in a middle school needs to allow for:

A.  Every student to be involved in government decisions
B.  Leadership opportunities for large numbers of students
C.  Opportunities for students to work toward all of the objectives stated in Part I
D.  Student government activities to be a part of the curriculum and schedule of the school
E.  Structure and adult guidance
F.  Balance between student and adult leadership and involvement

III. *A model for middle school student government*

A.  Every student will be a member of a *town meeting* group. Each town meeting group will:
1. have about 120 members, the students and teachers of one teaching team
2. break down into several small groups (such as home base groups or social studies classes)
3. debate problems
4. make decisions about rules and plans affecting that group of students
5. decide what to recommend to other town meetings about school-wide rules and plans
6. use rules of order and procedures that students have learned
7. use an agenda gathered from the small groups, individuals, and the coordinating committee
8. elect two leaders for a term of one semester to conduct the town meetings, to prepare the agenda, and to serve on the coordinating committee. Leaders shall not succeed themselves.

B.  Every student will be a member of a *small group*. Several small groups will make up a town meeting group. Each small group will:
1. be a regular school group, such as home base group or third period class, that will give some of its time to student government matters
2. work on ideas, plans, and research to take to town meeting
3. study rules of order and how groups work
4. elect leadership to conduct the small group's work
5. make decisions affecting the small group

C. Coordinating committee
   The two leaders from each town meeting group will form a coordinating committee. This group will perform the executive role of the student government, carrying out what is decided by two-thirds of the town meeting groups. The coordinating committee will:
   1. have adult advisors
   2. set up subcommittees as needed to carry out its work
   3. suggest items for the agendas of town meetings
   4. work with the school administrators to clarify what policy and decisions should be made in town meetings and what should remain with administrators and teachers

# ACTIVITY 3
## Gather information about students.

A teacher in a class is like a man in the woods at night with a powerful flashlight in his hand. Wherever he turns his light, the creatures on whom it shines are aware of it, and do not behave as they do in the dark. Thus the mere fact of his watching their behavior changes it into something very different. Shine where he will, he can never know very much of the night life of the woods (Holt, 1964).

Gathering information about students—reasonably accurate information—is more difficult than it seems. Young people show a different side of themselves in school than they show out of school. When they know that a teacher is the collector of information they may consciously or unconsciously alter their reports or their behavior to impress or tease or please the teacher. Moreover, a teacher cannot simultaneously conduct classroom events and be a careful observer of the events. These are conditions and precautions to be kept in mind as you gather and interpret information about students.

## TECHNIQUES FOR COLLECTING DATA ON STUDENTS

### General Directions

The activities described in section A provide some means of identifying the level of social maturity of students. Follow at least one of those activities. Also, if you possibly can, conduct a "shadow study" as described in section B. Then choose any of the remaining activities in sections C through G that fit your purposes, needs, and circumstances. Make notes on each activity and save them to share with a colleague who is also doing these activities.

**A.** *Identify Students' Social Maturity.*    Differences in physical maturity are dramatically evident in middle grades. Yet transcents of the same calendar age can differ even more widely in social maturity; the differences are just less obvious. Here are three ways to examine the variations. Choose and follow at least one of them.

1. Select and observe five students who are the same chronological age, plus or minus two months. They should not be aware that you are observing them. Prepare a page of notes on each student dealing with (a) his or her relationships to teachers and peers—both boys and girls; (b) evidences of social responsibility; (c) apparent preoccupations and strong interests; and (d) evidences of apparent emotional states. Analyze the five sets of notes for similarities and contrasts.
2. Select (or have someone select for you) five middle grade students whom you do not know and have no way of knowing what grades they are in. This activity can be done most easily in schools that have multi-age grouping. Observe or work with the students (teaching, tutoring, or guiding activities). Make notes on the social behaviors of each. Then estimate the age of each in years and months.
3. Select five students to interview, one at a time. Ask them to tell six things they like best about school and six things they like least. Keep notes as you analyze their responses for social maturity patterns.

**B.** *Do a Shadow Study.* Essentially, a shadow study is an attempt to experience a school day as a junior-high/middle-school student does. Select a student's name at random from the school rolls, obtain permission of the student's teachers to attend each of the student's classes, and "shadow" the student through all the daily activities—classes, hallway conversations, lunch, P.E., etc. There are four guidelines to follow.

1. Try to observe all the events—even small and informal ones the student experiences; and try to do it without the student knowing you are shadowing specifically him or her.
2. Describe the events in a log, recording both verbal and nonverbal (e.g., body language) behavior. Be factual and specific.
3. Make log entries at least every ten minutes or whenever a change of event occurs, making entries in three columns: *situation* (including time, place, people, and activities), *behavior* of the target student, and your *reactions to and interpretations of* the behavior.
4. Watch especially for clues to the social and emotional life of the student.

If you now have full time teaching responsibilities, try to arrange some trade-offs with other teachers so you can make at least part of the day available for shadowing. Do not shadow one of your own students. Save your log.

**C.** *Have Students Write Journals.* Students usually enjoy writing journals when they know this is a special kind of person-to-person communication with the teacher. Some want a written dialogue with the teacher, an opportunity to talk seriously with someone who listens and responds seriously. Some use the journal to express feelings, others to talk about ideas. Jacobs (1970) found journal writing to be a powerful way to help students assess more carefully the events of the their lives. He saw the quality of students' composition skills improve noticeably as they developed the habits of more carefully observing, reflecting, and recording journal entries. His book contains many excerpts from journals you might read to students to help them understand the idea of journals. Mirthes (1971) assigned writing topics such as: "Who Am I?"; "The Block I Live On . . ."; "In My

House. . ."; "Acting Tough"; and "The Ideal School." Once the journal process was well launched, assigned topics were no longer needed. Jacobs used no assigned topics.

Journal writing works best when the teacher takes the needed time to read the journals regularly and respond to the entries. Grammar and spelling should not be corrected unless the student requests the corrections. Journal writing is not an activity to be started as a short-term novelty or merely to provide some immediate data about the social and emotional life of students. We suggest that you begin the activity with the intention of continuing and as a basis for a new means of personal communication between teacher and student. One system that works well is having individual folders or binders for student journals stored alphabetically on one bookshelf in the classroom. Students should agree on a privacy rule, such as, no one read another's journal except as the writer chooses to share a certain entry. Students may want a rule that they can mark any entry "CONFIDENTIAL" so that even the teacher will not read that one. Classroom time, about twenty minutes twice a week, can be designated as journal-writing time.

The students who have difficult problems at home or in the neighborhood may be reluctant to write about their concerns—especially if they feel the teacher will judge or not accept them. Writing may not be the way to start a trusting relationship with some of these students. For some, more concrete person-to-person contacts, such as tutoring or being given classroom helper roles, may secure enough trust to start the flow of journal writing. Make notes describing the journal activities.

**D.** *Take Inventory of Student Interests and Concerns.*   Students like to know how their interests compare with those of peers. Construct a poll or inventory sheet that combines questions that interest students with questions that will give you (and them) some insights into their social and emotional makeup. After you propose some questions, students may want to add others. They will enjoy tabulating the responses. Some possible topics to include: "My Top 10 TV Shows"; "Ten Things I Like to Do in My Spare Time"; "Three Things I Am Afraid of"; "Three Things I Am Proud of." The Chase (1975) book suggests many more possible questions. Students need not put their names on their response sheets.

**E.** *Have Students Make a "Who Am I?" Collage.*   Using posterboard or a section from a cardboard carton, students can paste pictures and captions from magazines to make a collage that expresses who they are. This kind of activity runs the risk of getting trite and perfunctory responses from some students unless they are given an orientation to the activity that will encourage care and thoughtfulness. They may respond well to a challenge such as: "You are unique. No one else in the world is just like you. So your collage should be unique and personal. Out of these magazines that are printed for millions and don't pay attention to peoples' uniqueness, can you find pictures that say something personal about you? About what you believe, like, dislike, hope, fear . . . about what you are underneath that doesn't often show?"

After the students make and display their collages, try to interpret them without asking students to help. Make notes. Then, in a private conversation, ask the student who made a particular collage to describe it and say why he or she selected the pictures and words used. After each conversation, jot down your reactions and insights.

**F.** *Have Students Keep an Activity Log.*   Ask students to keep a time log for one week that records all activities they engage in during their waking hours, both inside and outside of school. Save some classroom time each day for them to make entries, and suggest that they be as specific as possible, avoiding general phrases such as "playing," "working," "messing around." Have them arrange the log like a date book, by hours of the day.

They may wish to show the logs to you and to other students. If they do, have a discussion that includes their reactions to the patterns of time usage that the log reveals.

**G.** *Analyze Students' Verbal and Nonverbal Expressions.*   Students' slang, colloquial exclamations, adjectives, and expressions of approval or disapproval change from year to year, but they often reveal something about the values of young people. The meanings of some expressions are not obvious to adults, and some have meanings very different from adult usage. For example, young people in our city have a special meaning for *mean*, as in "He's a mean teacher." It means *strict*. But *mean*, as in "That's a mean jacket," means cool (attractive). *Cool* has been around for years, but *scag* is new locally. The ultimate scag is someone wearing "highwaters" and unmatched sox, and carrying a briefcase.

Make a list of such words used in your locality. Define them as well as you can. The students will be glad to help you with the list, and will be quick to point out your mistakes in definition and usage. Analyze the list for what it suggests about the social norms and expectations of transescents. For example, are more of the words complimentary or critical? What do the words imply about the quality of thinking, the shadings of values, and the feelings that lie behind them?

Consider also the nonverbal expressions you see in students; for example, what is meant by the rolling up of the eyes, and turning down the corners of the mouth? Make a list of these expressions and their meanings. Write out your analyses of these as described above.

## ACTIVITY 4
**Analyze responses to student behavior.**

### TECHNIQUES FOR OBSERVING RESPONSES TO STUDENT BEHAVIOR

**A.** *Observe Teacher-Student Interactions.*   Any two schools may have quite different standards and expectations for student social behavior. And any two teachers may react differently to the same student behavior. What reactions and standards are best for promoting students' social and intellectual development? One way to answer the question is to carefully observe the transescents you know best, inside classrooms and out. We suggest these steps to guide your observation and analysis:

1. First observe any groups of ten- to fourteen-year-olds outside the classroom, when they are not under the direct supervision of adults. Try to observe groups of two or more young people in such a way that your presence does not affect their behavior. Schoolyards, hallways, cafeterias, recreation centers, and parks are likely places.

Record what you see and hear as objectively and factually as you can. Later analyze your notes for patterns. What do their words and actions reveal about their social development? What sorts of groups do they form? What dominates their interest and attention? How do they differ from younger and older girls and boys?

2. Next observe some ten- to fourteen-year-olds interacting with adults outside the classroom. Make notes and analyze them to find patterns of behavior.

3. Finally, arrange to observe in the individual classrooms of at least three teachers. In each classroom, for twenty minutes or more, concentrate on the behavior of students. Record events as they happen, recording just facts. You may want to focus on four or five students so your notes can better follow the sequences of their behavior. For another ten minutes or more, concentrate on the teacher's behavior—particularly the teacher's reactions to student actions. Later, analyze your notes and consider these questions: How did students' out-of-class behavior differ from in-class behavior? Were students' social preoccupations evident in any way in the classroom? What patterns did you observe in the teacher's reactions to students? Based on your analysis of student social development and needs, what teaching techniques do you regard as best suited to those needs? Save your observation notes and analyses to share with a colleague who is doing these activities.

**B.** *Obtain Teacher Reactions to Student Behaviors.*   Your observations in Section A3 gave you some ideas about different teachers' reactions to student behaviors. Now ask those teachers you observed and three or four others to describe the social behaviors of students which frustrate them most. As you talk with them, you may want to share your observations of the patterns of student social behaviors in and out of the classroom. After the interviews, write down any conclusions you have made as to why teacher needs and student needs often clash with each other. Also record the ideas you may have for minimizing the clashes. Save these notes.

**C.** *Analzye School Structure in Relation to Social Needs.*   In the school in which you teach (or intern, observe, assist, etc.), examine the school routines, rules, schedule, physical layout, and expectations as these relate to the social development needs of the students. Make a list of items and activities that facilitate social development and another list of features that seem to ignore social needs. Save your lists.

**D.** *Plan and Assess a Change in Your Teaching.*   Researchers have shown that middle grade students imitate or model themselves after teachers much more than teachers are aware. You can find out for yourself by planning a deliberate change in your behavior and then observing student reactions before and after you make the change. Your work in Activity 3 and Activity 4 may suggest a change you would like to make in your behavior, for example, a mannerism, a way of greeting students, or a new word or expression. First decide what effect you would expect that behavior to have on students when you model it. Find a way to make a quantitative "before" record of student behavior. After you have made the measurement, adopt the new behavior without telling students what you are doing. Take your "after" measurement when you think enough time has elapsed. Keep notes on the experiment. To what extent do you think students' social maturing is influenced by what you *do*, as distinct from what you *say*?

## NEXT STEPS

We have two suggestions for next steps. Make use of the list of references which follows. We selected the sources carefully and believe they all have relevance to teachers. The second suggestion is to consider the school curriculum and your own teaching in light of the "Goals for Social and Emotional Development" listed in Activity 4. We believe these goals need more attention in most schools. Consideration of how to implement them within a balanced curriculum will generate more "next steps" than any one person can take.

## REFERENCES

ADELSON, JOSEPH. "The Political Imagination of the Young Adolescent," *Daedalus* 100 (4) (1971):1013-1050.

AIKEN, WILFORD. *Story of the Eight Year Study.* New York: Harper and Brothers, 1942.

ALMY, MILLIE. *Ways of Studying Children.* New York: Teachers College Press, 1959.

ARONSON, ELLIOT, and others. "Busing and Racial Tension: The Jigsaw Route to Learning and Liking," *Psychology Today* 8 (9) (1975): 43-50.

BAKAN, DAVID. "Adolescence in America; From Idea to Social Fact," *Daedalus* 100 (4) (1971): 979-996.

BIEHLER, ROBERT F. *Psychology Applied to Teaching.* Boston: Houghton Mifflin Co., 1971.

BLYTH, DALE, ROBERTA SIMMONS, and DIANE BUSH. "The Transition into Early Adolescence: A Longitudinal Comparison of Youth in Two Educational Contexts," *Sociology of Education* 51 (3) (1978):149-169.

CANFIELD, J., and H.C. WELLS. *One Hundred Ways to Enhance Self-Concept in the Classroom.* Englewood Cliffs, N.J.: Prentice-Hall, Inc., 1976.

CHASE, LARRY. *The Other Side of the Report Card: A How-To-Do-It Program for Affective Education.* Glenview, Ill.: Scott, Foresman and Company, 1975.

CITIZENSHIP EDUCATION PROJECT. *Laboratory Practices in Citizenship: Learning Experiences in the Community.* New York: Citizenship Education Project, Teachers College, Columbia University, 1958.

COMPTON, MARY F. "Who Are Transescents?" *Middle School Journal* 9 (3) (1978):24.

DAMICO, SANDRA, and KATHRYN WATSON. "Peer Helping Relationships: A Study of Student Interactions in an Elementary Classroom," Research Monograph No. 18. Gainesville: P.K. Yonge Laboratory School, University of Florida, 1976.

DEVIN-SHEEHAN, LINDA, and others. "Research on Children Tutoring Children: A Critical Review," *Review of Educational Research* 46 (3) (1976):355-385.

ELKIND, DAVID.   "Egocentricism in Adolescents," Childhood Development 38 (1967): 1025-1034.

FOX, ROBERT, MARGARET LUSZKI, and RICHARD SCHMUCK.   *Diagnosing Classroom Learning Environments*. Chicago: Science Research Associates, 1966.

GALLATIN, JUDITH.   *Adolescence and Individuality*. New York: Harper and Row, 1975.

GINOTT, HAIM.   *Teacher and Child*. New York: The MacMillan Co., 1972.

GLASSER, WILLIAM.   *Schools Without Failure*. New York: Harper and Row, 1969.

HILL, JOHN.   "Perspectives on Adolescence in American Society." Paper prepared for the Office of Child Developement, U.S. Department of Health, Education and Welfare, Washington, D.C., May 1973.

HOLT, JOHN.   *How Children Fail*. New York: Pitman Publishing Corp., 1964.

JACOBS, GABRIEL.   *When Children Think*. New York: Teachers College Press, 1970.

JOHNSON, D.W., and R.T. JOHNSON.   "Instructional Goal Structure: Cooperative, Competitive, or Individualistic?" *Review of Educational Research* 44 (2) (1974):213-240.

————.   *Learning Together and Alone*. Englewood Cliffs, N.J.: Prentice-Hall, Inc., 1975.

KAGAN, JEROME.   "A Conception of Early Adolescence," *Daedalus* 100 (4) (1971):997-1012.

KOHLBERG, LAWRENCE, and CAROL GILLIGAN.   "The Adolescent as Philosopher: The Discovery of the Self in a Postconventional World," *Daedalus* 100 (4) (1971):1051-1086.

LIPPITT, PEGGY.   *Students Teach Students*. Bloomington, Ind.: The Phi Delta Kappan Educational Foundation, 1975.

LIPPITT, RONALD.   "The Neglected Learner," *Social Science Education Consortium Newsletter* 8 (Feb. 1970):1-5.

LIPSITZ, JOAN.   *Growing Up Forgotten*. Lexington, Mass.: D.C. Heath and Co., 1977.

LOPES, JOHN, JR.   "A Classroom Experience: Early Adolescents and Self-Governance," *Middle School Journal* 8 (3) (1977):3, 16-17, 19.

MELARAGNO, RALPH. *Tutoring with Students: A Handbook for Establishing Tutorial Programs in Schools*. Englewood Cliffs, N.J.: Educational Technology Publications, 1976.

MIRTHES, CAROLINE.   *Can't You Hear Me Talking to You?* New York: Bantam Book, Inc., 1971.

NATIONAL COMMISSION ON RESOURCES FOR YOUTH, INC.   *Resources for Youth* (A newsletter distributed free of charge). NCRY publishes and distributes a number of books, pamphlets, films and video tapes on youth participation, including tutoring and community service projects. To obtain the newsletter and a list of resources, write to the Commission at 36 West 44th St., Room 1314, New York, N.Y., 10036.

PAOLITTO, DIANA.  "The Effect of Cross-Age Tutoring on Adolescents: An Inquiry into Theoretical Assumptions," *Review of Educational Research* 46 (2) (1976):215-237.

POMAINVILLE, MARTHA, CYNTHIA BLANKENSHIP, and BARBARA STANFORD. *Possibilities for Reading/Relating.* New York: Learning Ventures, 1977. (666 5th Ave., N.Y., N.Y. 10017).

SCHMUCK, RICHARD, and PATRICIA SCHMUCK.  *Group Processes in the Classroom*, Dubuque, Iowa: William C. Brown Company, 1971.

SCHOFIELD, JANET W., and H. ANDREW SAGAR.  "Peer Interaction Patterns in an Integrated Middle School," *Sociometry* 40 (2) (1977):130-138.

SHAFTEL, FANNY, and GEORGE SHAFTEL.  *Role Playing in the Curriculum.* Englewood Cliffs, N.J.: Prentice-Hall, 1982.

SHULMAN, JEROME, ROBIN FORD, and PATRICIA BASK.  "A Classroom Program to Improve Self-Concepts," *Psychology in the Schools* 10 (4) (1973):481-487.

STANFORD, GENE.  *Developing Effective Classroom Groups: A Practical Guide for Teachers*, New York: Hart Publishing Co., Inc., 1977.

THIAGARAJAN, SIGASAILAM.  "Madras System Revisited: A New Structure for Tutoring," *Educational Technology* 13 (12) (1973):10-13.

WASSERMAN, ELSA.  "Implementing Kohlberg's 'Just Community Concept' in an Alternative High School," *Social Education* 40 (4) (1976):203-207.

WURMAN, RICHARD, (Ed.)  *Yellow Pages of Learning Resources*, Cambridge, Mass.: MIT Press, 1972.

*The following two journals frequently have articles related to the content of this chapter:*

*ADOLESCENCE.*  Libra Publishers, Inc., P.O. Box 165, 391 Willets Road, Roslyn Heights, New York 11577. Quarterly.

*TRANSESCENCE.*  The journal on emerging adolescent education. Educational Leadership Institute, Inc., P.O. Box 863, Springfield, Mass. 01101. Yearly.

# PART TWO The School

Middle schools attempt to satisfy two important criteria. They strive to be unique schools, offering the students a structure and program that differs from elementary and high school. They are also designed to help students make the transition from elementary to high school. These twin emphases, uniqueness and transition, make middle schools places where special things happen.

This section of the text focuses on those aspects of the middle school program that, because they are both unique and transitional, require special efforts from teachers. You will find a chapter that helps you play the role of advisor with your students. There is a chapter dealing with your participation in an exploratory curriculum program, one that assists you in planning and teaching as a member of a team, and more.

These chapters ask for your active participation in planning programs meaningful to ten- to fourteen-year-olds. When you have completed the activities in these chapters we hope you will have developed an understanding of what makes a middle school special. You will be able to answer the question, "What is a middle school—really?"

# CHAPTER 5

# UNDERSTANDING THE
# MIDDLE SCHOOL CONCEPT

You are probably considering the possibilities of a career in teaching ten- to fourteen-year-olds, or you may be already teaching in a school that has middle grades. In either case, you may want to know more about distinctive ways of organizing intermediate education to match the needs of ten- to fourteen-year-olds.

Many beginning teachers are given little opportunity to become familiar with their school's philosophy. The purpose of this chapter is to help you extend your understanding of what middle level schooling is about: its goals, its program, and what you might expect to find happening in well-functioning schools. When you have completed this chapter, you will be able to describe a model for middle level schooling and you will have a clear understanding of the phrase, "the middle school concept." Also, you will be able to describe the rationale usually set forth to justify the reorganization of intermediate education. We have carefully organized the activities for this chapter and suggest you follow our sequence for best results.

Please keep in mind that the term *middle school*, as used in this chapter, does *not* refer to a school with a specific set of grades (such as 5-8 or 6-8) as distinguished from junior high school or upper grades in an elementary school. *Middle school* here means a school organization that takes its design specifically from the analysis of ten- to fourteen-year-olds, their characteristics, and their needs.

## ACTIVITY 1
### Visit a school.

**A.**   Now that you have worked through the chapters on the nature of the transescent, you have had an opportunity to learn about the characteristics of this group of students. Please take some time to review these materials and experiences and create two lists. The first list (8-10 items) should consist of a summary of those concepts that you consider to be essential to understanding the special nature of these learners. The second list (10-15 items) is an extension of the first and based on what you know about transescents, consists of criteria that you believe are a good set of guidelines for schools serving this age group. For example, you might have on your first list the "the onset of puberty" as a factor, and on your second list a guideline that schools "provide appropriate instruction in sex education."

Use these two lists to help complete the rest of this activity.

**B.**   If you are not now teaching in a school serving transescents, arrange to spend a few hours visiting one nearby. If you are teaching in such a school, it is desirable to visit another one. If you cannot visit a middle school, plan to spend some time organizing your thoughts and feelings about your own school experiences and use these as a reference. Using the following questions as a guide, react to the observations and experiences you had in the selected school.

1.  Do the students in the school look and act as you expected they would? Elaborate on this a little.
2.  Based on what you see or remember, how are the teachers and students organized for learning? By subjects? On teams? In some other way? Describe the situation fully.
3.  How does the climate of the school strike you? Is there a pleasant, warm, and supportive feeling, or is it a tense, hostile, and cold place? Somewhere in between? What makes you feel the way you do about the school?
4.  If you had to label this school, would you call it a traditional or an innovative school? Why did you make this choice?
5.  Does the school more closely resemble an elementary school or a high school? What is there about the school that makes it seem the way it does?
6.  If you know the school principal or another school leader and have a chance to talk with that person, does he or she seem eager to talk about the term *middle school?* If so, what do they say? If not, what conclusions can you draw about their involvement in the process of educating emerging adolescents?

Based on what you have seen and experienced in middle schools to this point, describe your thoughts about: the purposes of such a school; the characteristics of the students; your personal reaction to teaching in such a school, and the reasons for this reaction.

## ACTIVITY 2
**Read and write about the middle school concept.**

**A.**   Read these selections and make notes:

1.  "The Middle School Story."
2.  At least two of the many articles dealing with the middle school concept that appear in journals such as the *Middle School Journal, Educational Leadership, NASSP Bulletin, Principal,* or *Clearing House.*

## The Middle School Story

### DEFINITION

The middle school is a concept which, when operational, results in a program that attempts to meet the needs of children in the in-between years, usually from ages ten to fourteen. The middle school differs from elementary and secondary schools, and attempts to provide a bridge between these two phases of schooling. No particular grade organization is sacred, but usually some combinations of grades five through eight are included.

There are a few central elements which most fully functioning middle schools have in common. Among those considered most important are:

1. Every student has a home base and teacher-advisor.
2. The school day is scheduled flexibly, often with some form of block schedule.
3. Interdisciplinary team teaching is the preferred method of instructional organization.
4. Multi-age student grouping is preferred. For example, a group of 150 students, ages 10-14, will be grouped with an interdisciplinary team of 4-5 teachers.
5. The curricular program focuses on three major goals: personal development, skills for continued learning, and introduction to the areas of organized knowledge.
6. Instruction is personalized and students progress continuously at their own rates.
7. A wide range of exploratory activities is provided.

### THE GROWTH OF THE MIDDLE SCHOOL CONCEPT

The Middle School movement began in earnest in the early 1960s. By the beginning of the 1970s the movement had taken on the elements of dynamic growth. In 1965 there were 500 middle schools across the nation. Two years later a survey indicated the number had doubled, reaching slightly over 1,000. By the 1969-70 school year the number had doubled again; over 2,000 schools were counted in a study. Recent surveys indicate there are probably close to 5,000 middle schools in the nation today. This rate of growth has to subside soon, but the movement is here to stay.

### THE RATIONALE FOR THE MIDDLE SCHOOL

"Why a new school in the middle?" There are three general answers to this question. First, a program is needed that really focuses on the "in-between-agers" and their specific needs. Second, a school program is needed that provides real continuity in education on a K-12 basis. Finally, the middle school can facilitate the introduction and adoption of needed innovations in every phase of schooling.

Much of the case for the middle school comes from the standpoint of human growth and development. There is some evidence that children today are maturing at a much earlier age, both physically and socially. Puberty, for both sexes, arrives approximately one year earlier than it did for children twenty years ago. Socially, children are achieving sophistication earlier for a variety of reasons connected with the modern media and with child-rearing practices.

Educators' understanding of the intellectual development of children has been considerably enhanced by the work of Jean Piaget, Jerome Bruner, and other educational psychologists. We know that the middle school child passes from a phase of less able mental operations into one which permits much more powerful thought processes. The school program must fit this change in thought processes.

Finally, we know that with the approach of puberty and the subsequent changing mental operations and restructuring of values, the self-concept of the child is more than ever fluid and fragile. The power of peer relationships, the presence of turbulent emotions, and a variety of other transescent characteristics demand an appropriate school program.

In addition to the evidence from studies of human growth and development, the failure of previous attempts to meet the needs of this age group is evident. The junior high school has, on the whole, become a miniature version of the senior high school, leaving many needs unmet.

## CHARACTERISTICS OF THE TRANSESCENT CHILD

While no set of statements about an age group can apply to all in that group, this list of characteristics applies to most.

The transescent student:

1. possesses a new-found intellectual prowess and, for many, this means an ability to deal with symbolic ideas and abstract concepts.
2. is living under the impact of the onset of puberty and the appearance of new erotic sensations.
3. is bound by an overwhelming need, a craving for peer acceptance and approval.
4. is faced with a new body, in muscular and skeletal terms, that must be mastered all over again.
5. needs to assert autonomy and independence, and often exhibits a resentment of, and resistance to, adult authority.
6. possesses extreme idealism.
7. struggles with turbulent emotions.
8. needs to face the task of developing a new value system to fit his or her life and society.
9. is constantly developing, testing, and changing perceptions of self (self-concept).

10. is living through a major transformation in relationships with the opposite sex.
11. faces the task of sex-role identification.
12. has rapidly multiplying but superficial interests.
13. has a need for frequent periods of physical activity and movement alternated with periods of rest.

## INSTRUCTION IN THE MIDDLE SCHOOL

The overall aim of instruction in the middle school is a balance between teacher-directed and student-directed learning. The end product is intended to be continuous progress education, implemented through a variety of instructional strategies.

Interdisciplinary team teaching fits the middle school almost perfectly. Four or five teachers from a variety of areas of expertise become a team with the joint responsibility of instruction for a large number of students. Teachers may organize the division of labor within the team in a variety of ways. One team of middle school teachers reported that the advantages of working together include increased program flexibility, improved interpersonal relationships, fewer discipline problems, and easy scheduling.

Flexible grouping and scheduling are common in middle schools. Large blocks of the day are given to the team to plan as they see best. Students may be from one age-group/grade-level or from a number of different groups. There may be a team, for example, that deals only with sixth graders. Another school may have a team that has 150 students from ages ten to fourteen.

Problem-solving, inquiry-oriented methods help to increase the relevance of the middle school program. Inquiry methods, combined with independent study and other related approaches, help to develop increased self-direction and responsibility among middle school pupils, as do various methods of classroom management and behavior management used by teachers.

A variety of small-group methods are appropriate for the middle school. The use of teams, committees, and other groups for work and play seem to work especially well at this level.

## CURRICULUM IN THE MIDDLE SCHOOL

The key assumption of the middle school curriculum is that a learner has mastered some skills and basic knowledge, but is not yet ready for the academic specialization of the high school. The middle school attempts to provide a program that contains three basic elements:

1. *Emphasis on Personal Development.*  This means a deemphasis on high school type activities, positive health and sex education, physical education, more guidance, increased interest activities, wider exploratory opportunities, home base and teacher advisor for every student, and more opportunities to experience success.

The program includes a focus on the development of values and opportunities for physical movement and social activities, including out-of-school activities. Cooperative teacher-student planning and decision making complement the personal development dimension.

2. *Stress on the Skills of Continued Learning.* These skills include communication (writing, reading, listening, viewing), thinking (hypothesizing, questioning, inferring, contrasting and comparing, generalizing, predicting, critical analysis), and study skills (library tools, laboratory skills, organizing and presenting information).

3. *Introduction to the Areas of Organized Knowledge.* This includes identification of the big ideas and underlying generalizations of the major disciplines, experiences in organizing and using appropriate data and methods and opportunities to integrate these understandings in interdisciplinary problem-solving. Some middle school educators believe that a general tone of cultural affirmation should be present, i.e., cultural positives before negatives.

## THE MIDDLE SCHOOL TEACHER

What qualities describe the people who become competent middle school teachers? What kind of people are they? What understandings must they possess? What instructional skills must they have mastered?

1. Personal qualities: a positive, secure, concept of self; flexibility; respect for the dignity and worth of the individual; the ability to interact constructively with teachers and students; and a commitment to the education of transescents.
2. Understandings: they understand the nature of the transescent learner, of the teaching-learning process, of the American educational enterprise, and of educational research and evaluation that bear on their teaching responsibilities.
3. Instructional skills: they have ability in the areas of counseling; use of multi-media approaches; alternatives to expository instruction; techniques of teaching values; classroom management; teaching problem-solving and independent learning; teaching communication skills; and ability to work across disciplinary lines.

**B.** Compare the criteria you developed in Activity 1 to one of the readings in Activity 2A. Are the readings congruent with what you know of the characteristics of the student? For example, based on what you know about transescents, are there any serious omissions in the literature? Any significant misunderstandings?

**C.** Write a brief statement which synthesizes your school visit, your readings on the middle school concept, and your readings on the nature of transescents. Compare and contrast your visit (Activity 1) with the other two factors (middle school concept and nature of the student). Save this for a discussion to come.

## ACTIVITY 3
### Discuss the middle school concept.

Meet with a group to discuss further the material in Activity 2. Organize your discussion around the "Middle School Fact Sheet" and around the four questions which follow. Be certain you understand the concepts in the fact sheet. If you or your group want to learn more about the characteristics of a middle school or the rationale for the development of this movement, consult some of the references at the end of the chapter. Keep the notes on the discussion for inclusion in your portfolio.

1. Do you understand what it means to avoid the "little high school" or "big elementary school" approach to early adolescent education? Can you relate this to difficulties that K-8 elementary schools or 7-9 junior high schools may have in educating early adolescents?
2. Can you summarize the basic components of the middle school concept?
3. What is articulation and how does that idea apply here?
4. Share your reactions to your visits and to what you read. Which (school or readings) seemed more in tune with the characteristics of transescents? Can you explain why?

## Middle School Fact Sheet

A Definition: The Middle School is an idea. When it is operational, it is a program that attempts to meet the needs of students in the "in-between years," usually from ages ten to fourteen. It differs from elementary and secondary schools, but attempts to provide a bridge between these two phases of schooling. No particular grade organization is sacred, but the middle school should include some combination of grades 5, 6, 7, or 8.

While middle schools are developing in different parts of the nation under the direction of many different people, there are a number of frequently common elements. Some of these include:

1. Absence of the "little high school" or "big elementary school" atmosphere.
2. Absence of the "star system," where a few special students dominate everything, in favor of an attempt to provide success experiences for greater numbers of students.
3. An attempt to use instructional methods appropriate to the age group: individualized instruction, variable group sizes, multi-media approaches, beginning independent study programs, inquiry-oriented instruction.
4. Planned opportunities for teacher-student guidance, which may include a home base or advisory group program.
5. Flexibility in scheduling and student grouping.
6. Some cooperative planning and team teaching.

7. At least some interdisciplinary or multidisciplinary studies, in which opportunities are provided for students to see how different areas of knowledge fit together.
8. A wide range of exploratory opportunities, academic and otherwise.
9. Extensive opportunity for physical activity and movement, including more frequent physical education.
10. Early introduction to the areas of organized academic knowledge.
11. Attention to the skills of continued learning, i.e., those skills which will permit students to learn more effectively on their own or at higher levels of learning.
12. Emphasis on increasing the student's independence, responsibility, and self-discipline.
13. Flexible physical facilities.
14. Attention to the personal development of the student: values clarification, group process skills, health and family life education when appropriate, and career education.
15. Teachers who have been trained especially for, and who are committed to, the education of emerging adolescents.

## ACTIVITY 4
**Read about, visit, and evaluate a school.**

**A.**  Familiarize yourself with the "School Visitation Checklist." This checklist provides a method for evaluating school programs for ten- to fourteen-year-olds. You may wish to devise your own checklist or adapt this one for your own use. You will use this checklist in a visit to a middle school.

### SCHOOL VISITATION CHECKLIST

This checklist is intended to be used in conjunction with a visit to a school serving students in some combination of ages ten through fourteen in grades 5, 6, 7, or 8. As you tour the school or talk with the staff, note whether the following items are present in the school program. Use the ranking system below, placing the appropriate number in the space at the left of the item:

1. Well-developed
2. Moderate
3. Minimal
4. Absent

_____ 1. Elimination of the "little high school" program where the program is a pale shadow of the upper level of secondary school (e.g., elimination of elaborate graduation ceremonies, proms, ornate yearbooks, highly competitive interscholastic athletics, etc.).

_____ 2. Elimination of the "star system" (see Middle School Fact Sheet) ( e.g., elimination of elite cheerleading groups, status conscious student councils, class presidents, etc.).

_____ 3. Appropriate instructional strategies (e.g., individualized instruction, variable group sizes, less lecturing, use of media, independent study, etc.).

_____ 4. Teacher-student guidance (e.g., home base or advisory group programs).

_____ 5. Flexibility in scheduling and grouping (e.g., block or modular scheduling, multi-age grouping).

_____ 6. Team teaching (e.g., cooperative planning, differentiated instructional assignments, etc.).

_____ 7. Multidisciplinary studies involving teachers from two or more different academic areas.

_____ 8. Exploratory opportunities (e.g., intramurals, special interest programs, varied curriculum enrichments, etc.).

_____ 9. Extensive opportunity for physical movement and frequent physical education.

_____ 10. Introduction to the advanced academic areas (e.g., in social studies, a sampling of anthropology, sociology, and economics).

_____ 11. Attention to the skills of continual learning (e.g., developmental reading programs, programs in thinking skills, researching skills, etc.).

_____ 12. A written school philosophy tuned to transescent development.

_____ 13. Teachers trained especially for the middle level school (e.g., inservice programs, teachers certified through the university, advanced degrees in middle school education).

_____ 14. Flexible physical plant (e.g., collapsible walls, large and small group areas, etc.) or imaginative use of the physical plant.

_____ 15. Attention to student personal development (e.g., career education, sex education, frequent opportunities for success, etc.).

**B.**   Refer to parts of Chapters 1-4 on the characteristics of transesents. These chapters give you opportunities to deal with these characteristics in depth, but it is also necessary to consider them briefly while thinking about an overview of the middle school concept.

**C.**   Using the "School Visitation Checklist" and the ideas from Chapters 1-4, visit and analyze a middle school or arrange to apply these criteria in analyzing a school with which you are already familiar. During and immediately after your visit, summarize (in writing) your impressions of the school on the basis of these two sets of criteria. Include, as a part of your summary, written answers to the following questions:

1. How well is this school succeeding in helping students achieve developmental tasks?
2. What might the staff do to improve the school's capacity to help students in these areas?

3. How does the behavior of the students I observed match the characteristics described in Chapters 1-4? What evidence suggests that the students are dealing with the demands of these developmental tasks?
4. Which student characteristics can schools deal with most effectively? Which least? Why?
5. List any other reactions you might have to your visit of schools and the needs of students.

Prepare to discuss these questions and include all materials in your portfolio.


## ACTIVITY 5
### Identify program components.

In the section entitled "Middle School Schedules," you will find the schedules of three exemplary middle schools—schools which actually exist. Study each schedule, following the brief description given, and try to apply your new knowledge of the middle school concept to these situations. All three schools have proved to be outstanding examples of the unique and transitional role of the middle school, and all three operate in different forms. The programs, however, are very similar in the most important aspects.

As you examine each schedule, try to identify the most basic components of the middle school: time for a teacher guidance role, interdisciplinary team organization and planning time, flexible student grouping, an exploratory curriculum, and a block schedule.

If you find it difficult to interpret the schedules, do not be discouraged. While the schedule will tell a lot about a school, it often requires experience to be able to draw out all of the information contained there. If you are confused, someone with administrative experience in education should be able to help you.

If you cannot identify the basic program components, make a list of your questions and bring them with you in Activity 8.


## Middle School Schedules

### MIDDLE SCHOOL ONE

This school of approximately 1,000 students in grades 6, 7, and 8 is organized into six interdisciplinary teams of 150 students, multi-age grouped, with 50 students from each of the sixth, seventh, and eighth grades. Each student has a faculty advisor and belongs to an Advisory Group that meets every morning from 8:40 to 9:10. The day is scheduled into three large blocks of time, two of which include the basics and physical education, and a third that is a special exploratory program based on the interests of students and teachers.

## Middle School One

| | G Team & T Team | W Team & S Team | C Team & B Team |
|---|---|---|---|
| 8:40—9:10 | — — — — — — — — — | *Advisor-Advisee Time* | — — — — — — — — |
| 9:10—9:55<br>9:57—10:42 | SKILLS | EXPLORATORY | CORE & P. E. |
| 10:44—11:29<br>11:31—12:16 | CORE & P. E. | SKILLS | EXPLORATORY |
| 12:16—1:10 | — — — — — — — — — — — | *Lunch* | — — — — — — — — — |
| 1:12—1:57<br>2:00—2:45 | EXPLORATORY | CORE & P. E. | SKILLS |

On Dec. 1 — G & T take W & S schedule
W & S take C & B schedule
C & B take G & T schedule
On Mar. 15 rotate ahead one block to complete cycle

MIDDLE SCHOOL TWO

This school houses approximately 1,100 students in grades 6, 7, and 8. It is organized into nine interdisciplinary teams of about 120 students. Students are in grade level teams, but some flexibility is provided for students whose development is really unusual. Teachers from the academic areas serve as advisors in a small group guidance format (notice the "SGG" time), and meeting with a small number of their advisees each morning while the remaining students go to physical education. The daily schedule includes both periods and a block time which allows opportunity for intrateam flexibility while providing whole school stability. Specialists provide a tremendously wide variety of exploratory opportunities. A special reading team provides remedial reading to each grade level.

## Middle School Two

| TEAM | 1 | 2 | 3 | 4 | 5 | 6 | 7 |
|---|---|---|---|---|---|---|---|
| 6A (4) | ACADEMIC BLOCK | | | | | Plan | SGG |
| 6B (4) | ACADEMIC BLOCK | | | | | Plan | SGG |
| 6C (2) | ACADEMIC BLOCK | | | | | Plan | SGG |
| 7A (4) | BLOCK | SGG | Plan | ACADEMIC BLOCK | | | |
| 7B (4) | BLOCK | Plan | SGG | ACADEMIC BLOCK | | | |
| 7C (2) | BLOCK | SGG | Plan | ACADEMIC BLOCK | | | |
| 8A (4) | ACADEMIC BLOCK | | | Plan | SGG | ACADEMIC BLOCK | |
| 8B (4) | ACADEMIC BLOCK | | | SGG | Plan | ACADEMIC BLOCK | |
| 8C (2) | ACADEMIC BLOCK | | | SGG | Plan | ACADEMIC BLOCK | |
| Physical Education (5) | Plan | 7 | 7 | 8 | 8 | 6 | 6 |
| Exploratory (7) | Plan | 7 | 7 | 8 | 8 | 6 | 6 |
| Reading (3) | 6-7-8 | 6-Plan-8 | 6-Plan-8 | 6-7-Plan | 6-7-Plan | Plan-7-8 | Plan-7-8 |
| Art and Music (4) | 6-7-8-6 | 6-8-6-Plan | 6/Plan/8/6 | 6/7/6/7 | 6/7/6/7 | Plan/7/Plan/8 | 7/Plan/7/8 |
| Special Education (6) | Planning Varies Depending upon Exploratory and P. E. | | | | | | |

school day for students: 7:30 a.m. — 1:55 p.m.
periods: approximately 45 minutes long
student body: 1,100

## MIDDLE SCHOOL THREE

This small school of approximately 360 students in grades 5, 6, 7, and 8 is organized into three units or teams with mixed grade levels. Unit One contains students who would normally be classified as older children, Unit Two includes preadolescent and pubescent students, and Unit Three has the young adolescents. Each student spends two years in one of the units, depending upon the birth date and developmental characteristics he or she displays. The academic teachers often share in the teaching of the P.E. and Expressive Arts, because of the small size of the school. A block schedule is obvious, as is the advisor-advisee time at the start of every day.

## Middle School Three

| TIME | UNIT I | UNIT II | UNIT III |
|---|---|---|---|
| 8:00 — 8:55 | Teacher Planning Time | | |
| 8:55 — 9:25 | Advisor – Advisee | | |
| 9:30 — 11:00 | Reading/ Language Arts | P. E./ Expressive Arts | Reading/Math |
| 11:00 — 11:30 | P.E./ Expressive Arts | Social Science | Social Science |
| 11:30 — 12:00 | P.E./ Expressive Arts | Social Science | Social Science |
| 12:00 — 12:30 | P.E./ Expressive Arts | Lunch | Social Science |
| 12:30 — 1:00 | Lunch | Math | Spelling/Language Arts |
| 1:00 — 1:30 | Social Science | Math | Lunch |
| 1:30 — 3:05 | Math | Reading/ Language Arts | P.E./ Expressive Arts |
| 3:05 — 3:30 | Teacher Planning | | |

# ACTIVITY 6
## Evaluate and discuss your priorities.

Respond to the questionnaire "Middle School Priorities." Then select one of the following alternatives.

**A.** If you are now teaching in a middle school, arrange to meet with two or three of your colleagues, each of whom has also completed this questionnaire. In your small group, discuss each other's priorities until you reach a consensus on the top five priorities for your school. You should try to arrive at the point where all of you agree, without voting. Put a copy of your group's decision in your portfolio.

**B.** If you are not teaching in a middle school, arrange to meet with some members of another small group (e.g., classmates), each of whom has completed the form. Discuss your individual priorities until the group reaches a consensus on the top five priorities for a model middle school.

## Middle School Priorities

Below is a list of fifteen relatively important aspects of modern schools for the "in-between-ager." Examine the list and make a decision based on your opinion about the relative importance of each item. Choose your top ten and place them in rank order, with the number 1 to the left of the item you consider the highest priority, number 2 beside the item that, in your opinion, is next in importance, and so on until you have given the number 10 to the last of your "top ten."

\_\_\_\_\_ 1. Absence of a "little high school" approach or a "big elementary school" approach.

\_\_\_\_\_ 2. Absence of the "star system" in favor of an attempt to provide success experience for greater numbers of students.

\_\_\_\_\_ 3. An attempt to use instructional methods more appropriate to this age group: individualized instruction, variable group sizes, multi-media approaches, beginning independent study programs, inquiry-oriented instruction.

\_\_\_\_\_ 4. Planned opportunities for teacher-student guidance, may include a home base or advisory group program.

\_\_\_\_\_ 5. Flexibility in scheduling and student grouping.

\_\_\_\_\_ 6. At least some cooperative planning and team teaching, interdisciplinary or otherwise.

\_\_\_\_\_ 7. At least some multidisciplinary studies where teachers from a variety of academic areas provide opportunities for students to see how different areas of knowledge fit together.

\_\_\_\_\_ 8. A wide range of exploratory opportunities, academic and otherwise.

\_\_\_\_\_ 9. Extensive opportunity for physical activity and movement, including more frequent physical education.

\_\_\_\_\_ 10. Early introduction to the areas of organized academic knowledge.

\_\_\_\_\_ 11. Attention to the skills of continued learning, i.e., those skills which will permit students to learn more effectively on their own or at higher levels of learning.

\_\_\_\_\_ 12. Emphasis on increasing the student's independence, responsibility, and self-discipline.

\_\_\_\_\_ 13. Flexible physical facilities.

\_\_\_\_\_ 14. Attention to the personal development of the student: values clarification, group process skills, health and family life education when appropriate, and career education.

\_\_\_\_\_ 15. Teachers who have been trained especially for, and who are committed to, the education of emerging adolescents.

## ACTIVITY 7
**Think about some unanswered questions.**

There are a number of what might be called unresolved issues in middle level education, questions which continue to produce debate and differences of opinion on a local, state, and national basis. Here are a few of these questions:

1. Is the middle school, in practice, really any different from older school organizational patterns (i.e., the junior high school)?
2. What is the relationship between the middle school concept and the open space school ("school without walls")?
3. Is team teaching essential to a middle school, and if so, what type of team teaching?
4. Which grades are most appropriate for the school in the middle?
5. What kind of student competition is appropriate for the middle school?
6. Is the middle school "watering down" the junior high school curriculum or "toughening up" the elementary school curriculum? Neither?
7. What kind of teacher is best for the middle level schools?
8. How likely are most middle schools to become models of the middle school concept, given limited funding, inadequate time for teachers to make the changes, and other restricting factors?

As a result of completing Activities 1 through 4 in this chapter, you may have recognized other unresolved issues. Write these issues in question form and write out brief answers to all the questions, based on what you have learned from this chapter, your experience, and your own opinions. Keep the answers in mind as you use the rest of this book. If you have a plan for the use of this book or a contract with an instructor, you may want to revise that plan or contract in light of these unresolved questions or issues.

## ACTIVITY 8
**Two additional activities from which to choose.**

Choose either A or B—both require a considerable amount of thoughtful preparation and professional maturity.

**A.** Several years ago Lounsbury and Marani (1964) engineered an evaluative study of junior high schools which had a unique design. On the same day and at the same time, dozens of educators across the nation visited a number of junior high schools. This simultaneous multiple observation of a number of schools provided the group with a sample of what was going on in the junior high schools of that time.

If you are working or learning with a group of at least three people, a similar approach might yield interesting results in terms of evaluating several middle schools in one or more districts. It would require at least three middle schools in order to make a meaningful comparison possible. A group of six or more people could, for example, divide themselves equally among the number of middle schools which have been made available for visitation. The observations would occur on the same day(s), with the same evaluative criteria and instruments, aimed at gathering data on the same topics. After the evaluations, the group can meet to discuss what was seen and compile a report which describes the "state of the middle school" insofar as your group's sample can generalize. The report could be delivered to a class, a faculty group, a district staff, or given to an instructor. It might even be a good topic for a professional journal. If you decide to do this activity, it will be a good idea to locate and study Lounsbury and Marani's work prior to your own school visits.

Your group might want to design its own evaluative instrument or use something from this or other books. If you choose to do your own, the following items might be included in the design:

1. *Curriculum:* scope and sequence, balance, relevance
2. *Instruction:* balance, variety, appropriateness
3. *Student behavior:* physical, verbal
4. *Program components:* advisor-advisee program, interdisciplinary team teaching, multi-age grouping, exploratory program, etc.
5. *School climate:* absence of little high school; absence of star system, lack of tension, etc.
6. *Schedule:* flexibility, simplicity, teacher control, etc.

Are there any other items you would include? Be certain to include copies of all relevant materials in your portfolios.


**B.**  It has been said that there are three types of middle schools currently functioning in the public school systems of our nation. Type One includes those which have managed to come as close to being fully functioning middle schools as allowed by current conditions of funding and staff development. These schools almost always have faculty and administration who understand the middle school concept and who are conversant with appropriate models of curriculum and instruction. Type Two middle schools can best be described as aspiring to be fully functioning middle schools. These schools usually have a number of administrators and faculty who understand and who are committed to the middle school concept but who have been unable, for various reasons, to implement it fully. The remaining middle schools (Type Three), some argue, can be described as middle schools in name only. The schools usually have a large complement of faculty and administrators who either do not understand the middle school concept, do not care, or both. When both the administration and a large group of the faculty fit this category, the school is often a dreary place, with only rare instances of truly student-centered efforts.

This activity attempts to give you an opportunity to demonstrate that you are at the point where you are sufficiently well-versed in the rationale for middle schools to recognize when a middle school fits one of the above three general descriptions and when it does not. You are asked to do several things.

First, write three brief case descriptions, each about two typewritten pages in length, each describing a Type One, Type Two, and Type Three school. These descriptions may be drawn from three real but unidentified schools, three totally imaginary situations, or a combination of the real and imaginary. The task is to write about each of the three schools, detailing what you identify as significant descriptions of each.

Second, exchange these case descriptions with an appropriate individual or small group and receive from them the cases that they have prepared. Your tasks are (1) to correctly categorize the three schools; (2) to note significant differences and similarities between each pair of cases; (3) to return the case studies to the writer and discuss items in (2) above. If you are in a credit-earning course, your instructor will want to see what you have written and to sit in on the discussions of the cases. As always, include the materials in your portfolio.

This activity can be done in small groups as well as individually.


## ACTIVITY 9
### Evaluate what you have learned.

Now that you have completed the learning activities, you may have achieved the objectives for this chapter. The following activities provide two ways to check the level of attainment you have reached.

**A.**  Write a one or two page statement entitled "The Emerging Middle School: Who, What, Why?" Summarize the essentials of the rationale of the middle school movement and the basic elements of a fully functioning middle school.

**B.**  Assume you are involved in a discussion with a parent who knows little about the middle school concept. The parent asks you several of the following questions which you want to answer well. Write out your answers to these questions.

1. "Why do we need to go to all the trouble of reorganizing the intermediate grades? Why is a middle school better?"
2. "Can you tell me, in a few words, just what a middle school is?"
3. "Can the middle school emphasize personal development and exploration without cutting down on attention to the basics?"

**C.**  Exchange your statements from section A or B with two or three colleagues and compare ideas. Discuss the differences. Insert the written material into your portfolio.


### NEXT STEPS

If you are interested in learning more about the middle school concept, the following resources may be helpful.

1. "The Modern Middle School." A series of four filmstrip/cassette tape packages on the following topics:
   a. An overview of the middle school and its students
   b. An in-depth examination of the program
   c. Organizing and operating the middle school
   d. A tour of an exemplary middle school

> Available from: Teacher Education Resources (About $115.00)
> Box 206
> Gainesville, FL 32602

2. Also available from Teacher Education Resources:
"What Is a Middle School—Really?" A unique handout designed by experts and written in language teachers and parents understand and accept. Perfect for workshops and as an office handout.

3. "Passing Through." A twenty minute filmstrip/tape resource focusing on the characteristics and needs of learners who are moving from childhood to adolescence. This film challenges school faculties to adjust to the needs of learners. It is available from the National Association of Secondary School Principals, Washington, D.C. (About $14.00)

4. "The Emerging Adolescent Learner." A package of six filmstrips with both six cassette tapes and six 33 rpm records. Each filmstrip was made by a different author. ASCD also has produced an excellent film, "Profile of a Middle School." Available from the Association for Supervision and Curriculum Development (ASCD), Washington, D.C. or from Educational Leadership Institute, Inc., Box 863, Springfield, Mass. 00100.

## REFERENCES

ALEXANDER, W. M. and PAUL S. GEORGE.   *The Exemplary Middle School.* New York: Holt, Rinehart and Winston, Inc., 1981.

DEVITA, JOSEPH, and others.   *The Effective Middle School.* Englewood Cliffs, N.J.: Parker Publishing Co., 1970.

GATEWOOD, THOMAS and CHARLES DILG.   *The Middle School We Need.* Washington, D.C.: Association for Supervision and Curriculum Development, 1975.

GEORGE, PAUL S. (Ed.).   *The Middle School: A Look Ahead.* Fairborn, Ohio: The National Middle School Association, 1977.

KENDRID, LESLIE, and others.   *The Middle School Curriculum.* Boston: Allyn and Bacon, Inc., 1976.

LEEPER, ROBERT C.   *Middle School in the Making.* Washington, D.C.: Association for Supervision and Curriculum Development, 1974.

LOUNSBURY, JOHN and GORDON VARS.   *A Curriculum for the Middle School Years.* New York: Harper and Row, 1978.

OVERLY, DONALD W., JON RYE KINGHORN, and RICHARD L. PRESTON.   *Middle School: Humanizing Education for Youth.* Worthington, Ohio: Charles A. Jones Publishing Co., 1972.

# CHAPTER SIX

# TEAM PLANNING AND SUPPORT SKILLS

Participating in a cooperative work group, such as a planning team, is not a natural, easy activity for most people. That's an assumption we have made in writing this chapter. We list nine other assumptions as well. See if they square with your perceptions.

1. Our culture emphasizes individual enterprise rather than group participation—particularly in schools. Hence, team teaching and group support skills are not well-developed in most people.
2. Many people enter teaching as a profession because, consciously or unconsciously, they are attracted by the belief that teaching is a solo job that requires a minimum of negotiation and collaboration with peers.
3. People often are wary of joining groups that may turn out to be gripe and gossip groups.
4. Some teachers have been burned or bored by problem solving groups they have worked in and as a result they see group work as a waste of time.
5. Groups such as teaching teams don't function well without trust between members—and the way most groups in schools or universities are formed does not encourage trust.
6. While self-analysis of one's teaching is essential to improving its quality, receiving analysis and feedback from a more objective source, such as a team member, is also vital.
7. Observing, listening, and responding to a colleague in a helpful way involves specific skills that can be practiced and certain attitudes that can be developed.
8. In the middle grades, instruction that is planned cooperatively by teams of teachers is more effective than instruction without team planning, provided that the team members are compatible.
9. Team planning and team teaching both involve skills and procedures beyond those that teachers need for individual planning and teaching.

Within the framework of these assumptions, we have assembled some readings that deal with the basic skills needed to conduct the work of a planning team and to support good communication among its members. Since this chapter involves the actual planning, implementation, and evaluation of a team unit, if you do not now have regular teaching responsibilities, you may want to locate a team of teachers who will cooperate with you in using the team teaching unit you produce. This ought to be done prior to moving very far into the activities. We have written the chapter to be used by a group, not by an individual. So if you are not a regular team member, arrange to attach yourself to a group that can plan and perhaps teach together, at least temporarily. You will plan a unit of instruction that draws upon whatever subjects the members teach.

In schools where team teaching is expected to occur, three factors usually determine whether or not such teaming actually happens. One of these factors is common planning time. When teams have little or no common planning time, very little teamwork will occur. If you are in a situation where your team has no such time, you will probably do better to defer any further work on this chapter until you are able to find a way to get the team together for some planning.

A second factor in determining the long-term success or failure of a team effort emerges from the nature of interpersonal communication. Team teaching is like marriage in many ways. When it is working well, it can be beautiful; when working poorly, it can be horrible. Much of the success or failure of the team depends upon how well the members communicate with each other. For that reason, the chapter includes activities concerning these skills: recognizing one's own behavior in group meetings; observing and giving nonjudgmental feedback; listening and responding effectively; analyzing and improving teamwork relationships; and guiding team problem-solving meetings.

The third factor that helps determine the success or failure of team teaching is the level of team planning skills present among the members of the team. To function effectively, team members must know how to plan for instruction as a group. Team planning is quite different from that done by individuals, although it is not necessarily more difficult or time-consuming. It will certainly seem so, however, if planning skills are not highly developed.

The activities will involve you with a model of team planning, focusing on helping your team plan and implement a unit of instruction. Your group will be asked to proceed through a number of steps in the process of designing and using a team teaching unit, and to analyze and evaluate what you do as a team as you proceed. We believe that you will find the process and its outcomes effective, efficient, and satisfying.

## ACTIVITY 1
### Analyze and discuss team organization patterns.

**A.**  Examine the thirteen descriptions of ways in which teachers can be organized to teach. Decide which situation most nearly fits your school, the school you are working with, or your idea of how teaching should be organized in middle grades. Which situation are you most comfortable with? There may be combinations of one category with another, and all the possibilities may not be described. The object of this activity is to analyze the current situation in which you are working (or a hypothetical one), to see how it fits on the continuum of teaching possibilities.

## Patterns of Teacher Organization

Below is a list of thirteen ways in which teachers have organized for instruction in middle grades. You will notice that the descriptions begin with a totally self-contained classroom setup and move along a continuum to a completely teamed and curriculum-coordinated framework. Each description moves a little further away from the self-contained and a little further toward complete teamwork.

**1.** Individual self-contained classrooms. Each teacher teaches all the major academic subjects, as well as art, music and other enrichments. Students remain with one teacher all day.

**2.** Individual classrooms, self-contained by subject. Each teacher teaches only his or her special academic area. Specialists are available for art, music, and other enrichments. Classes last for the largest part of an hour. Students change classes each period, spending one period with each of four to seven teachers every day.

**3.** Teachers are organized into teams on a disciplinary basis. Each team (e.g. social studies) provides instruction in that topic for all the students in the school. Team teaching exists only during rare curriculum meetings. No common planning time is regularly available.

**4.** Teachers are organized into grade level teams on a disciplinary basis as in "3" above. In this situation, however, team planning occurs regularly. During a regularly scheduled planning time (at least weekly) all the teachers from that team meet to plan special units, reorganize the scope and sequence of their area of the curriculum, etc. The teachers frequently teach special units across grade levels.

**5.** Teachers are organized into grade level teams on an interdisciplinary basis. Every team has one specialist from each of the major academic areas. Each member teaches only his specialty, to all the students in the team. Little common planning occurs. Teaming is limited to discussions of students, parent conferences, etc.

**6.** Teachers are organized on grade level teams as in "5" above. In this situation, however, several members of the team have discovered (usually quite randomly) that they get along well and enjoy working together. Whenever the planned units of these teachers seem to coincide, they arrange similar or complimentary assignments for students, joint field trips, etc. Other members of the team are not involved in team planning or teaching.

**7.** Teachers are organized into grade level teams on an interdisciplinary basis, as in "5" and "6" above. Several of the teachers in this situation are combined in ways which weld together common areas of the curriculum. These joint arrangements (e.g., language arts and social studies) are formalized with common scheduling and joint teacher planning time. Often the administrators and teachers in this school refer to their organization as core curriculum, cross curriculum, or multidisciplinary instruction.

**8.** Teachers are organized into grade level teams on an interdisciplinary basis. Each teacher teaches his or her specialty for the major part of the day. In this situation, the teachers do have a common planning time. As a result, several times a year, the teachers engage in teaming which can best be described as multidisciplinary or thematic. That is, the teachers choose a topic within which all their disciplines are represented (e.g., Latin American Ecology, Space, etc.) and each teacher is responsible for planning a unit on that general theme to be taught at the same time as the others. Occasionally, these units are very closely coordinated so that students perceive their studies to be unified or related.

**9.** Teachers are organized into grade level interdisciplinary teams. The members of the team have a shared responsibility for teaching all the major academic areas. That is, each teacher teaches mathematics, science, social studies and language arts, but because they have no common team planning time, little actual teaming occurs.

**10.** Teachers are organized into grade level interdisciplinary teams as in "9" above. Teachers have adequate planning time plus the commitment to work together. They decide on the topics for each subject unit together, and coordinate their plans for teaching these units on a regular basis. Each teacher teaches all four major academic areas, but on a thoroughly teamed basis.

**11.** Teachers are organized into grade level interdisciplinary teams as in "9" above. There is also adequate planning time and a commitment to teaming. Although each teacher spends a small part of each day teaching special academic skills, the major portion of the school day is devoted to the pursuit of a multidisciplinary or thematic unit which is thoroughly teamed, both in terms of planning and teaching. Often teachers disregard any special subject area boundaries and share responsibility for the total unit. Divisions of labor, regarding teaching, are as often on the lines of instructional expertise or other preference as upon subject matter training.

12. Teachers are organized into interdisciplinary teams but in a multi-age grouping basis. Four teachers might, for example, be responsible for teaching the major academic areas to a group of students representing what would have been grades five or six through eight. Grade level distinctions are blurred. Each teacher is responsible for teaching all four areas. Planning is based on the twin guidelines of continuous progress in skill areas and a three or four year cycle in the areas of literature, social studies and science. A great deal of teacher time is spent in team planning. The result is a very closely coordinated effort.

13. Teachers are organized into interdisciplinary teams on a multi-age grouping basis as in "12" above, with a small part of each day devoted to a highly structured skills time. The majority of teacher and student time is focused on multidisciplinary or thematic units which cross both subject and grade levels. Individualization is the key.

**B.**   Analyze the teaming arrangements in your team (or the team that has agreed to work with you on the unit). Write out the answers to the following questions and save them for Activity 2. You need not limit yourself to these questions, of course.

1. How much team planning time do the teachers have? Do they have additional personal preparation time? How much time is needed for each? Are there differences in opinion about how much time is needed?
2. How effectively are the team members communicating personally? Have they had any help? Are there differences in opinion about how well they are communicating?
3. Can you describe the planning process of the team? Do the members, in fact, plan together? If they do, is the process structured and regular? Describe the process.
4. Are the teachers satisfied with the teaming arrangement in this school? If they are less than satisfied, which of the three factors of time, communication, or planning skills seems to be significant?
5. Judging from the position of this team on the continuum in Section A, what type of unit would be appropriate?

## ACTIVITY 2
### Read about and analyze the team planning process.

The team planning process is particularly difficult to communicate in writing. You will probably have to reread each of the next activities several times before they will make sense to you. It is important that teams, regardless of the type, follow a structured model or process of team planning. Your team or group will need to find a way of planning that is comfortable and effective. Several models of team planning are presented here, but they have much in common. The objective of this activity is to help you develop a planning model that your team can use.

**A.**   Read: "The Planning Sequence," which follows.

**B.**   Find a team of teachers who plan and teach together frequently. Interview the team leader to determine the planning process used by this team.

C. When you have completed A and B, answer the questions below and save your answers to discuss with your team in Activity 4.

1. What do these two descriptions of the team planning process have in common?
2. List what seems to you to be the basic steps in team planning.
3. What are the differences between planning done by an individual teacher and planning done by a team of teachers?
4. Can your team or group plan in a manner similar to these models? Describe a possible model for planning in your team.

## The Planning Sequence

Planning, as we have come to see it, is a dynamic process. It is not static, but continually evolving and expanding to meet the everchanging needs of the learning community. The sequence we follow in planning any given unit of study is a progression of three phases, each one involving both preparation and action. In other words, each phase involves a "Get Ready" step (which is performed by the individual) and a "Do" step (which calls for the combined interaction of the team).

### THE ASSESSMENT SPECTRUM

The entire sequence takes place within the context of our continually increasing knowledge of students, content, and resources. Moreover, goal setting and design are not mutually exclusive functions which take place only in certain phases. Instead, they go on continuously throughout the planning sequence—changing only in specificity as the learning program progresses toward implementation and redirection.

### PHASE I

This phase usually begins about four to six weeks before we expect to launch the planned unit of study.

In the "Get Ready" stage of Phase 1, team members explore possible directions in which the Learning Community might proceed in developing the upcoming unit of study. Because they have worked with their advisees continuously over long periods within the supportive atmosphere of the learning environment, they have intimate knowledge of each student's individual goals and objectives and are thoroughly familiar with his or her progress as indicated by day-to-day contacts and assessment data. Drawing on this broad understanding of student needs, each staff member goes over in his own mind the skills and concepts he believes should be emphasized and gets his ideas in shape for interaction with other members of the team. If a member feels more up-to-date assessment information would be

---

FROM I.D.E.A. "The Planning Sequence," in *The Learning Environment*, Dayton, Ohio: Institute for the Development of Educational Activities, 1974, pp. 190–199. BY PERMISSION.

valuable, he sees that it is secured and uses it in working up his recommendations.

"As I said a moment ago, Cathy, goal setting is an ongoing function which takes place continuously throughout the entire life of the learning program. At the outset of planning, it focuses on long-range educational goals. Then, as planning becomes more specific, the focus narrows to broad objectives appropriate for almost all students. And, finally, as student assessment data accumulates and students participate more actively in the planning, the accent is on goal setting in the form of identifying and modifying specific learning objectives for individual students."*

**Get Ready**

Each Learning Community staff member:

- Reviews school-wide goals.
- Evaluates progress toward previously emphasized goals.
- Identifies skills and concepts to be accommodated in this unit of study.
- Thinks about possible designs and themes—if a resource teacher (or teachers) has already been identified, he will make a special effort here.
- Thinks about resources which might enhance the success of the learning program.

Next, the team members schedule a discussion to compare notes and make the necessary decisions for putting their ideas in motion—establishing goals, brainstorming broad objectives, and blocking out the rudiments of design.

**Do**

Team members interact to:
- Critique past efforts and identify goal priorities.
- Identify goals to be emphasized in this unit of study.
- Brainstorm possible broad objectives for promoting these goals and brainstorm design elements such as:

>   possible themes
>   complementary learning delivery systems such as learning stations,
>     short courses, CPU's,** and simulations
>   related activities
>   appropriate assessment procedures
>   facilitating grouping and scheduling arrangements

- Agree on a theme or general approach.
- Designate one or two resource teachers to draft a proposed learning program or have resource teachers in specific areas give the go-ahead to the appropriate person or persons.
- Set a date for team interaction on the proposed learning program prepared by the resource teacher(s). (Note: The proposal should be completed in

---

*The conversational material included from the original reading illustrates the team member interactions that sometimes accompany the development of this model.
**Cooperatively Planned Units

sufficient time for duplication and distribution to the entire team at least two days before the scheduled meeting.)

"This was the point the team had reached in its preliminary planning when Larry and I were delegated to research the area and draft a proposed learning program. The next phase of the planning sequence — Phase II — is the one we're in the midst of at present."

## PHASE II

This phase begins as soon as a resource teacher or teachers have been designated to design a given unit of study and present a comprehensive proposal. They have approximately two to four weeks, depending on the complexity of the learning program, to draft their recommendations and present them for team approval and modification. There is no break in momentum as the progression continues. Phase II is in operation as soon as the resource teachers have received guidance as to the team's intentions and continues until implementation begins.

### Get Ready

Resource teachers discuss means of following up the leads provided by their colleagues and decide who will be responsible for generating specific areas of the proposed learning program.

Resource teachers seek out the information needed to design a learning program proposal.

Advisors sample student interest in related areas as they discuss goals and objectives with their advisees and pass student suggestions on to the resource teachers.

Learning Community members keep their eyes and ears open for related information of value to the learning program and bring this to the attention of the resource teachers.

Resource teachers generate a learning program proposal and distribute it to the rest of the team several days before the scheduled Learning Community staff meeting. The proposal incorporates:

- goal setting—broad objectives based on the team's identified goals
- design
    - appropriate learning delivery systems
    - related activities
    - valuable resource materials providing background and other necessary information
    - suggested grouping and scheduling arrangements
    - complementary assessment procedures
    - tentative teaching assignments emphasizing team members' special individual strengths.

As soon as they have the resource teacher(s)' proposal in hand, the members of the team review it individually and make marginal notes indicating the additions and/or deletions they think may be necessary to modify the proposal for use as a learning program. Then, on the day of the first scheduled meeting, they get together and begin modifying the proposed learning program to team specifications. This process may go on for several additional meetings until the entire team is satisfied that the learning program is ready for implementation.

## Do

Team members voice their candid reactions to the resource teacher(s)' proposal.

Modifications are suggested in whatever aspects of the proposed learning program team members feel they are needed, and additions are mentioned and explored.

Assessment strategies are discussed and plans set up.

Agreement is reached on the overall design.

Staff assignments are made which reflect team members' strengths and special capabilities.

Tentative grouping and scheduling plans are devised.

Information about the coming learning program is prepared for release to students.

"If all goes well—and it should if today's meeting was any indication—we'll probably have the learning program shaped to our satisfaction by the end of the week. Meanwhile, we'll continue carrying out the 'Get Ready' and 'Do' steps concurrently—meeting whenever we feel the occasion calls for it to polish our learning program and refine grouping and scheduling arrangements.

"Since the planning sequence is a continuum, imagine for a moment that we're almost but not quite ready for the beginning of Phase III. Student interest is growing as each individual student assesses his progress and works with his advisor to modify announced learning options in the light of his personal goals to create specific objectives meaningful to him. At the same time, the team is assembling assessment data, organizing resources, and working to complete grouping and scheduling arrangements. If we were to diagram what's happening now, it might look something like this:

"Get Ready/Do"

Information about the broad learning options is released to students through posted descriptions and contacts with advisors. Broad objectives and related learning activities are described in detail to generate interest and spark student creativity.

Advisors discuss the options with their advisees and work with them to design individual learning programs which reflect:
— individual needs as pinpointed by continuous assessment
— individual goals and priorities that shape the choice of objectives
— individual learning styles, interest in subject areas, self-concept, peer relationships, and previous achievements.

Advisors and advisees work out individual student schedules and final grouping and scheduling arrangements are made for the entire Learning Community.

Team members continue individual preparation and research. Sub-teams get to work building learning stations and constructing assessments, work sheets, instructional materials, and other program needs. Necessary supplies and resources are assembled and further assessment procedures readied to facilitate movement of students who have mastered the initial skills and concepts.

"Throughout this phase, the accent is on things we can do with students and on ways we can incorporate additional means of meeting their needs into the learning program. Advisors work with advisees until all concerned are convinced that, based on available data, the best possible match of students with activities and grouping and scheduling arrangements has been made. When all this has been done to our satisfaction, we're ready for Phase III - implementation."

## PHASE III

"During this phase, all our planning and joint efforts are translated into action. The momentum accelerates as the learning is implemented with students. Daily situational conferences are held to identify problems and make on-the-spot arrangements for solving them. These situational conferences take place on two levels: students discuss progress with teachers and advisors and modify grouping and scheduling arrangements to accommodate new emphases in objectives and activities; team members interact to adjust elements of the design to bring them more in line with their goals and modify grouping and schooling arrangements to reflect student progress and provide reinforcement."

### Get Ready/Do - Continuing Implementation

Students hold situational conferences as necessary with their advisors to adjust their learning programs to their changing needs.

Team members interact daily on a 'command post' basis, briefing each other about changes in student needs. Together, they assess the impact of the various parts of the learning program and plan appropriate strategies for improving learning delivery systems and grouping and scheduling arrangements.

Team members develop additional and/or alternate instructional resources.

Outside resource persons are briefed, carry out their parts in the plan, and critique their performance to suggest possible improvements.

Students continue to assess their progress and modify their learning programs to provide necessary reinforcement, adjust objectives to accommodate changes in emphasis, and create new activities as their knowledge of concepts and skills increases.

Team members begin to think about the goals of the next learning program as they review current progress and evaluate the success of their present learning program.

This final phase lasts as long as the current learning program continues to meet the needs it was designed to fulfill. For example, we expect the learning program on which we're working now to last about seven weeks. However, whenever a learning program is in progress, we have three options:

1. We can continue in the same direction—extending the existing learning program and making appropriate modifications.
2. We can go back to Phase II and make a major change in goal emphasis— revising our broad objectives—and at the same time adjust our design to reflect new information.

3. We can start again at Phase I and begin work on a brand new learning program.

"You see, planning is something that goes on continuously in our Learning Community. We look on it as a regular part of our operating strategy instead of as an occasional activity. Consequently, we always have more than one learning program in the works at any one time as a way of being prepared for the contingencies that are bound to arise. For example, if students assimilate a given unit of study faster than we originally anticipated, we can go on to the next logical step without breaking stride. On the other hand, if assessments show the need for more reinforcement in a given area, we can see that it is made available without throwing other elements of the program out of kilter.

"Right now it sounds complicated, I'm sure, but you'll get the hang of it as soon as you've been through the sequence a time or two. We were unsure of ourselves, too, in the beginning and tried to 'bite off more than we could chew' in one learning program. Now, however, we know what we can accomplish in the time we have available and pace ourselves accordingly.

"Learning to teach in a Learning Community is like learning to ride your first two-wheeled bicycle. You need a lot of supportive guidance and practice until you develop balance, learn to steer a straight course, and build up your confidence. Later, when the rules of the road are second nature, you find success is simply a matter of staying alert and maneuvering intelligently. You have internalized all the criteria and you're riding smoothly and rapidly at a pace you couldn't have managed earlier."

"The whole thing seems a lot easier now that you've explained the process," Cathy agreed. "I had visions of something much more complicated and was afraid I'd have to go at it single-handed. I'm glad I have you and the rest of the team to serve as my 'training wheels' until I get my balance and learn to pace myself."

## ACTIVITY 3
### Read about and study team planning.

"The Team Planning Process," which follows, is a detailed description of the steps in planning. It is adapted primarily from the I.G.E. process you have just read about.

## The Team Planning Process

### TEAM MEETING ONE: PLAN PRELIMINARIES

Designate a temporary team leader for this unit. It will be this person's responsibility to shepherd this particular unit from beginning to end. If you are an interdisciplinary team and you are going to develop a unit in a particular subject, the team's resource teacher in that subject should probably be the leader for this unit. If it is not this particular situation, then the question of subject area expertise is not as crucial.

Designate a team "recorder" to take notes on a ditto master during team meetings and distribute copies to all concerned.

Gather copies of system-wide or school-level goals for learning and, as a group, choose which goal your unit will flow from. If there are no such developed series of goals, you may have to choose the theme of your unit some other way.

Now that you have a unit leader, a unit recorder, and a theme or topic for your team's unit, you are ready to begin planning.

## TEAM MEETING TWO: DEVELOP UNIT OBJECTIVES AND ACTIVITIES

The focus of this meeting should be on setting the goals and objectives for the unit. The school goals and course objectives should be at hand. As a team, now put the techniques of "brainstorming" to use. If you haven't already developed some skill in using precise instructional objectives, you will want to do some additional reading. Robert Mager's *Preparing Instructional Objectives* is a good place to start. The team should select objectives that everyone feels good about, that are realistic for your school situation, that students will be interested in, and that the average student can master in about one week (five hours) of classroom instruction. Then one or two team members should take the responsibility for preparing for the second step in the team planning process. These team members will take the list of objectives which the whole team has brainstormed, analyze and evaluate them, polishing those that seem most appropriate and prepare a tentative design for the unit. Their major duty is to prepare at least five learning activities for each objective. Variety is important.

## TEAM MEETING THREE: DESIGN THE UNIT

The design meeting has four purposes that must be accomplished. Someone on your team should take the responsibility for making certain that all four needs are met.

1. *Review:* The meeting should begin with a brief review of the activity of the previous (goal setting) meeting. Everyone should be familiar with what happened there. Use the notes taken at that meeting by the team recorder.
2. *Presentation:* The team members who assumed responsibility for designing this unit should now share the objectives and learning activities that they have selected and polished. They should also present the reasons for the choices and/or changes they have made.
3. *Critique:* The other members of the team now analyze and evaluate the unit in its tentative form. Suggestions should cover such areas as: available resources, teacher strengths, time constraints, variety, student interest, etc.

When the critiquing session is over, the unit should be complete (in skeleton form) and acceptable to everybody.

4. *Assignments:* It's now time for team members to choose teaching assignments for the unit. Teachers who are least comfortable with the focus of the unit should be permitted to choose first. This is especially true if it is a single subject unit (e.g., math) designed primarily by the resource teacher in that subject.

If it is truly a multidisciplinary unit in which all disciplines are interwoven, teacher assignments should be based on teacher strengths. This includes instructional strengths as well as curriculum expertise.

At the end of the design meeting the team members should have agreed on the theme, objectives, and learning activities of the unit. Each teacher should be clear about his/her assignments and obligations for the unit.

As you critique the developing team unit, there are a number of factors to consider. Here are some questions which might be part of your design and critique:

1. Are there provisions for any one-to-one learning (e.g., advisor-advisee, peer teaching, student with aide)?
2. Are there provisions for using a variety of small groups in this learning program (e.g., discussion, projects, review, etc.)?
3. Are there provisions for large group learning situations?
4. How many of the following are included in the learning program?

| | |
|---|---|
| _____ learning centers | _____ video tape |
| _____ unipacs | _____ television |
| _____ short courses | _____ transparencies |
| _____ group projects | _____ creative writing |
| _____ textbooks | _____ field trips |
| _____ newspapers | _____ resource people |
| _____ magazines | _____ programmed materials |
| _____ paperbacks | _____ oral and written reports |
| _____ library books | _____ short lectures |
| _____ reference books | _____ discussions |
| _____ filmstrips | _____ records |
| _____ films | _____ debates |
| _____ tape recordings | _____ other (describe) _____ |
| _____ drill | |

## TEAM MEETING FOUR: ORGANIZE THE UNIT

Several things need to be accomplished in the organizing meeting:

1. *Review:* The development and design meetings.

2. *Activity Checks:* The team needs to learn whether the individual teachers have in fact prepared the activities that they agreed to do. There may need to be modifications of plans if some ideas for activities haven't worked out.

3. *Assessment Plans:* The team needs to assess at least two things, as far as students are concerned—interest and achievement. Your team will need to know what student preferences are, and how much they already know prior to beginning the unit.

4. *Grouping Students:* On the basis of the above assessment data, plus factors such as peer relationships and learning styles, students should be organized for learning. Which students will go where? When?

5. *Scheduling:* Schedules for the length of the unit should be fixed. The entire team should be aware of beginning and ending dates, and how much time each day will be devoted to the unit. Each teacher's schedule should be firm at this point. Preparations should be made for any special scheduling of individual students (e.g., those who demonstrate superior knowledge on the preassessment may go on to "quest activities").

Now the unit should be ready to go. Are there any last minute details to be concerned about? You and your team should be just a few days away from "Day One" of your unit. Good luck!

## TEAM MEETING FIVE: SITUATIONAL MEETINGS

Once your team's unit is underway, you will discover reasons for having occasional meetings to discuss the inevitable problems which will arise and ways to solve them. You may also want to introduce new ideas and activities into the unit once you've started. Students may want to make individual or group program changes.

These meetings will continue to occur throughout the length of the unit. They may be as brief as thirty seconds, as long as thirty minutes, or longer.

## TEAM MEETING SIX: UNIT EVALUATION

The unit is over. Student assessment is complete. Student evaluation of the unit itself has been done and you and your colleagues have had a day or two to let the dust settle and mull over what has happened. The primary task of this meeting is to evaluate the learning program just completed.

You will again want to make use of the technique called "brainstorming." Take about five minutes to list all of the things that went really well during the unit. Have someone write them on the board as other members call them out. No analysis or criticism yet, just list them. Then take another five minutes to do the same for all of the things your team can think of that really went poorly.

Now, take some time to talk about those items on the board. Eliminate those that your group agrees are not really significant. Expand on those that seemed to make a difference in the success of the unit.

Another unit is now underway, or may be soon, depending upon how much actual teamwork your group may do. Take this opportunity to discuss ways in which your team can take advantage of what you have learned from your evaluation of this last unit.

## ACTIVITY 4
### Critique a team planning sequence and discuss the planning process.

**A.**   "Notes Taken at Team Planning Meetings" is a set of simulated notes taken by the team recorder of one team at several of the planning sessions of a middle school team. Team meetings two, three, four, and six are described: the development, the design, the organization, and the evaluation meetings, respectively. Study the notes of the meetings carefully. Then answer the questions that follow the notes.

## Notes Taken at Team Planning Meetings Two, Three, Four, and Six

### TEAM MEETING TWO—DEVELOPMENT

Date: September 7
School goal to be focused upon: Appreciation of our cultural heritage
Theme of the unit: Yesterday and Today
Primary content areas involved: Social studies, language arts, science
Teachers involved: All
Possible length of unit: 6-7 weeks, one hour per day
Objectives of the unit finally decided upon:

1. The learners will be able to define the word *bicentennial* and apply it to today.
2. The learners will be able to describe the core values of our society when it was founded and compare them to those of today.
3. The learners will be able to identify several major occurrences in the life of our society and tell what the impact of each has been on our lives: e.g., westward movement, space race, urbanization, television, etc.
4. The learners will be able to identify the major written documents in our nation's history and discuss the significance of each today.
5. The learners will be able to identify literary, musical, and artistic expressions of patriotism, both past and present, and describe the feelings which produce and surround such patriotic expression.
6. The learners will be able to compare and contrast the national ecological conditions of 200 years ago and today.

Mrs. Diane Dunlap (language arts), Mrs. Becky Stasio (science), and Mr. Jim Shearer (social studies) have assumed the responsibility for preparing the design meeting for this unit to be held on September 14.

## TEAM MEETING THREE—DESIGN TOPIC

Date: September 14

School goal for unit: Appreciation of our cultural heritage

Theme of unit: Yesterday and Today

Primary content areas: Language arts, science, social studies

Teachers involved: All

Length of unit: 6 weeks

Learning activities for the unit:

| | |
|---|---|
| Objective One (bicentennial): | —use dictionary<br>—use Latin book<br>—participate in small group discussion<br>—read handout<br>—ask ten people |
| Objective Two (values): | —learning center: "Values in 1776"<br>—panel of parents discussion: "My Values"<br>—short course on "Values Clarification"<br>—essay comparing values of yesterday and today<br>—film on contemporary society<br>—brief lecture on Kohlberg's "Moral Development" |
| Objective Three (major events): | —learning center on "Main Events"<br>—unipacs for each of five main events<br>—short course on the results of these events<br>—student drawn mural on events & results<br>—debate: "The Most Important Event"<br>—essay: "Main Events in the Future and the Results" |
| Objective Four (documents): | —films on documents and surrounding history<br>—learning center on historical documents<br>—public surveys on acceptability of Bill of Rights today<br>—rewriting historical documents<br>—writing the next important historical document for our nation<br>—skits depicting the events connected with historical documents |
| Objective Five (patriotic expression): | —small group discussion on the meaning of "Patriotism"<br>—learning center on "Patriotic Expression Today"<br>—student oral interpretation of poetry and literature |

—student playing of patriotic music
—short course on "Patriotic Art"
—student production of patriotic expressions
—listen to tape recordings of speeches

Objective Six           —short course: Historical Research on
(ecological situations):     "Ecology in 1776"
                        —map making: "Our State Then and Now"
                        —learning center: "Problems of Ecology"
                        —community resource speaker: "What's Next
                          in Ecology?"
                        —essay: "Comparing Ecology in 1776
                          and Today"
                        —murals and posters depicting slogans

Independent Study Projects and Quest Projects will be available.

Introductory Teamwide Activity: The mayor has agreed to come and speak.

Culminating Activity:  Each student will submit plans to involve the whole school
                    in the windup activity. Plans will be shared with whole
                    team.

Bob Shumaker (math) has agreed to design a paper and pencil preassessment based on the objectives, to be administered one week from now. Kids who score 85 percent or better will be assigned to a special quest group.

Assignments:  These teachers have agreed to assume the responsibility for each of the following:

Bob Shumaker:  1. Coordinate objective one
(math)         2. Order and show films and filmstrips
               3. Prepare tape recordings
               4. Supervise map making and mural production
               5. Read essays and other written products
               6. Assessments (large group)

Diane Dunlap:   1. Coordinate objective five
(language arts) 2. Prepare all learning centers

Becky Stasio:  1. Coordinate objective six
(science)      2. Conduct short courses on values, events, and arts
               3. Conduct introductory and culminating sessions

Jim Shearer:     1. Coordinate objectives three and four
(social studies) 2. Responsible for all student reports and displays
                   of student work
                 3. Lecturette on Kohlberg's "Moral Development"
                 4. Moderate debates
                 5. Short course on ecology

All assignments to be ready by October 1. Unit to begin October 8. Organizing meeting to be held on October 1.

## TEAM MEETING FOUR: ORGANIZING

Topic: "Yesterday and Today"

1. Diane Dunlap reviewed the two previous meetings dealing with the unit. Everyone is together.
2. All teacher responsibilities are being met. Some problem with one film, but Bob expects to be able to make it or to have a substitute film or activity.
3. Each teacher has conferenced with his or her advisees about the unit coming up.

Several groups of students want an objective on how our country actually celebrated the bicentennial in 1976 and what could have been done. Diane has agreed to design a group study around this objective for interested students.

4. Bob has completed the assessment. Fourteen students scored well enough to move immediately to quest activities. Becky Stasio has agreed to meet with each student to help design the individual or small group quest projects.
5. It was decided that the unit will run for approximately six weeks, from October 8 until Thanksgiving; an average of one hour per day. The skeleton schedule looks like this:

| | |
|---|---|
| Week One: | Introductory Activities |
| | Student Decisions & Contracting |
| | Student Special Scheduling |
| | Objective One |
| Week Two-Five: | Objectives Two-Six |
| Week Six: | Culminating Activities |
| | Assessment of Student Progress |
| | Student Evaluation of Unit |

6. The tentative daily schedule for the six weeks is included. (See next page.)

## TEAM MEETING SIX: EVALUATION

Date: December 2        Topic: "Yesterday and Today"

The team listed the following as strong points in the unit:

Timeliness
Disciplines well correlated
Speakers were good
Short courses worked out well
Students liked the learning centers
Students really enjoyed the amount of freedom they
had in scheduling and contracting

Weak Points:

Not well enough organized; too much chaos and not knowing where to be.

## Tentative Schedule for "Yesterday and Today"

| | Monday | Tuesday | Wednesday | Thursday | Friday |
|---|---|---|---|---|---|
| 1 | Introductory Activities | ← Student Decisions and Contracting → | | Student Scheduling | Objective One |
| 2 | Objective One | ← Students begin public survey → <br> ← All learning centers open → <br> ← "Documents" film → <br> ← Mapmaking → <br> ← Short course on values clarification → | | | "Bill of Rights" |
| 3 | Parents Panel | ← All learning centers open → <br> ← Short Course: "Major Events" → <br> ← Unipacs → <br> ← Essay writing → | | | |
| 4 | | ← All learning centers open → <br> ← Short Course: "Patriotic Art" → <br> ← Creative writing → | | Artwork | Film |
| 5 | Brief Lecture: "Moral Development" | ← All learning centers open → <br> ← Short Course: "Ecology in 1776" → <br> Unipacs still available | | | Speaker on Ecology |
| 6 | Debate: "Events" | ← Presentation and displays of student work → <br> Assessment of student progress | | | Mayor visits and speaks |

### NEXT TIME

The team will try to alternate units which maximize student choice and freedom of movement with those that are scheduled more traditionally. We agree that the next unit will have one objective for each teacher, and students will spend one week with each teacher, rotating through all objectives and teachers.

### ANECDOTAL RECORD OF THE TEAM PLANNING PROCESS

To help you understand this team's unit a little better, the narrative record, written by one of the team's teachers, is included here.

"We began planning this unit by choosing to focus on the schoolwide goal of 'appreciation of our cultural heritage.' We thought that the topic of 'Yesterday and Today' would be a good way to work on that schoolwide goal, one which would also allow us to work in at least three of the subjects that our team is responsible for teaching. The team thought we would aim for a unit that would fit in our schedule during the last period of the day, for about six weeks.

"Our objectives (one for each week) dealt with things such as defining *bicentennial*, comparing the present day with 1776, tracing the impact of major national movements such as urbanization, and learning about various ways to express patriotism.

"Then three of us volunteered to prepare a series of learning activities for each of the objectives. We ended up with a wide variety of methods, including these: handouts, lectures, textbook assignments, panels, short courses, essays, learning centers, discussions, visitors, films, mapmaking, murals, and many others. We made certain that each objective had at least five different learning activities. We also designed some independent and quest projects, and suggested some unit introductory and culminating activities for the whole team. Bob Shumaker volunteered to design a pretest for the unit, to see what the kids already knew. At this point each teacher knew what they were to teach and how they were to do it.

"At the next meeting (organizing), two weeks later, we checked on our progress, found that we were all on schedule. We examined the results of the preassessment. Finally, we agreed on a schedule which would free us during the last period of the day.

"Then the unit began. We had lots of situational meetings.

"At the conclusion of the unit, six weeks later, we talked among ourselves about its effectiveness. There were lots of things that went really well, and a few things that bothered us. Next time we're going to set up the unit in a way that does not disrupt our schedule at all. Each student will work on the objectives of the unit in each subject area with the teacher of that subject, during the regular class in that subject."

**B.**   Write out your answers to these questions:

1. How closely do the notes of this team's meetings follow the guidelines in Activity 3?
2. Is there evidence that the team ties its program to the broad goals of the school and community?
3. Were the objectives precise enough to permit the development of appropriate learning activities?
4. Did the objectives flow from the broad, school goal?
5. How well did the team build variety into the program?
6. How efficiently did the team members divide responsibilities for planning?
7. Does the schedule look realistic to you?
8. Do you agree with the comments in the evaluation session?
9. What did the team omit that you think should have been included?
10. What insights into your own team planning process do you derive from this simulation?

**C.**   Convene a meeting of your team or group. Select two recorders for the meeting. Your agenda will include three activities: (1) discuss answers to the four questions in Activity 2; (2) share notes from Activity 3; and (3) discuss Activity 4 answers. Include in your portfolio as much data from these discussions as seems appropriate.

## ACTIVITY 5
**Plan a unit.**

You have had the opportunity to become familiar with at least one model for the team planning process. Now it's time to apply the model in a real or simulated situation. If you and your group are members of a functioning team, go all the way! If you are not, try to find a functioning team that will agree to evaluate the unit you prepare. If you cannot, use another group or individual to react to your plan. Each of you should keep notes as if you were the recorder. First, read and become familiar with the "Team Planning Checklist" and "Key Practices in Group Problem Solving." These will be used in your team planning activities. Then follow the "Guidelines for Planning an Instructional Unit" as you plan your unit. Hold all the meetings described there and complete each step. Save all your notes, materials, etc., for later review.

## Team Planning Checklist

Directions: Answer *yes* or *no* to each question.

A. *Preliminary Planning*

___ 1. Have you set aside enough time for both team and individual planning?

___ 2. Do you have a set of broad, perhaps schoolwide or systemwide, educational goals from which you can fashion your team's learning program?

___ 3. Have you decided on a unit topic that emerges from one or more of the broad educational goals mentioned above?

___ 4. Are you certain the topic fits the goal?

___ 5. Have you considered the place of this unit in the scope and sequence of the curriculum as a whole?

B. *Development Meeting*

___ 1. Have you allowed at least one month in lead time before the learning program is to be implemented?

___ 2. Have you identified precise, specific learning objectives to be achieved by the students?

___ 3. Do these objectives clearly relate to the topic?

___ 4. Did you discuss the results of the evaluation of the last unit and take into account what you planned to do differently?

___ 5. Did the team decide which member(s) would prepare the unit for the design meeting?

C. *Design Meeting*

___ 1. Has the design meeting been held about ten days or so after the development meeting?

___ 2. Are there at least two weeks remaining before the beginning of the program?

___ 3. Have you developed at least five activities for each objective? Five ways students can achieve the objective?

___ 4. Have you included the maximum amount of variety in the learning activities?

___ 5. Have you agreed on teacher assignments for the preparation of the learning activities for each objective?

___ 6. Have you planned to assess both student interests and achievements?

___ 7. Have you planned large group introductory and culminating activities?

D. *Organization Meeting*

___ 1. Have you reviewed the decisions from the two previous meetings?

___ 2. Has each teacher prepared the activities for which he/she assumed responsibility?

___ 3. Do you have assessment data on student interests and achievements ready for this meeting?

___ 4. Have you decided how to organize the students for the unit?

___ 5. Have you decided when the unit will begin and when it is scheduled to end?

___ 6. Have you made any changes in your plans based on assessment data?

___ 7. Have you decided how much time will be scheduled for the unit each day?

___ 8. Have you decided the time and place for each learning activity?

___ 9. Have you prepared a master schedule of the unit for everyone involved?

E. *Situational Meetings*

___ 1. Have you had any situational meetings?

___ 2. Were you able to resolve any problems?

___ 3. Did you discuss the progress of the unit as it moved along?

F. *Evaluation Meeting*

___ 1. Have you analyzed and discussed student evaluations of the unit? Analyzed student post-tests? Other student work?

___ 2. Have you decided what the strengths of the unit were, and why?

___ 3. Have you discussed what the weaknesses of the unit were, and why?

___ 4. Have you decided what to do differently the next time around?

## Key Practices in Group Problem Solving

1. *Prepare for the meeting.*
   a. Have a clear idea of what the meeting is for.
   b. Think out what you want to put on the agenda.
   c. Prepare the materials needed.
   d. Block off the time needed for the meeting.

2. *Adopt a plan for managing the meeting.* There are five elements, relatively mechancial procedures, without which a meeting does not run smoothly. The group should have a plan for:
   a. Starting and stopping at agreed times.
   b. Agreeing on an agenda.
   c. Hearing from everyone who wants to contribute.
   d. Keeping on the topic, helping the group focus on the task.
   e. Keeping records during and after the meeting.

3. Analyze the problematic situation.
   a. Probe the situation facing the group, state the facts.
   b. Examine people's assumptions about the situation.
   c. Consider the boundaries within which the group works.

4. *Examine the possibilities for action.*
   a. Brainstorm ideas.
   b. Propose tasks or goals; suggest ways of organizing the products of brainstorming.
   c. Test alternative plans against the situations, assumptions, and boundaries already identified.
   d. Test the consequences of a plan.

5. *Decide on an action plan.*
   a. Carefully define the problem; clear up confusion and ambiguity.
   b. Design the plan.

    c.  Agree on work assignments.

    d.  Agree on a timetable and communication plan.

6. *Attend to the group's processes.* While the group is acting on its agenda and following the problem-solving sequence, some members must be giving attention to the interpersonal processes of the group.

    a.  Encourage members' participation and sharing.

    b.  Protect members' rights to have their opinions known and feelings aired.

    c.  Bridge differences and conflicts between members.

    d.  Help the group to be aware of its procedures and interactions, and to consider changes if needed.

    e.  Clarify, elaborate, and summarize ideas and suggestions; offer conclusions for the group to accept or reject.

    f.  Ask for clarification, elaboration or summary.

    g.  Ask for expression of feelings and concerns.

    h.  Try to ensure that everyone shares in the decisions being made.

    i.  Be constantly alert to what the group process needs at any moment to move it ahead.

7. *Carry out the meeting's decisions and plans.*

    a.  Refrain from altering the plan without the group's consent.

    b.  Keep complaints for the next meeting.

    c.  Protect the confidences of the meeting.

## Guidelines for Planning an Instructional Unit

### A. TEAM MEETING ONE: Preliminary Planning

*Step One:* Choose an overall schoolwide goal (e.g., Appreciation of the Cultural Heritage). List it.

*Step Two:* Choose a subject that is congruent with that goal. If you are a disciplinary team, focus on a single subject, or maybe a topic (e.g., "Yesterday and Today") that involves several disciplines. Discuss several. List them all and circle the one your team has chosen.

The above steps may have already been done by your team, by your school district planning, by a curriculum committee or by some other means of formalizing curriculum plans. If so, you may move directly to the next team meeting. Follow the guidelines below. List the objectives you finally agree on. Your team may have fewer than five objectives or many more.

### B. TEAM MEETING TWO, FIRST PART: Development

Date:

Schoolwide goal of the unit:

Topic of the unit:

Content area(s) and teachers involved:

Objectives for the unit:

1.

2.

3.

4.

5.

Teacher(s) who have assumed the responsibility for preparing for the design meeting: _____

_____.

In your notes of the design meeting include all the learning activities your team has agreed upon for each objective.


## C. TEAM MEETING TWO, SECOND PART: Homework for the Next Meeting

In addition to task assignments for the next meeting, here are two assignments related to your skills in helping the group members work well together.

1. *Analyze your group problem-solving skills and plan ways to improve them.*   Those who study the process of work groups recognize a number of key practices that separate effective groups from ineffective ones. We could list the good practices and suggest that you watch for them and try to follow them yourself. Unfortunately, having a list handy doesn't offer any more assurance of having an effective group than a paint-by-the-numbers set assures an artistic product. Artistry in group membership comes from members knowing what particular functions are needed, and when, and having the skill to perform the needed functions. The more members who are alert to the *need* for and *timing* of the functions and who have the *skills* to perform them, the more effective the group.

"Key Practices in Group Problem Solving" is an outline that includes preparing for a meeting, conducting a problem-solving process, and giving attention to essential interpersonal processes. Your group can use the outline as a set of guidelines, and you can use it specifically to consider the roles you typically play in group meetings and the roles you would like to become more skilled in performing. Study the guidelines and be ready to discuss them at the next meeting.

2. *Analyze your own behavior in work group meetings.*   What roles do you usually play in group meetings? We think you will benefit from identifying ways you typically act in work group meetings. Before the next group meeting, write at least six phrases describing recurring ways you participate in the meetings. Include actions you like and don't like. Visualize yourself in action, enacting each of the behaviors. Arrange the phrases in a sequence from the action you like best to the one you like least. Select *two* you don't like and write yourself a reminder of what you want to avoid or improve; put it in front of yourself at the next group

meeting. The purpose of the reminder is to help you visualize the new behaviors and practice using them prior to and during the meeting. Tell one other member what you are doing and ask that person to take notes on your participation and later give you feedback. Continue trying new behaviors and getting feedback as long as you need to. Keep a set of notes for your portfolio.

## D. TEAM MEETING THREE, FIRST PART: Design

Date:

Schoolwide goal of the unit:

Topic of the unit:

Learning activities for objective one:

Learning activities for objective two:

Learning activities for objective three:

Learning activities for objective four:

Learning activities for objective five:

Have you thought of any large group introductory or culminating activities?

Who has agreed to design the preassessment?

Who has agreed to coordinate Quest Activities for students who do unusually well on the preassessment (e.g., 85 percent)?

Now list the names of your team members and their responsibilities for this unit. Remember, there are several ways such assignments can be made:

1. One teacher for each subject
2. One teacher for each objective
3. On the basis of teacher instructional strengths and interests

Name _____

Responsibilities:

Name _____

Responsibilities:

Name _____

Responsibilities:

When should all preparations be finished?

## E. TEAM MEETING THREE, SECOND PART: Analyze Team Practices

As part of this meeting, set aside a half an hour to discuss the guidelines, "Key Practices in Group Problem Solving," and to consider how your group can use them. If you want to, you can tell the others what group skills you were deliberately practicing at this meeting.

Before the meeting is concluded, the group should decide which of the following activities to plan for the next meeting.

1. Make an audio recording of the next meeting. At a special meeting after Team Meeting Four, the tape can be played back and analyzed using the "Key

Practices" guidelines as categories for taking notes. If three people can analyze the tape together, have one person make notes on evidence relating to Categories 1 and 2 of the "Key Practices;" assign the second person to Categories 3, 4, and 5; and the third to Category 6. The latter should also tally the frequency of each process in Category 6. This can be done with a simple grid, with the nine processes along the margin and group members names across the top. In the analysis session stop the tape periodically to facilitate note taking. Report the results to the total group during Team Meeting Five. The group can then discuss the results and plan for any changes that may be desired.

2. Designate one member of the group to take the role of process observer at the next meeting or two—using the Key Practices list—and report observations during the meeting at appropriate times. Feedback from an observer while group dialogue is still fresh in everyone's mind is very effective in raising awareness of group processes.

3. One activity that sounds contrived and awkward but actually works well is the assignment of group members to specific roles to remind the others about needed group processes. Make a set of placards, 4″ × 8″ or a little larger, each bearing one of these words or phrases: "I like your idea," "Let's hear from. . .," "Recorder," "Please clarify," "Please summarize," "What are your feelings?," "The topic is . . .," "Say more about that," and "Do we agree on this?" Distribute all the cards among members of the group. More than one card per person is all right. The cards obviously refer to useful group functions: encouraging, bringing other members into the dialogue, etc. The person who draws the recorder card is, of course, the recorder. All the other cards are to be raised at appropriate times during the meeting to remind the other members of a process that needs group attention.

## F. TEAM MEETING FOUR: Organization

Date:

Goal:

Topic:

The first task is to review everyone's understanding of the plans thus far. This may be difficult to understand the first time through. Ask for help from someone who has done it.

The second step is to be certain all the teacher assignments are complete or near completion. Are they?

The third step is to report on teacher conferences with advisees. Has anything emerged from these conferences for which plans need to be made?

Has the preassessment been carried out? What has it revealed about student achievement in the topic to be covered by your unit?

How will the students be grouped for this unit?

How long (in days or weeks) will the unit last? How much time each day on the average, will be devoted to the unit? It could be, for example, one class period per day for eight weeks, two class periods per day for four weeks, all day for one week, etc.

Record a skeleton schedule here:

Week One:
Week Two:
Week Three:
Week Four:
Week Five:

|          | M | T | W | Th | F |
|----------|---|---|---|----|---|
| Week One |   |   |   |    |   |
| Week Two |   |   |   |    |   |
| Week Three |   |   |   |    |   |
| Week Four |   |   |   |    |   |
| Week Five |   |   |   |    |   |
| Week Six |   |   |   |    |   |

On a larger piece of paper, fill in this "Bird's Eye View" schedule for the unit. Refer to the simulated schedule on page 135.

### G.  TEAM MEETING FIVE: Situational

During implementation of this unit, there will have been several situational meetings. Record the subjects of these sessions and the decisions made. Save time to continue discussion of the group's progress in using skills for effective group work (using audio tape analysis or other data).

### H.  TEAM MEETING SIX: Evaluation

Date:
Goal:
Topic:

Evaluate the unit with your team, and if applicable, the other teachers who implemented the unit. Record this data and file in your portfolio.

Data used in evaluating this unit (e.g., analysis of student post-tests, other student work, student feedback):

Strong points of this unit:
Weak points of this unit:
What we'll do differently next time:

## ACTIVITY 6
### Analyze group relationships

This is a good time to consider how well the team members worked together in the planning process in Activity Five. Consider what the conditions are that make one work group effective and healthy in the long run and another not. Researchers in industry, in the military, and more recently in education have provided some answers. "Work Group Relationships," which follows, is a rating instrument based on research findings. You can use it to identify the relative strengths and weaknesses of any work group, particularly a professional group. Using the rating device is most effective when all members of the group can respond to it and then as a group analyze the patterns of responses. The activity may be inappropriate for some work groups; it is for groups that have some degree of trust and good will, and intend to stay together as a group. It is for groups that can define their problems in terms of relationships and behaviors, and not in terms of weak or strong persons.

The group can follow these guidelines:

1. Take plenty of time to do the rating. Each person completes the rating sheet privately.
2. Schedule time specifically to discuss the outcomes.
3. In preparation for the discussion, each member makes a personal selection of five items that represent the group's strongest assets. Each makes another list of five items most in need of attention and improvement. The latter list should include only items that the member believes really can be changed by group effort.
4. Before the discussion, one member hands ten small slips of paper to each person. Each member writes one "asset" number on each of five slips, and all are collected in one container. The other slips are for the "improvement" numbers, which go in another container. Tally the two sets of numbers.
5. The group then discusses the outcome by
   a. Seeking some agreement on the group's assets, and
   b. Trying to answer the question, "How can we use our assets to work on the needed improvements?"
6. If appropriate, the group then decides on a plan of action to make improvements. For ongoing work groups, the process of self-analysis and planning improvements needs a regular place in the schedule. Each group decides how frequently to cycle the activity. Each member keeps notes. For your own purposes, file your responses to the rating list and your notes on the meeting in your portfolio.

## Work Group Relationships

*Directions:* To rate the quality of relationships within your work group, score each item as follows: ++ strongly true, + somewhat true, − needs improvement, or −− a clear weakness.

\_\_\_\_ 1. Members have trust and confidence in each other.

\_\_\_\_ 2. Members feel free to act naturally with each other.

\_\_\_\_ 3. Members genuinely try to understand what others in the group think and feel.

\_\_\_\_ 4. The group can handle anger, tension, and conflict in constructive ways.

\_\_\_\_ 5. The group paces itself and allows for "ups and downs," cycles of hard work and relaxation, intensity and tension release, action and reflection, conflict and unity, as needed for productivity.

\_\_\_\_ 6. Asking for and giving help is expected and supported in this group.

\_\_\_\_ 7. The group regularly takes time and provides outlets for members to share ideas and solve problems.

\_\_\_\_ 8. Members take time to seek my reactions and ideas.

\_\_\_\_ 9. All members understand and feel personally committed to help achieve the common objectives.

\_\_\_\_ 10. The group works toward its goals with a minimum of inefficiency and wasted time.

\_\_\_\_ 11. The group's objectives accommodate rather than conflict with my individual goals.

\_\_\_\_ 12. Members serve as helpful sounding boards for each other's ideas.

\_\_\_\_ 13. Members give nonjudgmental feedback on each other's work.

\_\_\_\_ 14. The group uses integrative, constructive methods of problem solving rather than a conflictive or win/lose approach.

\_\_\_\_ 15. The group makes constructive use of the differences and diverse talents of the members.

\_\_\_\_ 16. Members have a sense of shared responsibility for getting a job done.

\_\_\_\_ 17. Members are conscientious about carrying out responsibilities that are theirs to do.

\_\_\_\_ 18. The work of the group is planned and accomplished without members manipulating each other.

\_\_\_\_ 19. Influence and power in the group are based on individual knowledge and skills, not on age, seniority, or organizational authority.

\_\_\_\_ 20. The leadership pattern of the group fits the group's needs.

## ACTIVITY 7
### Meet to discuss the team planning process

By now you have been involved in team planning and have a base of experience from which to reflect on the process. The following questions may help you analyze and evaluate the experience. Write out your own answers to the questions and then convene a meeting of your group to discuss the members' answers. Save your written responses in your portfolio.

**A.** The following statements are often proposed as advantages of team teaching. According to your experience in planning and possibly conducting a team unit, does your experience confirm or deny the following proposed advantages of teamwork? Comment briefly.

1. The pupil is known better through teacher sharing.
2. Teachers make better use of their particular strengths.
3. Teachers can refine and improve their teaching skills as the team develops.
4. Giving help to each other is easier for teachers in team situations.
5. Teacher morale is higher because of continued contact with adults.
6. Opportunities for leadership present themselves.
7. Greater flexibility is provided for instruction.
8. Greater variety in instructional strategies is provided.
9. The correlation of subject matter through cooperative planning is improved.
10. Student interest and motivation are increased.
11. Student achievement improves because of coordinated planning.
12. Curricular continuity is improved.

**B.** How do you feel about team planning now? What are its strengths for you? Its weaknesses?

**C.** Do you have any suggestions for changes in the team planning model to make it work better for your team?

**D.** Do you prefer teamwork or some other method of teacher organization? Why?

**E.** What questions about team teaching do you need to have answered?

### NEXT STEPS

You are now at the point where you have participated as a team member in the planning and possibly the implementation of a team-planned unit; you may want to go further. Some of these activities may be appropriate.

1. Try another unit. Evaluate this unit on the basis of how much your team has improved its planning skills.

2. Find another team that is doing that same kind of thing. Arrange to "fishbowl" some of their planning sessions, and they yours. Engage in some mutual helping critiques. You might even be able to follow each other from preliminary planning to evaluation.

3. Invite your principal or instructor to your meetings. Ask for his or her critique of what you are doing.

4. Put on a team planning workshop for the other teams or teachers in a school. Invite their reactions.

5. Contact the nearest facilitator for the Kettering Foundations' Institute for the Development of Educational Activities. Ask to have a "Clue In" conference held at your school. Be especially concerned about studying the six filmstrip-cassette tape packets on "Planning and Managing I.G.E. . . ." These are among the finest materials on the process of team planning and team teaching.

6. Consider arranging for a workshop, making use of materials developed at the University of Texas at Austin. There are two volumes that may be ordered: a workshop manual, *Interdisciplinary Faculty Teaming;* and a second volume of supplementary materials, *A Handbook for Interdisciplinary Faculty Teaming.* They may be ordered from:
   > Communications Service
   > The Research and Development Center for Teacher Education
   > Education Annex 3-230
   > The University of Texas at Austin
   > Austin, Texas 78712

7. Read Chapter Five, "Interdisciplinary Team Organization," in William M. Alexander and Paul S. George, *The Exemplary Middle School,* New York: Holt, Rinehart and Winston, 1981.

8. Examine a copy of Pumerantz, Philip, and Ralph Galano *Establishing Interdisciplinary Programs in Middle Schools,* West Nyack, New York: Parker Publishing Company, 1972.

# CHAPTER 7

# EXPLORATION IN THE CURRICULUM

Over a half century ago, the developers of the junior high concept focused on the need to provide opportunities for students to explore the world of knowledge. Junior high educators reasoned that students who were able to become acquainted with broad areas of academic and vocational effort would be able to make more effective choices when they reached high school. Exploration of several areas in junior high school would be followed by in-depth study in high school. By the time the students arrived at the high school they would be able to choose wisely from among the academic, the vocational, or the general tracks, having determined their interests and abilities in the junior high school. This was a relatively reasonable approach and the middle school continues to honor it.

Today's middle schools have other good reasons for encouraging exploration in the curriculum. Perhaps the most compelling reason is the knowledge of the close relationship between an exploratory curriculum and student skill development—the more exploratory, even experimental, a school's curriculum, the more basic skills are developed. So, even in a "back to basics" milieu, there are important reasons to continue an emphasis on an exploratory curriculum.

Middle school educators know that their students have entered a combustive period of their lives, a period of rapid physical growth, intellectual blossoming, tumultuous social and emotional change. It is a time when they begin to see their world in wholly different ways; a time of life when exploration of their many potential selves becomes paramount. The most effective schools for emerging adolescents ought, logically, to be those which recognize and facilitate this process of exploration that is so central to their developmental process. Providing for exploration, then, becomes a primary goal of the fully functioning middle school.

There are many ways this goal can be achieved. The unified arts program has traditionally been the major avenue for exploration in schools for transescents. There have been strenuous efforts to mold the academic programs in individual classrooms to more effectively meet student interests. Whole school efforts have included the development of mini-courses, independent study programs and special interest activity programs.

The goal of this chapter is to help you review and evaluate opportunities for exploration in a school program.

Look at the following questions. The more affirmative answers you can give, the more likely you will find the activities helpful.

1. Are you convinced of the need for middle schools to foster increased opportunities of exploration in the curriculum?
2. If you are now teaching in a middle school, are most of your colleagues convinced of this need?

3. Would the school with which you're most familiar profit from the inclusion of mini-courses or a special interest program in the curriculum?
4. Would the community where your school is located support this sort of program if its members were informed of the purposes and results of such an effort?

## ACTIVITY 1
### Respond to inventory and discuss exploratory opportunities.

The "Exploratory Program Inventory" deals with your opinions about exploratory opportunities in the school with which you are most familiar. Please complete the inventory on your own. You may then want to compare your responses with others who are familiar with the same school. You may even want to devise a way of tabulating the results of the responses which you and your colleagues make, as a way of evaluating the school's exploratory program. When you finish, answer the discussion questions below.

1. In your opinion, how effectively does this school meet the goal of providing an exploratory emphasis in the school curriculum?
2. How satisfied is the faculty regarding the exploratory opportunities now provided?
3. If you and the faculty agree on the need for improvement, which areas do you think are most in need of this improvement?
4. What factors might make such improvement difficult? What could be done to remove the barriers to the improvements?

If you decide to continue designing improvements for the exploratory function of a school, the following learning activities should prove helpful. These activities are focused on only one practical way of infusing the school with an improved exploratory emphasis. If well-designed, such an exploratory program should and can involve the areas of Unified Arts, Independent Learning, Academic Inquiry, and Special Interest Activities mentioned in the "Exploratory Program Inventory." Doing something about the areas of Expanding Horizons in Disciplines, and Interest-based Academics are not specifically dealt with, although they are also involved.

All of the activities that follow deal with the establishment of a Pilot Special Exploratory Program in a middle school—a program which constitutes a formal part of the daily or weekly schedule and which has its own place in the evaluation of student learning and can be another category on the report card. If you (and the school's faculty) have decided to design such a program, these activities should be helpful to you. Or, if you find yourself in a school where such a program is already operating, these activities should help you understand the program and work well within it.

## Exploratory Program Inventory

### DIRECTIONS

Please evaluate the exploratory emphasis of the school in question by responding to the items below. Place the appropriate number in the space to the left of each item.

4: Active and extensive program in this area.

3: Happening somewhat in this area.

2: Very little in this area.

1: None.

###### EXPLORATORY AREA ONE: UNIFIED ARTS

Teachers in the areas of the curriculum which extend beyond the four basic academic areas are numerous. Among the opportunities offered to students, most of the following are included: art, choral music, instrumental music, physical education, home economics, career education, industrial arts, foreign language. Students have the opportunity to enroll in all or almost all of these unified arts areas before leaving school. Year-long and even semester-length courses are few, compared to the number of six,- nine,- or twelve-week options. The teachers in the unified arts areas see themselves as teachers of exploratory courses, as opposed to teaching high school style content and emphasis. The academic faculty recognizes that the extended curriculum (unified arts area) is of critical importance to the schooling of transescent students.

###### EXPLORATORY AREA TWO: ACADEMIC INQUIRY COURSES

The school schedule is organized to permit students and faculty to spend part of their day going beyond the basics, into what might be called *mini-courses.* Such courses are taught by the regular academic teachers in addition to the core subjects of language arts, social studies, science, and math. These mini-courses are, however, tied to academics. Students have a day that includes skill and content work in each of the basics for, perhaps, forty minutes, and one or two forty minute mini-courses which promote academic inquiry. These courses are offered regularly and students are held accountable for their participation; however, evaluation is flexible enough to permit exploration without fear of failure. Students are able to choose from a variety of academic inquiry mini-courses which are intended to be relevant, exciting, and fun. The courses are for everyone, not just for a particular ability group. (See examples of these courses later in this chapter.)

###### EXPLORATORY AREA THREE: INTEREST-BASED ACADEMICS

The faculty in all areas recognizes that the traditional curriculum offered to the in-between-ager has sometimes been so irrelevant to their lives as to be almost foreign. As a result, teachers make a serious attempt in their daily classes to be certain that the curriculum has the interests of the students involved. If you asked students in the school about their studies, they would probably tell you how interesting their teachers made the classes. They would be able to see how the course content fits into the present concerns. Literature, composition, social studies, science, and perhaps even math, are focused on the developmental tasks of transescents. Students have a great deal of choice regarding what they learn in all of these areas.

###### EXPLORATORY AREA FOUR: INDEPENDENT LEARNING

Students in the school have an opportunity to participate in a formally organized program of independent study. This means that students have a time separate from their other regular classes, when they are engaged in choosing topics and learning independently, but with guidance from the teachers. It may be scheduled daily, weekly, or otherwise, but it is scheduled. In this program students become more aware of their interests and talents, learn how to select a topic for independent learning, and are helped to become better at growing on their own. Growth in self-discipline and responsibility are as important as the topics that students learn. Students are evaluated in this area as they are in the regular academic program. Perhaps most important, this part of the academic program is open to all students regardless of previous grades.

###### EXPLORATORY AREA FIVE: EXPANDING THE HORIZONS IN THE DISCIPLINES

Every teacher in the school understands the exploratory needs of transescent learners and attempts to translate this into his or her own class. In terms of curriculum, this means that all subject areas are designed to offer the learner a glimpse of a wide array of areas of investigation. Every subject area offers an introduction to most of the major areas of that part of the world of knowledge, on the assumption that exploration in earlier grades will allow students to make reasonable choices at the high school level. In social studies, for example, students are able to explore anthropology, sociology, economics, psychology, and political science, as well as traditional world history, geography, and American history. In science, students are introduced to oceanography, ecology, zoology, astronomy, and other new sciences, as well as earth science and "general science." Other areas of the curriculum follow suit.

###### EXPLORATORY AREA SIX: SPECIAL INTEREST ACTIVITIES

Recognizing the need to help students use their leisure time effectively, now and in the future, the school provides a regular opportunity for students to gather together on a special interest basis. These interests include hobbies, crafts, music, dancing, games, sports, forensics, and others. Time for these activities is scheduled on a regular basis in the school day, thereby providing an opportunity for all students to participate.

## ACTIVITY 2
### Read about the rationale for exploration.

Read the selection "Exploration: A Rationale." Note your questions and concerns.

## Exploration: A Rationale

In the past century, educators seem to have assumed that children approaching adolescence need to make decisions, to focus sharply on a narrow set of interests, to chart an often irrevocable personal course for the future. This may be at least part of the reason why generation after generation of Americans reached adulthood with many talents undiscovered, many interests unrecognized, many personal resources undeveloped. Now, however, educators seem to recognize that one of the identifying characteristics of emerging adolescence is a veritable explosion of personal interests—physical, sexual, social, intellectual. Emerging adolescents are growing, blossoming, changing—reaching out to explore the world now seen by them in a different perspective.

If this is an accurate picture of early adolescence, then the most effective schools for this age group will be those offering programs that facilitate rather than retard this exploratory urge, programs that are authentically exploratory.

In light of this new understanding of the nature of early adolescence, and of the proper way to nurture these emerging characteristics, middle schools across the country are experimenting with a variety of ways to implement exploration. One of the more popular approaches is the development of Special Exploratory Programs which are an addition to the regular academic program. Such programs are developing differently in different schools in various parts of the country, but most have certain elements in common.

Such programs, to be effective, have to be part of the regular schedule of the school day or week. Attempting to schedule the exploratory program before or after school just doesn't seem to work. Transportation is a problem, but this is not the only reason before-and-after-school programs fail. How and when a part of the school program is scheduled tells students, parents, and teachers how important it is. Placing the exploratory programs before and after school communicates a lack of commitment to such  activities. They usually collapse without much support. So, they must be worked into the school day if they are to survive.

Successful exploratory programs also involve everyone in the school, both academic and unified arts personnel. To avoid being criticized as a frill, the exploratory program must be substantial in an academic sense. The program must convince parents that their children will be able to become involved in rigorous academic activity at an earlier age through the exploratory program. Stultifying academic repetitiveness can be avoided if unified arts alternatives are available. Furthermore, effective exploratory programs depend on the frequency with which the class or groups meet. A balance between too frequent and too infrequent meetings must be achieved for the program to work. Experience indicates that if the exploratory classes meet on a daily basis, the duration of the classes should not be longer than six weeks and not shorter than three weeks. If the classes meet twice weekly, four to six weeks seems to be an appropriate length, with nine weeks as an appropriate maximum time.

Successful exploratory programs also hold students accountable for their participation. That is, some method of providing evaluation of student efforts must be included to communicate to students and parents that students are expected to work hard in the exploratory program. But it must also allow for exploration without excessive fear of failure. Some students will not take the program seriously if they are not held accountable, and some will not explore unfamiliar areas if the risk of failure is too great. How feedback is given to students about their efforts communicates how the program is valued by the faculty.

Finally, effective exploratory programs are built upon the interests of both teachers and students. If the interests of either are not adequately considered, the program will falter. If faculty members do not consider it fun, the program will be seen as a burden, an additional preparation. When students have enough varied choices, they are likely to be enthusiastic participants.

In short, effective exploratory programs consider the following factors: time of day for best reception; balance of academics and unified arts; length of program and frequency of meetings; evaluation of student work; and teacher and student interest. Programs which do not deal effectively with these issues simply don't last long.

## ACTIVITY 3
### Examine exploratory options in several schools.

**A.**   Now that you know something about the basic ideas of a Special Exploratory Program, finding out some specifics about how others are doing it should be helpful. Read the three descriptions of middle school exploratory programs:

1. "Lincoln Middle School Exploratory Program;"
2. "Baker County Middle School; Mini-course Program;"
3. "The Co-curricular Program at Niphur Middle School."

**B.**   When you have studied the three programs, answer the following questions.

1. What are the strengths and weaknesses of these programs from your point of view?
2. Do these programs strike you as something in which you, personally, would like to participate?
3. Do you think these programs would have an appeal to middle school students? To parents? Why or why not?
4. Which of the three programs might work in the school with which you are most familiar? Why?
5. What changes would have to occur before such a program could become a part of the curriculum of your school?

## Lincoln Middle School Exploratory Program

### INTRODUCTION

This handout is a capsule of information concerning the exploratory program at Lincoln Middle School.

These samples of procedures and representative classes are only tokens of a profound commitment toward meeting individual student needs and implementing middle school philosophy at our school.

John P. Spindler, Principal

## PROCEDURE

The following is an outline of the procedure used to implement the exploratory program at Lincoln Middle School.

All students at our school take two exploratories each six weeks. The vocational and music courses are available to all students. Each of our six teams has exploratories taught by core teachers from that team, which are open mainly to team students. There are some instances when cross-teaming occurs. Each core teacher teaches two exploratories daily with an average enrollment of twenty-five.

We feel it is beneficial for all of our students to have an experience in vocational agriculture, industrial arts, home economics, and music during their three-year stay at our school. This influences us as we guide undecided students into specific classes. We also encourage some of our weaker students into academically oriented exploratories.

The procedure, in brief, consists of the following steps.

1. Teachers decide what courses they will sponsor or teach, depending on student needs, desires, and interests. As teachers, we can select our own hobbies or specific skills that we possess to teach as an exploratory. It is also possible for a group of students to become interested in a specific topic in an academic class and convince the teacher to offer it as an exploratory. In this way, students take part in planning their own learning program. Teacher interest, enthusiasm, and support are vital.

2. Publication of offerings for students and parents to look over and discuss.

3. Students select a first, second, and third choice in each of two groups of courses—one group for each period.

4. Homeroom teachers assign students to exploratories based on student choices and what the teacher feels will benefit the student. As you could expect, balancing class teaching loads and funding implications occasionally influence our decisions to make certain assignments.

5. The homeroom teacher lists the names of his students to attend a specific class on a team roll sheet. After all team teachers have posted their students' names, the list is given to the exploratory teacher as a roll.

6. Students are informed as to which classes they are to attend.

7. The roll sheet is returned to the team at the end of the six weeks with the students' grades posted on it.

8. Our exploratories are graded on an E, S, U system. E = Excellent, S = Satisfactory, and U = Unsatisfactory.

By Permission Of Lincoln Middle School, Gainesville, Florida. John P. Spindler, Principal.

## Sample Exploratory Sign-Up Sheet

Student Name _____ Grade _____ Homeroom _____

Please choose a 1st, 2nd, and 3rd choice for each mod. If you have made special arrangements with a teacher to be an aide, write aide in at the place marked OTHER.

| MOD 3 | MOD 4 |
|---|---|
| _____ Follow the Leader | _____ Fall Vegetable Gardening (12 weeks) |
| _____ Let's Find Out about Home Economics | _____ Fun with Decorating |
| _____ Industrial Arts | _____ Woodworking |
| _____ Piano Lab—Beginning | _____ Piano Lab—Advanced |
| _____ Beginning Band | _____ Art |
| _____ Library Aide (12 weeks) | _____ Library Aide (12 weeks) |
| _____ Five Faces of Man (Enrichment) | _____ Five Faces of Man (Enrichment) |
| _____ Typing | _____ Crafty Creators |
| _____ One Word Leads to Another | _____ Get Ready, Get Set, Go! |
| _____ String Design | _____ Cartoon Comics |
| _____ OTHER ( _____ ) | _____ OTHER ( _____ ) |

## COURSE TITLES

| | |
|---|---|
| SPANISH | IT'S RAINING CATS AND DOGS |
| BEGINNING BAND | EXPLORING HOME ECONOMICS |
| INTERMEDIATE BAND | IT'S ALL GREEK TO ME |
| THE OLYMPICS | GET READY, GET SET, GO! |
| EXPLORING HOUSING | SOFT SUMMER BREEZES |
| NUMBER POWER | THE JOYS OF BEING A FEMALE |
| TYPING | WALK A MILE IN MY SHOES |
| PIANO LAB | A JOURNEY TO SOUTH AMERICA |
| UP, UP AND AWAY | WRITE ON WITH READING |
| INTO THE UNKNOWN | FAMOUS SCIENTISTS |
| NEWSPAPER PRODUCTION | LOTS OF KNOTS |
| STRING DESIGN | EAT WHAT YOU GROW |
| SOCIAL SEMINAR | THE AMERICAN INDIAN |
| WORKING WITH WOOD | WILD, WILD WEST |
| FOUNDERS OF FREEDOM | MEDIA MANIA |
| NAME THAT TUNE | C TROUPE–STAGE |
| IN THE NEWS | SPIRIT OF SPORTS |
| IT' ALL AN ACT | CURIOSITY CORNER |
| WORD POWER | FALL VEGETABLE GARDEN |
| FAR OUT FICTION | FIVE FACES OF MAN |
| SCIENCE FAIR '75 | MIDDLE EASTERN DANCE |
| THE WHY OF IT ALL | THE DEVIL MADE ME DO IT |
| THE DIG | ART'S A MESS |
| HUMAN LIFE SYSTEMS | AMERICAN INDUSTRY |
| PHYSICAL FITNESS | CARTOON COMICS |

READING FOR FUN

LEATHER

MAKE IT WITH DENIM

MAN POWER

BLACK HISTORY

GEE, I'M A TREE

DISCOVERY

SCI FI

SHARKS

SPIRIT OF '76

MASTER MATH

AUTOMOTIVE MECHANICS

COME FLY WITH ME

BIOLOGY

DECIDING????

IT'S A SMALL WORLD

WORLD OF CONSTRUCTION

CRAFTY CREATORS

SMART ART

HAPPY BIRTHDAY! AMERICA

PIANO LAB

JOB JARGON

ONLY THE SHADOW KNOWS

PERSONAL BUSINESS

SLAVERY AND THE CIVIL WAR

FUN WITH DECORATING

MUSIC FOR THE JOY OF LISTENING

STAYING IN SHAPE

GEOLOGY

MACRAME

CREATIVE STITCHERY

IT'S ALL IN THE GAME

CREATIVE WRITING

LET'S SPEAK ENGLISH

## COURSE DESCRIPTIONS

**Wild, Wild West!:** This course will be offered simultaneously with an exploratory course on American Indians taught by another teacher on this team. Classes will be combined for audio-visual presentations and other resource presentations.

Wild, Wild West will be an in-depth study of the life styles of early American pioneers to the western part of our country. Family and community life, as well as the history of this period and locale will be explored.

Students will learn square dancing and perform in the joint chorus and band spring concert to be held at the end of this six weeks based on a western theme. Also, students will construct the set used for the performance.

**Joys of Being a Female:** This is an exploratory course that is strictly for girls. We will be discussing the human anatomy using the series "Reproduction and Human Development 1A" and "Human Growth and Development" International Teaching Tapes. We will study childbirth and marriage and the family.

Girls will be taught to interview so they can get firsthand information on the woman's role in her profession. We will also interview husbands to see how men see the role of wives. Fashion, dieting, breast cancer, and cosmetology are some of the areas the girls want to include. Films from different department stores and guest speakers will be used for these areas.

**The Devil Made Me Do It!:** Have you ever wondered why we behave the way we do? We'll probe into the innermost depths of the human mind to discover the why and wherefore of it all! Superstitions, folklore, myths, and challenging literature will blow your mind!

**Fall Vegetable Gardening:** The joy of growing your own vegetables—that's what it's all about. Eat them in the field or at home. Watch out! Those radishes are hot! Here's a chance to be outside part of the time planting, fertilizing, watering, weeding, and harvesting. While back in the classroom we will be exploring the pathways of food from the field to your table and all the different kinds of jobs necessary in order for us to eat. This course will cost you $1.00 for your seed and fertilizer. Remember, this is a twelve-week course.

**Spirit of '76:** A study into the lives of the men who signed the Declaration of Independence and helped establish the United States of America. A thumbnail sketch will be presented for each of the fifty-six signers with additional emphasis upon those signers who distinguished themselves as leaders in the early years of the United States. Films, filmstrips, individual study, and lectures will be employed during the course of study.

**Do It Your Way—Shorthand:** Create your own symbols for writing. Learn how to write your notes in SHORTHAND. Enjoy the fun and thrills of creativity. Pupils will want an introductory course in shorthand which includes learning and writing the alphabet. They will also be responsible for writing letters, symbols, and phrases. Supplies: Transcription pad and pen.

**The Write to Type:** Everyone will learn the basics of typing. We will learn the letters on the keyboard and the simple mechanics of the machine. Each person will progress at his own speed, working individually. We will learn to type letters and short stories toward the end. We will play Blind Man's Bluff. Each student will have to provide his own typing paper and a clean handkerchief.

**The Dig:** A brief exploration of the development of civilization through archaeological finds. A simulated dig will be conducted between two teams with the students developing an imaginary culture complete with religious morals, ethics, monetary system symbols, slogans, and laws. The students will make artifacts representing the ideas of the culture. The artifacts will be buried so that a dig may take place. Each team will dig up the other's artifacts and try to make generalizations about the culture represented.

**South of the Border:** Ole! Viva el Espanol! South of the Border opens the doors of friendship and international relations. Learning Spanish is more than just a "foreign language," it is a way of life. In the six-week course, students will learn many useful phrases and questions as well as patterns of culture and customs. Any student will gain immeasurably in South of the Border.

**It's Raining Cats and Dogs:** This is a course on pet and animal care. We will be learning and sharing ideas about all kinds of pets, both domestic and wild. Outside guests include someone from the humane society, from the Santa Fe Zoo, a dog trainer, and a veterinarian. They will come in and help us study animals. Whether your pet is on a leash, in a cage, or in a tank, you can learn ways to make its life better.

**The Klassy Keyboard Kids:** The Piano Lab is equipped with *Keyboard Magic* filmstrips and cassette tapes. In addition to narrated instruction, the tapes contain many musical examples and a variety of songs played by a combo of professional musicians. Students have the opportunity to hear the music and the pleasure of accompanying the combo music for meaningful playing experience. Elton John will have nothing on you after this class.

**Lincoln Lingo:** This course is intended to give students (from at least two teams in the school) an outlet for journalistic interviewing and writing while producing a newspaper for the entire school (*The Lincoln Lingo*). Students should learn to: 1. Write an inverted lead and news story. 2. Conduct an interview from a list of questions and then write up a news or feature story from the interview.   3. Draw up a page layout. 4. Create and count a headline of two lines. 5. Know the difference between news, editorial, feature, and sports stories and demonstrate writing in all four. A field trip to the *Gainesville Sun* offices is a part of the course, as is viewing of newspapers from other middle and high schools.

**Middle Eastern Dance:** We're going to tone our muscles and learn to control them by doing simple exercises that stretch muscles. The exercises prepare the body for a form of dance which is a combination of Greek, Turkish, and Lebanese. A simple routine will be taught. Those students who wish will be encouraged to make costumes.

**The Five Faces of Man:** *Monday:* The Cultures of Mankind from Prehistoric to the Present. (A study of differences and similarities); *Tuesday:* The Communication Media of Mankind. (How these are used and may be used to enrich life); *Wednesday:* The Beliefs of Mankind. (Exploring the answers mankind has for questions beyond his knowledge); *Thursday:* The Literature, Arts and Music of Mankind. (How the spirit and attitudes of the times are expressed in art forms); *Friday:* The Great Games of Mankind. (Chess and Bridge)

**Walk a Mile in My Shoes:** Students are given the opportunity to become more aware of their own and others' needs and to develop the ability to cope with personal and group frustrations. We will use the interaction of the social seminar to examine and evaluate personal attitudes and biases toward drugs and drug-related issues.

We will use films and printed materials developed by the National Institute of Mental Health and field tested by the National Training Lab.

**The Olympics:** This exploratory course will be offered in conjunction with an interdisciplinary unit on ancient Greece taught during the core block. Aspects of the Olympics, the values of physical health, competition, and sporting conduct, will be stressed. A comparison of the modern games with the ancient games will be made with special reference to how world politics and economics have interfered with the modern games.

At the completion of the course, a special Olympics Day will be held for the whole team with the exploratory class in charge of organizing and officiating.

**Acting is Believing:** This course is designed to bring out the "ham" (which is in all of us) in students who feel they can better meet their needs to really express themselves only by acting or playing a part. The emphasis in this course is on creative dramatics. Students will participate in and be expected to show some proficiency in: (1) stage movement; (2) pantomine; (3) oral interpretation; (4) stage crafts; (5) stage make-up; (6) finally producing a one-act play.

Guest artists and speakers from the community—Hippodrome, Florida Players, Santa Fe Community College—will aid the class in an exploration of the theatrical arts. Materials needed for this course are scene paint, muslin flat boards, and stage make-up. The final class project will be filmed for showing on Channel 5.

## Baker County Middle School Mini-Course Program

### INTRODUCTION

Mini-courses are not clubs. They are exploratory activities for students and are planned the same as courses. Mini-courses meet Tuesday and Thursday during homebase, after students are scheduled. Mini-courses run nine weeks, with each course having around twenty-five students. Students choose their mini-courses.

Larry E. Kondas, Principal

Teacher: Mrs. C. Albury
Room: 402
Mini-course: Slim and Trim

A short course to help those who wish to start on a program to slim down and get in better shape for the coming year.
Fees: $2.00 for exercise book.

Teacher: Mr. A. Barrios
Room: 236
Mini-course: Space-Age Spanish

Basic Beginning Spanish. I am going to teach the following:

1. Common daily expressions used in conversation.
2. Numbers
3. Colors
4. Names of people
5. Words that teach: (a) the living room; (b) the grocery store; (c) the school; (d) the house; (e) the restaurant; (f) words used in traveling; (g) the family; and (h) the park.
6. The alphabet

Fees: None

Teacher: Ms. Batdorf
Room: 107
Mini-course: Mosaics
  Course starts out with paper mosaics working toward a seed mosaic done on wood.
Fees: $1.00

Teacher: S. Boutwell
Room: 400
Mini-course: Crocheting
  Students will learn the baisc steps in crocheting and make a simple item.
Materials: Students will purchase materials needed.
Fees: None

Teacher: C. Broomfield
Room: 103
Mini-course: News-Lab
  Course designed to help you learn about newspapers and the information you can get from them. Also, hints on how to report as it happens.
Materials: Students must furnish 1 newspaper per week.
Fees: None

Teacher: Ms. Burian
Room: 303
Mini-course: Chess
  Learn history and beginning moves in game. Build up gradually to proficient level of playing.
Materials: Chess sets
Fees: None

Teacher: Mr. Coleman
Room: 502
Mini-course: Conservation
  It will deal with ways to improve and save our air, water, and soil. Also, noise pollution will be covered.
Fees: None

Teacher: Sherrie Conrad
Room: 101
Mini-course: Introduction to Decoupage Art
  Decoupage is the art of blending pictures on various materials such as wooden plaques or pieces of tile.
Fees: $1.75

Teacher: Mrs. E. Gazdick
Room: Gym

Mini-course: Folk Dancing and Rhythms
  Rhythms—dance steps (depends on group).
Fees: None

Teacher: Mrs. G. Griffis
Room: 102
Mini-course: Embroidery
  Learn basic embroidery stitches used for pillowcases, aprons, dresser scarves, etc. We will complete one item of design by the end of the nine weeks.
Materials: Students must furnish their own 6-strand floss, needles, thimble, and a design to work on with a pillowcase, scarf, etc.
Fees: None

Teacher: Mrs. J. Griffis
Room: 302
Mini-course: Fun with Ceramics
  We'll begin with a plaster mold of your choice, use some paint, stain, and lots of imagination. The end product should be pretty enough to hang on any wall or set on any table.
Fees: $5.00

Teacher: Ms. Hartley
Room: 403
Mini-course: Beginner's Crochet
  This short course is to teach students how to use their time wisely and enjoyably while making useful articles that can be used in the home.
Materials: Must have a crochet hook, knitting yarn, and a beginner's crochet book.
Fees: None

Teacher: Mrs. Angie Hinson
Room: 404
Mini-course: Latin Heritage
  An introduction and general study of the Latin language, Roman history and mythology and English derivatives.
Fees: None

Teacher: Mrs. B. Hobbs
Room: 108
Mini-course: The Art of Painting
  Students will each do an original painting in acrylic paint.
Fees: $1.00 (Students who were in art club last year and already paid their $1.00 may finish the paintings they started and do not have to pay.)

Teacher: Ms. Huffington
Room: 301
Mini-course: String Art
   To learn how to create your own design using paper and colored pencils, then make your design using plywood, nails, thread, and yarn. Each student will furnish his own materials.
Fees: None

Teacher: Mr. R. James
Room: 401 (Band)
Mini-course: Music Appreciation
   We will listen to records, mostly classical, with the goal of learning to understand classical music. (If we can get a record player.)
Fees: None

Teacher: Mrs. S. Jasonek
Room: 408
Mini-course: Chess
   Students will have an opportunity to learn how to play chess, names of chess-men and what moves to make.
Materials: Chess set.
Fees: None

Teacher: Mrs. D. Kirkland
Room: Gym
Mini-course: Gymnastics
   Will cover stunts and tumbling, balance beam, rhythm, jumping rope, and others.
Fees: None

Teacher: Mr. R. Kline
Room: 501
Mini-course: Model Rockets That Fly
   Students will learn the basics of what makes a rocket fly, thrust ratio, aerodynamics, etc. Students will then build their own rocket kit and launch it. Students may keep their rockets.
Fees: $5.00

Teacher: Mr. L. Kondas
Room: New Cafe
Mini-course: World Records
   Using the Guiness Book of World Records, the students will identify various world records through the use of games, puzzles, discussions, etc.
Materials/Fees: Guiness Book or $2.00

Teacher: Mrs. D. Kramer
Room: 406
Mini-course: Newspaper
   The students will write and print a monthly newsletter about what is going on around the school. We hope to keep the student body aware of what is happening through this monthly newsletter.
Fees: None

Teacher: J. Kramer
Room: 207
Mini-course: Pen Lettering
   Use India ink, pen lettering pen points, and pen holders. Students will learn to letter in fancy styles for posters, charts, etc. without guides.
Fees: $2.00—$3.00

Teacher: Danny Lamb
Room: 405
Mini-course: Danny's Dynamic Drawing
   This mini-course will be designed to aid the semi-skilled person who has an interest in drawing. Helpful hints will be taught for giving dimension and clarity to drawn objects.
Fees: None

Teacher:
Room: 103
Mini-course: Parliamentary Procedure
   This course is designed to enable a student (through individual participation and practice) to conduct a business meeting using ten of the most frequently used parliamentary procedures.
Fees: None

Teacher: D. Melton
Room: 105
Mini-course: Shape Up (Girls only)
   Controlled exercise. Tips on personal grooming, cosmetology, and diet.
Fees: None

Teacher: Mr. E. Register
Room: 240
Mini-course: Macrame
   To learn the art of creative knot-tieing.
Fees: $2.00

Teacher: Brenda Rhoden
Room: 237
Mini-course: Basic Needlepoint

Beginning tips and basic stitches in needlepoint will be taught. A kit will be required (I will purchase) and a finished product will be kept by each student.
Fees: $4.50

Teacher: King S. Ruise, Sr.
Room: Gym
Mini-course: Gymnastics
Improvements in stunts and tumbling, wrestling and weight lifting.
Fees: None

Teacher: T. Scott
Room: 304
Mini-course: Smoking, Alcohol, Drugs
This is a course designed to allow the students to explore the effects of smoking, alcohol, and drugs on their lives.
Fees: None

Teacher: Marsha Starling
Room: 211
Mini-course: Crewel Embroidery
Students will learn simple crewel embroidery techniques.
Materials: Students will purchase.
Fees: None

Teacher: T. Starling
Room: Gym
Mini-course: An Appreciation of the Classic Books
To become aware of and appreciate the classics. Club will meet in the Media Center. Students should have above average reading ability and be able to give oral presentations to the rest of the groups.
Fees: None

Teacher: B. Taylor
Room: 407
Mini-course: Meet the Theatre (An Introduction to the Theatre)
This course will introduce the student to the various aspects of the theatre, such as history, architecture, construction, directing, acting, and art. It will be taught through lecture, study, films, slides, projects and field trips.
Fees: May be charged for projects and field trip materials.

Teacher: Ms. Tedrick
Room: 238
Mini-course: Quilling (or crochet)
Make a snow-flake using the old method of twisting paper on a quill.
Fee: $1.50

Teacher: Mr. Voorhees
Room: 104
Mini-course: Speech
A course designed to explore facets of speaking and oral communications. Public speaking, theatre, drama, etc. will be covered.

Teacher: J. Weldon
Room: Media Center
Mini-course: Make-Show-Tell
Each student will learn to make slides by using the Visual Maker and a cassette tape. The finished product could be used to illustrate a class project.
Fees: $5.00

Teacher: D. Kingdom
Room: 269
Mini-course: Improving Learning and Memory Skills
Students will be taught that learning is through the five senses; that learning is retained best when one is attentive; that recall (memory) is best when one associates new knowledge with old knowledge.
Fees: None

Teacher: J. Williams
Room: 235
Mini-course: Line Design and String Pictures
The students will learn some geometry, will do some line designs on paper, and then some string drawings with thread and needle.
Fees: $ .40

## Niphur Middle School Co-curricular Program

### INTRODUCTION

The Co-curricular Program at the Niphur Middle School is an important part of your total educational program. It is designed to give you a chance to explore a variety of areas that we hope will interest you.

How often have you found something interesting and wished you could learn more about it? Here is your chance! You might find that teachers have interests very much like your own. How much you learn depends on you! The choice is yours.

### SCHEDULE OF SESSIONS

The Co-curricular program, consisting of eighty different courses, will be offered during the last periods of the day on each Wednesday and Friday. Six different four-week sessions have been scheduled (three each semester), having either seven or eight class meetings each. The number of meetings depends upon whether a holiday might fall on a scheduled Wednesday or Friday.

The sixth grade will participate in each of the six sessions, while the seventh grade will alternate intramural activities with their co-curricular courses. The class time for each period will be 59 minutes in length. This time will be made available through the shortening of each "mod" throughout the day. A calendar showing the dates of the co-curricular sessions and the dates when registration will take place follows.

#### CO-CURRICULAR PROGRAM DATES

| | |
|---|---|
| October 6 and 7 | Registration |
| October 10 through 29 | 1st Session |
| November 3 and 4 | Registration |
| November 12 thru December 10 | 2nd Session |
| January 5 and 6 | Registration |
| January 7 thru 30 | 3rd Session |
| February 5 and 6 | Registration |
| February 11 thru March 5 | 4th Session |
| March 11 and 12 | Registration |
| March 17 thru April 9 | 5th Session |
| April 22 and 23 | Registration |
| April 28 thru May 21 | 6th Session |

### REGISTRATION PROCEDURE

1. Assemblies will be held for both the sixth grade and the seventh grade classes for the purpose of explaining the entire program, its course offerings, and the registration procedures to be followed.

2. Each session will last four weeks, with the fifth week left open for registration for the next session.

BY PERMISSION OF Niphur Middle School, Kirkwood, Missouri. Tom Moeller, Principal.

3. Seventh grade students will be given first choice in all courses, as they have to alternate with intramurals. Thus, the seventh grade students will have three full intramural sessions and three co-curricular sessions. The sixth grade will be able to participate in all of the co-curricular sessions, as they will have their intramural activities on a day to be set aside during their physical education period. Scheduling for this year makes this arrangement necessary. A rotation system for registering by teams will be set up for each grade to ensure as much fairness as possible in getting first-choice chances.

4. Students will be given a Co-curricular Handbook at the co-curricular assembly.

5. Students should then study the handbook and make decisions regarding which courses they might wish to take.

6. Students are encouraged to take the handbook home and discuss possible choices with their parents.

7. After discussion with their parents and having given thought to the choices they might wish to make, students should make a list of the order of those choices, i.e., first choice, second choice, etc. Make at least five in rank order of preference. This is necessary due to the fact that some courses may be found to be filled when you attempt to register.

8. A student wishing to register for a given course and finding it filled in that session would then go immediately and register for his or her second choice.

9. Students cannot be permitted to repeat courses and will be required to choose from a different course area each session.

10. Registration will take place in the cafeteria, where tables will be set up by subject matter area, i.e., Language Arts, Social Studies, Science, etc.

11. Each course is numbered within a given subject area, i.e., Language Arts is the 100 series, Social Studies is the 200 series, etc. Every course has a number code and a title. Thus, for example, Creative Writing is LA (Language Arts) 101 and Ancient History is SS 201.

12. Each student, having been given an enrollment card, will go to the subject area table to register for the course of his or her choice. If the course is NOT FILLED, the student will be enrolled and his enrollment card will be placed in the course packet to be given to the teacher of that course. The student will be given a slip (receipt) that will list his name, the number and name of the course, and the number of the room in which it is to meet. A copy of this receipt will be given to his or her homeroom teacher.

13. At the end of the course, the teacher of the course will send the enrollment card to the students' home-room teacher to be used again for registration for the next session. A rating scale to report the degree of the student's cooperation and conduct is provided on the enrollment card but no grade, as such, will be given.

14. All students are required to participate in the co-curricular program, however, in exceptional cases, going to the library for study is a possible option.

15. Transferring from one course to another is to be discouraged. In an exceptional case, a student may change his course, but he must have the permission of the two teachers involved and then obtain the approval of the Co-curricular Coordinator, Mr. Pennycuick.

16. Due to costs that are involved in some courses for materials, rental of a facility (swimming pool), or transportation, a nominal fee will have to be charged. Fee courses and the amount of the fee are listed with the description of the course in this Handbook.

17. Some courses may require your bringing some material or a tool from home. Your co-curricular teacher will let you know what you must bring.

## LANGUAGE ARTS—100

**LA 101: Creative Writing** Want to visit strange and exotic places? Create weird monsters? Describe the real world? Release your feelings? Writers do this and so can you!

Mr. Greg Mayer                    Room 207 H

**LA 102: Dramatics** This course will offer basic techniques in creative drama with all the fun of acting and self-expression. The class will emphasize pantomime, original skits, and improvisation.

Mrs. Jeannette Corrigan              Room 100 S

**LA 103: Great Books and Short Stories** We will read and discuss one full-length classic such as *Robinson Crusoe* or several short stories chosen by the group.

Mrs. Virginia Dennison
Mrs. Ginny Clark                          Room 204 S

**LA 104: Haiku** Have you tried to paint with words, to express color, sound, or movement? We'll write, paint, draw, print, and sew using Haiku.

Mrs. Maxine Mace                          Room 204 N

**LA 105: Journalism** We will study the function of a newspaper versus that of television and radio in the dissemination of news. We will write news stories, human interest stories, sports stories, editorials, columns, headline writing, etc.

Mrs. Lemoyne Peters                       Room 214 N

**LA 106: Mythology** Learn all about Greek, Roman, and Norse mythology—the stories of their gods and goddesses.

Mrs. Frank Fisher                         Room 102 N

**LA 107: Newspapers (How to Read Them)** Can you read the newspaper? Do you know that the newspaper contains more than the comic page to interest you? Enroll—and discover the inside story.

Mrs. Clare Hogerty                        Room 108 S

**LA 108: Penmanship** Would you like to improve your handwriting? This course will focus on legibility. Letter formation, size, slant, spacing, and alignment will be stressed.

Mrs. Mary Armistead                       Room 211 N

**LA 109: Poetry** Enjoy poetry by reading and writing various types of poems. We will begin with simple poems and progress on to the more complex forms of poetry.

Mrs. Dixie Crawford                       Room 210 N

**LA 110: Public Speaking** Afraid to speak up? Conquer the fear the easy way by enrolling in Public Speaking. This course will give students the opportunity to do television and radio commercials as well as funny monologues.

Mr. Vernal Beckmann                       Room 109 N

**LA 111: Puppetry** Learn how to make your own puppet from scratch. We not only will make our

puppets, but we will make our own scenery and produce our own plays.

Mrs. Martha Wagner                        Room 205 S

**LA 112: Reading Games** This will be a course designed to create and construct various reading games to be used within the classroom during the twenty-three minute reading mod.

Mrs. Margaret Cowden
Mrs. Nancy Lors                           Room 112 N

**LA 113: Short Stories** This course is to trace the background of the short story in world literature, and to learn something about great writers of short stories that will appeal to teenagers. Films of some of the great short stories will be shown. An opportunity to write a short story will be given to you in the last two meetings.

Mrs. Elizabeth Via                        Room 105 S

**LA 114: Application of Stage Make-Up** Ever wonder what it might feel and look like if you were transformed into your favorite monster character, circus clown, or animal figure? This course will provide you with some of the basic techniques in applying a stage make-up through the use of materials employed by professional actors.

Mrs. Susan Tanton                         Room 210 S

## SOCIAL STUDIES 200

**SS 201: Ancient History** Why be concerned with what happened long ago? We'll explore some phases of early Greek and Roman civilization to see if they have any importance for us today. Research, reading, relating.

Mrs. Connie Coomer                        Room 213 N

**SS 202: Black History** The course will consist, basically, of Black History from slavery to contemporary trends. Various sources will be studied and discussed.

Mr. Eldridge Bryant                       Room 101 S

**SS 203: Civil War** This course will be a general overview of the strategies and major battles of the war.

Dr. James Fox                            Room 105 N

**SS 204: Colonial History** Films on colonial Williamsburg showing early American crafts followed by six lessons on the great variety of American crafts.

> Mrs. Betty Summar   Room 102 S
> (Sessions 1, 2, and 3 only!)

**SS 205: Current Events** Reading and discussion of what's going on in the world right now. Newsweek magazine will be used. Students will select events of interest to follow over a four-week course.

> Mrs. Lois Spano   Room 205 S

**SS 206: Geography (Missouri and Its History)** Indian lore in connection with names of rivers, counties, and regions. Hopefully, we will have time to explore some bicentennial stories and data.

> Mrs. Grace Ferrier   Room 208 N

**SS 207: Heraldry** Originally the designs the warriors put on their weapons and shields were to tell friend from enemy. Now used to tell from which family a person comes. Learn what their designs mean and how you can design your own coat-of-arms.

> Mrs. Patricia Fitzroy   Room 108 N

**SS 208: "Kids and Cops" (Students and the Law)** The course is designed to acquaint young adults with a variety of interesting topics in today's field of law enforcement. Included are a field trip and guest speakers.

> Officer Michael Chastain   Counselor's Office
>
> Kirkwood Police Department  Conference Room

**SS 209: National Parks and Camping** Ever discover wild skunks at your feet? Share in funny and potentially disastrous camping experiences. Discussion and demonstration of equipment . . . food, clothing, and first aid. Visit National Parks through slides.

> Mrs. Frances Bonebrake   Room 103 N

**SS 210: World Travel** We will talk about countries I have visited, using reference materials, pictures, and objects (money, jewelry, etc.). Students will then bring materials and information about countries they have visited or know about.

> Mrs. Charlotte Biggs   Library

**SS 211: World of Work** This course will trace the World of Work from ancient times through the middle ages into modern industrial society, with a close look at a twentieth century industry of our choice.

> Mrs. Ruth Coombs   Room 104 N

## SCIENCE 300

**SCI 301: Animals** A general discussion which will be accompanied by live specimens (when available) of the many species of birds, mammals, reptiles, and amphibians found throughout the world.

> Mr. George Brandon   Room 5 S

**SCI 302: Astronomy** We will explore what we know about the universe, including the sun, moon, and planets, as well as those bodies outside of our solar system.

> Miss Bonnie Meyer   Room 106 N

**SCI 303: Basic First Aid** This is a course in basic first aid which you will use for the rest of your life. This course is a confidence builder to help keep you cool and calm in times of accidents or emergencies while caring for yourself and others.

> Nurse Rosemary Diaz   Nurse's Office

**SCI 304: Gardening** Exchange of information about planning a garden and starting seedlings. Sharing magazines, particularly those concerned with organic gardening. Guest speakers from Shaw's Garden and government agencies.

> Mrs. Betty Summa   Room 102 S
> (Sessions 4, 5, and 6 only.)

**SCI 305: Model Building** Emphasis will be placed on talking about model building techniques. Showing of completed models and movies about model building will be featured. There is a possibility of field trips depending upon the interests of the group.

> Mr. Robert Westerdale   Room 113 N

**SCI 306: Photography** Develop your skill in taking pictures. Learn about cameras and their features as well as film development and enlarging techniques. Students must have their own camera and film.

> Mr. Brian Natheny   Room 1 S

**SCI 307: Plants** In this course we will grow plants from seeds and cuttings, make clay pots and macrame hangers, learn to transfer hanging plants properly, to grow a miniature garden, and to plant a terrarium.

Mrs. Helen Meatte                    Room 4 S

## MATHEMATICS 400

**Math 401: Slide Rule, Calculators, and Adding Machines** Students will learn how to multiply, divide, square numbers, and find square roots using the slide rule. Students will also have the opportunity to learn how to use calculators for addition, subtraction, multiplication, and division.

Miss Vickie Kurczynski              Room 106 S

**Math 402: Bridge** This course will include basic skills for playing the world's most popular card game, contract bridge. You will learn to count points, bid, and practice playing out hands.

Mrs. Frances Maginnis               Room 201 S

**Math 403: Chess** Attack! Capture! Checkmate! Move into co-curricular chess. Join the tournament. Match wits with other experienced players. Challenge other schools. Improve your game.

Mrs. Julie Bradbury                 Room 202 S

**Math 404: Computers** Learn about computers and how they are used. Solve problems.

Mrs. Cathy Ahillen                  Room 207 S

**Math 405: Darts** In this course the rules of various dart games will be learned, as well as the basic techniques and strategies in throwing darts. The emphasis will be on practicing dart throwing skills by playing various dart games. A tournament will be held during the last two meetings.

Mr. Terry Diehl                    Cafeteria (SW)

**Math 407: Introduction to Navigation** Historical background of navigation. Relationship of time, direction, latitude, and longitude. Importance of maps, charts, tables, etc. How instruments such as compass and sextant are used. Construction of simple instruments models. (Time and material permitting!)

Mr. Russell Eddington              Room 203 S

**Math 408: Word Games and Puzzles** Mind stretchers and brain teasers of every variety.

Mrs. Jane Chambers                  Room 6 S

## ART 500

**Art 501: Artificial Flower Making** Students will make an arrangement of fabric flowers in a container plus large tissue paper flowers, yarn pom-poms, Kleenex boutonnieres, burlap flowers, and aluminum foil roses.

Mrs. Mary B. Marshall               Room 110 S

**Art 502: Clay Sculpture** Create your own compositions by modeling and carving clay. If at first you don't succeed, remold, and try again.

Mrs. Dorothy Nassler                Room 208 S

**Art 503: Decoupage** Decoupage consists of cutting paper to be applied to a surface, usually wood, and covered with coats of modge-podge to produce beautiful objects.

Mrs. Norma Owen                     Room 113 N

**Art 504: Drawing** Drawing techniques will be developed through the use of pencil, ink, felt pens, and charcoal. The student will draw from posed models and nature studies.

Mr. Ken Webber                      Room 209 S

**Art 505: Linoleum Block Printing** Students will carve original designs into linoleum blocks, and use the blocks to print on paper and cloth.

Mr. Barry Buchek                    Room 214 N

**Art 506: Macrame** Macrame is the ancient art of knot-tieing. We will learn the two basic macrame knots and their variations. They will enable you to make belts, bracelets, wall-hangings, plant or candle holders, etc.

Mrs. Cathy Ahillen                  Room 207 S

**Art 507: Paper Quilling** Quilling, also known as paper filigree, paper mosaic, or paper lace, is the art of rolling thin strips of paper into various shapes and using the shapes to form designs.

Mrs. Peggy Presley
Mrs. Mary Adolphsen                 Room 201 N

**Art 508: Pottery and Clay Sculpture** This course will concentrate on the methods of building a pot or sculpture piece from clay. Work will be fired or glazed. If the class is small, there will be an opportunity to work on the potter's wheel.

Mrs. Donna Weber                    Room 208 S

**Art 509: Shadow Boxes** This class will learn to create the shadow box effect on a plaque. We will develop the art of paper cutting in order to achieve a three-dimensional effect on a plaque.

Mrs. Shirley Kleiman                Room 202 N

**Art 510: Stained Glass** Students will make small items from stained glass. They will design the item, select and cut out glass, and lead the glass together.

Mr. Ray Kelly                          Room 9 S
(Session 5 only!)

**Art 511: Watercolor** The students will be taught the proper use of their equipment and materials, how to blend colors, various watercolor techniques, and perhaps painting from nature or still life. We hope to plan at least one outside painting experience.

Mrs. Virginia Hopmann
Mrs. Ila Bruns                         Room 212 N

## SHOP AND HOME ECONOMICS 600

**SHE 601: Bachelor Cooking** A basic introduction to cooking. Students will become familiar with cooking techniques and terms. By the end of the course, the bachelor will not become a junior chef but he will know his way around the kitchen. Fee $2.00.

Mrs. Estelle Smith                     Room 110 S

**SHE 602: Christmas Decorations** Learn to make Christmas wreaths and other Christmas decorations out of pine cones and other materials. A great hobby and a lot of fun. Fee: $1.50

Mrs. Brenda Matthews                   Room 9 S
(Sessions 1 and 2 only!)

**SHE 603: Crewel Embroidery** Beginners will be taught the basic stitches to embroider. A picture, pillow, or other project in colorful yarn will be a project goal. Experienced embroiderers are also welcome.

Mrs. Judy Cassidy          Office Conference
                                          Room

**SHE 604: Diet and Nutrition** You are what you eat! Learn how to eat the right foods daily to build the best you.

Mrs. Marydelle Thomaides               Room 101 N

**SHE 605: Dip-N-Drape Dolls** Dolls are made on a soda pop bottle with styrofoam balls for head and hands. These are covered with a Dip-N-Drape fabric (dipped in a solution and draped on the bottle), dried, and then painted. Fee $1.00

Mrs. Sue Trog                          Room 9 S
(Sessions 1, 3, and 5 only!)

**SHE 606: Home Repair** Typical home repair problems: electrical, plumbing, painting, replac-

ing, and fixing. Learn to be handy around the house. Save money!

Mr. David Young                        Room 3 S

**SHE 607: Beginning Knitting** This course will include such things as casting on, straight knitting stitch, and purling. A simple project of the student's choice will be made.

Mrs. Pat Cravens                         Library

**SHE 608: Needlepoint** Student will learn to needlepoint (make a design on needlepoint canvas using a needle and yarn). Each student will create a design, transfer it to a 6″ × 6″ canvas, and stitch it with various colors of yarn.

Mrs. Saralee Edler                     Room 107 S

**SHE 609: Patchwork Pillows** Would you like to make an attractive patchwork pillow for your bed or for a gift? In this class, you will learn how to design, cut, and sew material to make a pillow.

Mrs. Lois Mueller                      Room 206 S

**SHE 610: Sewing** Learn how to sew! The various sewing techniques will be taught in this course.

Mrs. Tomasina Hassler            Counselor's
                                    Office Area

**SHE 611: Wood Carving and Decorative Painting** Learn to create interesting and useful wood objects. Woodcarving is fun and easy to do. Make holiday gifts.

Mrs. Gloria Simms                      Room 8 S
(Sessions 2 and 4 only!)

## FOREIGN LANGUAGE 700

**FL 701: French** Learn conversational French, French words, phrases, their origins, and meanings. Songs, games, and stories will be taught.

Mrs. Doris Shreve                      Room 206 N

**FL 702: Russian** Introduction to Russian conversation and culture. We will look at the alphabet, listen to songs, try Russian food, have discussions about the Soviet Union, and see slides and souvenirs from Russia.

Miss Joy Dressel                       Room 205 N

**FL 703: Spanish** Did you ever want to speak another language? Well, here's your chance! In this course, you will learn easy and useful Spanish phrases.

Miss Sheri Schwarzbach                 Room 110 N

## COMMERCIAL 800

**C-801: Audio-Visual Equipment** This course is designed to teach students how to operate movie projectors, video equipment, television camera, etc. Students may produce their own television show on video-tape.

Mrs. Laneta Chadwick     Room 209 N

**C-802: Shorthand** Shorthand is an easy to learn technique in writing words in brief forms. Learn to take your notes in shorthand. A lesson with a future!

Mrs. Alma Webb     Room 203 N

**C-803: Typing** This course teaches the basic skills needed to operate a typewriter and to type by the touch method. This course is designed for those not presently enrolled in typing.

Mrs. Gail Humphrey     Room 111 N

## MUSIC 900

**MU 901: Singing** This course is designed to give students experience in singing music in harmony and to show that singing is fun. Current songs of the day will be used.

Mrs. Lorene Puchbauer     Room 10 S

**MU 902: Grand Opera** This course is designed to introduce the student to operatic music. What an opera is; types of singing voices; and how they are used in a musical play.

Mr. J. E. McCann     Faculty Room
(Sessions 3 and 4 only!)

**MU 903: Musical Comedy or Light Opera** The course will include learning and singing songs from many favorite musicals such as "Oklahoma" and "West Side Story." We will also study the plots and perform some scenes within the class.

Mrs. Carol Minichiello     Faculty Room

**MU 904: Music Fundamentals** A basic course describing the theory and harmony of music.

Mr. Stan Topfer     Room 11 S

**MU 905: Recorder** Learn to play a recorder! This course will give you the basic instruction necessary to learn to play this simple, yet unique, instrument.

Mr. Ken Black     Room 103 S

**MU 906: Rock Music** Why does Alice Cooper act the way he does? Whose style is Mick Jagger imitating? What is a "phase shifter"? An echoplex? Everything you always wanted to know about ROCK but were afraid to ask!

Mr. Greg Mayer     Room 207 N
(Sessions 4, 5, and 6 only!)

## PHYSICAL EDUCATION 1000

**PE 1001: Baton** This course will cover the fundamentals of baton twirling and the basic techniques of footwork. Note: A student interested in enrolling should have his or her own balanced and measured baton.

Mrs. Donna Ahlquist     Student Center

**PE 1002: Football (How to watch it!)** This course is designed to introduce the student to football, its history and development, and terms and rules. It is particularly recommended for girls, who may have had less exposure to this sport than boys have had.

Mr. J. E. McCann     Cafeteria
(Sessions 1 and 2 only!)

**PE 1003: Ice Skating** Skating instruction for beginners and pleasure skating for the more advanced skaters. Instruction will be given in both hockey style and figure skating for those who desire instruction.

NOTE: Students who sign up for this course, which will be held at the Kirkwood Park Ice Rink, will have to arrange for their own transportation home after the session! A bus will get you there, but will not be able to bring you back to school! Also, to help defray the costs involved in transporting you to the rink, a fee of $1.50 will have to be charged for the course.

Mr. Thomas Moeller - Supervisor
Mrs. Betty Jo Harper - Instructor
Mrs. Joanne Kramer - Instructor
Mrs. Jean Szpak - Instructor     Kirkwood
Ice Rink

**PE 1004: Riflery and Gun Safety** This course is designed to instruct the young person in the basic skills of shooting with special emphasis on firearm safety. BB rifles ONLY will be used. Rifles furnished for use.

Kirkwood Police Officers     Cafeteria

**PE 1005: Swimming** This course will be designed to afford the students the opportunity for recreational swimming as well as teaching the basic strokes. Time will be allowed for water games and contests.

NOTE: Students who wish to sign up for this course will be transported to Meramec College but will not be brought back to the school. Each student will have to arrange his own transportation home. In addition, due to the costs involved in pool rental and bus transportation (one way), a fee of $2.00 for the course will be required. Students should bring their own swimming suit and towel. (Cap is required.)

Mr. Mike Reger
Mr. Doug Pott          Meramec College Pool

## ACTIVITY 4
### Develop a version of your own.

Based on your knowledge of Special Exploratory Programs and the examples from Activity 3, in one page or so, describe your own version of the Special Exploratory Program. Consider the following factors before you begin.

1. How will the emphasis be balanced between academic and unified arts perspectives?
2. How long will the basic time period be (in terms of weeks)?
3. How frequently will students be involved? That is, how much time per week?
4. How will student effort be evaluated?
5. How will the interests of both faculty and students be taken into account?

Save your "thumbnail sketch" of the Special Exploratory Program to share with your colleagues or classmates. Be certain to ask them for feedback on your ideas.

## ACTIVITY 5
### Analyze the school schedule.

**A.** Get a copy of the master schedule of your selected school. Examine the schedule closely. What does the school schedule reveal about the nature of the exploratory emphasis? Record your analysis and save it to share.

**B.** Examine the master schedule again. This time, suggest some ways the schedule might be changed to allow for the implementation of one of the exploratory programs from the readings or your own version. Prepare to share the redesigned schedule with others and to get their feedback on whether it seems workable or not.

## ACTIVITY 6
### Develop a single roster of exploratory courses.

Compare the three sample programs in Activity 3 and prepare a single list of activities by eliminating duplication or combining those which overlap. Then add to this list all the others that you can think of. (If you are working with a group, combine all of your lists into one master list. Then brainstorm and add as many others as your group can think of.)

What do you think of your final list of offerings? Is it comprehensive enough to cover both academics and unified arts? Does it look broad enough to cater to the interests of both teachers and students? Will almost everyone be able to choose something that will interest them? Are the activities on your list capable of fitting into the time frames which have been recommended earlier? Does the school have adequate resources for most of these items? Have you kept to a minimum the ones which require large fees or special equipment?

Share your final listing with others in the school for which you have designed the program. Ask for their reactions and include all the materials in your portfolio.

## ACTIVITY 7
### Design a pilot program.

This activity invites you to design a faculty proposal for piloting a Special Exploratory Program in a selected school. Here are some things that are important to consider before such an undertaking:

**A.** Prepare an evaluation of the school's current exploratory efforts that involves the school's faculty.

**B.** Assuming that this evaluation reveals a need to improve the exploratory aspects of the curriculum, secure the permission of the faculty to design a proposal to investigate alternative methods. Invite volunteers to serve on an ad hoc committee.

**C.** Seek several interested parents and students to work on the ad hoc committee.

**D.** Prepare a briefing for the committee members on the purpose of the exploratory emphasis. Be sure to include the three examples of Special Exploratory Programs from Activity 3.

**E.** As a committee, design a Special Exploratory Program pilot proposal which will be presented to the faculty. Consider the following tasks:

1. Write the objectives of the program in a convincing way.
2. Compile a list of tentative offerings that will involve everyone. You will need to adapt it later, based on the talents and interests of teachers and students.
3. Design a way of choosing which of the list of tentative offerings will be a part of the pilot program taught by the faculty and others.
4. Design a method of registration. Some schools register students through homebase advisor-advisee groups, others use a process similar to college course registration. It is important to build in as much student choice as possible.

5. Scour the community for resource people to teach offerings for which no faculty member volunteers.
6. Investigate the possibility of students teaching some activities with faculty guidance.
7. Devise a way to pilot the program without major changes in the school's present schedule.
8. Make suggestions for the length of the pilot program (e.g., six weeks), frequency of sessions (e.g., three times a week), and a way of holding students accountable for their participation.
9. Design a method of evaluating the program at the end of the pilot period which allows for input from faculty, students, and parents. Include these data in the decision of whether to implement the program on a permanent basis.

**F.**    Present this pilot program to the faculty and administration. If they decide to implement the pilot program, the faculty should form an Exploratory Program Committee. Allow at least six weeks lead time between the decision to try the program and the beginning of the program itself. The Exploratory Committee should supervise the following activities:

1. Final design of the list of program offerings and schedule.
2. Explanation of program to parents, students, etc.
3. Registration for program offerings.
4. Assignment of students to program options.
5. Monitoring the pilot program.
6. Evaluation of the pilot program when completed.
7. Providing results of evaluation to all concerned.

Remember to keep careful notes on all of these activities for inclusion in your portfolio.

## ACTIVITY 8
### Create your own mini-course.

This activity presumes that you are or may soon be a teacher in a school that has a functioning Special Exploratory Program. If this is the case, you will be expected to participate in the program, and this implies that you will be designing exploratory experiences for you and your students.

**A.**    Examine the earlier learning activities in this chapter for examples of the types of exploratory mini-courses with which you may be dealing. From the list of mini-courses, select those in which you are interested enough to serve as teacher or facilitator. You may want to share the list of your selections with someone in the school who has the responsibility for organizing a Special Exploratory Program.

**B.**    From your list in section A, select one mini-course that you haven't taught but would like to teach. Assuming that you have a total of fifteen to twenty class meetings, develop a course description which includes the title, the subject area(s), course objectives, planned learning activities, tentative schedule, and a method of evaluating student work. Submit your final product to the instructor or other person responsible for designing the Special Exploratory Program. Keep careful notes.

## ACTIVITY 9
**Evaluate what you have learned.**

If you have completed this chapter successfully, you should be able to report and share information and materials on:

- The rationale for an exploratory curriculum in modern middle schools.
- Ways in which effective middle schools infuse their programs with an exploratory emphasis.
- Examples of special exploratory programs.
- Ways to modify a school schedule to accommodate a greater emphasis on exploration.
- Your version of an exploratory mini-course.
- The process of designing, implementing, and evaluating special exploratory programs.

## NEXT STEPS

If, after completing this chapter, you want to further your interest in the exploratory curriculum, here are a few suggestions:

1. Visit another school that has an effective exploratory program. Compare this program to those with which you are already familiar.
2. Secure a place on the annual conference program of your state middle school association. Share what you are doing in your exploratory program with those who attend.
3. Develop an informational brochure describing the exploratory program in your school. Circulate it to interested community leaders and nearby schools.
4. Arrange a teacher workday when the focus of the day is on improving the exploratory program. Design the process and the schedule for the day.

# CHAPTER 8

# THE TEACHER AS ADVISOR

This chapter will yield the maximum amount of learning to teachers who are or wish to be involved in a school day which sets aside a regular period of time devoted to affective education. Some schools call it a homebase or homeroom time; others call it advisor-advisee time, small group guidance, or even the "fourth R" (relationships). If you are involved in such a situation, are familiar with one, or anticipate finding yourself in one soon, you are probably also one of the many teachers in middle schools all over the nation who are struggling to make the most of the opportunity. This chapter is designed to introduce you to resources, and to help you design an *effective, affective* education program.

Two special concepts, then, add up to affective education: the development of growth-producing interpersonal relationships between teachers and students; and, that part of the school day which focuses primarily on the socio-emotional development of students. Both are important parts of the emphasis on personal development in fully functioning middle schools. This chapter focuses on the second of the two functions as a context within which better teacher-student relationships can develop. If you agree that this is important, and you want to learn more, proceed to the learning activities.

## ACTIVITY 1
### Examine the idea of affective education and how it is practiced.

**A.**   Activity 1 is intended to give you an overview of what affective education means and how it is implemented in middle level schools. Read, "Affective Education and the Advisor-Advisee Program: One Teacher's View." When you have finished, make some notes on your answers to the questions that follow. Save the notes.

1. What percentage of the middle school teachers that you know would be comfortable with the concepts and commitments presented in this selection?
2. What concerns do you have about these ideas?
3. How does the program in your school, or schools you know about, match up with the descriptions offered in these readings?
4. How do you think students in your school would (or do) respond to a program like this? Parents? Administrators?
5. What are the advantages of such a program, for you? The disadvantages?

**B.**   If you are involved in some type of regular affective education program with students, the first step toward improving what you're doing is an analysis of how things are working now. If you are not now involved, this chapter will be more meaningful to you if you become familiar with a program in operation in a school that you can visit. Prepare a summary description and analysis of the program you select, using the following questions as an outline.

1. What are the key features of the affective education program? Describe it in enough detail that an outsider would have a clear mental picture of it. Why is it being done? If the school you know about does not have such a program, why not?
2. Is the faculty familiar with the program's objectives? What about the students? Parents? Administrators?
3. What percentage of the faculty agrees with and seems comfortable with the whole idea—if the percentage is small, have you any hypotheses about why this is so?
4. How do the students respond? Why do you think it is this way?
5. What are the facts about the schedule? How much time do you have each day or week? Is this enough? Does the time of day during which the program occurs communicate anything about its importance relative to the other things in the schedule?
6. Describe, in as much detail as possible, what seems to happen in the program. What sort of activity is typical? Do the activities match the objectives? What are your personal reactions?

If these questions have totally confused you, it is probably because the idea of a formal affective education program is new to you. Find someone who has had some appropriate experience and seek clarification from them. Perhaps this is a good time for more reading about such programs.

## Affective Education and the Advisor-Advisee Program: One Teacher's View

As the back-to-basics movement sweeps the country, middle schools are being shaped and reshaped in response to the public's demand for accountability in education. Indeed I am concerned about our acknowledged failure to teach basic skills to many of our country's children. It is evident to me that such skills are in fact survival tools for those attempting to function effectively in our diversified and complex society. Even so, as I watch our pedagogic pendulum swing back to the three R's, I am concerned that we are losing touch with what is equally basic—our role in helping kids become happy, self-actualized, and fully functioning human beings.

As evidenced by the difficulties inherent in adolescence and by the continually recurring adolescent tragedies, kids in the middle grades need special help in

Nancy Doda, By Permission, From *The Middle School Journal*, Vol. VII, No. 3, September 1976, pp. 8-10.

their struggle to grow. If we fail to provide help, I am afraid that not only will many children grow up without the skills to read but they may grow up never fully realizing all of their potential capabilities and talents, never learning how to make decisions and formulate values, never learning how to relate to others in a meaningful and satisfying way, and never acknowledging their worth as human beings.

Middle schools and middle school teachers have a unique and exciting opportunity to finally make the thousands of affective objectives written in the hundreds of curriculum guides come to life in viable school programs. As a teacher in a relatively new middle school, I have experienced the struggles and the successes in an attempt to start an affective education program and I am eager to share my discoveries and conclusions.

## I. The Schoolwide Picture

Persons involved in the middle school readily concede that one of its fundamental goals is that of bridging the gap between the elementary school and the high school. With regard to teacher-student relationships and student personal development, this bridging characteristic is particularly important.

One way middle schools have attempted to serve this bridging function is by having some small-group, affective education program. Typically, these programs have been labeled Homebase, Advisor-Advisee, or Small Group Guidance. Basically, an advisor-advisee program, as an example, consists of assigning every teacher, specialists included, a small group of approximately twenty-five students which would meet as a group for some scheduled part of the school day. In this advisor-advisee class, the teacher serves as the advisor, school expert, and affective guide for each child in the group.

Implementing a program like the one roughly defined is an involved task. In fact many difficulties arise because of a failure to consider the time, planning and commitment necessary for success. Here are some suggestions to consider:

1. Staff development appears to be an essential prerequisite for successful affective education programs. Often difficulties result because teachers, and thus students, don't know what such a program is designed to do nor how they could achieve effective results. Programs attempted without adequate teacher preparation could make the affective education program disappointing to both teachers and students, resulting in increased discipline problems, extra, unrewarded work for teachers and a tendency to turn off to the idea of affective education altogether.

2. If possible, an advisor-advisee class should be smaller than the average academic class of thirty to thirty-five. One way some schools have managed to cut down on the teacher-pupil ratio is by involving almost every available adult in the school.

3. It seems to be important that these classes, although nonacademic, meet every day at a regularly scheduled time. Further, in some schools it has been more readily accepted and valued by students when it is scheduled at the opening of the school day. In doing so, teachers and administrators are openly admitting its importance and students are less apt to view it as free time. Opening the school

day with such a program has other advantages as well. It gives those students with problems from home a chance to work through difficulties before beginning their academic work. Naturally, students will be better able to learn if they are not troubled or upset. Scheduling such classes at the start of the day is certainly not the only workable arrangement. It should be scheduled, however, at a place which does not suggest it is merely an appendage added on to an already complete school day.

4. In schools where homebase or advisor-advisee classes are in operation, the length of the class ranges from twenty to thirty-five minutes long. If the period is to be uninterrupted, twenty-five minutes seems to be adequate with often-restless middle school kids. On the other hand, if schoolwide announcements, scheduling and related paperwork are to be continually interrupting factors, more time may be desirable.

5. Teachers ought to have freedom and flexibility in designing their own homebase or advisor-advisee classes. It would be advisable, however, if prior to implementing such a program, schoolwide affective goals could be determined. Whether or not career education and sex education, for example, are to be taught via these special classes is something to be decided for the entire school. Then, copies of these objectives ought to be available for all teachers for use in designing their class activities.

6. Counselors can play a vital role initiating and maintaining a complete affective education program in the middle school. In the beginning stages, they are a number one source for teacher-training and they can continue to aid teachers in the designing of special units or activities for their individual classes. In addition, the fact that kids are now in groups especially designed for affective reasons could make it possible for counselors to meet with many more students for counseling and testing purposes.

This list is not intended to rule out other considerations, perhaps more specific, which deserve attention. It is simply to serve as a guide for those in the planning stages.

## II. Inside the Classroom

Though decisions made concerning the schoolwide structure of an affective education program are critical and may either hinder or help individual classroom teachers, I am convinced that what goes on in the advisor-advisee class between the teacher and her students is the final proof of the program. Organizing this class in a way that allows the teacher to be the advisor, school expert and affective guide for each student is of supreme importance, and decisions concerning its design should be made with great care.

In offering suggestions to teachers it would be of little value to simply state what works for me since teaching styles always reflect our individual personalities. Rather, I would like to make some general suggestions which could be applicable for almost any teacher in any middle school who is beginning with an affective education class. Behind all of my suggestions are some broad goals which seem to have constantly demanded attention in my own experience with an advisor-advisee group. Under two expansive topics they are:

I. Self-knowledge
   A. Getting to know each student exceedingly well.
   B. Letting students get to know you well.
   C. Helping students get to know each other.
   D. Helping students get to know themselves.
II. Group effectiveness
   A. Helping the group care about the group itself.
   B. Helping the group learn to work/play together.
   C. Helping the group to talk/listen together.
   D. Helping the group be self-directed.

Each of these goals can be articulated in advisor-advisee class. To do so the group must have variety in the nature of the activities they do. A continuing intensive encounter group would be no more desirable than an affective education class in which the students did art work every day. Balance of emphases is the key!

For some teachers achieving a balanced program is best facilitated by a permanent weekly schedule. A sample schedule that I have used may help to illustrate this point. The schedule had four basic components with one repeated part. They were: (1) Creative Expression; (2) The Valuing Process; (3) The Group Time; (4) The Valuing Process; (5) Individual Conference and Academic Work Time. This sample weekly schedule, which is designed to be ongoing, is only one means of establishing a multifocused program. These categories, however, are each broad enough so as to encompass a wide array of activities. Using these same components, a teacher could choose her own activities and achieve a complete and balanced advisor-advisee program.

Even with a well-balanced class schedule other factors can interfere with the success of your advisor-advisee class. The following are recommendations to promote success.

1. Have a set of overall goals for your affective education class. If one is not provided by the school, write your own. Any successful instructional program rests on valued goals and objectives. Moreover, affective education assumes that we can in fact teach kids to understand themselves, others, and their living experience. It's up to us to decide *what* as well as *how*.

2. Orient both your students and their parents to the concept of advisor-advisee early in the program. Parents are remarkably receptive to the concept and they are often willing to participate. Students are more eager to cooperate when they know the program's rhyme and reason.

3. As the school expert on each child, try to meet with the parents of each child several times during the year. Knowing the parents will help you to function more effectively as that child's advisor and affective guide.

4. As difficult as it may be, it is advisable, as advisors and affective guides, to maintain a nonmoralizing attitude. What middle school kids need and want least is

to be told what to do. More than ever they need our unconditional, positive regard coupled with a clarifying, questioning, and guiding voice. It is best if we can help students examine their own behavior and feelings to help them do so in the future. Some part of a balanced program ought to be devoted to this task but the process of helping kids clarify values should be continuous.

5. Teachers can be more effective advisors if they can be more effective listeners. Middle school kids want to be heard. Letting kids know we want to hear them really makes a difference. Moreover, it presents an inviting model for students to copy.

6. Make it a point to have group outings. This, as always, encourages a very needed sense of unity. The advisor-advisee class could be like a family at school.

7. Spend time with students individually. Some students get lost in a group and every child needs to know that you really care about all of him—his work at school, his life at home, his problems and his successes.

8. Share yourself with your kids. Let students know as much about you as you are willing to disclose. Students in your advisor-advisee class have the opportunity of getting to know you, perhaps far better than any of the other children you teach. Your willingness to share also sets a pattern of behavior students may choose to model.

A list such as this could never be complete enough. I hope, however, that it can help teachers just beginning with an affective education program or those for whom such a program has not yet seen success. If you as a teacher can help your middle school design an affective education program and if you can design an affective education class which really lets you make a difference in the lives of the children you teach, then you are to be proudly hailed. For, to the middle school, affective education is basic; to the middle school teacher, it is a chance to make a difference; and to the middle school child, it is the difference.

## ACTIVITY 2
### Read and share resource materials.

Developing a quality affective education program involves being familiar with available resources. The objective of this activity is to review some of the books that have been written to help teachers with affective education. "Books on Affective Education" contains an annotated bibliography on the subject. (But remember that new books are appearing each year.)

This activity may take a while to complete, depending upon the availability of the books. You may even want to get some of them on special order from a bookstore, from the company, at your district learning resources center, through interlibrary loan, from instructors, or from friends. If you are working on this chapter with a group, divide up the responsibility so that each of you will do part of the work of locating and reading the resources.

**A.**   If you have several other people to work with, divide the list in some fair way.

**B.**   Acquire as many of the books on the list as you can, either by purchase or loan.

**C.**   Familiarize yourself with each of the books that you, individually, have acquired.

**D.**   Share the contents of the books with other members of your group. Consider devising a standard form for the reports. Describe the contents and distribute samples of some of the materials. Share samples of some of the activities contained in promising books.

**E.**   Some of these books contain lists of other books, materials, films, and additional resources. Contribute what you find to form an expanded joint bibliography for affective education. Also, add new publications that have become available recently, those that you might now find in the bookstore.

## Books on Affective Education

1. Barr-Johnson, V., D.E. Hernandez, and S.L. Hiett. *Helping Kids Behave*. Des Plaines, Ill.: Nickerson & Collins Co., 1975.
   This book briefly describes a few of the methods used in enhancing classroom communication (e.g., transactional analysis, teacher effectiveness training, etc.). Also included are several strategies and games designed to facilitate interpersonal communication, self-awareness, and affective exploration.

2. Canfield, Jack and Harold C. Wells. *100 Ways to Enhance Self-Concept in the Classroom*. Englewood Cliffs, N.J.: Prentice-Hall, Inc., 1976.
   Affirms the strong relationship between self-concept and learning. 105 activities for use in the classroom with explicit instructions on how to use them.

3. Carswell, E.M., and D.L. Roubinek. *Open Sesame*. Glenview, Ill.: Scott, Foresman and Co., 1974.
   *Open Sesame* is a primer on open education, primarily for the elementary grades, that includes articles and activities on such affective topics as trust, understanding, openness, and love. Instead of writing a text to be read from cover to cover, the authors have organized a series of short articles and open-ended exercises that focus on the awareness and understanding of feelings that children seldom deal with in traditional educational approaches.

4. Casteel, J.D., and R.J. Stahl. *Value Clarification in the Classroom: A Primer*. Glenview, Ill.: Scott, Foresman and Co., 1975.
   The rationale and purpose of value clarification are clearly defined in this book. The primary emphasis is on what teachers can do to facilitate student learning of

the valuing process. Several in-depth strategies/exercises, ranging from social to self-exploration, are included in order "to stimulate and channel student behaviors related to value clarification."

5. Castillo, G.A. *Left-handed Teaching: Lessons in Affective Education.* New York: Praeger Publishers, 1974.
   The author's goal is to share classroom exercises that involve the student's affective domain—"not to teach cognitive or affective lessons, but to have cognitive and affective dimensions available in each and every learning situation." Simple exercises on trust, communication, and negative feelings are included.

6. Chase, L. *The Other Side of the Report Card.* Glenview, Ill.: Scott, Foresman and Co., 1974.
   A down-to-earth, step-by-step how to do it program in affective education. Fits middle school programs beautifully. No homebase program will be complete without reference to it.

7. Chesler, M., and R. Fox. *Role-playing Methods in the Classroom.* Chicago: Science Research Associates, Inc., 1966.
   The theoretical basis for role-playing introduces role-playing as a teaching practice that allows "children to look at themselves, to look at the actions and behaviors of others, and to look at social life in general." The authors present several role-playing strategies, including implications and limitations for the classroom. Teacher preparation and evaluative procedures are also discussed. (This is one of three booklets dealing with classroom problem diagnosis and corrective strategies.)

8. Dinkmeyer, Don and Lewis E. Losoncy. *The Encouragement Book: Becoming a Positive Person.* Englewood Cliffs, N.J.: Prentice-Hall, Inc., 1980.
   This book focuses on encouraging self-examination of one's attitudes. The authors include many practical exercises.

9. Ernst, K. *Games Students Play (and What to Do about Them).* Millbrae, California: Celestial Arts Publishing, 1972.
   The author presents a transactional analysis point-of-view of several disruptive games that are played in the classroom. The motivation behind game playing is explored and methods for stopping game transactions are discussed. Several of the game descriptions would make excellent classroom discussion topics—especially when dealing with unexpressed feelings. The author also presents a brief history of transactional analysis.

10. Fox, R., M.B. Luszki, and R. Schmuck. *Diagnosing Classroom Learning Environments.* Chicago: Science Research Associates, Inc., 1966.
    Emphasis in this booklet is on the gathering of information concerning the students learning environment. Several simple data-gathering tools are outlined along with means for analyzing and organizing the data. These diagnostic tools are oriented toward interpersonal relationships (student-teacher, student-student), the learning environment, outside influences on pupil learning, and the student's self-concept. The purpose of these diagnostic measures is to give teachers information

about the "actual state of affairs" so that appropriate changes can be made in the classroom learning environment. (This is one of a series of three booklets dealing with classroom problem diagnosis and corrective strategies.)

11. Freed, A.M. *TA for Kids*. Sacramento, California: Jalmar Press, 1971.
This book is a basic transactional analysis primer that is designed to explore feelings, stroking patterns, basic communication, and contracts. There are several group exercises (e.g., identifying ego states) that serve to enhance self-understanding, self-expression, interpersonal communication, and goal attainment.

12. Gillies, E. *Creative Dramatics for All Children*. Washington, D.C.: Association for Childhood Education International, 1973.
Gillies discusses some very basic verbal and non-verbal approaches for helping children become more aware and more in tune with themselves. In addition, there are sections devoted to creative dramatics with emotionally disturbed children, with the brain-injured child, and with students whose second language is English. There is also a short, annotated bibliography on creative dramatics for classroom use.

13. Glasser, W. *Schools Without Failure*. New York: Harper and Row, 1969.
Glasser's description of classroom meetings and his outline for implementing this approach provide the teacher with a simple method for initiating group discussions on a wide range of topics, from problem resolution to feelings catharsis.

14. Gorman, A.H. *Teachers and Learners: The Interactive Process of Education*. Boston: Allyn and Bacon, Inc., 1969.
In an effort to enhance the teaching and learning process, the author has described in detail the history of teaching and learning behavior, the contextual environment for teaching, and methods for improving and evaluating communication (intellectual and emotional) in the classroom. Several group interaction activities, including role-playing, are graphically outlined and discussed.

15. Greer, M., and B. Rubinstein. *Will the Real Teacher Please Stand Up?* Glenview, Ill.: Scott, Foresman and Co., 1972.
A series of short exercises to stimulate interpersonal interaction is interspersed with articles/exercises on humanistic education. The focus of the exercises is on self-discovery, as well as self-disclosure with group members.

16. Howe, L.W. and M.M. Howe. *Personalizing Education: Values Clarification and Beyond*. New York City: Hart Publishing Company, Inc., 1975.
The authors have described the process of values clarification as a total approach to teaching rather than as a series of unrelated teaching strategies. Additional values clarification strategies are included, but the primary emphasis is on the process of valuing and clarification of underlying feelings.

17. Hubel, K.H., and others. *The Teacher/Advisor System*. Dubuque, Iowa: Kendall Hunt Publishing Co., 1974.
Includes an introduction to the role of the teacher/advisor in an affective education program. The bulk of the book is made up of affective education excercises appropriate for middle school homebase programs. Very practical.

18. Hunter, E. *Encounter in the Classroom: New Ways of Teaching.* New York: Holt, Rinehart and Winston, Inc., 1972.
The author developed this book as a means for changing the process of teaching. She felt too much emphasis was placed on the content of education because of clamor for relevance and student participation. Activities that provide for student involvement in the education process are included. The primary focus is on the use of encounter and sensitivity group techniques to "increase personal and interpersonal effectiveness." Skills to improve classroom communication are also included.

19. James, M. *What Do You Do With Them Now That You've Got Them?* Reading, Mass.: Addison-Wesley Publishing Company, 1974.
Although this guide to transactional analysis was written for "moms and dads," it contains important material for anyone working with children. Emphasis is on dealing with feelings and behaviors that arise; questions that elicit feelings and thoughts about feelings are included.

20. James, M., and D. Joneward. *Born to Win: Transactional Analysis with Gestalt Experiments.* Reading, Mass.: Addison-Wesley Publishing Company, 1973.
This book is primarily designed to describe the content and structure of transactional analysis. Exercises to enhance self-awareness are included at the end of each chapter. Some of the exercises are ideal for initiating group activities in affective education.

21. Mattox, Beverly. *Getting It Together: Dilemmas for the Classroom.* San Diego, CA: Pennant Press, 1975.
Based on Kohlberg's theories of moral development, this book offers dozens of discussion-style dilemmas for use in the classroom. The dilemmas are divided into those appropriate for different age groups. An excellent resource.

22. Morrison, E.S., and M.U. Price. *Values in Sexuality.* New York City: Hart Publishing Company, Inc., 1974.
This series of small and large group activities deals with a variety of topics, from sex roles to physiology to values clarification. Also included is a "discussion starters" section that emphasizes emotional rather than cognitive responses to the presentation. Each activity clearly outlines the objectives, the rationale, materials needed, time required, and the procedure. (Especially good for the middle school age group!)

23. Pfeiffer, J.W., and J.E. Jones. (Eds.) *A Handbook of Structured Experiences for Human Relations Training.* (Vol. I–IV) La Jolla, California: University Associates, 1969–1974.
This series of four handbooks is specifically designed to help group leaders facilitate human relations training. The editors present a number of clearly outlined activities including goals, group size, materials needed, time required, and procedures, many of which are appropriate for classroom awareness experiences. Exercises range from the self-disclosing encounters ("Who Am I?") to the more cognitive task-oriented problems ("Joe Doodlebug" and "Group Problem-solving").

24. Raths, L.E., M. Harmin, and S.B. Simon. *Values and Teaching*. Columbus, Ohio: Charles E. Merrill Publishing Co., 1966.
The authors have outlined a methodology for the clarification of values. Emphasis is on providing the classroom teacher with a means for helping students clarify their own values. The strategies are adaptable to all age groups and are aimed at emotions underlying valuing.

25. Read, D.A., and S.B. Simon (Eds.). *Humanistic Education Sourcebook*. Englewood Cliffs, New Jersey: Prentice-Hall, Inc., 1975.
The authors have compiled articles exploring the humanistic education movement. The emphasis is on generating ideas to enhance a humanistic philosophy in a classroom setting. This is not a "strategies" book, but the articles within provide a sound springboard for creating effective exercises.

26. Schmuck, R., M. Chester, and R. Lippitt. *Problem Solving to Improve Classroom Learning*. Chicago: Science Research Associates, Inc., 1966.
This is the first in a series of three booklets dealing with classroom social structures, individual and group attitudes toward learning, significant environmental forces influencing both teachers and students, and the nature of the student-teacher relationship. The authors discuss such issues as the identification of problems in classroom life, the selection of appropriate diagnostic measures to analyze these problems, and the development of plans for changing the classroom environment. Teaching practices (and methods of evaluation) to improve the classroom atmosphere are also included.

27. Schmuck, R.A., and P.A. Schmuck. *Group Processes in the Classroom*. Dubuque, Iowa: Wm. C. Brown Company, 1971.
The authors have focused on the group interaction process in the classroom so that teachers can make more effective use of that process. Group process, leadership, and communication are some of the general topic areas explored. Included in these discussions are descriptions of classroom practices that have proved effective in facilitating communication and in taking advantage of group dynamics to promote learning.

28. Schrank, J. *Teaching Human Beings*. Boston: Beacon Press, 1972.
Schrank has described strategies, books, films, and games which are designed to help teachers "prevent school from handicapping kids." The emphasis is on exploration of sensory modalities, feelings, and values. Several topic areas, such as the effect of death on young people, are explored. The book was originally written for high school classrooms, but many of the ideas and strategies are easily adaptable for the middle school audience.

29. F. Shaftel and G. Shaftel. *Role-Playing in the Curriculum*. Englewood Cliffs, N.J.: Prentice-Hall, Inc., 1982.
An update of their classic work. A how-to-do-it guide for the use of role-playing in situations akin to the advisory role.

30. Simon, S.B., L.W. Howe, and H. Kirschenbaum. *Values Clarification*. New York: Hart Publishing Company, Inc., 1972.

This is the follow-up book to *Values and Teaching*. This book is primarily concerned with providing a number of strategies to initiate classroom discussion, but also provides a concise outline of the valuing process.

31. Stevens, J.O. *Awareness: Exploring, Experimenting, Experiencing*. Lafayette, California: Real People Press, 1971.

The active world of fantasy and awareness is explored in this book. Exercises on communication of feelings and sensory awareness for individuals and groups are included. There are also chapters devoted to the mechanics of group activities.

32. Wittmer, J., and R.D. Myrick. *Facilitative Teaching: Theory and Practice*. Glenview, Ill.: Scott, Foresman and Co., 1974.

In addition to providing a guide to facilitative responses, the authors have also included a series of fantasy and "feeling" exercises (with discussion) to enhance self-awareness and to explore the affective domain.

# ACTIVITY 3
**Begin to design an affective education program.**

The readings in Activity 1 suggest that planning for affective education is often done on a daily or weekly cycle. With early adolescents this sort of scheduling seems to legitimize each type of activity and sets up their expectations to the point that they look forward to each new topic without flinching. We also know that middle level students get bored quickly so that, for example, spending three straight weeks on values clarification, or on a special project of any one focus, is likely to be counter-productive. These students need both variety and structure. Teachers involved in affective education need to develop a schedule for small group time with students.

"Ideas for Affective Education" contains a list of activities that can be a part of a year-long program. Most of the activities can be used effectively once a week and can be repeated each week of the school year, or they may become the focus of a week-long affective education unit that would not be repeated. Using a separate sheet of paper for each idea, describe how each activity could be implemented in your situation. Then add, if you can, at least two other ideas of your own. The objective is to provide yourself with a resource file of ideas which makes it unnecessary to have a different lesson plan for each small group guidance day. Many teachers, when first encountering the advisor role, see it as an additional daily preparation, but it need not be so. When properly designed, as much as 80 percent of an entire year's program can be conducted without planning on a day-to-day basis. Write your file in a form that can be shared easily.

## Ideas for Affective Education

**1. Getting to Know You:** One student from the group is chosen for a day in which the focus of the group's activity is on him or her, exclusively: "This is YOUR day!" During the small-group time we may learn some of the following: biographical data, such as age, birthdate, family, pertinent facts about the past; favorite things, such as colors, clothes, animals, academic subjects, etc.; short- and long-range plans for the future; values; and, many other possibilities. With twenty to twenty-five students in your group this activity will, in itself, require almost 20 percent of small group time for the entire year. Can you describe how you would use this?

**2. Small Group Special Projects:** Early adolescents really enjoy working together cooperatively or competitively. Projects which permit working together allow students to get to know each other well in a low-threat manner, and help them make contributions to the school or community which can provide a much-needed feeling of value. Projects can include murals, collages, etc., to which all contribute, letters to newspapers or public officials which they all help to compose, cleaning up the school or community aid projects of all kinds, which may even be planned in school but be carried out after school hours. How many other kinds of special projects can you think of?

**3. Values Clarification/Moral Development:** A tremendous amount of popularity now surrounds the topic of values and moral decision making. Students can have a lot of fun with this, and also move toward the development of an integrated philosophy of life. If you are not familiar with these areas, a good place to begin is the June 1975 issue of *Phi Delta Kappan* magazine. If you've moved beyond this stage, you may find the bibliography from Activity 2 helpful. Are you comfortable enough with the values clarification approach to use it in your classroom? If not, turn to Activity 4.

**4. Supervised Study Time:** In any classroom, some students are always in need of help with their academic work, particularly with learning how to learn. The advisor's role, more than any other adults', certainly implies knowing more about the academic side of each advisee's life, with the possible exception of parents. During supervised study, the advisor can focus on the skills of continued learning, provide remedial help, counsel academically, and generally aid the student's academic progress. This time is particularly well spent when data need to be collected for parent conferences, special staffings, etc. Can you elaborate on how this kind of activity might be useful to you? Can you think of additional activities, such as a library day?

**5. Educational Games:** A regular day when students are permitted to engage in relaxed but educational pursuits can be extremely valuable. Providing a time when students can ease away from highly structured teacher-directed academic activity is very important; students need breaks as much as teachers. An opportunity to be together when no one is giving input and no one is receiving it, can be the exact time when students are available to the teacher for important one-to-one or small group (3, 4) counseling, or just personal, informal contact. While most of the students are reading, playing math games, doing word puzzles, or challenging each other in "think type" games like chess or checkers, the teacher can casually contact those students who require most personal attention at that time.

**6. Self-Awareness Sessions:** Several models for involving students in discussions which have as their purpose the development of the student's social and emotional maturity are available. One of the most well-known is the "schools without failure" approach developed by William Glasser. He advocates the use of "class meetings" to develop students' thinking, to get teachers involved with them, and to make school more relevant. Larry Chase's *The Other Side of the Report Card*, mentioned earlier in this chapter, is an excellent book which provides an approach to self-awareness sessions which could last an entire year or longer. You'll want copies of both books for your own library.

These sessions are basically student-centered, small-group discussions which focus on concerns directly relevant to the social and emotional growth of the student. Productive self-awareness discussions should have a low level of personal threat, but should try to involve everyone who wants to be involved. Here are just a few of the possible topics (suggested by Chase): friendship, fear, sensory awareness, trust, attention, self-control, tolerance. Can you list some other topics that are appropriate? The whole area of group dynamics, for example?

**7. Health and Family Life Education:** Homebase programs can also spend time, profitably, on those topics which are basically physical, but which are closely connected to social and emotional growth. Sex education, drug education, and health education efforts are all quite appropriate. Are there some topics in this category on which you could be prepared and with which you could be comfortable in handling as an advisor?

**8. Field Trips, Films and Friends:** Scheduling one day each week for field trips, films or invited guests can be fun and instructive. Field trips that go with the special interests of your group are great—the more time you spend together outside the school, the better you'll get along inside. Thousands of short films and filmstrips can be used to produce discussions of significant topics. Your community will have dozens of resource people who can be induced to come in for small group "public interviews." Students can often be relied upon to schedule all of these activities, relieving you of that burden. How does this fit in with your conception of ways to use advisor-advisee time?

**9. Group Dynamics:** Young adolescent students have discovered that the group exists. Prior to this time in their lives they perceived significant others largely in terms of individuals. They now need a great deal of help in understanding themselves as group members. The affective education program can help the student learn about groups. Setting aside some time on a regular basis to become involved in role-playing, sociodrama, simulations and other group activities can be extremely valuable. Here are several resources for you to use in designing these activities and in extending your search for useful ideas:

  a. Chester, M. and R. Fox. *Role-Playing Methods in the Classroom*. Chicago: S.R.A., Inc., 1966.
  b. Epstein, C. *Affective Subjects in the Classroom*. Scranton, Pa.: International Textbook Co., 1972.
  c. Fox, R., M. Luszki, and R. Schmuck. *Diagnosing Classroom Learning Environments*. Chicago: S.R.A., Inc., 1966.
  d. Gorman, A. *Teachers and Learners: The Interactive Process in Education*. Boston: Allyn and Bacon, Inc., 1969.
  e. Hunter, E. *Encounter in the Classroom*. New York: Holt, Rinehart and Winston, 1972.
  f. Schmuck, R., M. Chester, and R. Lippitt. *Problem-Solving to Improve Classroom Learning*. Chicago: S.R.A., Inc., 1966.
  g. Shaftel, F. *Role-Playing in the Curriculum*. Englewood Cliffs, N.J.: Prentice-Hall, 1982.

**10. Rap Sessions:** Students need to feel that there is at least one adult in the school to whom they can complain and with whom to share excitement, and there needs to be a time for this to happen. Otherwise this sort of ventilating of feelings will occur at inappropriate times. One way to facilitate this sort of discussion is to follow an "open microphone" format, where anyone who wishes may take the floor and express himself. Traditional small-group topical discussions are also effective. Are you comfortable with this? Are there specific modifications or ground rules that you would use?

**11. The Arts:** All too often music, art and drama get crowded out of the curriculum. Sometimes the school is too small to afford the special teachers. But whatever the emphasis on the arts in other areas of the curriculum, the affective education program is particularly well-suited to some informal experiences with the arts. A week-long unit on contemporary music, with an examination of the lyrics and how each person in the group relates them to their own lives, is a popular and very appropriate idea. Devoting one day a week to some form of artistic expression of self is another example. Play reading is also a great way to involve the arts in affective education. How would you use this particular idea?

**12. Sharing Time:** Middle school kids are full of ideas, feelings, and options that they would like to share, but often cannot express in a rap session format. Talking about some things in groups is difficult, yet they need feedback just the same. There are several methods to facilitate this process which can fit in the affective education program. Some teachers use the "Dear Abby" or "Dear Mrs. Thompson" format of soliciting anonymous contributions which are later discussed with the group. Other teachers use a "Diary Day" approach, with students writing in a journal which (only) the teacher reads and then writes back to the student. Still others use a "Me Book" approach to get students to write and discuss personal concerns.

**13. U.S.S.R.:** Uninterrupted Sustained Silent Reading. Once or even twice a week everyone in the group brings something appropriate to read, silently. Everyone, including the teacher, is reading something. Nothing interrupts.

**14. U.S.S.W.:** Uninterrupted Sustained Silent Writing. This activity is similar to U.S.S.R., except that journal writing becomes the focus. The teacher may write in his or her own journal too. Teachers may or may not read and write comments in the student journals. Try it both ways before you decide which works best for you and your students.

**15. Small Group Newspaper:** Students write articles describing themselves, others in the group, extra activities of the group, school or team, etc. The group performs the tasks of typing, duplicating, collating, assembling and distributing the paper.

**16. Read Aloud:** Middle school students are young enough to enjoy having someone read aloud to them. Choose a high interest book or story and simply read to students for one or more days a week. After selecting the story, this activity requires little teacher preparation. Questions for discussion following the reading might deal with values and moral dilemmas.

Other methods of getting to student concerns are important. Having a regular day on which each person brings something they care about to share (Book, poem, song, picture, etc.) rises above the show-and-tell stage, but still permits young people to let others in on what is important in their lives.

How can you adapt this strategy for use in your classroom? Are there other ideas that occur to you? Now prepare your own resource file as indicated at the beginning of this activity.

## ACTIVITY 4
### Review nonprint media on affective education.

"Films, Filmstrips, and Games for Use in Affective Education," is a selected list of materials that can be used in affective education programs. If you are working on this chapter with a group, divide the list so that each member is able to locate and preview several of the films and other activities. You may have to rely on a school district's media director for help in acquiring the materials for preview. Also search all available resources and catalogues for recent additions to this list.

For each item that you preview, record the following information:

1. The topic of the item
2. The grade level
3. Running time

4. Ideas for using it that occurred to you as you watched it
5. Other ideas about this item's place in your affective education program
6. Your evaulation of the item's worth

Keep all notes and other materials and plan to share your results with your work group.

## Films, Filmstrips, and Games for Use in Affective Education

### FILMS

1. *"All the Wishes of the World"*   Two friends save an enchanted fish, who grants them a reward. One boy is granted all his wishes, and the other gets double the amount of the same wish. The remainder of the film dwells on the rivalry that ensues and the attempts of the first boy to eliminate the second boy. (10 min., animated, color)

   > Contemporary Films/McGraw-Hill, Inc.
   > Princeton Road
   > Hightstown, New Jersey 08520

2. *"Art and Perception, Learning to See"*   This film is aimed at art classes, but has general appeal. Visual awareness is the topic, and students are encouraged to focus on such elements as color, line, texture—all with the express purpose of reacting to mood and life experiences around them. (17 min., color)

   > Bailey Film Associates
   > 2211 Michigan Avenue
   > Santa Monica, California 90404

3. *"Black and White: Uptight"*   This film explores the ways in which racial prejudice is learned and shows government and business leaders (black and white) working together in an attempt to eliminate such prejudice. (35 min., color)

   > Bailey Film Associates, 1969

4. *"Black Thumb"*   A white man automatically assumes that a black man who is doing some gardening is an employee of a white home owner; in actuality, the black man owns the house. Prejudice that produces such assumptions is explored. (28 min., black and white)

   > King Screen Productions, 1970.

5. *"Blindness"*   This film follows the life of an active, young man who is learning to accept his blindness. (28 min., black and white)

   > National Film Board of Canada, 1965.

6. *"Boundary Lines"*   This is an animated film exploring man's use of lines to express ideas and the imaginary lines (fear, possession, greed, and color) people have created to isolate themselves. (10 min., color)

   > International Film Foundation, 1948.

7. *"The Boy Who Couldn't Walk"*   Glenn Cunningham overcomes his physical disability—the result of severe burns—and walks again. (10 min., black and white)
   Films, Inc., 1964.

8. *"Brotherhood of Man"*   This short, animated film deals with the absence of basic differences between races of the world (adapted from a pamphlet by Ruth Benedict, "The Races of Mankind"). (11 min., color)
   Anti-defamation League of B'nai B'rith, 1946.

9. *"A Chairy Tale"*   In this fantasy without words, a young man tries to sit in a common kitchen chair, but the chair refuses to be sat upon. The chair withstands the young man's attempts at mastery, and the boy changes tactics—struggling to understand the chair. (10 min., black and white)
   National Film Board of Canada, 1957.

10. *"Chickamauga"*   Death in war is experienced through the eyes of a deaf boy, who is able to fantasize and to cope with death as long as it does not have personal meaning for him. When he encounters the death of his mother, however, he does not understand. His personal tragedy revolves around war, death, and deafness. (33 min., black and white)

    | Contemporary Films/McGraw-Hill, Inc. | Pyramid Films |
    | Princeton Road | Box 1048 |
    | Hightstown, N.J. 08520 | Santa Monica, CA 90406 |

11. *"A Christmas Fantasy"*   Music from the harp, celeste, and flute add to the enchantment of Christmas lights and the wonder of children's faces—the expression of Christmas "magic." (8 min., color)
    National Film Board of Canada, 1963.

12. *"The Dot and the Line"*   A straight line, who falls in love with a dot, feels hopeless and plain because the dot loves a squiggle, which is seemingly more interesting. Eventually, the line learns how to "break out" of his drab existence and he wins the love of the dot. Excellent study of growth and self-exploration. (9 min., color)
    MGM, 1965.

13. *"Flatland"*   A little square who lives in a two-dimensional world inhabited by other geometric figures is inquisitive, but is only brushed aside until he encounters a three-dimensional sphere and his world. He is scorned and jailed for heresy when he attempts to convince his elders that there is more than a two-dimensional world. (12 min., color, animated)
    Contemporary Films/McGraw-Hill, Inc.
    Princeton Road
    Hightstown, New Jersey 08520

14. *"The Greater Community Animal"*   This cartoon demonstrates society's intolerance of creative individuals and nonconformists. Society (represented by an animal) must digest and normalize the nonconforming elements. The question that remains is: Can society survive without the nonconformist? (7 min., animated, color)

Pyramid Films
Box 1048
Santa Monica, CA 90406

15. *"Invisible Walls"*   This is a film about our personal "space" and spatial distance between people. People are "caught in the act" of protecting their personal space—sending nonverbal signals that personal space can be violated and that such violations might provoke defense against the "attack." The focus of the film is on how Americans learn to restrict touching behavior. A question is posed: What can we do when city size and increasing population no longer permit the personal space we are accustomed to? (12 min., black and white)

Extension Media Center
University of California
Berkeley, California 94720

16. *"Kevin"*   This film focuses on how a young blind boy (age 10) experiences his world through other sense modalities. (20 min., black and white)

Churchill Films
662 N. Robertson Blvd.
Los Angeles, CA 90069

Pennsylvania State Univ.
Audio-Visual Services
University Park, PA 16802

17. *"The Monkey Who Would Be King"*   When the lion retires as head of the animal kingdom, a monkey wins the crown—and the ensueing trials and tribulations that accompany such responsibility. (11 min., color)

Encyclopaedia Britannica Films, 1957.

18. *"Mr. Grey"*   Mr. Grey is a businessman caught in his nine-to-five, Monday-to-Friday social role. The film emphasizes Mr. Grey's feeling of being trapped as a result of his daily routine. (20 min., color)

Mass Media Ministries
2116 N. Charles Street
Baltimore, Maryland 21218

19. *"The Red Balloon"*   This is a fantasy exploration of a boy's experiences with a balloon. After he befriends the balloon, he tries to protect it from mischievous boys who want to destroy it. (34 min., color; non-narrated, filmed in France)

Brandon Films, 1959.

20. *"The Searching Eye"*   Through the play of a ten-year-old boy, the viewer is able to share the world he sees and the world he cannot see; the purpose is to increase the viewer's awareness of the "invisible" world around him. (18 min., color)

Pyramid Films
Box 1048
Santa Monica, CA 90406

Extension Media Center
University of California
Berkeley, CA 94720

21. *"Silent Snow, Secret Snow"*   This film is an adaption of a Conrad Aiken short story about a boy who withdraws from the real world to live in his private, imaginary world of snow. The adults in Paul's world badger and question him until Paul decides to withdraw permanently. This is a study of schizophrenia, but

offers good discussion possibilities about fantasy worlds. (17 min., black and white)

> Audio/Brandon
> 34 Macquesten Pkwy. South
> Mount Vernon, New York 10550

The following twenty-one films can be rented from:

> Instructional Media Center
> Florida State University
> Tallahassee, Florida 32306

1. *"Agression-Assertion"*   Designed for all age levels, this film focuses on five alternatives: Aggression, Sarcasm, Destruction of Property, Cowardice, and Compromise; it provides an excellent opportunity to air student thinking on this subject. (8 min., color)

2. *"Boy Creates Toy"*   A six-year-old boy constructs his own version of a plane—after watching a twelve-year-old friend fly a model plane. He also creates a sailboat. (6 min., color)

3. *"Family in the Purple House"*   A seven-year-old child expresses his feeling about growing up in a fatherless home. The subject of families affected by divorce is discussed here. (13 min., color)

4. *"Farewell to Childhood"*   Even though this is a 1952 production, the moods, swift emotions, and uncertainties of adolescence are clearly portrayed by a teenager, named Susan. The film also captures her parents' bewilderment as they try to understand her rebellion. (23 min., black and white)

5. *"From Generation to Generation"*   This film emphasizes the functional, emotional, and spiritual aspects of human reproduction, without too much precise physiological detail of the process and organs involved in the process. (27 min., color)

6. *"Getting Along with Parents"*   Common problems between parents and teenagers are explored. Six teenagers in conflict with their parents generate discussion. Emphasis is on understanding points of view and feelings in order to arrive at mutually acceptable solutions. (15 min., black and white)

7. *"Hello, Up There!"*   Through the use of drawings, children voice feelings of anger, jealousy, hurt, and love in their attempts to understand the adult world—especially when one is so small that he must cry "Hello, up there!" in order to be noticed. (8 min., color)

8. *"How Friends Are Made"*   An elementary grade boy describes his wonder and excitement in making a friend. (11 min., color)

9. *"Love Is for the Byrds"*   This film follows two young married people, who make adjustments in solving their problems; the film emphasizes the importance of developing and maintaining good communication between mates. (28 min., color)

10. *"Mom, Why Won't You Listen?"*   How to get parents to listen is the topic of this film. Communicating is something more than finding the right moment and approach. (13 min., color)

11. *"What to Do about Upset Feelings"*   Four ways of overcoming upset feelings—understanding your feelings, facing your responsibility, talking your feelings out, and taking action—are viewed in three parallel situations. Designed for primary grades, the purpose of this film is to give children a means of dealing constructively with their upset feelings. (11 min., black and white)

12. *"What Will Barbara Do?"*   Barbara, a pre-teenager, finds the constant company of her friend, Pat, stifling. How should she handle friendly overtures from others when she knows that Pat will be jealous and hurt by being excluded? (6 min., color)

13. *"What Will Bernard Do?"*   Bernard has been helped (legitimately) in the past by a friend. Now that friend wants to copy Bernard's geography paper, what should Bernard do? (6 min., color)

14. *"What Will Christy Do?"*   Christy sees her younger brother break a window and then tell the principal that another boy did it. Family loyalty and feelings for an innocent victim do not make Christy's course of action easy. (6 min., color)

15. *"What Will Jonathan Do?"*   A fifth grade class has fun leading a substitute on. The class tries to convince her that they are supposed to see a film they saw the day before. Jonathan thinks the game has gone far enough, but what can he do? (6 min., color)

16. *"What Will Kathy Do?"*   Kathy has promised her vote to a candidate for seventh grade student council, but now she has found a better-qualified candidate. What should she do? (6 min., color)

17. *"What Will Kevin Do?"*   Kevin has a conflict between responsibility and his desire for fun. Should he keep his commitment or should he lie in order to keep his teacher's high opinion of him? (6 min., color)

18. *"What Will Linda Do?"*   Should Linda protect her little sister or should she let her handle her own problems? How can she be helpful, but not over-protective? (6 min., color)

19. *"What Will Patty Do?"*   Patty's friend has received a valentine from one of the most popular boys in the class. However, the card was really sent by members of Patty's group as a joke. If Patty warns her friend, she risks being expelled from her group. (6 min., color)

20. *"What Will Pete Do?"*   A ring disappears during a classroom activity, and everyone believes it is stolen. Pete sees a classmate in the principal's office and starts a rumor that the boy stole the ring. However, the ring is soon found in some materials. How does Pete handle the situation? (6 min., color)

21. *"What Will Ted Do?"*   Ted, an average student, comes to "hobby day" with a great collection of ships. Ted implies that he has made them rather than collected them. Under intensive questioning, Ted must decide whether or not to maintain the bluff. (6 min., color)

## FILMSTRIPS

1. *"Exploring Moral Values"* (by Louis E. Raths)   This comprehensive packet of materials includes a recording, a teacher's guide, and fifteen film strips. Specific

values areas such as prejudice, personal values, authority, and honesty, are death with. The teacher's guide has a description of each film strip and a list of supplemental readings.

> Warren Schloat Productions, Inc.
> Pleasantville, New York 10570

2. *"Freedom and Responsibility"* (by Hugo J. Hollerorth)  Designed primarily for upper middle school grades, this packet has sections on freedom and responsibility, sensitivity, honesty, love, non-conformity and the independent person, self-discipline, self-identity, and the adventurous person. The set includes a detailed guide, four recordings, information sheets, pictures, slides, cards, and four books.

> Division of Education and Programs
> Unitarian Universalist Association
> 25 Beacon Street
> Boston, Mass. 02108

3. *"Identifying Affective Objectives"* (by W. James Popham)  Designed for teachers, this program outlines a strategy to help specify affective objectives. Popham hopes this will facilitate the task of affective education. Included is a filmstrip and an instructional tape (reel to reel).

> Vimcet Associates
> P.O. Box 24714
> Los Angeles, CA 90024

4. *"A Strategy for Teaching Values"*  This set of three filmstrips, guide, and a recording outlines a strategy for applying the theory of moral development in the classroom situation. Although the packet is primarily designed for elementary grades, it provides an excellent background of Kohlberg's theory of moral development and, therefore, a solid basis for using the values approach in the classroom.

> Guidance Associates
> Pleasantville, New York 10570

5. *"Teaching Children Values"*  This set of six filmstrips (including a cassette recording and teacher's guide) is designed for elementary and intermediate grades. The animated filmstrips cover the following values areas: integrity, courage, moral courage, responsibility, justice, reverence, kindness, love of freedom and brotherly love.

> Educational Activities, Inc.
> Freeport, New York 11520

6. *"Understanding Your Parents"*  Interviews with young people and parents develop insights into conditions affecting parent-child relationships. This program, two filmstrips and two records or cassettes, is designed to help students begin productive dialogue centered on building satisfying relationships in the home.

> Guidance Associates
> Pleasantville, New York 10570

Here is a list of individual filmstrips which may be obtained from the following address:

> Churchill Films
> 662 North Robertson Blvd.
> Los Angeles, CA 90069

Essentially, each filmstrip deals with one particular emotion or event and is designed to elicit discussion from children concerning their feelings about that event. The subtitled filmstrips can be used for large or small group presentations or, in some instances, in individual situations.

A. "Is Anyone to Blame?"
B. "Have You Felt Hurt?"
C. "A Place in the Family"
D. "Have You Wanted to Be Alone?"
E. "How Do You Feel about Your Community?"
F. "How Do You Feel about Your School?"
G. "How Do You Feel about Your Home and Family?"
H. "How Do You Feel about Animals and Plants?"
I. "How Do You Feel about Other Children?"
J. "How Do You Feel about Being Alone?"

## GAMES

1. *"Blacks and Whites"*   This is a role identity and neighborhood action game. Participants experience the ghetto, live on welfare, try to build in a white suburb, and shake up the status quo. The game is ideal for small group interaction and is recommended for seventh and eighth grade use.

   Publisher: Didactic Systems, Inc.                    Cost: $6.95
   6 North Union Avenue
   Cranford, NJ 07016

2. *"Body Talk"*   Participants express emotions through nonverbal cues which are limited by various emotion cards. The game exposes students to an affective vocabulary; it also enhances awareness of nonverbal communication. Game variations and additions are possible. (Works best in small groups, but could involve the whole class.)

   Publisher: Communications Research Machines, Inc.      Cost: $6.00
   (Available in most stores.)

3. *"Culture-contact"* (Simulation)   This is a role-playing simulation for twenty to thirty students. The focus is on misunderstandings and potential conflicts when two very different cultures first meet and try to relate.

   Publisher: ABT Associates, Inc.                       Cost: $30.00
   55B Wheeler Street
   Cambridge, MA 02133

4. *"Family"*   This series of seven games can be used in small or large groups and can be played in 20 minutes. Emphasis is on teaching friendly feelings and coopera-

tive efforts in order to solve problems. Either all players win or all players lose!
Producer:  Family Pastimes                                    Cost: $2.50
           RR 4; Perth, Ontario

5. *"Feel Wheel"*  Through the use of an emotion chart and tokens, players can express feelings (and feeling intensity) toward other players. The game works well in small group situations and is especially useful in familiarizing students with several affective words.
Publisher:  Communications Research Machines, Inc.         Cost: $8.00
           (Available in many stores.)

6. *"The Games People Play"*  This game is for one to eight players and helps students develop skill in recognizing social actions and their consequences.
Producer:  MACSCO                                             Cost: $10.00
           P.O. Box 382
           Locust Valley, NY 11560

7. *"Generation Gap"* (Simulation)  This simulates interaction between parent and adolescent son or daughter with respect to certain issues on which they may have opposing attitudes. Conflict is presented within the context of rules which reflect structure of power and interdependence in the family.
Publisher:  Didactic Systems, Inc.                           Cost: $15.00
           6 North Union Avenue
           Cranford, NJ 07016

8. *"Hang-up"*  Small groups of three to six players role-play, often outrageously, to rid themselves of hang-ups. Empathy and nonverbal action are especially emphasized. Players are encouraged to express hang-ups and then to respond empathically to others' expressions. Suitable for seventh and eighth graders.
Producer:  Synectics Education Systems                       Cost: $15.00
           121 Brattle Street
           Cambridge, MA 02138

9. *"Happiness"*  "Tracks" of faith, hope, health, friendship, knowledge, and love are traveled; travelers get "keys" to these areas of life. The player may travel along the self-improvement track. The object is to obtain all the keys to happiness. Middle school students should have no problem understanding the principles of this game.
Publisher:  Milton Bradley                                   Cost: $6.49
           Springfield, MA
           (Available in many stores.)

10. *"Insight"*  The objective of this game is to evaluate the personality of every other player and to compare one's self-evaluation with that of others. Each player tests his powers of perception of personality. From two to twenty students can play.
Producer:  Games Research, Inc.                              Cost: $8.00
           48 Wareham Street
           Boston, MA 02118

11. *"Interaction"*  This game involves small groups of people who have specified likes and dislikes. Players must guess the attitudes of opponents.
    Producer:  Simulation, Inc.                          Cost: Unknown
              P.O. Box 140
              Carmel, Indiana 46032

12. *"Powderhorn"*  "Powderhorn" is a version of "Star Power," adapted for middle school students. It is an interactive game involving both competition and cooperation. The game is for large group activity and invites a great deal of vigorous (verbal) interaction.
    Producer:  Simile II                                Cost: $12.50
              Box 1023, 1150 Silverado
              La Jolla, CA 92037

13. *"Star Power"* (Simulation)  This simulation can handle up to sixty players and is best suited for seventh and eighth graders. Players are divided into three social groups and are designated as squares, circles and triangles (equivalent to upper, middle and lower class). Squares are given more decision-making powers than other groups. Social mobility, decision-making processes and group cohesiveness are explored (along with all the attendant feelings).
    Publisher:  Simile II                               Cost: $25.00
              Box 1023, 1150 Silverado
              La Jolla, CA 92037

14. *"Timao"*  Game variations are possible for this exercise in expressing values, understanding how values are interrelated, understanding others' values, and awareness of multivalued events (including enhancement and deprivation of values).
    Publisher:  Pennant Educational Materials            Cost: $3.50
              San Diego, CA 92120

15. *"Ungame"*  This game can be used in any middle school classroom. It is designed to draw out the participant's true thoughts and feelings regarding his self-concept. Topic areas covered are hope, fear, joy, sorrow, philosophy, ambition, etc.
    Publisher:  Au-Vid, Inc.                             Cost: $7.95
              P.O. Box 964
              Garden Grove, Ca 92642

16. *"Values"*  Designed for small group activity, this game faciliates self-disclosure of players' values. Players attempt to do the best job of clarifying their own values. The message of the game is that each individual counts and has value as an individual, that everyone has values, and that it is good to discuss themselves and their values.
    Producer:  Friendship Press                          Cost: $5.95
              P.O. Box 37844
              Cincinnati, Ohio 45237

17. *"Why Am I Afraid To Tell You Who I Am?"*   Students role-play or verbally describe personality types designated on character cards (e.g., cynic, crank, pouter, etc.). There are a variety of activities for individuals, dyads, and small and large groups.

   Publisher:  Argus Communications                          Cost: $2.95
                    (Available in many stores.)

## ACTIVITY 5
**Experience and evaluate activities in affective education.**

Arrange to join a group of your colleagues who are interested in affective education. They may be members of your class, or on the faculty in the school where you teach. This group should consist of six to ten people. Let this group become a simulated advisor-advisee group in which you select activities which will (1) help you get to know each other better and (2) engage in trying on some of the affective education techniques described elsewhere in this chapter. Each person should share equally in the responsibility for designing and conducting the activities.

   Meet for at least six sessions of thirty minutes each. Keep an individual record of what transpires and your own reactions to the simulation. The last session should provide an opportunity for the group to evaluate what has happened.

   You might use the following questions to help evaluate the simulation:

1. Did you enjoy the time you spent with this group? Why or why not?
2. Did you learn anything new or clarify any earlier insights about yourself?
3. Did you learn anything new about the other members of the group? What?
4. Has your relationship with the members of the group changed in any way during the simulation?
5. Have your feelings about affective education been altered? Why do you think that is?

## ACTIVITY 6
**Outline a year-long sequence in advisor-advisee activities.**

Assuming that you are or soon will be participating in a formally scheduled advisor-advisee program of some sort, in this activity we ask you to design a homebase program for your own use. Drawing on the materials and ideas of previous activities in this chapter, your task is to design a skeleton outline for a year-long advisor-advisee program that fits you, your school, and the number of students with whom you will work. If you work in a school that does not provide scheduled time for advisory groups, for the purposes of this learning activity assume that you have been given 30 minutes at the beginning of each day for the advisor-advisee program and design the year's program accordingly. Or, you can make a plan that can be used in some other teaching assignment.

You will probably want a schedule that is a balance between things which occur once-a-week on a regular basis, and those which last for a week or more and do not recur during the year. For example, you may want to begin the year with a week's worth of get-acquainted activities and orientation for new students and then you could establish a semi-regular routine interrupted every so often by special three, four, or five day activities, after which the regular routine resumes. Now do the following.

A. Describe a typical week's schedule.

B. List all the special kinds of activities that might occur over a nine month period.

C. Combine the results from (A) and (B) into a brief (one page) "September-June" skeleton schedule.

D. Be certain that you add a description of your reasons for choosing activities.

E. If there are others in your learning group who are working on this chapter, exchange these plans with them. Ask for their reactions to your plans and share your response to theirs. If you are working with kids, see what they think.

F. Arrange to meet (individually or as a group) with a school counselor. Let this person know that this meeting is designed for you to receive help on homebase-advisor ideas and techniques. Prior to the appointment, you may want to share this chapter with the counselor, asking for help in as many ways as possible. After the meeting, summarize your findings and include all of the materials (e.g., handouts) you receive.

## ACTIVITY 7
### Design answers to problem situations.

This activity assumes that you have designed an affective education program to be used with students. You will undoubtedly encounter a variety of discussion situations, or you may already have some questions about small group guidance that begin with "What if. . .?" The best answers to these questions will probably come from you or from colleagues who share similar situations.

Read each question and the suggested answer(s) and list at least one other way of dealing with the problem situation that seems appropriate to you. Keep the notes.

## What If. . .

1. During group discussions, students copy one another's verbal contributions?
   a. Try to focus on the feelings involved.
   b. Accept their comments and then ask them to say a little more.
   c.
   d.

2. During group discussions students tell you only what they think you want to hear?
   a. Let them know that it makes you feel good to know that they want to say things that please you, but that their own special thoughts are what please you most.

b. Use that very thing (saying what you think is wanted) for a discussion topic.

c.

d.

3. During group discussions, students ramble on and on, using up everyone's "air time?"

   a. Clearly state that those who didn't have a chance to talk today will start tomorrow.

   b. Use a rotation system of some kind.

   c.

   d.

4. Students will not listen to each other?

   a. Use the "echo rule"—everyone who speaks must paraphrase what the preceding speaker has said.

   b. Analyze *your* listening—are you modeling good listening?

   c.

   d.

5. Students interrupt?

   a. Ignore the interruptor as much as possible, keeping the focus on the child who is having his turn.

   b.

   c.

   d.

6. Students do not speak at all?

   a. Use a technique which requires anonymous written contributions.

   b. Break the group into twos or threes with some nonthreatening tasks.

   c.

   d.

7. Students ridicule each other?

   a. Deal immediately and directly with the subject of ridicule and all the associated feelings.

   b.

   c.

   d.

8. Students "act out" because they are uncomfortable, anxious, or in need of the attention of the group?

   a. Try to design a situation in which the child can be obviously successful, even if it is something as simple as helping you choose who will speak next.

   b.

   c.

   d.

9. Students will not attempt tasks?

   a. Let them pass—that should be their privilege.

   b. Start with something less objectionable or anxiety producing.

   c.

   d.

10. Students aim all their comments at the teacher and not to each other?
    a. Be quick to ask the opinion or reactions of other children.
    b.
    c.
    d.
11. Students always talk about the same thing?
    a. Accept the contribution and then ask if the student can also add something about the current topic.
    b. Sit by him or in some other way let him know that you notice him.
    c.
    d.
12. Students complain that a topic is too personal?
    a. Remind the group that it is okay not to talk about a topic if they choose not to.
    b. Explore the possibility with the rest of the group. They may be right.
    c.
    d.
13. Students say that a topic or activity is boring?
    a. Explore the possibility with the group. If they all feel this way, there are plenty of other things to do.
    b. Does it bore you too? If so, change the topic.
    c.
    d.
14. Students engage in cruel or negative talk about someone else outside the group?
    a. Remind them that the ground rules don't permit it, and make certain it stops.
    b. Talk about *your* feelings when you hear things like that.
    c.
    d.

# ACTIVITY 8
## Evaluate what you have learned.

If you have worked through the activities successfully, you will:

1. Be able to describe affective education and its place in the middle school. Can you?
2. Be able to analyze the status of affective education in your school and be able to recommend improvements. Can you?
3. Be aware of a large number of activities that can be used in designing your own affective education program. Are you?
4. Be familiar with a list of films which are useful in affective education. Are you?
5. Have designed an affective education program for you and your students. Have you?
6. Have probed some of your concerns about what goes wrong in affective education. Have you?

Now, organize the products which have resulted from your work in this chapter for inclusion in your portfolio. Share what you have accomplished with your instructor or peers, specifically the results of activities that you have accumulated.

## NEXT STEPS

1.  Join a group of your colleagues who are also involved in affective education. Meet regularly to share ideas until you have assembled a bank of activities that can be used comfortably in your classroom.

2.  Explore the idea of an affective group for you and your colleagues. In today's society a sense of community is hard to find. You may be surprised to learn that a number of your colleagues would favor meeting regularly to focus on doing the kinds of things that you may be doing with your students.

3.  Try pairing up with another teacher and his or her homebase group for a week. You might want to try this several times during the year, with several different groups.

4.  Read Chapter Four, "Providing Teacher Guidance" in Alexander, William M. and Paul S. George, *The Exemplary Middle School,* New York: Holt, Rinehart and Winston, 1981.

# PART THREE

# The Strategies

Knowing the characteristics of transescents and knowing about the new middle school being designed to enrich their educational experience will help you function more effectively in the day-to-day activities of the classroom. That knowledge is necessary, but not sufficient to ensure effective teaching. We have, therefore, included a section with a few specific strategies that good teachers have used successfully for many years.

As you will see, most of the strategies described here are methods of individualizing instruction, because middle school educators have long been committed to that concept. There are chapters on learning centers, learning activity packages, mastery learning, and on developing responsibility in your students. Individualized instruction and the middle school concept are not completely synonymous, however. Many large group, teacher-directed learning experiences are also appropriate and desirable.

As were previous chapters, these chapters are based on the premise that the most effective, meaningful way to learn is to *do*. Each chapter, therefore, involves you in the active exploration of a particular technique. There are many other successful strategies which might have been included. We have chosen methods that we believe lighten the burden of the teacher who chooses to personalize instruction. These strategies work in harmony with the goals, objectives, and staffing designs that middle schools have adopted to serve the needs of transescent learners.

# CHAPTER 9

# THE OTHER SIDE OF DISCIPLINE: HELPING STUDENTS TAKE RESPONSIBILITY

Comments heard from middle school students:

> "I hate it when we have free time. There's nothing to do here."

> "Am I learning anything? I don't know. Well, I must be. I got 85 on the last test."

> "Not many kids work hard at this school. I'm not learning. Nobody drives me."

> "Some kids act wild and out of control in our class. I think it's because they're scared. They feel dumb. They feel they don't have any control over what happens to them in the classroom."

Comments from middle school teachers:

> "Whenever I'm out of the room, chaos reigns. I even got their agreement on a special set of classroom rules. Didn't work. They just don't have the self-discipline it takes."

> "You see the kind of bind I'm in. I believe in having the students make decisions about what we study and how we do it. But it takes so much time and we can't cover all the required curriculum if we do it that way."

> "The students' low scores on the minimum competencies test have just one message for me—kids today feel less and less responsible for their own learning."

> "It's like pulling teeth to get these kids to work independently. I took this group to the library and told them they had to pick out a book on the period in history we were studying, read it, and write a report on it to give in class. And you know what? Eighty-five percent of them asked me to pick the book for them! Now what am I supposed to do? How can they work independently? They can't even pick a book by themselves."

When students fight or daydream or deface school property or don't do their assignments, some people find the causes for this behavior in the students themselves. "They don't appreciate school. They don't have respect or self-discipline. They don't know how to get along." Some people blame parents for not teaching their children respect, self-discipline, or appreciation for school. Some blame television. Others blame the teachers for not being firm enough or compassionate enough or well prepared.

We find much more power in another view: Blaming teachers and parents doesn't help. Blaming sets off a useless cycle of counter-blaming that drains off energy needed for more constructive things. Wholesale blaming seems a sure sign that the *system* that prescribes behavior and relationships isn't working adequately. If the finger must be pointed, we vote for blaming the system.

All of us associated with schools have inherited a system that no longer works well. In many ways the rules and procedures and norms of the system do not fit our times. The structure of schooling has not really changed, while our society has. When a shift is made from blaming each other to blaming the system, energy is released to work on the common target: fixing the system to serve us better.

In this chapter the focus is on ways that you can change the system so that it encourages students to be more self-disciplined and self-reliant. Of course, this means changing the part you play in the system, too. More specifically, the chapter is intended to help you:

- Analyze how the system discourages responsibility taking
- Use some new techniques of managing a classroom so as to prevent discipline problems
- Administer first aid for discipline problems after they occur
- Analyze your own tendencies to encourage or discourage responsibility-taking
- Try out techniques of helping students move toward independence
- Implement some plans for developing students' social responsibility

## ACTIVITY 1
**Consider how school social structure affects students' sense of responsibility.**

American schools and classrooms have a structure that prescribes roles for teachers, students, and others. The structure is remarkably consistent from generation to generation and from place to place. Some of its features are helpful and right for today's needs, some are not. "School Social Structure and Individual Responsibility: Letting Kids in on the Secret" presents our views. Read it first and then use the suggestions that follow it to make your own analysis of ways that school structure affects students' taking of responsibility.

## School Social Structure and Individual Responsibility: Letting Kids in on the Secret

Americans who have studied Soviet schools have found striking similarities in the structure of classrooms in the U.S. and the U.S.S.R.[*]

- One teacher and approximately thirty children work separately from others. (Teams of colleagues are rare. If a second adult is present, it is a helper, not another teacher.)
- Children of the same age are grouped together; interaction or instruction across ages is not commonly seen.

---

[*]See, for example, Urie Bronfenbrenner, *Two Worlds of Childhood: U.S. and U.S.S.R.*, New York: Russell Sage Foundation, 1970; and Susan Jacoby, *Inside Soviet Schools*, New York: Hill and Wang, 1974.

- The groups of thirty stay together; they do not change from day to day or week to week.
- School work is broken up into subjects which stay separate from the others.
- Students follow a regular sequence through the separate subjects.
- A predetermined schedule regulates the movement from subject to subject.
- The curriculum is predetermined and organized according to subjects and age of the students.
- Almost all instruction is verbal, either oral or written; hence, paper and pencil, textbook and workbook, and recitation are at the center of classroom activity.
- Instruction emphasizes right answers to predetermined problems or tasks.
- The informal social structure of students (peer relationships from outside school) is regarded as not appropriate for classrooms and so it is actively discouraged.
- The teacher actively directs and monitors student behavior as agent of the school authorities; rules, procedures, and behavior norms are predetermined by the authorities.

There are other similarities and many differences between U.S. and U.S.S.R. schools. The comparison is made here to highlight some of the structural features of American classrooms that often are unseen and unexamined because they are so familiar. Structure is a given, an obvious fact of life, until it is examined seriously. Then it may be seen as a condition that has the possibility of being tested for its effectiveness, and perhaps changed.

Middle schools in the United States are testing all of the givens mentioned above. Such experiments give us reasons to believe that many of the most common structual features of classrooms actually discourage student self-discipline and responsibility-taking. In the paragraphs that follow, we argue that certain structural features of American schools are particularly detrimental to developing student responsibility.

When student discipline and apathy are problems, when teacher morale is chronically low, there are strong reasons to suspect that the system today's teachers have inherited does not fit the times. Today's teachers have had better training and bring no less good will and intentions to the profession than teachers in earlier generations. Children are no less intelligent or healthy, and parents are no less hopeful of the school's educative potential. When people who have good will, intelligence, hope, and skills have increasing trouble in making a system work, the system is suspect. Our suspicions focus on six major structural features of the system of schooling this generation has inherited.*

---

*The authors are grateful to James Coleman for several of his insights that are reflected in our analysis. See his article, "The Children Have Outgrown the Schools" in *Psychology Today*, February 1972, pp. 72–75, 82.

### 1. The Sheltering Structure

When American schools began, each served a relatively homogeneous community. The school was expected to give instruction in the values held by that community. More importantly, the school was expected to perform a sheltering function, to keep children from being exposed to alien values until the community's values were fully accepted and built into the children's habit patterns. The sheltering process became assured by a structure of curriculum and teaching patterns.

Today's schools operate in a radically different situation. Schools do not serve homogeneous communities. They are mixing pots, not really melting pots, of values. Through television and other sources, children are exposed to a bombardment of conflicting values, beginning long before their first day of school. They experience a confusion of competing values. Unfortunately, the school structure has not changed. Schools continue to try the sheltering process—to proscribe and prescribe, to censor and pretend that certain values do not exist as forces in the children's lives.

The inherited school structure does not encourage young people to take responsibilities for their own values. What they need is a curriculum and teachers that understand the realities of the student's world, that help the student face the conflicting values squarely, to use intelligence in analyzing consequences of acting on this or that value. In effect, to help each student *find* a set of values worthy of commitment. That is the first priority for structural change that we propose—for every child the continuous development of a personal ideology.

### 2. The Holding Pattern

When American schools began they had a limited curriculum: writing, reading, and computing. Later, because children typically traveled no more than thirty miles away from the place they were born, books were added that introduced children vicariously to places and people they would never see. This curriculum of reading, writing, computing, and vicarious experience was remote from daily life, but made sense in those days because the school day and school year were short and because all of the practical, concrete knowledge and skills a child would need could be gained outside the school. Every child worked at home or in the community. Each was expected to be a productive contributor; gathering eggs, bringing in firewood, feeding animals, peddling papers, working in father's shop.

Today's urbanized and automated culture has many fewer opportunities for children to be contributing members, to feel their efforts are worth something to someone. And today the schools still emphasize reading, writing, computing, and vicarious, abstract experiences. During school hours children spend their time trying to master the symbolic tools of the culture, and after school, do they have the chance to put the tools to productive use? A recent survey of 5,000 middle school students confirmed suspicions; the vast majority of the students spent their afternoon and evening hours watching television (*more* vicarious experience) or playing with their friends. Some did report having chores or jobs, of course, but they tended to be unrelated to the tool skills they were studying in school. Those young people we know who do have jobs baby sitting or mowing yards seem to thrive on the responsibility, the sense of contribution, and the independence that comes with earning their own money.

American society is telling its children we have no productive place for you, no functional, social identity for you until you become an adult. So the children remain in a holding pattern, waiting for the signal to join the adult world. It is not difficult to find a relationship between this nonfunctional condition assigned to children and the apathy, the vandalism, and all the self-deprecating behavior they exhibit.

As opportunities for young people to take responsibilities have dried up in our society generally, the structure of schooling has remained essentially the same and children have no additional opportunities for taking responsibility within the school setting.

Thus the second priority we propose for the schools of older children and adolescents is a program that stretches the school out into the community, helping students find personal meaning in concrete, responsible social roles—a program that then brings the community experiences back into the school to be analyzed, interpreted, and integrated into each student's sense of self. There is no way to learn responsible behavior except by taking responsibility in various life roles.

### 3. The Spectator Learner

American schools began when information was scarce. Very little printed matter existed, so it was natural for schools to be a place for accumulating the scarce material. And it was natural for the teacher to assume a role of disseminator. The student's role, one that we described in the introduction to this book, was that of a relatively passive receiver or spectator. The information had already been collected, organized, and predigested for student consumption. That structure was appropriate when information dissemination was a major need in our culture.

The pattern persists. Schools disseminate information as if it were a scarce commodity. Despite the information explosion of this century, the school is still structured to be a center of gathered information—gathered in textbooks, in audio-visuals, and in teacher's notes—to be dispensed as if school were the only significant source of the culture's information. The student's responsibility is limited essentially to being a spectator of whatever the textbooks choose to display of other people's knowledge about the culture. Therein is our third priority for changing the structure of the schools: that students be given the opportunity and responsibility to actively seek and sort and screen and critique the substance of the culture; to be problem solvers and to learn how to test information in the crucible of problem solving.

### 4. The Student as Taker

The fourth problem is related to the third. When school occupied a smaller space in a child's life, and the curriculum mainly dealt with language and math skills, the model of teaching that seemed most natural was that of the teacher telling and the student reciting lessons. The teacher was giver and the student was taker. Learning was a taking process. Through the years, that structure has persisted and developed to the point that today's consummate student is a narcissist centered in upon the process of academic self-agrandizement. The best student is the one who can store up the most the quickest. Students are encouraged to believe in and to take pride in an essentially self-centered process of learning. After twelve or sixteen years of schooling devoted to being an academic taker, students are expected to go out to contribute to our social institutions, and the elders wonder why the young people have trouble meshing their talents with those of others. For sixteen years they build habits of taking, and then are told, "Go out and give of yourselves." As if giving did not require any habit development.

Our fourth priority is for a new school structure that encourages learning through sharing and giving. That means helping students take on the responsibility of contributing and of participating in group efforts that have social meaning beyond narcissistic interest. In our experience, people learn best when they have harnessed themselves to a task that transcends their own private needs to develop skills.

## 5. The Myth of Social Stability

When American schools began, teachers were not trained to deal with the social and emotional development of students. That omission was natural because children not only had nuclear families to attend to their development, but extended families were part of most children's lives. Children knew family rules, had various adults around who would attend to a child's business, had ample opportunities to learn correct social behavior in face-to-face groups other than with parents and siblings. Most children had a supportive circle of relatives who accepted them, warts and all, not because they proved themselves as worthy group members, but just because they were family. Acceptance was unconditional. So schools did not need to provide what the families and communities already supplied.

Today the same structure of schooling persists while the social conditions of children have changed radically. Mobility, not stability, is the reality for most families. Few families have roots down in one place for five years, let alone a generation. Extended families located in one community are extremely rare. And it is the children that are most affected. How wide is the circle of adults and young people within which today's child finds unconditional acceptance?

We propose a fifth priority: that today's schools have within them extended family groups and curriculums that help students learn the responsibilities and skills of face-to-face supportive group relationships. We are proposing that every school place high priority on giving each student the experience of being a member of a group that accepts him or her unconditionally, warts and all. Some of society's survival skills will be learned only in that context.

## 6. The Myth of Obvious Goals

None of us doubts that people work hardest and best when they have a clear goal to which they are committed, and when they agree on how to pursue the goal.

When the structure of schooling developed 200 years ago, the goals of the school were more simple, more clear to everyone, including students. Through the years, society's goals for schools have become less and less clear and there is great disagreement about how to pursue them. At the same time, the goals and the means have become less and less clear to the students.

As the authority status of elders has changed in our culture, youngsters are less and less willing to follow the elders on faith and on authoritarian pressure toward some school goal they do not understand. So two choices are left to the elders: step up the authoritarian pressure or persuasion, or find some way that students can see school goals as intelligible and valuable to themselves. The traditional structure of school knows only the method of pressure or persuasion. That seems to be what is happening as teachers try to become more and more skilled in sophisticated discipline techniques.

Our sixth priority is to have students brought into the planning process—into the process of goal-finding, goal-setting, task definition, and the making of work assignments. With the authoritarian solution getting poorer and poorer results, the logical solution is a democratic one—shared planning and decision making. Tasks that students plan and commit themselves to will bring out more intelligent action, greater responsibility, and better learning.

These six ideas are not pipe dreams. We have been in a number of schools where kids *are* being let in on the secret: *the system does not work well and everyone's help is needed to change it.* In that attitude is the best hope for encouraging student responsibility and for improving the structure of schooling.

## ACTIVITY 2
**Analyze your own school.**

If you have your own classroom, here are two activities that may help you analyze some conditions that promote or inhibit students in taking responsibilities.

**A.** *Student responsibility inventory.*   Young people act more responsibly in some situations than in others, as do we all. Your students can compare their own responsibility taking in school, home, job, and other situations. Their analysis can be helpful to them and to you. Here are some suggestions for writing a student questionnaire.

### STUDENT SURVEY

1. In each of these situations, how responsible do you feel for your own actions? (Circle a number for each item. A (1) means very responsible, a (5) means not responsible, and the other numbers mean in between.)
    a. At *home* I feel:
       very responsible 1..2..3..4..5..not responsible for myself
    b. At *school* I feel:
       very responsible 1..2..3..4..5..not responsible for myself

   c. At *job(s)* I feel:
      very responsible 1...2..3..4..5.. not responsible for myself
   d. With my group of *friends* I feel:
      very responsible 1..2..3..4..5.. not responsible for myself
   List below *other* situations, such as organizations, sports teams, church, etc.
   e. _____ I feel:
      very responsible 1..2..3..4..5.. not responsible for myself
   f. _____ I feel:
      very responsible 1..2..3..4..5.. not responsible for myself
   g. _____ I feel:
      very responsible 1..2..3..4..5.. not responsible for myself
2. When I feel responsible at school it is because: _____
   _____
   _____

3. When I *don't* feel responsible at school it is because: _____
   _____
   _____

The survey will be a good basis for class discussion about conditions that help students take responsibility and conditions that make them feel irresponsible. Make notes on the results of the survey and discussion, and save them to share with a colleague.

**B.** *Examining school structure.*    Using the results of the survey and the reading you did in Activity 1, analyze the structure of your school to identify features of the structure that *discourage* students from acting responsibly or developing more responsibility. An example may help you. Philip Cusik (1973) analyzed the structure of a high school and found that the time schedules of the school caused responsibility problems. While students moved in and out, from class to class, with no apparent problems, the tight schedules caused students to hurry and made them tense. The built-up tension became hostility and aggression that was vented frequently during the day. Most likely, teachers felt the same pressure. The penny-wise, pressing schedule was pound-foolish in effectiveness of teaching and learning.

In analyzing the structure, it may be helpful to consider what rules are frequently broken, what procedures frequently neglected. They may offer clues to a structure that promotes more irresponsibility than it prevents.

Write out your analysis to share with a colleague.

## ACTIVITY 3
### Analyze the structure in lesson plans.

As students play their parts in your lesson plans and strategies, how much opportunity do they have to take initiative and make decisions about the learning tasks? Here is a way for you to analyze the initiative patterns in your teaching. Consider that instruction involves four main ingredients in various relationships:

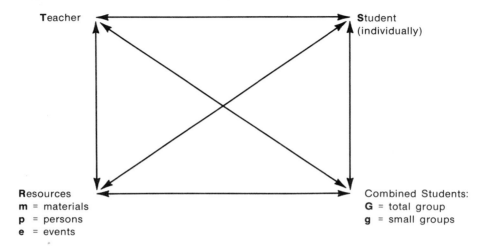

**Teacher** — **Student** (individually)

**Resources**
**m** = materials
**p** = persons
**e** = events

**Combined Students:**
**G** = total group
**g** = small groups

For example, the most typical pattern in middle grade classrooms has been: The teacher (T) decides what the students should study and gives the same assignment to each student (S) in the class. The students use resource materials (Rm) to do their assignments. Then the teacher leads a recitation session with the whole group (G). That sequence could be represented by the diagram:

T → S → Rm → T → G → T → G, etc. We can add three more symbols to make the pattern more clear:

    o = responsibility for deciding tasks
    * = providing a stimulus
    ... = extended time.

With these symbols added, the diagram above would be:

(T)* → S → Rm ... → T → G → T → G, etc. Meaning: the teacher (T) has the responsibility (o) of deciding and defining an assignment; provides a stimulus (*); and makes a common assignment to each student (S). Students individually use resource materials (Rm) for an extended time (...) and then report to the teacher in a recitation session (T → G → T → G, etc.).

The students' need for variety can only partially be satisfied by changes in the *content* of activities. If the same initiative pattern is repeated over and over with only the Rm changing, the formula gets monotonous and boring.

Out of many possible patterns, here are four that put the initiative and stimulus in other places:

    1. T → Re* → G → (g) ... → S → Rm → g → G. In this pattern, the teacher provides an event that stimulates the total group to plan some activities. Tasks get divided among small groups that carry the initiative and responsibility over an extended time. Individual student members of the small groups take on some jobs, using

resource materials, and then they report back to their groups. Finally, the small groups report to the total group. Here are three other patterns:

2. $g^* \rightarrow \text{G} \rightarrow g \rightarrow Rm \rightarrow G \rightarrow g \rightarrow Rp \rightarrow G$

3. $S^* \rightarrow G \begin{smallmatrix} \text{S} \cdots \\ \\ \text{T} \cdots \end{smallmatrix} G$

4. $T \rightarrow Rm^* \rightarrow \text{g} \rightarrow Rm, \; RP \ldots \rightarrow S \ldots \rightarrow g \rightarrow G$

So that you can better understand your own teaching patterns and can consider ways to vary them:

1. Translate the three patterns above into your own terms.
2. Diagram your own most typical patterns.
3. Devise or select several patterns that differ from what you usually use and briefly sketch lesson plans to fit them.
4. If you have students, conduct the lessons you have planned and make notes on the results.
5. Share your outcomes with a colleague or two.

Changing classroom patterns so that students are given more responsibility is easier to plan than to do. The proof, of course, is in the doing. Besides any doubts and reservations *you* may have about the changes, the students' habits and attitudes will work against the changes until they learn through experience that there *can* be:

- more than one expert in the classroom
- more than one correct answer (the one in the teacher's head)
- more than one way of deciding what is studied
- more than one source of payoff—the teacher
- more ways to get the payoff than by being smart, quick, neat, and compliant.

## ACTIVITY 4
**Analyze school rules with students.**

Students are regarded as acting responsibly when they follow school rules and as acting irresponsibly when they don't. What are the school rules? Do all students understand them? Most schools have lists of rules that apply to students. All schools have unwritten rules, some of which are more powerful than the written ones.

**A.**   Plan to discuss school rules with one class for a period or longer. Obtain a copy of the written school rules for each student. First discuss the written rules to be sure students understand them.

- Are the rules really followed and enforced as they are written?
- Are most of them related to student misbehavior? Why?

- Are some of them confusing, seeming to create problems?
- Should recommendations be made for changing any of the rules?

**B.**   Next, ask students to identify some unwritten rules. "If you thought about school as a game in which some students win and some lose, what are the unwritten rules for winning at this game?" You may want to start them off with a few unwritten rules you know about. Two students can record on the chalkboard, and two on paper to be saved. Have the group also decide if they want to recommend to the principal or student council any changes in the school policy or rules—in light of their analysis of the unwritten rules.

**C.**   Finally, if you are their regular teacher, you can ask students to discuss the rules for this classroom. If the class already has a set of written rules, they can be analyzed for adequacy and effectiveness. If the rules have not yet been reduced to writing, have the students help you state the rules that they are willing to abide by. This is also an excellent opportunity to have the students consider whether the teacher should be enforcer of all the rules or whether some enforcement responsibilities can be delegated to students. Ask the students to consider whether the rules and routines actually interfere with their relationship with you and with their learning. One researcher's analysis suggests that rules and routines often replace interaction with the teacher, so that the student might only experience interaction with the teacher when he or she violates a rule, alters a routine, or defies a regulation (Cusik 1973).

   Rules and procedures that result from this activity can be written and posted in the room. Save a copy of the recommendations, the list of unwritten rules, and the classroom rules that result from this activity. Also make summary notes as needed so that the process and outcomes can be shared with a colleague or two.

## ACTIVITY 5
### Consider your "ideal" and "real" teacher images.

Those of us in the teaching profession have inherited not only a strong mind set of what schools should be and do, but also a powerful image of what the ideal teacher is and does (Greenberg 1969). We continually compare our own performances against the ideal we have inherited. Is that true for you? Below are twelve statements often regarded as standards for teachers. Do they operate as standards for you? For each of the twelve items, place an *IT* on the scale where you think the *Ideal Teacher* would be, and put an *I* on the scale where you believe you actually perform. If you think any of the statements are not appropriate standards for teachers, write "Not a good standard" on the line.

   1. Ideal teachers/I am: calm and even tempered.
      high _____ low
   2. Ideal teachers/I: follow the rule of moderation.
      high _____ low

3. Ideal teachers/I: regard children's feelings as more important than the teacher's feelings.
   high _____ low

4. Ideal teachers/I: accept and respect all the children.
   high _____ low

5. Ideal teachers/I: trust the children.
   high _____ low

6. Ideal teachers/I: protect the children from negative feelings they/I have about the children.
   high _____ low

7. Ideal teachers/I: can hide feelings from the children.
   high _____ low

8. Ideal teachers/I: do not have favorites among the children.
   high _____ low

9. Ideal teachers are/I am: able to answer all the children's questions.
   high _____ low

10. Ideal teachers/I: do not have prejudices about some children.
    high _____ low

11. Ideal teachers/I: can diagnose each child's needs and prescribe appropriate instruction for each.
    high _____ low

12. Ideal teachers/I: can conduct the classroom without distress and conflicts.
    high _____ low

Consciously or unconsciously, many teachers accept these standards. The greater the distance they see between their performance and their ideal, the more guilt they feel for not reaching the ideal. The guilt saps one's energies and undermines self-confidence. We agree with Greenberg (1969) that these ideals are strong myths and they are fantasies that do more harm than good. The intent of this set of scales is not to make you feel guilty for accepting any of the twelve standards. One load of guilt is as heavy as the other.

We reject the twelve myths because they set unattainable goals, superhuman expectations. They are part of the giant myth that schools should perform a sheltering function, keeping out all the "lower" human traits and values, modeling only the ideal virtues, until the twig is bent in the right direction.

We believe the school can be an arena where students encounter typical human problems — progressively, developmentally — as they are ready. In this setting, the teacher shows students how to take responsibility for their own feelings, behavior, and learning by *being responsible* for their own feelings, behavior, and learning. The way the teacher shows students these attributes is by presenting an authentic self rather than a facade of the ideal teacher. This chapter offers several alternatives to the "sheltering" model.

## ACTIVITY 6
### Analyze your use of sanctions.

Respond to the questionnaire that follows, score your responses, and interpret the score using the materials provided.

## Teacher Approval and Disapproval

This is a questionnaire you may use to examine your uses of sanctions (approval and disapproval) with students. Answer it as objectively as you can and score your responses with the key. Then read "Interpreting Your Sanctioning Score," and analyze what the outcome means to you.

Below is a list of actions teachers often take in managing a classroom. For each item decide if it is *like* you or *unlike* you to take that action or a similar action. Circle the L for Like or the U for Unlike.

The term *praise* as used below means to evaluate favorably, and *reprimand* means to evaluate unfavorably or to scold. *Punish* is used broadly to mean causing unpleasantness for a student, and *reward* means causing pleasantness.

| | | | |
|---|---|---|---|
| L | U | 1. | Physically escort the student back to his/her seat after telling him/her several times to be seated. |
| L | U | 2. | Praise a student for reading the right kind of literature outside of class. |
| L | U | 3. | Reprimand a student for loud talking in the library. |
| L | U | 4. | Give a reward when a student has indicated on a performance chart that he/she has consistently improved. |
| L | U | 5. | Punish or deny a student something when you catch him/her telling a lie. |
| L | U | 6. | Reward a student (who is often tardy) for being on time for a month. |
| L | U | 7. | Punish or reprimand a student for stealing money from another student. |
| L | U | 8. | Praise a student for coming to school with no make-up when she usually wears too much. |
| L | U | 9. | Make a student think in order to come up with the right answer when you know he/she knows the answer. |
| L | U | 10. | Promise your students a film if they perform an activity acceptably. |
| L | U | 11. | Punish or threaten to punish if a student continues to disrupt the class when you've asked him/her not to. |
| L | U | 12. | Set up a system whereby your students can earn some kinds of rewards if they do their work regularly. |
| L | U | 13. | Punish or scold a student for not cleaning up the work area when he/she knows it is a requirement. |

---

The authors are grateful to Ernest Coats for suggestions of items and to Thomas Gordon whose "Use of Parental Authority" questionnaire in *Parent Effectiveness Training* (Wyden, 1970, pp. 316–20) suggested the format for this questionnaire and score key.

L U 14. Set up some system of rewards as an incentive for your students to perform better on tests.

L U 15. Threaten to send a student out of the room if he/she continues to be disobedient.

L U 16. Praise or reward a student for doing a good job on a required project.

L U 17. Reprimand a student for not starting to work on an assignment after you thought he/she had begun at the right time.

L U 18. Praise your students for promptness in cleaning up after an activity.

L U 19. Punish or reprimand your students for fighting.

L U 20. Promise your students a party or some other such reward if they will stick to their study schedule to improve their grades.

L U 21. Punish or reprimand a student you see bullying and embarrassing another student.

L U 22. Praise your students for observing safety precautions during an experiment or other activity where safety is a factor.

L U 23. Punish or scold your students if they chew gum or eat during class.

L U 24. Tell your students that you are proud of them for behaving so well during a field trip.

## DIRECTIONS FOR SCORING

_____ Write here the number of *L's* circled beside *odd* numbered items. This figure suggests your tendency to control students by punishing or using other means of showing *disapproval*.

_____ Write here the number of *L's* circled beside *even* numbered items. This figure suggests your tendency to control students by using praise or other means of showing *approval*.

_____ Write here the total of the two numbers above. This figure suggests your tendency to control students by using sanctions, both approving and disapproving.

You may use this table to rate your uses of sanctioning.

| Use of Disapproval | | Use of Approval | | Use of Both Kinds of Sanctioning | |
|---|---|---|---|---|---|
| Score | Rating | Score | Rating | Score | Rating |
| 0-3 | Very Little | 0-3 | Very Little | 0-6 | Anti-Sanctioning |
| 4-6 | Occasionally | 4-6 | Occasionally | 7-12 | Moderate User of Sanctioning |
| 7-9 | Often | 7-9 | Often | 13-18 | Regular User of Sanctioning |
| 10-12 | Very Often | 10-12 | Very Often | 19-24 | High User of Sanctioning |

## INTERPRETING YOUR SANCTIONING SCORE

How much should a teacher use sanctions? A classroom must have structure and a certain level of order for learning to happen. Some students who come to you at the beginning of the year are self-disciplined and need very little control from you. Others, accustomed to a high degree of control by some adult, require authoritarian behavior from you—or they may spoil the learning situation for everyone.

Too little control means chaos, but too much is also dangerous. Research on teaching now shows a clear set of findings:

1. Classroom *structure* (rules, understood procedures, expectations) is essential for classroom learning. Teachers who rely on moment-by-moment *control* tactics to keep order, who neglect to develop classroom structure, actually discourage learning. "Cool" control tactics (commands, veiled threats) that do not help establish or clarify structure are harmful. For example, a teacher command such as "Stop that!" probably won't help the student relate his/her behavior to the classroom structure; but "Remember our rule about that?" affirms the structure. How you use the sanction is as important as how often (Soar and Soar 1976).

2. A teacher's use of approval, such as praise and rewards and a smile, is irrelevant to achievement. Students who learn well do so *not* because their teacher praises them, and the absence of teacher praise is *not* the reason that some students don't learn well. Teacher *empathy* is related to learning, but not teacher praise—when it is delivered mechanically, without empathy and genuine appreciation. Praise and rewards may often cause a student to *attend* to the task at hand, but studies of hundreds of classrooms show that most teachers' use of praise and rewards does not correlate with student achievement (Brophy and Evertson 1976, Roebuck and Aspy 1974, Rowe 1973).

3. Teacher disapproval, such as criticism and reprimand, is directly related to *lower* student achievement. The adverse effects of criticism are magnified among low social-economic group students. (Criticism is distinguished from an appropriate critique of a student's work, which can be helpful.) (Soar and Soar 1976)

In using reprimands, warnings, and punishment, teachers generally have good intentions: to teach respect, responsibility, honesty, self-discipline, etc. And these disapproval tactics often have short-term positive values. They give teachers a safety valve for their frustration and anger. They assert the rules and authority structure of the school. And they actually cause a student to stop an unacceptable behavior. Unfortunately, the natural longer-term consequences of reprimands, warnings, and punishment far outweigh the possible short-term benefits. The ultimate consequences are likely to be resentment, hostility, vengefulness, defiance, fear, resignation, and self-depreciation. There is no doubt that these emotions interfere with learning and with responsibility taking. Some of them may sometimes get students to comply with procedures and rules. They are "motivators," but they do not promote learning that lasts and integrates into one's behavior and they cannot produce responsible behavior.

4. The more a teacher uses sanctions (praise, criticism, rewards, threats, etc.), the less initiative students take in problem solving, and the less responsibility they take for managing their own learning. Teacher sanctions encourage a student to search for "right answers;" whether the answers are understood or not is irrelevant to the search. Teacher sanctions discourage group cooperation in problem solving. One researcher colorfully noted that teacher sanctioning encouraged students individually to hoard "right answers" and to release them only when they could get little pellets of praise from the teacher. When students feel the necessity of

"doping out" or "psyching out" what the teacher wants and likes, they are turning away from the responsibility of analyzing their own learning needs. They are not making connections between new knowledge and their prior experience (Rowe 1973).

5. Your sanctioning score also says something about who makes decisions in the classroom. Students need the opportunity to make decisions and choices. For complex, abstract tasks (e.g., vocabulary development, composition, and social concepts), students learn best when they have more chances to decide and choose; these tasks also need more student interaction and less drill. Simple, concrete learning (e.g., spelling, handwriting, and concrete facts) is accomplished better when students have fewer choices, the teacher makes the basic decisions and recitation and drill are used more. If your sanctioning score was high, you may be making classroom decisions that should be delegated to students. If your score was low, you may be leaving too many decisions to students (Soar and Soar 1976).

We suggest you reread these five sets of research findings, perhaps several times. These are not the outcomes of single studies, but conclusions based on the findings of many distinguished researchers through many years of work. To summarize:

1. Teacher sanctions are harmful when they only control student behavior and do not clarify or strengthen the structure of the classroom.

2. Teacher praise and other kinds of approval are irrelevant to achievement unless they genuinely express empathy and appreciation.

3. Teacher criticism and other kinds of disapproval are harmful to achievement, especially for students of low socio-economic backgrounds.

4. Teacher sanctions discourage problem solving and encourage dependency on the teacher.

5. For abstract, complex tasks, students learn best when they have the responsibility of choosing and deciding activities; a low level of student choice is appropriate for simple, concrete tasks.

In developing self-reliance, self-discipline, and responsibility, a student moves away from dependence on the teacher. When teachers use sanctioning sparingly and with care, they help students make that move.

## RELATING THE RESEARCH TO PERSONAL EXPERIENCE

For each of the five sets of research findings given in the material, write a personal reaction based on your experiences.

Save your reactions and analyses to share with colleagues. Note: If you feel discouraged about the outcomes of this activity, it may help to know that Activities 7 and 8 deal with skill development in sanctioning and control techniques.

## ACTIVITY 7
### Analyze and change your uses of praise and criticism.

A teacher's uses of sanctions are clearly related to students' taking responsibility. This activity is designed to help you be clear about your typical uses of approval and disapproval, to recognize some more constructive teacher responses, to plan any changes you want to make, and to practice the alternatives to sanctioning.

**A.**   Set a tape recorder going during a period when you are conducting a class discussion and interacting with students in other ways. (You may already have a tape made for other purposes. Decide whether it suits this purpose.) The object is to record some typical ways you interact and lead discussions. If you are unable to record your teaching, complete only section E of this activity.

**B.**   Afterwards, as you listen to the tape, jot down a list of the words you use that show approval or disapproval: good, bad, that's right, clever, silly, careless, etc., and tally the number of times you used each. Save the taped dialogue for analysis of a different kind in Activities 8 and 12.

**C.**   Write down your reactions to your use of these sanctioning words. Save it to share with your colleagues.

**D.**   Decide on some goal for yourself: Reducing the use of certain words or reducing the frequency of the total number of sanctioning words used per minute. To make your plan work, to actually reduce the quantity of either verbal or nonverbal sanctioning, you probably will need to increase your use of *nonjudgmental* responses as explained in section E.

**E.**   Read "Kicking the Sanctioning Habit," which follows, and complete the activities described there.

**F.**   Put your plan into action, making use of the tape recorder to catch the changes you are trying to make. An alternative is to ask two students to be observers. Show them how to recognize and tally your nonjudgmental reaction and feedback statements. Students often are intrigued with this kind of task. Average the two sets of tallies. Write reaction notes after each observation session and save them to share with your peer panel. Note any changes you see in student participation and other behavior. Don't expect rapid changes.

## Kicking the Sanctioning Habit

The teacher's job requires directing and correcting, supporting and encouraging students, frequently, every day. The conventional way of doing that is by stating approval or disapproval of student actions. Research clearly shows that the conventional way is not the best way. Higher teacher use of sanctions is directly linked to higher student dependence on their teachers and lower student initiative and responsibility taking. The case against praise is expressed well by Ginott (1972). "Praise, like a drug, may make a child feel good—for the moment. However, it creates dependence. Others become his source of approval. He relies on them to quench his craving and establish his value. They must tell him his daily worth." The case against criticism and punishment has been well-articulated and is based on substantial research evidence: the higher the level of criticism in a classroom, the lower the achievement scores (see the summary of research findings in the previous reading.)

If teachers must correct and direct, support and encourage students, what alternatives are there to sanctions? Clearly, sanctioning responses cannot simply be removed without substituting other kinds of responses. We have identified six kinds of teacher responses that are essentially nonjudgmental, one of which should fit any kind of situation: (a) a structuring response; (b) an "I" message; (c) a response to feeling rather than content; (d) a response that accepts and uses the student's idea or contribution; (e) a response that shows appreciation; and (f) a response that shares in the student's pleasure or satisfaction. The first three are alternatives to disapproval, criticism, reprimand, warnings, and punishment. The (d), (e), and (f) responses are alternatives to praise and rewards.

## A STRUCTURING RESPONSE

The general rule for responding to problem situations can be stated in three sentences. When a student makes a mistake, breaks a rule or norm, disappoints the teacher's expectation or the group's expectation, or interferes with the teacher's work or plans, a structuring response is needed. *If* the problem triggers the teacher's anger or other strong emotion, then an "I" message needs to come before a structuring response. *If* the student's emotion in the situation may be blocking his or her ability to hear the structuring response, then a response to the student's feelings must come before the structuring response.

What is a structuring response? Below are two sets of teacher's responses, nonstructuring and structuring, for different situations. Study them and identify in your own words, as precisely as you can, the attributes of a structuring response—what it is and what it is not.

| Situation | Nonstructuring Response | Structuring Response |
|---|---|---|
| One small group is talking loudly while others work quietly. | "Quiet down. Can't you control your voices? You're not thinking about the rest of us." | "When you talk loudly it's hard for the rest of us to concentrate." |
| John, who has a record of causing problems, makes three students angry by annoying them. | "John, if you can't control yourself any better than this, I really am going to send you to the time-out room." | "John, you have a choice. You can abide by the rules of this class or go to the time-out room." |
| Ann, a large eighth grader, bumps into the teacher while running in the hall. | "Ann, why are you running? "Don't you know the rules? Don't you know you could really hurt somebody?" | "Ann, our rule about running in the halls is a good rule. Imagine what might have happened if I were a small sixth grader you just ran into." |
| Two girls start swinging at each other outside the classroom door just as the period begins. The teacher steps between them. | "Break it up. Fighting is stupid. It doesn't solve anything. What's the problem?" | "You two are obviously so angry, it's dangerous for you to be near each other. Jan, sit over there. After class, if you two need my help, tell me." |

| Situation | Nonstructuring Response | Structuring Response |
|---|---|---|
| The teacher, coming into the classroom, sees two boys fighting furiously. The teacher stops them with a loud voice. Then the boys start yelling and accusing each other. | "I don't care who did what or who said what. You're both guilty of fighting. Report here after school so we can decide what should be done." | "Hold it. You are too angry to talk now. Both of you sit down and write out what happened... The whole story, and what you think should be done about the situation." |
| While the teacher is filling out reports at her desk, six students crowd around her with science graphs they have been preparing. | "Can't you see I'm busy? I've got these reports to do. Go back to your seats and wait. I'll get there when I can." | "I would like to help each of you, but I must do these reports right now. How about each of you taking a partner and helping each other?" |
| At the beginning of class, a student says to the teacher, "I don't have my assignment finished." | "Why haven't you finished it? It wasn't a hard assignment." | "That makes a problem for you and for me. What should be done? Think about it and give me your answer in a few minutes." |
| Responding to the teacher's question, a student says that Miami is the capital of Florida. | "Wrong. That's one you were supposed to study. Who can tell me the right answer?" | "Miami is the largest city in Florida, but not its capital. Why might a capital not be the largest city of a state?" |
| Janice has complained six times in twenty minutes about one student or another bothering her—taking her pencil, moving her books, etc. | "Janice, your whining is really annoying. If it doesn't stop, I'm going to put you at the back of the room where no one can get near you." | "We are all trying to work quietly and we need to protect our quiet. Put your complaint in writing and put it in this box. From now on this is our complaint box." |

After you have written your own definition of a structuring response, compare yours with ours, below.

A structuring response has four basic attributes:

1. It is a *factual statement* about the immediate problem. The intent is to clarify the nature of the problem.

2. It is *nonjudgmental*. It does *not* question a person's motives or imply weakness of character. All of the nonstructuring responses above either questioned motives, blamed the student and implied a character flaw, or both. The problem with a judgmental response is that it tears down the student, allows resentment to build and offers no way for the student to save face in the situation.

3. A structuring response either *affirms an existing structure* (norm, procedure, or rule), as in the first three examples above, or *it provides a new structure* to deal with the situation, as in the other examples. A structuring response always implies that the school and classroom are governed by a respect for the general welfare that overrides the idiosyncracies and whims of individual students, teachers, and others.

4. It *places with the student the responsibility* for his or her own behavior. All of the nonstructuring responses above label the student(s) as irresponsible. That label, pasted on the student day after day, must affect the student's self-image. In

contrast, the structuring response avoids labeling and emphasizes the student's continuing responsibility for present and future action. Note that in most of the nonstructuring responses the teacher assumed responsibility for the situation and in effect diminished the student's need to be responsible.

In summary, a structuring response is a factual, nonjudgmental statement about the immediate problem that affirms structure and leaves the student responsible within the structure.

## AN "I" MESSAGE

Thomas Gordon (1974) has provided the key insights about teacher responses that deal effectively with teacher anger and other strong emotions. Swallowing the anger and pretending it isn't there is less than useless, it is harmful. Suppressed anger interferes with communication. Anger expressed with restraint is the objective. When a structuring response is needed, but the situation has triggered strong emotion in the teacher, an "I" message must come first to deal with the emotion, to release it without destructive consequences.

As with the structuring response, an "I" message has some distinctive attributes. Below are several statements. What makes the "I" messages different from the others? Can you identify the features of an "I" message?

| Not "I" Messages | "I" Messages |
|---|---|
| "When you are sloppy and leave glue and paper scraps all around the tables I really get angry." | "When I find glue and paper scraps all around the tables, I really get angry. I'm stuck with cleaning it up or having the custodian mad at me." |
| "We agreed on a plan. Why didn't you do your part? You're a real disappointment to me." | "I'm really disappointed. We agreed on a plan and you didn't do your part. That spoils our schedule." |
| "Your brawling makes me furious! Can't you keep yourselves under control?" | "Your fighting makes me furious! I get panicky with fear when people are so violent with each other." |
| "When you are inconsiderate of other people, you offend them and make me unhappy, too." | "When people make loud noises like that and interrupt the speaker, I get very annoyed and have a hard time controlling my temper." |

Before reading our definition of an "I" message, write your own to compare with ours.

An "I" message has five attributes:

1. It reports a teacher's problem. The teacher *owns* the problem (a mess to clean up, a spoiled schedule, panic, temper control).

2. It conveys a factual report of what is creating the problem for the teacher. A *nonblaming description* of what is unacceptable is the best kind of report.

3. It conveys the *tangible or concrete effect* on the teacher of the specific behavior described in the message.

4. It states the *feelings* the teacher is having because he or she is tangibly affected.

5. It leaves with the student the responsibility for his or her own behavior.

Note that an "I" message is like a structuring response in that it includes a nonblaming description and it leaves responsibility with the student. What an "I" message distinctively adds is the report of the teacher's feelings about a problem the teacher is concretely experiencing.

For most teachers, their first reaction in a stressful situation is not an "I" message. Much more common is an inquisition question, "Why did you do that?" The teacher's intent may be to help the student see how to choose better behavior, but the question is an inquisition to the student. It implies blame, induces guilt feelings, and prompts excuses that may not be truthful. Even worse, the "Why did you . . . ?" question takes the student's mind away from constructive alternative behaviors. None of these effects encourage responsibility taking.

If the teacher is annoyed or hurt by the student's behavior, an "I" message can convey feelings without discouraging the student from finding better behavior.

## A RESPONSE TO FEELING RATHER THAN CONTENT

When a student's emotions are immediately involved in the problem, they must be acknowledged before a structuring message can have any value. The content or substance of the problem comes second in the sequence.

A student comes to the teacher's desk. "I don't understand why I got this stupid low score on the test." The teacher, instead of beginning structuring response, says: "You're really disappointed with the score." "Yes." "Especially after all the time you spent studying for it." "Yeah, I spent a lot of time." "You're worried about how your parents will react." "I sure am . . . Can you show me what I did wrong?" By responding to feelings first, the teacher set up conditions for a dialogue about content. Teacher: "Do you ever check your work systematically before you turn in your test?" "No. Can you show me how?" "Yes, I'll show you with some of these problems, then you use the system to check the others and see how many errors you can detect without my help."

Panicked at the thought of making a presentation to the whole class, a student says, "I can't do it. I'll throw up." Avoiding easy reassurances, or prodding, the teacher responds, "It really is a scary thing to do . . . Makes you feel nauseated just thinking about it . . . You'd be very frightened up there." After the student gives some signs of feeling the teacher's empathy, the teacher makes a structuring suggestion: "Can you think of some ways to make presentations less scary for people?" The teacher leaves the problem with the student and offers a new vantage point.

Responding constructively to students' fear, anger, hostility, and frustration not only requires practice but also a desire to know their feelings and to deal with them. The books by Ginott and Gordon offer helpful suggestions (Ginott 1972, and Gordon 1974).

## A RESPONSE THAT ACCEPTS AND USES THE STUDENT'S IDEA OR CONTRIBUTION

The three kinds of response already described are constructive substitutes for teacher disapproval messages. These last three are constructive alternatives to teacher praise and rewards—which tend to heighten student dependency and lower initiative.

When students display their efforts—through words, crafts, paintings, models, maps, displays, movement skills, etc.—the teacher can provide support and encouragement by giving *thoughtful, nonsanctioning attention* to the students' efforts. Attention can take various forms.

**A.** *Acknowledging:* "Well, you got it done! Congratulations! It was a big job."

"I can see you have given the problem a lot of thought."

**B.** *Clarifying:* "Let me be clear about your idea. You're saying the author meant to throw us off the track and this is a misleading clue. Right?"

"Then your reason for supporting Bakke is really different from Walt's reason. Is that true?"

**C.** *Describing:* "Your display is really set off by the contrasting colors. The letters are big and the description cards are all mounted where people can see them easily." (Note: Any description is selective. In this case the teacher probably selected features for comment according to some criteria for designing displays. Probably the teacher is supporting the judgments the student made in designing the display. These kinds of teacher comments can encourage independent judgment—provided that the display features really respresented the initiative of the student.)

**D.** *Developing:* "Suppose we took your idea one step further, George. Suppose there was a ban on manufacturing any car that didn't get twenty-five miles to the gallon. What would be the consequences?"

"Jean, your plan for the experiment has two variables. What would happen if we added a third—perhaps temperature differences?"

**E.** *Summarizing:* "You're saying that the can-collection drive has too many teams, that each home-base group should be a team, that we should set a deadline, and the whole school should decide how to spend the proceeds—regardless of who wins. Have I got it all?"

**F.** *Inferring:* "If your hypothesis is correct, then we should get a deep blue color by mixing these two. Right?"

"Your painting tells me you wanted to show a stormy mood, angry and troubled. Was that what you meant?"

What these six kinds of responses have in common is a deeper attention to the intellectual and feeling messages of students, deeper than can be conveyed by conventional praise responses: "Good," "I like that," "I'm proud of you," "You should be proud of yourself," "What a clever idea." When the essence of the student's message is recognized in the teacher's response, all the students—not just the speaker (or displayer)—receive a clue that this teacher cares enough to listen and observe with sensitivity.

## A RESPONSE THAT SHOWS APPRECIATION

The difference between a praise response that binds and an appreciation response that frees is subtle but vitally important. Far more often than we suspect, students know when our praise is mechanical or when it comes from the teacher role and not from the person inside the role. The subtle difference is difficult to convey in the printed word because tone of voice and context often are the only carriers of the difference. Nevertheless, we make the attempt.

| | |
|---|---|
| "Your paper is much neater this time. Congratulations." | "Your careful spacing of the problems made your paper *much* easier to read. I'm grateful." |
| "I'm very proud of you for your great work on the play. Super!" | "Your work on the play helped me see a new side of you. Thank you." |
| "John, you stuck to your contract and didn't hassle me all day. I said you could do it, and you did! You should be proud." | "I was tense in the beginning of class, wondering if you would keep your 'no hassle' agreement. You did, and it made my day! Thank you." |
| "Thank you for sharing your cartoon with us. You're really an artist." | "Grace, your cartoon made me chuckle every time I walked past the bulletin board." |
| "You are a very thoughtful girl who knows how to please her teacher. The supply cupboard looks much better!" | "Your taking time to help me with the supply cupboard saved me a lot of work. Thank you for your thoughtfulness." |

We hope you can detect the differences in tone we mean to convey in the two columns. Appreciation is personal. It is a message that reveals something of the person sending the message. It speaks about the tangible effect the person has felt. It is meant to close the distance between people, not to keep them at a formal distance, as between a judge and a person being judged. The appreciation response does not tell the students how or what they should feel ("You should be proud!") or what interpretation to put on the teacher's comment. As with other nonjudgmental responses, this one leaves with the students the responsibility for their own thoughts, feelings, and actions.

## A RESPONSE THAT SHARES IN THE STUDENT'S PLEASURE OR SATISFACTION

When students choose to display their work or ask for a reaction to it, they have different reasons for doing so. Some want other people to share in their pleasure. Others are asking for a critique with the serious intent of improving the quality of their work. Still others only want their daily dose of teacher approval and don't know whether to take pleasure in their work until the teacher tells them its worth. And a few students in every group ask for teacher reaction just to see how the teacher plays the game. With a great flourish of eagerness and anticipation, these students present work they know is not their best and thus test the teacher to see how high the teacher's expectations and quality standards are. This is the mini-max game: do just enough to get good pay-off and no more.

A response that shares in a student's satisfaction is a safe and constructive way to respond to all four kinds of requests. Students who really want a critique will persist in asking for it.

The teacher should not use this response without being reasonably sure of the level of satisfaction the student feels in his or her own work.

Student: How do you like my map?

Teacher: I saw you working at it with a lot of concentration. What parts of it did you especially like doing?

Student: Well, I like the symbols I made to show the products of the countries . . . The rest was mostly boring. I don't like making maps very much.

Teacher: The symbols show your careful work. They are bright and it's easy to understand what they stand for. Maybe next time you can team up with someone who likes doing other parts of maps and you could do the illustrations and symbols.

The teacher is faced with a different situation when a student proudly presents work of uneven quality.

Teacher: You seem really pleased with your short story.

Student: I am. I like it. What do you think of it?

Teacher: I like your choice of characters—ordinary people, like people we already know. What do you especially like about your story?

Student: Well, I like the mystery part of it, the surprises that happen to Anne.

Teacher: Yes. I bet you had fun thinking up those surprises. That's a new feature in your stories. I'm glad you are looking for ways to strengthen your writing.

Note that these responses, too, are nonjudgmental. The teacher expresses personal pleasure without presuming to put an objective value on the student's work.

## CONVERTING APPROVAL AND DISAPPROVAL RESPONSES

To help you practice phrasing nonjudgmental responses, we have compiled a list of frequently used teacher sanctioning statements that need to be converted. For each one, compose a nonjudgmental response using the guidelines given in the six sections above. By the time you reach the last third of the list, the nonsanctioning phrases should be coming to you fairly quickly. When your list of responses is finished, save it to compare with those of your peer panel members.

Composing nonjudgmental responses is a useful, probably essential, step in kicking the sanctioning habit. But it is an armchair activity remote from the pressures of the classroom. The most vital step, which we cannot structure for you, is your own plan to make specific changes and to monitor your progress. Working through the list below may suggest to you some particular targets for your plan.

Convert each of these teacher responses to a nonjudgmental form.

1. "Matt, your handwriting seems sloppier than ever. Aren't you trying any more?"

2. "Karen, your papier-maché rabbit is just as handsome as you said it was. You should feel very proud."

3. "Having hand-me-down clothes is nothing to be ashamed of. I wore them as a kid. Anyway, other students don't notice clothes as much as you think they do."

4. "Your manners are disgusting! How can you expect other people to respect you when you are so offensive?"

5. "You see? You're smarter than you thought . . . every problem is worked right."

6. "Stop the noise! I leave you alone for five minutes and the roof blows off the classroom. Why can't you be orderly without me here?"

7. "I'm very proud of all of you. We've gone two whole weeks without anyone coming late to class. You really can do it when you want to."

8. "Jim, why are you late? You know how late arrivers always disrupt things."

9. "Jean, your design is beautiful. You're a real artist."

10. "George, you have a knack for interrupting. Now I've lost my train of thought."

11. "If we can make it to Friday with no litter on the floor at the end of each period, I'll give you all a half-hour of free time as a reward."

12. "The way you went through the halls to assembly was a disgrace. Third graders do better. Tomorrow we'll practice doing it right, and we'll get it right or miss the next assembly."

13. "The way you acted during the assembly was great. You were ladies and gentlemen."

14. "Who's got the hall pass? Why isn't it on my desk? How can we have an orderly classroom unless things stay in the place they belong?"

15. "Lisa, what are we going to do about your writing? Many sentences are run-on. You've neglected to start some sentences with capitals. And there are at least six other kinds of errors. I don't think you're making any progress."

## ACTIVITY 8
### Analyze classroom control strategies.

Anyone familiar with middle grades classrooms knows that they easily drift into disorder unless a social system is working to maintain order. Some classrooms have a strong and clear *structure*—those norms, procedures, and expectations that students follow with little need for reminders. Classrooms without a strong and clear structure must obtain most of their order from teacher *control*, the moment-by-moment directing of students—telling them what to do. Even in well-structured classrooms, regular teacher directives are needed. Teacher control strategies differ widely in quality. The better ones encourage student responsibility taking and strengthen the structure of the classroom so that the teacher spends less time controlling and more time instructing.

This activity gives you a means to analyze your own control strategies and to consider what controls might be delegated to students.

## IMPROVING CLASSROOM CONTROL TECHNIQUES

**A.**  *Your Controlling Behaviors.* Teachers spend a large amount of time giving directions, organizing, directing traffic, and otherwise getting students ready for instruction or keeping them on track. One researcher (Hughes 1959) found that, on the average, half of a teacher's time is spent in controlling student actions, while less than one-fifth of the teacher's time is given to the *content* of instruction. The research findings show substantial variation from teacher to teacher. The findings also suggest that some teachers have discovered means of keeping their classrooms under control through structure, thus reducing the amount of teacher time spent on controlling student actions and leaving the teacher more time for the content of instruction.

Controlling, unlike sanctioning, does not involve judging students' work or behavior. It is telling students what to do, not giving a reaction to what they already have done. Controlling is:

| | |
|---|---|
| Setting goals | Directing attention |
| Defining tasks | Specifying content |
| Regulating who will do what | Specifying the answers to be sought |
| Regulating how it will be done | Directing traffic |

Teacher phrases that control student actions are familiar ones:

"First we are going to work on our . . ."

"John, you write on the first question; Lee, you take the second one . . ."

"Your graphs should have five things in them . . ."

"Ben and Russ will work together; Jan and Sue . . ."

"We need three illustrators. Let's see, Jim, Mary, and John . . ."

"You four bring your chairs over here. Work quietly. Use standard size paper. Check each other's work when you are done. Then one of you come and get the answer key . . ."

"We all should be on page 61, second paragraph."

"Keep your eyes on the balance beam."

"The topic for your paper should be, 'What I Did on My Summer Vacation.' Tell about things that really happened."

"That may be true, but that's not the answer I'm looking for. Who else . . . ?"

"Don't sharpen pencils now. Take your seats, please."

Controlling classroom events is an integral part of the teacher's job. However, research indicates that teachers must be alert to the risks of over-control. Student growth in responsibility taking depends on the delegating of some teacher-held controls to students, individually and collectively.

What proportion of your time is spent controlling student actions? What control statements are typical of you? If you wanted to spend less time on controlling and more time on the content of instruction, could you find some ways to do it?

1. If you are now teaching, make a tape recording when you are conducting typical classroom activities. Record one period, or at least twenty minutes. You may wish to use a previously recorded tape. Listening to the tape, make a list of all the controlling statements you made. Remember to exclude statements of approval and disapproval and those that are substance or content-of-instruction statements.

2. Make an estimate of the ratio of time (on the tape) spent on controlling to your time spent on the content of instruction. Do you want to devote more of your time to instructional content? You can get some clues about how to reduce your directing and controlling time by analyzing your list of statements. Use the following questions in your analysis and keep notes to share later with your colleagues.

   a. Do your statements include instructions for routines that students probably could carry out without your verbal instructions—if they had a checklist or a signal, or if the routine were delegated to particular students? For example, directing the flag salute, watering plants, preparing attendance reports.

   b. Do your statements include efforts to fine-tune student behavior beyond what is needed for an orderly class? "Put away your spelling lists now. That means everybody. You, too, April. John. George. Put them in your notebooks. Now put the notebooks in your desks. Clear off the desk-tops. Sit up straight, Ralph. Everybody sit up straight. I see three desktops that aren't clear. Now everyone get out a clean piece of paper so we can do some writing . . ." Could such instructions be simplified to a single directive statement?

3. For whatever you intend to change in the way you direct and control students, write out an action plan for yourself, collect at least two additional talk-samples in the classroom, and keep a log of your progress. Share your plan, procedures, and log with a colleague. Set realistic goals for yourself and be persistent.

**B.** *Avoiding Commands.* Some teachers' controlling methods are too heavily loaded with commands. Commands don't invite participation or action, they order it. Everyone has experienced the unpleasant pressure and feeling of resentment that comes from an overload of commands. Unfortunately, teachers are not always aware of when they use commands or over-use them.

People don't mind commands when they are obviously necessary for order and for everybody's welfare—as when the policeman directs traffic, the surgeon calls for instruments from the nurse, and the choreographer commands the dancers. Commands of that kind are, most likely, part of a collaboration, an agreement about relationships, and they imply mutual respect. Commands that don't have those features, that seem to be just an exercise of power, are ones that promote resentment.

Commands leave no room for student judgment or choice. Students have no way to improve the quality of their judgments except by making judgments, analyzing the value of them, and trying again. Few commands are actually required in most classrooms. They can be replaced by other techniques that leave room for student judgment. We hold the view that commands should be replaced by other forms of control whenever possible. Then, when a command is truly needed, it is more likely to be heeded. We recommend replacements such as these:

"Everybody stop what you're doing and clean up your tables."

"It's 2:00. Time to clean up."

"Pull your foot in out of the aisle."

"Your foot is in the traffic path."

"John, turn off your sink faucet when you're not using it."

"John, your sink faucet is running."

"Stop talking. Sit down. Give me your attention so we can get started."

"It's time for us to begin now."

As suggested in these examples, commands often can be replaced by simple statements of fact about the timing, pacing or orderly management of the classroom. To offer you some practice in finding replacements for commands, we have listed ten commands for you to convert to non-command statements. Please note that a command with the word "please" on the front is still a command. Save your list to discuss with a colleague.

"Take this envelope to the office for me."

"All of you who have not already finished your reports must finish them as homework tonight."

"Clean up and put away your equipment now. Wash out the glass pieces carefully. Wipe them. Put the towels back. Put each piece in its place in the tray. (Etc.)"

"Don't speak out of turn. Raise hands when you want to speak."

"Get ready to go to the auditorium. Remember what I said about your behavior in the hall."

"Give your full attention to each speaker giving a report. Be courteous."

"Take out your textbook everybody. Turn to page 189. John, page 189. Rona. Do it now. Find the six questions at the bottom of the page. This side of the room write out answers to the odd-numbered items and this side answer the even-numbered items. All right? Go to work. Quietly."

"Give me your attention. Eyes up here. Quiet. All right, listen while Jack reads the morning announcements."

"Stop the talking. You may talk *quietly,* but don't let your voices get loud again."

"Hand me your admit slip."

**C.** *What controls can students exercise?*  At the University Elementary School of the University of California, Los Angeles, teachers have trained themselves to automatically ask themselves a question whenever a decision must be made in the course of daily instruction: Is this a decision the student can make, a decision the student and I should make together, or a decision I must make? This technique is powerful in reminding the teacher to help students assume as much responsibility as they can handle.

Each controlling statement a teacher uses represents a decision made, usually made by the teacher alone. Whether the decision could have been made by the student, given appropriate structure, is often not considered.

We invite those readers who have full charge of a group of students to conduct a brainstorming session with your students to consider the distribution of authority to make decisions within your classroom. Here is a format you may follow.

1. Ask students to brainstorm all the various sorts of decisions that are made in this classroom. If *brainstorming* is a term unfamiliar to them, you can explain its objective of

producing as many items as possible, with no one stopping to criticize or analyze. Have two or three students at the chalkboard to take turns writing items. You may wish to get them started by using examples like those used in the preceding pages. They probably will need some help to recognize the wide range of decisions that are made each day. If you think it will be useful, have each item on the board marked to indicate who typically makes each decision: teacher, student, or both together.

2. Next ask each student to write three personal lists:
   a. Decisions I should make for myself.
   b. Decisions the teacher and I should make together.
   c. Decisions the teacher should make.

Students may need help in starting their lists. You can suggest items which they then can place on one of the three lists. For example: how to use my study time; choosing the topic for research projects and for papers I write; how much individual study time to have each week; what words should be added to my vocabulary/spelling list each week; what should be in our individual study contracts; and choosing what major topics we work on during the year. The list of items, of course, is likely to be much longer. After the student lists are completed, before interest begins to wane, organize students into trios to compare and discuss their lists. Before you collect the lists, save a few minutes for the total group to discuss the outcomes.

3. Analyze the students' lists. Consider (a) how realistically each student has judged his or her capacity for responsibility; (b) what the lists suggest about individual contracts with the students; and (c) what structural changes in your classroom procedures are suggested by the lists. Your analysis should give you some agenda items for a classroom meeting on these topics. The students may have related agenda items to suggest as well.

4. Of course, the process of adjusting authority and responsibility does not end here. It does not end at all. This activity can initiate a dialogue that continues. Students' lists can be kept in their classroom folders. The lists and some narrative record should be available so that you can discuss them with a colleague.

## ACTIVITY 9
**Analyze the classroom emotional climate.**

### EMOTIONS AND RESPONSIBILITY

**A.** *The responsibility range.*   Students feel responsible under some conditions and not others. As with the ecology of plant life, responsibility seems to grow in some classroom climates and not in others. The emotions, attitudes, and motivations that make up a student's sense of responsibility can be strongly influenced by the classroom structure provided by the teacher.

For each student there is a range of classroom conditions within which responsibility taking is supported. As suggested in the table that follows, the responsibility range falls between too little stimulation or challenge and too much.

**Too Little Stress** ◀─────────────────────────────▶ **Too Much Stress**

| | | |
|---|---|---|
| "I'm not responsible for anything except sitting quietly and following directions." | | "The teacher leaves me responsible for managing too many things." |
| Expectations for the student are too low | THE RESPONSIBILITY RANGE | Expectations for the student are too high |
| too cut and dried | | too much to attend to |
| too little variety, too much predictability and routine | | too little security and routine work |
| APATHY/BOREDOM | | ANXIETY/PANIC |

We know of no practical way to measure with exactness a responsibility range for individual students. However, students' reactions to a few straight questions can give a teacher some useful clues about adjustments that may be needed in the classroom climate. Below are ten questions students can answer anonymously. Tally their responses by item. Even-numbered items marked *true* reflect their judgment of too little stimulation. There are no objective standards to compare their responses to. Draw your own conclusions. The questionnaire serves as a good discussion vehicle. You can have students help tally the responses (by having them exchange papers and raise hands item by item) and then have them discuss their interpretations and make suggestions. Keep notes and the tally sheet to share with a colleague.

Teacher's Name _____ *No Student Names, Please*

### Student Survey

Please respond to these items by marking a *T* for true next to any item that is true *for you*. Mark as many as are true for you.

_____ 1. In this class I feel a lot of pressure and tension.

_____ 2. This class needs more variety; we do too much of the same thing.

_____ 3. The teacher leaves me responsible for managing too many things.

_____ 4. Too much of the work is all planned out; we don't have enough chance to plan and change things.

_____ 5. The teacher expects too much from me, more than I can really do.

_____ 6. The teacher expects too little from me; I can do better work.

_____ 7. In this class there are too many things to pay attention to and to keep track of.

_____ 8. In this class I'm not responsible for anything except sitting quietly and following directions.

_____ 9. This class needs fewer surprises and less complicated work.

_____10. This class is not stimulating; mostly I feel dull in here.

**B.** *Reducing the fear of failure.*  Taking responsibility means taking risks. Risk involves the possibility of failure, and fear of failing or losing face is a powerful reason for avoiding responsibility.

Have a discussion with students along these lines: "People seem to have a strong fear of failing. They hate to make mistakes. That's true in school, too, isn't it? Why is that so?" After they share their views, ask for ideas of how in this class the fear of failure can be reduced. You can have bumper-sticker size paper ready and have students work in pairs to convert their ideas into mottos to post around the room. Make notes to discuss with colleagues.

## ACTIVITY 10
**Analyze classroom practices that promote responsibility and irresponsibility.**

### INCREASING STUDENTS' SENSE OF OWNERSHIP OF SCHOOL AND CLASSROOM TASKS

People take responsibility for things and events in which they feel a sense of ownership. Some schools have dramatically reduced vandalism by finding ways for students to develop a sense of ownership in school property. The same principle applies to curriculum, classroom activities, school rules, homework, and other aspects of school life.

Researchers who study how groups function have had some potent insights into group planning and individual responsibility. When a group of people is given a problem to solve and a task to accomplish, it naturally goes through three stages, as suggested in the diagram:

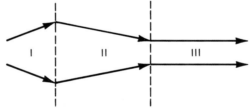

Stage I, called *exploration,* is represented by the diverging arrows. The group members search and brainstorm to clarify the situation and to consider alternatives. In the second stage, *evaluation,* the members assess the various alternatives and narrow the options down to a single plan of action. The plan specifies who will do what, and how. *Task accomplishment,* the third stage, is the effort to carry out the plan.

Out of the research on group functioning has come these two principles, among others:

1. The quality of a group's accomplishment is directly related to how adequately it does its work in Stages I and II. If either of those stages is shortcircuited, ignored, or dominated by one or two members, the quality of accomplishment tends to be lower.

2. How well individuals in the group do their work, and how responsible they feel for the group's effort, depends directly on how they feel about their participation in Stages I

and II. The more they believe their ideas and judgments are woven into the group's plan and task, or at least were considered, the more responsibility they take and the better their work.

Schools, unfortunately, have inherited a very different structure. All that the students see of the school's plan is:

Students are given a task to perform that was decided by someone else, and they are expected to accept it as their responsibility. Explanations of why the task is important for them, and other "motivators," do not adequately substitute for their being involved in Stages I and II. If students are to have a sense of ownership in the curriculum and school operations, it is most likely to happen through their genuine involvement in the planning—involvement of a kind that matches their maturity.

Consider the array of plans and decisions made in schools, made *for* the students but not *with* them. Consider what aspects of classroom and school life require planning. Concentrating on just one school, your own or one you know well, decide which of those planning processes students could participate in. If the students are not accustomed to responsible roles in planning, can some tasks be selected that offer them a good chance of success as participants in planning? Organize your ideas on paper and share them with a colleague.

Chapter Four, "Social and Emotional Development," includes several suggestions for projects in which students can take major planning responsibilities.

## CLASSROOM MANAGEMENT TO PROMOTE RESPONSIBLE BEHAVIOR

After spending several years in frustrating research trying to find the most effective ways of dealing with discipline problems, Jacob Kounin (1970) concluded that teachers unknowingly permit or promote most of the irresponsible student behavior by the way they manage classroom events. He studied classrooms that ran smoothly and those that did not and found that teacher management of the classroom differed dramatically between the two groups.

Classrooms in which students did not take responsibility and were frequently "off-task" had teachers who:

- were not alert to budding disruptions
- often reprimanded the wrong students
- became distracted easily
- had difficulty attending to more than one thing at a time
- broke into students' concentration
- made awkward or slow transitions from one activity to another
- became preoccupied with trivial details

- dragged out activities that could have been done quickly
- asked questions in a way that caused nonreciters to lose interest
- offered little or no variety in the learning tasks.

Kounin found that teachers usually were not aware of what behaviors of theirs were related to student "off-task" behavior. There was no ready vocabulary to use in discussing the teacher behaviors, so he gave them descriptive names. The "Classroom Management Self-Rating," which follows, is a checklist based on Kounin's research. It contains his phrases for the teacher behaviors he found to relate strongly to smooth-running classrooms and student attentiveness to work. Use the self-rating, to analyze your own tendencies, and consider any of your behaviors that may need attention.

## Classroom Management Self-Rating

### WITHITNESS

(1) I let my students know that I know what's going on in the classroom.

(2) I stop the right disruptive individual or group of individuals (i.e., the instigator/s).

(3) I stop the disruption before it increases in seriousness.

(4) I stop the disruption before it has spread to others.

### OVERLAPPING

(5) If there are two matters to handle at the same time, I somehow attend to both issues simultaneously.

(6) If I am teaching a group and a student from another group intrudes with a question, I somehow attend to both the group and the student-intruder.

(7) If I am in a recitation setting with a group and a disruption occurs in another part of the room, I somehow attend to both.

### SMOOTHNESS

A. Avoiding *Thrusts*

(8) At a transition point, when groups need to shift places in the room, I pause a few moments to see if the group members are alerted and ready for the move.

(9) I avoid "bursting in" on students' activities with an order, statement or question without evidence of their readiness to receive my message.

BASED ON the research reported in Jacob Kounin, *Discipline and Group Management in Classrooms.* New York: Holt, Rinehart and Winston, 1970. The authors are grateful to Lynn Smolen for ideas in the construction of the instrument.

B. Not being *Stimulus-Bound*

   (10) While working with one group I don't suddenly become deflected from the main activity by reacting to a stimulus that is not intrusive or interfering in any noticeable way. (Suddenly noticing someone's lunch bag has been left on the floor.)

C. Avoiding *Flip-Flops*

   (11) I avoid stopping one lesson, beginning another one, and then suddenly going back to discuss something about the earlier lesson.

D. Avoiding *Dangles*

   (12) I don't suddenly drop an activity or line of thought and leave it "hanging in midair" by going off to some other activity.

## MOMENTUM

A. Avoiding *Overdwelling*

   (13) I don't go on and on about how my students are behaving or are supposed to behave (nagging).
   (14) I don't overdwell on a small part of a task to such a degree that it detracts from getting on with the major task.
   (15) I don't overemphasize props (pencils, books, paper) used in an activity to the point of temporarily losing the focus on an activity.
   (16) I don't overelaborate explanations and directions beyond what would be necessary for most students to understand.

B. Avoiding *Fragmentation*

   (17) I don't break an activity or unit of behavior into smaller components when it could be performed as a single, uninterrupted sequence.
   (18) I don't have individual students take turns at something which a group could do as a single unit.

## GROUP FOCUS

A. *Group-alerting*

   (19) I ask a question *before* selecting a respondent.
   (20) I create suspense by pausing after a question and looking around before selecting a respondent.
   (21) I pick reciters randomly so that no one knows ahead of time who will be called on.
   (22) I create a challenge with statements such as "This is a tricky question."
   (23) I don't become immersed in single respondents without giving signs of attending to others.
   (24) I call on different students.
   (25) I alert nonperformers that they may be called on in connection with what a reciter is doing.

B. *Accountability*

(26) I call on a large number of students to perform or recite as a means of holding them accountable and responsible for the material.

(27) I circulate and check products of non-reciters during a student performance.

### PROGRAMMING TO AVOID OVERLOAD

(28) I adjust the length and difficulty of assignments so that students have a sense of progress and mastery.

(29) I structure student work so that there is variety in the learning activities and contrast from activity to activity.

## ACTIVITY 11
**Observe for classroom management techniques.**

**A.** Have one or more of your classes of students respond to the "Student Survey of Classroom Management," which follows. It can be reproduced from the book. Student perceptions about your management skills are important data for your analysis of your teaching. How or by whom the survey is given to the students may influence their responses. Plan its administration so students will want to give honest answers. After they respond, tally the answers. You will be able to match the items to the categories (withitness, overlapping, etc.) on the self-rating questionnaire, and to identify behaviors the students say you need to work on.

**B.** Arrange for a colleague to observe your classroom. Agree on what behavior(s) will be observed. Have the observer record the target events with as much factual detail as possible.

**C.** Discuss and analyze the outcomes, plan changes, and repeat these steps until you are satisfied with the results.

Teacher Name _____   *No Student Names, Please.*

### Student Survey on Classroom Management

A note to students from the teacher: Your honest answers to these questions will help me know how to do my work better. Circle one answer for each question. Thank you for answering them.

1.  When there is a misbehavior, does the teacher show the class that he/she knows what's happening?

| 1 | 2 | 3 | 4 | 5 |
|---|---|---|---|---|
| Not Ever | A Little | Sometimes | Many Times | All the Time |

2.  Does the teacher ever speak to the wrong student about a misbehavior?

| 5 | 4 | 3 | 2 | 1 |
|---|---|---|---|---|
| Not Ever | A Little | Sometimes | Many Times | All the Time |

3.  Does the teacher ever pay attention to a small misbehavior and not see a more important one?

|  |  |  |  |  |
|---|---|---|---|---|
| 5 | 4 | 3 | 2 | 1 |
| Not Ever | A Little | Sometimes | Many Times | All the Time |

4.  Do misbehaviors ever spread from student to student before the teacher stops them?

|  |  |  |  |  |
|---|---|---|---|---|
| 5 | 4 | 3 | 2 | 1 |
| Not Ever | A Little | Sometimes | Many Times | All the Time |

5.  Do misbehaviors ever get serious before the teacher actually steps in?

|  |  |  |  |  |
|---|---|---|---|---|
| 5 | 4 | 3 | 2 | 1 |
| Not Ever | A Little | Sometimes | Many Times | All the Time |

6.  When two things need the teacher's attention at the same time, can the teacher somehow take care of both at once?

|  |  |  |  |  |
|---|---|---|---|---|
| 1 | 2 | 3 | 4 | 5 |
| Not Ever | A Little | Sometimes | Many Times | All the Time |

7.  Does the teacher ever forget what he/she is doing during an activity and go off to something else?

|  |  |  |  |  |
|---|---|---|---|---|
| 5 | 4 | 3 | 2 | 1 |
| Not Ever | A Little | Sometimes | Many Times | All the Time |

8.  Does the teacher ever interrupt an activity with unimportant things?

|  |  |  |  |  |
|---|---|---|---|---|
| 5 | 4 | 3 | 2 | 1 |
| Not Ever | A Little | Sometimes | Many Times | All the Time |

9.  Does the teacher ever start an activity, leave it hanging by going on to another one, and then return to the first activity?

|  |  |  |  |  |
|---|---|---|---|---|
| 5 | 4 | 3 | 2 | 1 |
| Not Ever | A Little | Sometimes | Many Times | All the Time |

10.  Does the teacher ever interrupt an activity to go to something else, and then forget to return to the first activity?

|  |  |  |  |  |
|---|---|---|---|---|
| 5 | 4 | 3 | 2 | 1 |
| Not Ever | A Little | Sometimes | Many Times | All the Time |

11.  Does the teacher ever do things that slow down or drag out a classroom activity?

|  |  |  |  |  |
|---|---|---|---|---|
| 5 | 4 | 3 | 2 | 1 |
| Not Ever | A Little | Sometimes | Many Times | All the Time |

12.  Does the teacher ever spend a lot of time on things that are not important to the activity?

|  |  |  |  |  |
|---|---|---|---|---|
| 5 | 4 | 3 | 2 | 1 |
| Not Ever | A Little | Sometimes | Many Times | All the Time |

13. Does the teacher ever go on and on about how students are behaving or are supposed to behave?

| 5 | 4 | 3 | 2 | 1 |
|---|---|---|---|---|
| Not Ever | A Little | Sometimes | Many Times | All the Time |

14. Does the teacher ever divide activities into small parts when they could all be done together?

| 5 | 4 | 3 | 2 | 1 |
|---|---|---|---|---|
| Not Ever | A Little | Sometimes | Many Times | All the Time |

15. Does the teacher help you keep interested while other students are answering or performing?

| 1 | 2 | 3 | 4 | 5 |
|---|---|---|---|---|
| Not Ever | A Little | Sometimes | Many Times | All the Time |

16. Does the teacher keep you "on your toes" by calling on you when you don't expect it?

| 1 | 2 | 3 | 4 | 5 |
|---|---|---|---|---|
| Not Ever | A Little | Sometimes | Many Times | All the Time |

17. Does the teacher keep students wondering who will be called on next?

| 1 | 2 | 3 | 4 | 5 |
|---|---|---|---|---|
| Not Ever | A Little | Sometimes | Many Times | All the Time |

18. When the teacher is working with one or two students does she/he ever forget about the rest of the class?

| 5 | 4 | 3 | 2 | 1 |
|---|---|---|---|---|
| Not Ever | A Little | Sometimes | Many Times | All the Time |

19. Does the teacher call on a lot of different students?

| 1 | 2 | 3 | 4 | 5 |
|---|---|---|---|---|
| Not Ever | A Little | Sometimes | Many Times | All the Time |

20. When asking questions, does the teacher give you enough time to think?

| 1 | 2 | 3 | 4 | 5 |
|---|---|---|---|---|
| Not Ever | A Little | Sometimes | Many Times | All the Time |

21. Does the teacher ever have you do some activities over and over so that they become boring?

| 5 | 4 | 3 | 2 | 1 |
|---|---|---|---|---|
| Not Ever | A Little | Sometimes | Many Times | All the Time |

22. Does the teacher have you do new and different things that are interesting?

| 1 | 2 | 3 | 4 | 5 |
|---|---|---|---|---|
| Not Ever | A Little | Sometimes | Many Times | All the Time |

BASED ON the research in Jacob Kounin, *Discipline and Group Management in Classrooms.* New York: Holt, Rinehart and Winston, 1970. The authors are grateful to Diana Carroll for assistance in the writing of the instrument.

## ACTIVITY 12
**Read about and analyze dialogue patterns. Read the section below and complete the activities described.**

### TEACHER-STUDENT DIALOGUE THAT ENCOURAGES RESPONSIBILITY

Research suggests that teachers who encourage responsibility in their students conduct classroom dialogue differently from other teachers. In one study (Tuck 1971) teachers rated by students and administrators as high in encouraging students to assume more responsibility for their own learning did indeed teach differently from teachers rated low in that trait. The study concentrated on verbal interactions during classroom discussion. The table summarizes the findings.

| Teachers who were rated *high in encouraging responsibility* | Teachers who were rated *low in encouraging responsibility* |
|---|---|
| —talked less | —talked more |
| —had students talk more | —had students talk less |
| —accepted and used student ideas more | —lectured more |
| —accepted feelings more | —praised more |
| —asked more divergent questions | —asked more memory questions |
| —had students initiate more talk | —asked more for recitation-type responses |
| —more often had students' initiatives structure the dialogue | —received more predictable responses from students |
| —tended to use public criteria when praising or criticizing students | —tended to use no criteria or private criteria when praising or criticizing students |

The results are consistent with the findings of other research described in this chapter. The key differences in the two sets of classrooms seemed to be that the high-rated teacher asks divergent, open-ended questions; the teacher accepts and uses student ideas; and in these classrooms, students initiate comments and questions that shape the dialogue.

One way to measure your success in encouraging students to take responsibility for the quality of classroom work is to record kinds of student talk. Student talk can be sorted into two general categories:

**Type A:** Contributions, helpful comments, new ideas, statements, or questions that add something to the classroom inquiry. This kind of student talk indicates responsibility taking.

**Type B:** Dependent or predictible responses or questions, recitation responses, questions about procedures on assignments, asking the teacher to make a judgment or to control. This kind of student talk leaves the responsibility with the teacher.

The research shows that Type A student talk was much more frequent in the classrooms of teachers rated as encouraging responsibility taking (Tuck).

If you have your own classroom, we suggest that you complete section A that follows. If not, section B can help you recognize the two kinds of student talk.

**A.**   Locate a previously recorded sample of classroom dialogue (twenty minutes or longer). As you listen to it, tally each instance of student talk as either Type A or Type B. This is your "before" sample.

Either now or as soon as you feel ready, tape another twenty minutes or more as your "after" sample. Classify the student talk into the two categories and then compare the percentage of Type A talk in the two samples.

Consider what the comparison means. Decide whether you will put additional work into changing the way you conduct classroom discussions. Repeat as needed until you are satisfied with the results.

**B.**   Analyze the dialogue of a classroom, either live or on tape. Classify the student talk as either Type A or Type B. Then consider what relationships you see between the teaching techniques and the type of student talk recorded.

## ACTIVITY 13
### Prepare plans for students' independent study.

> Children are dependent on their teachers, and dependency breeds hostility. To reduce hostility a teacher deliberately provides children with opportunities to experience independence. The more autonomy, the less enmity; the more self-dependence, the less resentment of others (Ginott 1972).

This statement may not be true for all situations, but independent study is important for all students, not a special few. Some degree of independent activity can be planned for every student, even those who are highly dependent. You will find guidelines for doing it in "Planning Independent Study for Each Student."

## Planning Independent Study for Each Student

Students, particularly those in middle grades, differ widely in both the amount and kind of independent activity they are ready for in school. In finding the right match of student and independent activity, the teacher reaps the reward not only of increased student learning,* but also of having more time freed from controlling students—time to be put to better uses.

The objective of an independent study program is to have every student working with just as much independence as he or she can manage. The key to a successful program is a planned system for managing it, the subject of the paragraphs below. As with  any other instruction, the teacher is in charge, and must

---

*One study showed that second graders (!) completed significantly more study tasks under conditions of self-management than they did under regular teacher-managed instruction. Margaret C. Wang and Billie Stiles, "An Investigation of Children's Concept of Self-Responsibility for Their School Learning." *American Educational Research Journal.* Vol. 13, No. 3, (Summer 1976): 159–179.

make basic decisions about objectives, resources, activities, space and time usage, records, and evaluation. However, careful planning is more important in independent study programs because some of the basic decisions must be made with students, or delegated to them. The textbook, the workbook, published kits and teacher guides typically do not include planning to promote self-direction.

## BASIC PROGRAM DECISIONS

Program decisions can be sorted into three groups: those decisions the teacher makes for students without their participation—the *prescriptive* component; those decisions that teacher and student make together—the *negotiated* component; and those decisions the student makes without the teacher—the *open* or *exploratory* component. We believe that every program for the middle grades should have all three and that every student should have experiences in all three.

Picture in your mind's eye two students you know fairly well, one who is highly dependent and one who is relatively self-directed. It should be fairly easy to think of negotiating objectives and activities with the latter student or having that student design exploratory studies without your management. But think of the dependent student. Is there *some* aspect of the present prescribed curriculum that could be negotiated with or delegated to that student? Pursue the thought until you have identified some objective, or activity, or circumstance that student could handle independently. We support the view that every student needs some negotiated or exploratory components every day.

If you are accustomed to planning and teaching with some individualized procedures—learning centers, individual contracts, learning activity packets, diagnostic-prescriptive kit materials, etc.—then analyzing and adjusting your procedures to emphasize independence and self-direction is a fairly simple process. You already have a management system operating. Using the seven categories of planning as a checklist, you can decide how much of what kinds of responsibility to delegate to each student.

1. *Objectives*—In what areas can this student decide what objectives to pursue? Do we negotiate the objective(s) or does the student decide alone? Does the student have the prerequisite skills?
2. *Resources*—For what objectives could the student manage the necessary resources? With teacher assistance or student initiative only?
3. *Activity Plans*—For what objectives (prescribed, negotiated, or open) can the student take responsibility for deciding *how* to use the resources and manage his or her own activities?
4. *Space*—Is *where* the student works something I must manage or can the student decide that?
5. *Time*—Are the timing and pacing of the student's work something I must manage or can the student manage that?
6. *Records*—Are the records for managing and reporting student progress something I must handle or can some of them be kept by the student?

7. *Evaluation*—Do I decide what shall be evaluated; how and by what criteria; do the student and I decide together; or is the student's self-evaluation appropriate here?

Bring back to mind the two students you thought about before. With each one go through the seven planning categories and specifically, with some particular objective, answer each of the questions. Write a one-paragraph description of each student to go with your plan for each.

If you are now using an adequate system for managing individualized instruction, then it need only be supplemented by an "independence profile" for each student—perhaps a page for each student in your plan book, a place to keep an anecdotal log of the kinds of independence encouraged and the student's response. We also suggest coding your regular record or student activity sheets so that you know not only what the student accomplished, but how—in terms of independence and responsibility.

If you are not accustomed to conducting an individualized program, we suggest you begin modestly with a few alternatives for students and gradually add new ones. Here are our ideas for beginning your plan. Use any of them that fit your situation. Whatever you decide, the objective is for you to construct and try out (if you possibly can) a plan that helps each student toward more responsible self-direction. Write out your plan in a form you can share with colleagues.

A. Probably the easiest significant step to make away from an all-prescriptive classroom is to arrange for students to have some choices in the uses of time and space. Without changing the prescription of work assignments, you can give them command over their uses of time. One successful plan is to tell them they may work at their own pace, and when the week's prescribed work is completed, they may use the remaining time in whatever exploratory ways they choose. Having an ample supply of games and craft materials on hand is a good incentive. A sixth-grade teacher describes the plan very well in Chapter 1 of Rogers' *Freedom to Learn* (1969). Students in a flexible time classroom generally need some choices in the use of space, and freedom to move about the room—so long as they do not interfere with other people's work. A games area and crafts area need to be provided. A quiet zone and an area for quiet talking is needed, as well as a seating arrangement that allows easy access to resource materials and to the teacher. Some students may be able to work responsibly outside the clasroom—in the learning resources center, patio, etc.

B. Also within an all-prescriptive curriculum, students can easily learn to manage most of their own work records. Coming into the classroom, students can take their name cards from the roll board and put them in the appropriate places on a weekly progress chart. That eliminates calling roll. Students can keep work report forms up to date in their individual folders. While students are working independently, you can circulate and talk with individual students about their work reports. A few students will need frequent attention, at least at first. Clear, easy-to-use record forms are important. Blackburn and Powell (1976) have included in their book three dozen typical forms that can be reproduced.

C. If you have a prescriptive curriculum and activities that involve checking a lot of answers (math solutions, correct spelling, etc.) with an answer key, consider having student management of the answer-key book. A binder book with answer sheets sandwiched between celluloid sheets works well. Students can rotate through the job of being responsible for checking other students' work, so that only about one thirtieth of a student's time is taken up with this responsibility. Students working in learning teams can follow a rule that requires a member to check work and try to solve difficulties within the team prior to coming to you for evaluation or help.

D. Students can be taught to use all the audio-visual equipment available to the classroom. With operator skills, students are able to use any of the resources as the work plans call for them—without dependence on you as operator. This flexible use of resources will be important as you begin to use learning centers and activity stations.

E. Learning centers bring a surprising amount of variety and novelty to a classroom, even when the curriculum is totally predetermined. When they also include negotiated or open/exploratory curriculum options, they represent a modest revolution in schooling.

Several books listed at the end of the chapter offer guidelines and concrete suggestions for developing learning centers. If you are an intern or student teacher, operating a classroom with learning centers is an appropriate part of your training. Find the opportunity to do so, even if centers are not commonly used where you are teaching. If you are a regularly employed teacher, we suggest that you start developing learning centers as a joint project with other teachers. Several centers need to be in use at one time, so sharing the construction and use of them with other teachers is the practical approach. Most teachers we know who have started with centers are committed to them as a regular part of their instruction plans.

Centers can vary dramatically in the amount of independence they require of a student. At a minimum, the student using a center is removed somewhat from the teacher's supervision of space and time. Toward the other end of the spectrum, a center can provide raw materials and suggestions that evoke creativity and independent problem solving. Well-designed centers offer students choices according to how much independence they want. Or a teacher can prescribe that a student use certain components of a center according to the amount and kind of independence the components require.

F. Learning activity packs, the subject of another chapter, are natural partners with learning centers. In some classrooms where both are in use, an outside observer cannot distinguish which students are using which. The main difference is that the center, physically, is the source of instructions for student activities, while each student's pack is the source of instructions on ways to use various resources in the classroom and beyond. LAPs can incorporate the same spectrum of student dependence-independence as centers can.

G. Individual student contracts are the most flexible means of planning negotiated components or open components with students. Any of the seven elements of planning can be negotiated to match the responsibility the student is ready to take. Any of the seven can be open to the student's independent judgment. Your vital task in arranging a contract is to be reasonably sure that the quality of the learning is not sacrificed by overestimation of the student's capacity for self-direction. The Blackburn and Powell book, previously cited, contains suggestions and forms for contracts. Some students in middle or junior high schools will be able to contract for the kind of independent study that is found in well-planned high school programs. Most certainly they should have the opportunity. Most probably a teacher will be unable to see the need for the independent work unless that teacher is using a plan to promote independence and self-direction, a plan such as suggested in these paragraphs.

In a classroom where students are working with as much independence as they can manage, one is likely to see diversity:

- Resource centers, learning centers, a games area—all in use
- The teacher having conferences with individuals and small groups
- Resource people from the community
- Students working alone or in learning teams, moving about and talking according to the needs of their work
- Work records kept systematically by students
- Demonstrations, displays, and dramatizations for those who are interested
- Classroom meetings to solve problems, to change the group's rules and procedures, and to plan classwide projects.

Perhaps the teacher's highest obligation to students is to help them be self-directing people who can make sound choices and pursue their own interests as self-propelling, lifelong learners.

## REFERENCES

BLACKBURN, J.E., and W.C. POWELL. *One at a Time All at Once*. Glenview, Ill.: Scott, Foresman and Co., 1976.

BRONFENBRENNER, URIE. *Two Worlds of Childhood: U.S. and U.S.S.R.* New York: Russell Sage Foundation, 1970.

BROPHY, J. E., and C. M. EVERTSON. *Learning from Teaching: A Developmental Perspective*. Boston: Allyn and Bacon, 1976.

COLEMAN, JAMES. "The Children Have Outgrown the Schools," *Psychology Today* (February 1972).

CUSIK, PHILIP. *Inside High School: The Student's World*. New York: Holt, Rinehart and Winston, Inc., 1973.

FUCHS, JULIUS E., JAMES D. FERA, and JOHN T. REID. "An Approach to Student Misbehavior," *NASSP Bulletin* 62 (414) (January 1978): 104-111.

GINOTT, HIAM. *Teacher and Child*. New York: MacMillan Co., 1972.

GORDON, THOMAS. *P.E.T.: Parent Effectiveness Training*. New York: Peter H. Wyden, Publisher, 1970.

————.*T.E.T.: Teacher Effectiveness Training*. New York: Peter H. Wyden, Publisher, 1974.

GREENBERG, HERBERT M. *Teaching with Feeling*. New York: Bobbs-Merrill Co., 1969.

HUGHES, MARIE, and ASSOCIATES. *The Assessment of the Quality of Teaching: A Research Report*. U.S. Office of Education, Cooperative Research Project No. 353. Salt Lake City: The University of Utah, 1959.

JACOBY, SUSAN. *Inside Soviet Schools*. New York: Hill and Wang, 1974.

KOUNIN, JACOB S. *Discipline and Group Management in Classrooms*. New York: Holt, Rinehart and Winston, 1970.

NATIONAL SCIENCE FOUNDATION. *Early Adolescence: Perspectives and Recommendations*. Washington, D.C.: Superintendent of Documents, 1978.

RADZ, MICHAEL. "Responsibility: Is It the 4th R in Education?" *Illinois School Research and Development* 14 (2) (Winter 1978): 85-89.

ROEBUCK. F. N., and D. N. ASPY. "Response Surface Analysis," National Consortium for Humanizing Education, Interim Report No. 3, 1974. ERIC ED 106 732.

ROGERS, CARL. *Freedom to Learn*. Columbus, Ohio: Charles E. Merrill Books, 1969.

ROWE, M. B. *Teaching Science as Continuous Inquiry*. New York: McGraw-Hill, 1973.

*School Science and Mathematics*. November, 1980. (The entire issue is focused on the ten- to fifteen-year-old student.)

SOAR, R. S., and R. M. SOAR. "An Attempt to Identify Measures of Teacher Effectiveness from Four Studies," *Journal of Teacher Education* (3) 27 (Fall 1976): 261–267.

TUCK, RUSSELL R., JR. "Some Relationships Between Teachers' Encouragement of Students to Assume More Responsibility for Their Own Learning and the Patterns of Verbal Interaction in Their Classrooms." Doctoral Dissertation. George Peabody College, 1971.

WANG, MARGARET C., and BILLIE STILES. "An Investigation of Children's Concept of Self-Responsibility for Their School Learning." *American Educational Research Journal* 13 (3) (Summer 1976): 159-179.

# CHAPTER 10

## MASTERY LEARNING

Most teachers have an eager interest in teaching strategies that promote learning, increase motivation, are inexpensive and relatively easy for one person to implement. There are, naturally, very few of these methods available, even though many claim to satisfy the above criteria. One method of managing instruction, which seems to have more promise than others, is known as mastery learning.

The subject of this chapter is based on a radical assumption in modern education—the belief that almost all students can master what they are taught! Mastery learning strategies, properly implemented, purport to enable 75 to 90 percent of the students to achieve the same level of excellence that the best students reach under traditional instructional strategies, with perhaps as little as 10-15 percent more time. Mastery learning advocates also boast that this method makes learning more efficient than conventional approaches, takes less time, and produces higher levels of motivation and better attitudes in students than conventional classroom approaches. Quite a series of claims, no?

This chapter will explain what mastery learning is and how to organize your classroom to give it a try. You will be involved in analyzing your curriculum, developing smaller units and objectives, designing appropriate learning activities, evaluating student progress somewhat differently, and performing several other tasks. You will also read about how several other teachers have tried to implement mastery learning in their classrooms.

Look at the following questions. If you find yourself answering "yes" to them, this chapter may be a practical one for you.

Would you like to improve the systematic nature of the way you manage individualized instruction?

Have you noticed that some of your students seem to be able to learn well if they have a little extra time?

Are you dissatisfied with the "bell curve" distribution of grades and its effects on motivation?

Do you have a variety of learning activities for your classes, but don't seem to be able to find time to use them all?

Do you know how to write precise objectives for learning?

Mastery learning does not, of course, fit all learning situations; not all learning consists of following preselected activities toward teacher-selected objectives. Keep this in mind as you work through the chapter.

## ACTIVITY 1
### Read about mastery learning.

**A.** Go to your library and locate one or more of the four books listed below. Read as much of the recommended sections as possible. (The three books by Block are brief and somewhat overlapping.)

1. Bloom, Benjamin S. *All Our Children Learning.* New York: McGraw-Hill Book Co., 1981.
2. Block, James H. (Ed.) *Mastery Learning: Theory and Practice.* New York: Holt, Rinehart and Winston, Inc., 1971. (Entire volume.)
3. Block, James H. (Ed.). *Schools, Society, and Mastery Learning.* New York: Holt, Rinehart and Winston, Inc., 1974. (Entire volume.)
4. Block, James H., and Lorin W. Anderson. *Mastery Learning in Classroom Instruction.* New York: MacMillan Publishing Co., 1975. (Entire volume.)

**B.** Here are four additional readings on mastery learning. The first presents the theory briefly, and the others describe how three different teachers applied the ideas in their own styles. When you have completed the readings, answer these questions. Save your notes and answers.

1. Describe, in your own words, the basic assumption of mastery learning.
2. Rewrite, in your own language, the concepts associated with the terms: optimal instruction time, aptitude, quality of instruction, perseverance, formative evaluation, and summative evaluation.
3. With how much of the case in favor of mastery learning do you find yourself in agreement?
4. Describe how this approach is different from the way your classroom is now organized for instruction.
5. Do you believe that a much higher percentage of your students could achieve much higher levels under other instructional conditions than those which currently exist in your classroom? What evidence could you offer to support your answer?
6. Can you imagine any ways in which you might rearrange the instructional conditions in your room to enable larger groups of students to achieve more successfully?

## Mastery Learning: An Overview

It can be argued that the most serious problem in American education is simply that students are learning too little. For far too many students early failure leads to more and more frequent failure, continually accumulating until the students fall so far behind that they drop out, physically or mentally. Mastery learning promises to change that. In today's cultural and educational climate, any such promise deserves a hearing.

The startling contention of mastery learning is that all but perhaps five to twenty percent of any given student population can master what the school asks them to learn. By properly managing each student's instruction, almost all students can achieve a level of excellence now attainable only by a few.

Mastery learning advocates maintain that if each pupil is allowed to spend the time needed to learn to some level and actually spends the required time learning, then he or she can be expected to reach mastery level. When students are not allowed to take the time they need, they fail to learn what is required. There is a direct relationship between learning and time spent on learning. Technically speaking, learning is a function of the ratio of the time actually spent in learning to the time needed. John Carroll (Block 1971) expressed it this way:

$$\text{Degree of Learning} = f \ \frac{\text{Time actually spent}}{\text{time needed}}$$

Remember the normal (bell) curve? One implication of the normal curve is that if you give the same quality of instruction and provide the same amount of learning time to a randomly grouped class of students, then achievement looks something like the curve. That is, there is a relatively small number of students who achieve mastery of the subject, a relatively small number who exhibit little or no achievement, and a large group stretches out between. This is because students have different aptitudes for learning. Block (1971) illustrated it this way:

Uniform Instruction/Time
Per Learner

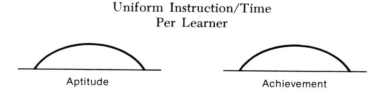

According to Block, if time and instruction are held constant, aptitude for learning will cause achievement to be distributed like the normal curve. Advocates of mastery learning, however, maintain that if each learner receives the optimal quality of instruction and the learning time each requires, there will be little or no relationship between aptitude and achievement. Block represents this situation like this:

Optimal Instruction/Time
Per Learner

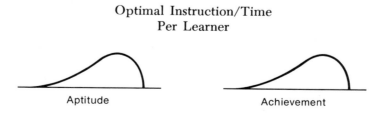

# WHAT ARE THE VARIABLES IN MASTERY LEARNING?

In 1963, John Carroll outlined the basic components of a mastery learning approach to individualizing instruction (Block 1971). First, one must rethink the idea of aptitude. Instead of referring only to a student's general ability to learn, Carroll viewed aptitude as "the amount of time required by the learner to attain mastery of a learning task," not the possibility of learning it well. This, of course, carries the implication that given enough time, almost all students can theoretically attain mastery of any learning task. Some students need more time and help, and need to expend more effort but almost all are capable of learning what the school demands.

Second, the quality of instruction is an important factor. Carroll said that quality of instruction means that "degree to which the presentation, explanation, and ordering of elements in the learning task approaches the optimum for a given learner." Helping larger numbers of students achieve mastery levels, therefore, involves providing learning activities which are capable of being adapted to individual learning styles. A variety of learning activities from which students can select those which most closely fit their learning styles becomes crucial.

Third, perseverance, or the time the learner is willing to spend in learning, is another important consideration. If a student needs ten hours to achieve mastery of a learning task, but is willing to spend only five hours on the task, he or she will not achieve the desired level. Perseverance is, however, a malleable quality, and can be modified by different frequencies of reward, learning success, and better instruction.

Fourth, and perhaps most important, is the time allowed for learning. While the amount of time needed by different students to learn the same task may vary by as much as a ratio of six to one, this ratio can be cut to as little as three to one by modified factors described above. An effective mastery learning strategy must, nevertheless, find ways of altering the time individual students need for learning, and providing the necessary time, whatever the length.

The above four factors can be expressed as an equation with the degree of learning again a function of time allowed plus perseverance, and aptitude is the quality of instruction matched to each individual.

$$\text{Degree of Learning} = f \quad \frac{\text{1. Time allowed} \qquad \text{2. Perseverance}}{\text{3. Aptitude} \qquad \text{4. Quality of Instruction}}$$

In addition to the factors described above, there are several other factors which affect the success of mastery learning strategies. One is the requirement that the learner complete the necessary prerequisites before beginning a learning task. No one can learn a new task well without having learned the earlier tasks upon which the new task is based. This is, of course, no different from conventional approaches to instruction.

Formative evaluation performs the twin functions of feedback and guidance. Given at the end of each unit or objective along the way, these tests allow the learners to determine how well or how poorly they have performed. Formative evaluation helps determine whether the student should move on to a new objective or review the present one. Most often, these formative evaluations are ungraded, in the sense of having no permanent effect on the learner's final grade.

The formative evaluation also provides feedback and guidance to the teacher. It tells the teacher which aspects of instruction have been most effective, and which least. It indicates what may need reteaching and what may need less emphasis in the future.

Summative evaluation is just that, a final test of whether or not the learner has achieved mastery. If the formative tests have indicated success all along the way, the summative evaluation should present no new challenges. The final evaluation, taken only when the student is ready, forms the basis for grading. If the mastery learning approach has been successfully implemented, a much greater percentage of these final evaluations will be at the "A" level, and far fewer at the "D" or "F" levels.

## WHAT ARE THE STEPS IN IMPLEMENTING MASTERY LEARNING?

Later activities in this chapter will involve you in implementing mastery learning in your classroom. You can follow these basic steps:

*Step One.* Analyze your curriculum and break it down into smaller units or objectives which can be taught in one to two weeks (for the average student).

*Step Two.* Design learning activities which present a variety of approaches to mastering the objective. As a rule of thumb, a minimum of five learning activities per objective works well.

*Step Three.* Develop formative evaluations for each objective which specify the level of attainment which constitutes mastery.

*Step Four.* Prescribe learning correctives for students who fail to attain mastery after working through learning activities. Basically, these learning correctives are either additional learning activities which the student did not choose the first time through or are special remedial techniques, reserved for recycling.

*Step Five.* Administer summative evaluations to students who have arrived at the appropriate point.

## WHAT ABOUT MY CLASSROOM?

Like so many other strategies available to teachers, there is no exactly correct way to implement mastery learning in your classroom. As a professional educator, you will naturally adapt and modify this strategy to fit your own unique classroom situation.

Basically, there are two methods of teaching or organizing instruction with mastery learning. One approach, designed by Bloom, begins with large group instruction for each objective followed by a formative test which lets students know whether they are on their way to mastery without further work. Students who need extra work turn to learning correctives, while also participating in the next large group presentation. At the end of a set period of time, a summative evaluation is given with grades to follow. This approach is particularly useful when specific time limits are necessary. A second approach, the Keller model (Block 1974), does not use the large group instruction process, and relies on counting the number of objectives completed to arrive at a grade for each student. The approach you take will depend upon the needs and preferences specific to your situation.

## My Mastery Learning - Contract Program
### Mrs. Loretta Jackson, Belleview Middle School, Pensacola, Florida

After coming back to Belleview Middle School from an exciting summer school workshop at the University of Florida (1974-75 school year), and being introduced to many new teaching methods in a course called Middle School Practicum, I was extremely motivated to do a better job of teaching.

I began my program the next fall by introducing contracts, mastery learning, learning centers, unipacs, behavior modification, and many new ideas which I had brought back with me.

The first step was to rearrange my room. I placed the desks in groups of six for group work, peer help and togetherness. I also made one group of desks separate (for the testing area) in which no talking was permitted. I had each group select a captain, and this person was placed in charge of keeping the noise level down, placing a check on a chart at the end of the period on each person's effort for that particular day, and for getting materials for the group at the beginning of each period. This helped out in moderating the level of traffic congestion in the room.

Next, I set up my regular math classes on a program developed from the theory of mastery learning. A contract was written for the first week to introduce the students to the concept of a contract. The contract was simple and was for a period of one week. To get an "A" for the first week students were required only to take the county pre-test, put a book cover on their mathematics books and do two "math box" questions.°

---

° A "math box" was a special activity developed from laminated magazine pictures which involved the students in some sort of fun math activity.

By Permission of Loretta L. Jackson, teacher of mathematics, Belleview Middle School, Pensacola, Florida.

The students were excited about the option of selecting what grade they wanted out of a course. Most of them chose to work for A's and B's. A few students had problems working on their own. They seldom got around to working on their contracts unless the teacher stayed on them to do so. I would check about twice a week to see how far each person was on his/her contract. This made it necessary to place an approximate finishing date for each contract and a final finishing date. This kept the students who tended to fall behind on a contract from doing so. It also kept most of them from trying to do a complete contract at the last minute.

The second contract for the year was on adding and subtracting integers. I had already made a learning center in the Middle School Practicum which I used on this contract. We also had some filmstrips in the library on the subject. This contract contained activities from many sources and the students could select which activities they wanted to do. They seemed to like the idea of choice. There were some "quest" activities which were considered as extra activities for the better student. These activities involved doing such things as making math games, making math box questions, making posters for the subject we were studying, doing extra work in the library, or doing extra work out of other textbooks or dittoed materials.

Quest projects stimulated students to think. On the integer contract they made up card games using integers, they made dice games using negative and positive numbers on the dice, and they made up their own rules on games they made. It was good that students were actually deciding what to do themselves instead of someone dictating exactly what to do and how to do it. It worked out great! Students could use the games after making them.

After the second contract was finished, I had written some happy-grams for some students who never got any recognition. These students were elated upon receiving these little sheets of paper. I also made it a point to call about five parents of students I knew had really posed problems for teachers in the past. I told the parents (after seeing progress in moving from a negative attitude) that I wanted to commend their child's progress in mathematics thus far and thought that he/she deserved a reward of some type from home. Most of the parents were shocked and very quickly asked, again, who I was. This had probably been the first positive contact they had ever had from schools. Anyway, I got increasingly good responses from these students for the rest of the year, just from taking a few minutes to make these telephone calls. I also made it a habit to make a couple of calls per week to some parents of a student who had really been working for me.

I let the students check all of their own work and make all corrections before coming to my desk for the post test. The post test was given to the student if he/she had fulfilled this part of the contract. If a student's work on the contract did not meet the criterion, he/she would go back and make improvements before receiving a post test. The post test was checked by me. The good thing about the post test was that the students knew that they had more than one chance to pass this test. Those who failed it the first time went back and reviewed activities and came back to retake it. If they failed it the second time, they still had a third chance. After getting help from someone in the room (another student or me), a student could retake it the third time. If the student failed it this time, we sat down for a discussion on his/her problem and designed something specifically tailored to this individual.

I soon needed someone to help with questions, with grading of tests, with group discussions, etc. I was able to get a teacher aide two periods a day to act as a remedial math teacher with my basic math class; two students from the University of West Florida helped as did students of my own, serving as math assistants. It worked out just fine. There was a time before I got any help that I had to make some numbers for the students to take from my desk if they needed to see me during the period. Then I would call numbers all period (like a short order cook) and the student would bring the problem up for discussion.

I rewarded students in many different ways if they worked diligently on their contracts and completed objectives. They were allowed to run errands, work on Student Council projects, work on bulletin boards, play records for a day, read books, play math games, etc. If they finished their contracts ahead of the time limit, they were rewarded by having free time. I made many behavior modification games in which some students were allowed to participate, such as a monopoly game board, a box to draw fortune cookies out of, flip cards to gain free time, a spinning wheel of fortune, and several others.

The students were given a chance to evaluate the mastery learning program and the use of contracts. Approximately 90 percent of the students favored the use of contracts. I decided, in self defense (and facetiously) that the remaining 10 percent were mainly students who were immature and would not have done well in any program. Some of the comments concerning contracts were as follows: "I like to work on my own," "I like to work at my own rate," "I don't have to listen to teacher lecture every day," "I don't have to do homework except when I want to do so or when I allow myself to get behind," "I don't get bored because there are choices of things to do," "I like them because I can make good grades," "It makes me more independent," "I know exactly what I have to do for a certain grade," "Contracts are fun to do," "I like the free time after finishing a contract," and "Don't stop them."

The one thing mentioned most about disliking contracts was that some of them were too long. This was good advice and I have tried to make them shorter and more to the point after this advice. It seems to have really helped because the students can see progress a lot quicker.

I eliminated the use of mastery learning contracts for one unit just to give the students an idea of the difference in my classroom. They begged to go back to contracts. I liked the program, the students liked the program, and the parents were all for the program.

This program definitely kept the teacher busy. I had to keep ahead of the smarter ones in my planning while trying to get the slower ones caught up. I had to be organized; this is the key word—organization. I doubt that just any teacher could pull this program off, because a teacher must have the desire, and above all a teacher must care about the students.

## Mastery Learning and a Sixth Grade Social Studies Curriculum
**Ms. Susan Bush, Lincoln Middle School, Gainesville, Florida**

### MASTERY LEARNING IN MY CLASSROOM

Mastery learning in my classroom is an individualized method of instruction based specifically on student rate rather than aptitude, with the curriculum broken down in small segments of observable behaviors. My students are required to master each segment at a predetermined level before progressing to the next segment.

I have adapted social studies at the sixth grade level to mastery learning. My curriculum has been broken down into small segments, drawing on the six social science disciplines of anthropology, sociology, economics, political science, geography, and history. This article will explain my reasons for changing to a mastery learning approach, the initial plan, the implementation, the problems, the resolutions to the problems, the current concerns, and the rewards of the system.

My year began with total group instruction in a lecture/activity approach, but the ineffectiveness of this method of teaching became apparent to me almost immediately. The students with a relatively low aptitude in social studies struggled for a short time to keep up and understand, but eventually quit. The students with a relatively high aptitude in social studies rapidly became bored. This left a small percentage interested and the majority turned off and creating behavior problems. This age group of children has a very difficult time sitting for any extended period of time on a daily basis, fifteen to twenty minutes being about as long as their attention span will allow. Judging from the number of vacant eyes, it became impossible to believe that any effective teaching or effective learning was taking place. I needed to change, desperately and quickly.

In looking for a change in the approach used for teaching sixth grade social studies several needs had to be met. I wanted a curriculum that was individualized specifically on rate, to eliminate the pressure on students with lower aptitudes to keep pace with the rest of the class and to eliminate the boredom experienced by students with high aptitudes who did not need the slower rate.

I was deeply concerned about the attitudes of students toward social studies. They had to feel that they were capable of learning and succeeding. The curriculum in itself had to reduce the incidence of discouragement and failure. Students needed encouragement through experiencing success. If this was to be done, then a curriculum which included almost instant feedback had to be adopted. In addition, students with a higher aptitude in social studies must not be overlooked. Individualized rate so as to eliminate boredom is not enough; these students need a challenging curriculum which demands high levels of thinking.

Mastery learning meets all of the preceding concerns. It is an approach based specifically on rate. Students progress from one concept to the next at their own speed with a consequent reduction of pressure and boredom. The very nature of

---

By Permission of Susan Bush, Lincoln Middle School, Gainesville, Florida.

mastery learning insures success unless if becomes apparent the maturation level of the student suggests switching him or her out. Mastery learning enables rapid feedback which informs students of their success or where more work is needed. No grades are recorded which fall below the mastery level and corrections are made while they still have meaning. Thus, failure is eliminated and student self-concepts become more positive.

Mastery learning can be adapted to a highly challenging curriculum by gearing each observable behavior to some level of Bloom's *Taxonomy of Educational Objectives - Cognitive Domain*. Students will be required to think on higher levels of the taxonomy rather than just on the knowledge level.[1]

With this general definition in mind, I built an actual plan based on sixth grade world history and the six social science disciplines. Goals, objectives, a table of specifications, activities, types of evaluation, and determination of a level of mastery all became vital elements of my mastery learning strategy.

- Goals were formulated from the six social science disciplines of sociology, anthropology, economics, political science, geography, and history.[2]

- Objectives were written based on the goals. These objectives were designed behaviorally and dealt with only small pieces of information that could be easily observed.

- A table of specifications was drawn up which indicated where each objective fell along Bloom's cognitive taxonomy. This table gives a clear indication of the desired outcome of the objectives—that of getting students to think on higher levels rather than just on the first level of knowledge.

- Formative and summative evaluations were employed. Formative evaluation, a brief systematic means of evaluation to improve curriculum learning, was used for checking mastery. Each student was evaluated after completing those activities necessary for an objective. Only grades which reached the predetermined mastery level were recorded.

- Summative evaluation, an assessment of all knowledge covered and retained for the assignment of a grade, was used to test the student's retention of the material covered. This evaluation was given only after several objectives had been covered and about six or seven weeks had passed. The summative evaluation is given only once, with no level of mastery involved.

- The criteria of formative mastery were eighty percent and ninety percent. An assignment of grades B and A respectively went along with these two levels of mastery. A lower level of mastery allowed students to make sev-

1. Benjamin S. Bloom, Ed., *Taxonomy of Educational Objectives, The Classification of Educational Goals, Handbook I: Cognitive Domain* (New York: David McKay Company, Inc., 1966), 207 pp.

2. Leonard S. Kenworthy, *Social Studies for the Seventies* (Waltham, Massachusetts: Blaisdell Publishing Company, 1969), pp. 22, 25, 28, 31, 34; *The Social Sciences: Concepts and Values*, Teacher's Edition (Atlanta: Harcourt Brace Jovanovich, Inc., 1970), pp. T-14–T-25.

eral mistakes and possibly not to have truly mastered the work. Any higher level of mastery must be determined by the caliber of the majority of the students involved.

The actual implementation of the plan involved a series of six steps that each student went through with each objective:

1. The goal is presented to the class for a discussion of the teacher's meaning and the student's meaning.
2. Only one of the objectives relating to the goal was presented to the students with each one having an individual copy. On this objective sheet is listed all the activities needed to master the objective. The student may do as many or as few optional activities as he or she chooses. (The student is, however, encouraged to do at least two optional activities.)
3. When the student has completed the required activities and as many optional ones as he or she chooses and has received an S (each activity must be 100 percent correct in order to receive an S) on all of them, he or she is ready to be evaluated.
4. The evaluation is given in a short period of time with immediate feedback. If eighty percent mastery is not achieved, the student is referred back to more activities to achieve mastery.
5. After the student completes the prescribed activities, he or she is ready to be reevaluated.
6. Upon mastery of the objective the student is given fifteen minutes of free time and then moves on to the next objective.

## PROBLEMS IN IMPLEMENTATION

Shortly after this curriculum plan was put into practice, many problems surfaced which demanded my attention. Dealing with these problems in many cases has been long and tedious work and has involved a great deal more teacher planning time. The result, however, has been a more efficient and satisfactory program for me and my students.

Perhaps the most difficult problem was getting the students adjusted to a new way of learning. For many students it was the first time they had ever been given any big responsibility. They were all fairly well conditioned to the teacher totally directing all learning and all activities. I think a very important factor involved in this reorientation is the teacher's personality and his or her reactions to student progress during this adaptation. It is very possible that a teacher with a personality different from mine might be able to shorten this adjustment period.

Many students just did not know how to begin or what to do, even though directions had been given. They would sit and do nothing which, if they were quiet, made them initially very inconspicuous. Later, a quick survey over the room periodically was all that I needed to check for the silent nonworkers. Then a brief question as to what they were doing or how they were coming along got them back on course. (It is important to add here that this program is designed to reduce the number of nonworkers but, of course, the total involvement of all students at all times is not possible.)

A number of problems concerned the implementation of various aspects of the program and student reaction to them. Of primary importance was the need for remedial activities when mastery was not achieved on an objective. For students just to be rerouted through previously completed activities was not beneficial to achieving success; students became bored and frustrated. Consequently, with each objective at least two extra activities were planned and saved specifically for remediation. These were not among the activities first presented with the objective.

There were several problems which involved the activities themselves. Students on the whole did not like long reading assignments and did not do them well. This can be attributed to the fact that the average reading level of these sixth graders is on grade five.° In addition, the textbooks used were all well above the sixth-grade level. Putting the assignments on tape at a listening station did not help; students still did not understand what they were hearing. The solution, for me, was to limit reading assignments to a maximum of five to seven pages and have them all read aloud by either the teacher or a teacher aide with an explanation to students with low aptitudes in reading.

Study questions were met with the same response as long reading assignments, which again relates to this age group's need for activity. Therefore study questions were used only occasionally and were limited to a maximum of five questions. Another answer to the study question problem, and for that matter all activities, was to allow students to work together. This was highly acceptable in that students learned from one another, helped one another, and challenged one another. This collaboration was a totally reinforcing method of learning.

After the students worked together on reading assignments and small projects they asked for activities that specifically called for groups. Middle school students inexperienced in group work perform exceptionally well in groups when they are given a specific task to accomplish. A particularly favorite group activity was short skits; all were eager to be center stage. Both changes, small group work and collaboration, increased productivity and interest.

With all the added group work many students wanted more large group discussion. In the beginning this approach had been eliminated so that as much time as possible could be put toward working directly on objectives. A change in routine was needed and therefore Fridays were turned over to large group discussions including films, filmstrips, value clarification activities, and the discussion of current events.

The short formative evaluations presented an unexpected difficulty. Because the evaluations were brief, answers were quickly passed around. This made it necessary to construct several forms of the same quiz. As students became aware of this change they realized the fruitlessness of memorizing the answers to one form of the evaluation.

Because the objective work process is cyclical in that as soon as one is completed another is begun, some students felt that they were on a treadmill with no means of stopping the momentum. They indicated, and the teacher agreed, that

---

°Reading levels were assessed by the Comprehensive Test of Basic Skills.

they needed a break between objectives. No matter how long it took for completion, after each objective each student was given twenty minutes free time to do whatever he or she wanted as long as he did not disturb others. (Twenty minutes proved to be too long for most and the time was eventually shortened to fifteen minutes. This satisfied both the students and the teacher.)

Gearing each objective to the aptitudes of the slower students was another difficulty. All objectives were written on one level and it was necessary to alter the expected outcomes on activities and evaluations for them. This change enabled these students to have feelings of worth, accomplishment and success—a vital component of this program.

The one single aspect of this program which caused the most concern and probably deters more teachers from individualizing their curriculum is the large amount of bookkeeping that is necessary, especially with 120 students. It was in this area that the most radical changes had to take place. All activities and evaluations were, initially, teacher-scored; along with keeping records of what activities and evaluations were being completed by each student. (Each objective usually involved between four and seven activities with a student accomplishing at least one activity a class hour and an evaluation every fifth class hour.) I was only record-keeping and grading; not teaching. Students waited in line to be checked or graded.

The first change in this area was to make answer keys for all activities and post them on the wall for self-correction and correction by other students. At this point, teacher-recording involved keeping account of activities covered and the grading and recording of evaluations. This provided some relief, but did not totally rectify the problem of tying up teacher time.

The next change in this area was to move to a student record-keeping system to free even more of the teacher's time. Each student was given a folder in which to keep his or her work. Stapled to the inside was an activity checkoff list (see below) which included a space for both required and optional activities to be checked off upon completion.

Objective 1    Activity  °1 _____
                         °2 _____
                         °3 _____
                          4 _____
                         °5 _____
                         °6 _____
                          7 _____
                          8 _____
                          9 _____

(° indicates a required activity)

Students had the teacher check their folders only when they were evaluated. I would scan the work quickly and check for all required activities. The result of this switch was a waiting line of students that lasted for the first ten to fifteen minutes of the hour, then left the rest of my time free for small group work on specific objectives and individual attention.

At first, as students finished a set of objectives based around a particular goal or goals from one of the social science disciplines, they were not sufficiently aware of closure. No discussion about what had been covered was being provided. This is one point in particular with which this teacher still must deal. Perhaps this idea can be tied in with the summative test. Instead of having this large evaluation after a certain number of weeks, it could be given after a certain number of objectives based around a goal(s) from a social science discipline. The students would have a sense of closure from the test. I need to carry out some further experimentation on this point.

Although there have been problems in creating this program, the rewards have been so numerous and so substantial that I think they completely outweigh the difficulties. Students' motivation and interest have never been higher in social studies (one of the least liked subjects in school). Behavior problems are at a minimum. Most important, students of all aptitudes for social studies are feeling that they are capable of success in school mainly in the positive proof of A and B work. Frustration is reduced, as well as the incidence of failure. And last, I feel that this is a very effective method of instruction and that real learning is taking place in my classroom.

Mastery learning is a method of instruction based specifically on rate where students work on small pieces of observable behaviors until they are learned or mastered. This is a program which initially takes a great deal of planning and constructing. (The program was in progress for four months before all major problems were ironed out.) The rewards of seeing students look alive, interested and concerned about social studies, however, far outweigh any and all difficulties.

# Mastery Learning in a College Classroom
**Paul George, University of Florida**

One of the authors of this book has found that mastery learning works as well at the graduate level as it does in the middle school. I regularly teach a graduate course in middle school curriculum. It is a ten week course that meets once a week for four hours over a period of ten weeks. As you will see, I, too, have modified mastery learning to fit my own style and situation.

Included here is the syllabus for the course and the list of objectives and learning activities that accompany the objectives.

## COURSE SYLLABUS

### A. GOALS

This course is intended as an opportunity for students to become more competent in the following areas:

1. Identifying the objectives and characteristics of the middle school in relation to other school organizations.

2. Analyzing curriculum and instruction in middle schools in relation to criteria derived from the nature of middle school age children and other factors.

3. Planning curriculum, instruction, organization, and evaluation for the middle school.

4. Using appropriate sources in studying problems of curriculum, instruction, organization, or evaluation in a middle school.

## B. CONTENT

Each student will have the opportunity to achieve greater mastery in the following general areas:

1. The rationale of the middle school
2. The middle school child
3. The curriculum of the middle school
4. The instructional strategies of the middle school
5. The organizational structure of the middle school
6. The evaluation of the middle school
7. The teacher in the middle school

## C. MOTIVATION AND THE INSTRUCTOR'S ROLE

It is assumed that each student possesses an authentic interest in learning more about the middle school. The instructor sees his role as more of course coordinator than as the source of knowledge on the subject of middle schools. These two factors should produce a situation unlike the traditional course where the professor pontificates and the students struggle. At the same time, however, the instructor recognizes his responsibility to provide structure and to take a role in evaluating the work of the students.

## D. EVALUATION AND STUDENT RESPONSIBILITIES

This quarter EDM 6005 will be structured somewhat differently. The instructor is attempting to improve his teaching style. The approach this quarter will be a modified mastery learning style, attempting to individualize instruction to the rate of learning.

*Eleven objectives* have been developed. These objectives and the learning activities constitute the major part of the course. In addition to the evaluation of each objective, there will be a summative evaluation in the form of an exam/paper alternative. Students have the choice of an in-class essay exam or a paper on "The Ideal Middle School" due in the last week of the quarter.

Each objective is weighted (15, 20, or 25 points). Each "evidence of completion" will receive an evaluation of 1, 2, 3, or 4. This factor will be used as a multiplier with the weight of each objective. Taken together, the basic weights of the eleven objectives add up to 200. With the multiplier, therefore, there is a possibility of amassing up to 800 points on the formative evaluation via the objectives. These accumulating points should help you perceive how you are doing in the class as well as contributing to your final grade.

The *summative evaluation* is in the form of a choice between an essay exam based upon the eleven objectives or a paper in which you describe in detail (15-20 pages) your concept of the "Ideal Middle School." This paper should also be based upon the objectives, so that what is required is an integration of what you have learned earlier in the quarter rather than a new and different assignment. A total of 500 points is attainable.

Finally, there is something called an *involvement factor*. This includes several somewhat vague and arbitrary, but nonetheless important, items: (1) helping in the process of developing a productive learning experience for yourself and your classmates—including panel discussions, arranging visitors, peer teaching, setting up and returning media and other equipment, etc.; (2) attendance; (3) participation; and (4) enthusiasm. A total of 200 points may be obtained.

The scale for final grades looks like this:

$$A = 1200 - 1500$$
$$B = \phantom{0}900 - 1200$$
$$C = \phantom{0}600 - \phantom{0}900$$
$$E = \phantom{00}0 - \phantom{0}600$$

| | | |
|---|---|---|
| Objectives 200 × a maximum of 4 | = | 800 |
| Summative Evaluation 125 × 4 | = | 500 |
| Involvement Factor 50 × 4 | = | 200 |
| Total Possible | | 1500 |

### E.  Textbooks

1. Alexander, William and Paul George. *The Exemplary Middle School.* New York: Holt, Rinehart and Winston, Inc., 1981.
2. Leeper (Ed.). *Middle School in the Making.* ASCD, 1975.

## LEARNING OBJECTIVES AND ACTIVITIES FOR EDM 6005

### GREEN OBJECTIVE (15)

The student will be able to describe the rationale for the middle school movement.

1. Alexander, *Emergent Middle School,* pp. 3-59
2. Module, "The Middle School Concept"
3. Filmstrip-tape, "The Middle School Story"
4. Small group discussion observed by instructor
5. Other readings (e.g., *Middle School in the Making*)
6. Student designed activity
7. Peer teaching

*Evidence of completion:* A brief (one-two page typed, single-spaced) essay entitled "Reorganizing the School in the Middle: Why?"

### RED OBJECTIVE (15)

The student will be able to list and describe at least seven characteristics of middle school students, and discuss the implications for schools.
1. Alexander, *Emergent Middle School,* pp. 23-43
2. Filmstrip-cassette tape, "The Middle School Story"
3. Filmstrip-cassette tape, "Passing Through from Childhood to Adolescence"
4. Filmstrip-cassette tape, "Characteristics of Emerging Adolescence"
5. Modules on middle school student traits
6. Shadow study at a local middle school
7. Other readings (e.g., *Middle School in the Making)*
8. Student-designed activity
9. Peer teaching
*Evidence of completion:* Written quiz.

### BLUE OBJECTIVE (15)

The student will be able to explain the following terms as they apply to the curriculum of the middle school and describe ways in which they might be implemented: "personal development," "skills of continued learning," "introduction to the areas of organized knowledge."
1. Alexander, *Emergent Middle School,* pp. 63-82
2. Filmstrip-cassette, "Middle School Story"
3. Small group discussion observed by the instructor
4. Question-answer sessions with class members, class guests, or other middle school educators
5. Panel discussions on controversial issues
6. Other readings (e.g., *Middle School in the Making)*
7. Student-designed activities
8. Peer teaching
*Evidence of completion:* A brief (one-two pages typed, single spaced) essay entitled, "The Middle School Curriculum: Three Emphases."

### WHITE OBJECTIVE (15)

The student will be able to describe the terms "disciplinary," "interdisciplinary," and "multidisciplinary," as applied to team and curricular design, describing the advantages and disadvantages of each for the middle school.
1. Alexander, *Emergent Middle School,* pp. 104-109
2. Lecturette by instructor
3. Panel discussion, "Teaming Yes, But What Kind?"
4. Question-answer sessions with class members, guests, and other middle school educators
5. Other readings (e.g., *Middle School in the Making)*
6. Visitations to local middle schools
7. Student-designed activities
8. Peer teaching

*Evidence of completion:* A brief (one-two pages typed, single spaced) essay entitled "Disciplinary, Interdisciplinary, and Multidisciplinary Organization: My Preferences."

## YELLOW OBJECTIVE (20)

The student will be able to describe the most appropriate instructional strategies for middle school learners.
1. Alexander, *Emergent Middle School,* pp. 83-97
2. Filmstrip-cassette tapes on Individually Guided Education ("Planning and Managing, II")
3. Perusal of booklets and modules on learning centers, unipacs, mastery learning, etc.
4. Attendance at class presentation by instructor and others on "Individualizing Instruction in the Middle School"
5. Visitation to local middle schools
6. Other readings (e. g. *Middle School in the Making*)
7. Student-designed activity
8. Filmstrip-tape, "Instructional Strategies for Emerging Adolescents"
9. Peer teaching

*Evidence of completion:* Written quiz

## PINK OBJECTIVE (25)

The student will be able to describe a model for effective team planning and demonstrate its use in the planning of a team unit.
1. Alexander, *Emergent Middle School,* pp. 106-113
2. Module on "Team Planning" with others
3. Filmstrip-tape packages on Individually Guided Education ("Planning and Managing IGE, I, II, III")
4. Filmstrip-tape packages on Individually Guided Education ("Planning and Managing IGE, IV, V, VI")
5. Share your team's unit with other teams; receive feedback on what you have designed
6. Offer your team's unit to a group of local middle school teachers who agree to: try it out or give you feedback on its strengths and weaknesses
7. Sit in, observe a team planning session of others in the class or a team in a local middle school
8. Other readings (e.g., *Middle School in the Making)*
9. Student-designed activities
10. Peer teaching

*Evidence of completion:* (a) Team unit; (b) written comments from other team(s)

## ORANGE OBJECTIVE (20)

The student will be able to design a homebase advisor-advisee program appropriate for use in the middle school's program for affective education.
1. Module on "The Teacher as Affective Guide"

 2. Filmstrip-tape, "The Fourth R"
 3. Filmstrip-tape, "Adult Models for Emerging Adolescents"
 4. Question-answer sessions with class members, guests, and other middle school educators
 5. Visitation to local middle schools
 6. Participation in small group discussion on "The Teacher as Guidance Person: Pros and Cons"
 7. Readings
 8. Student-designed activities
 9. Peer teaching

*Evidence of completion:* A brief (one-two pages typed, single-spaced) essay: "Affective Education in the Middle School: Who, What, Where, When, Why, How?"

### BLACK OBJECTIVE (20)

The student will be able to describe the variety of ways in which the middle school emphasizes the process of exploration.
 1. Alexander, *Emergent Middle School,* pp. 69-71
 2. Attend a lecturette on "Exploration in the Middle School"
 3. Module on "Exploration in the Middle School"
 4. Question-answer sessions with class members, guests, and other middle school educators
 5. Visitation to local middle schools
 6. Other readings
 7. Student-designed activities
 8. Evaluation of illustrative middle schools for exploratory emphasis
 9. Peer teaching

*Evidence of completion:* Written quiz

### BROWN OBJECTIVE (20)

The student will be able to analyze and evaluate schools for emerging adolescents, describing how well various schools fulfill the requirements of the middle school concept.
 1. Alexander, *Emergent Middle School,* pp. 129-149
 2. Attend lecturette on "Evaluating the Middle School"
 3. Attend small group discussion observed by the instructor to familiarize the student with "Middle School Review" form
 4. Using the "Middle School Fact Sheet," evaluate Spring Hill Middle School and Steele Middle School via slide tape presentations. Write up your analyses.
 5. Other readings (e.g., Wiles, "Developmental Staging")
 6. Using the "Middle School Review," analyze one or more of the text's "illustrative middle schools." Write up your analyses.
 7. Student-designed activities
 8. Peer teaching

9. Visitations to other middle schools

*Evidence of Completion:* (a) Written summary of readings; (b) Reports from activities four and six.

## PURPLE OBJECTIVE (20)

The student will be able to identify problems and unresolved issues in the implementation of the middle school concept, and areas of critical concern for the future of the middle school movement on local, state, and national levels.

1. Module, "The Middle School Concept"
2. Other readings
3. Panel discussions on unresolved issues
4. Personal statements from national leaders
5. ASCD monograph, "The Middle School We Need"
6. Attend National Middle School Leadership Seminar sessions
7. Student-designed activities
8. Question-answer sessions with class members, guests, and other middle school educators
9. Filmstrip-tape, "Operational Problems in Educating Early Adolescents"
10. Peer teaching

*Evidence of Completion:* Two page (typed, single-spaced) essay entitled "The Future of the Middle School: Problems and Priorities"

## CALICO OBJECTIVE (15)

The student will be able to describe the characteristics of effective middle school teachers.

1. Alexander, *Emergent Middle School*, pp. 54-55, 87-88, 97, 101, 122-125
2. Filmstrip-tape, "The Middle School Story"
3. Filmstrip-tape, "Adult Models for Emerging Adolescents"
4. Panel Discussion "Middle School Teachers—Animal, Mineral or Vegetable?"
5. Other readings
6. Question-answer session with class members, guests, and other middle school educators
7. Student-designed activities
8. Examine lists of teacher competencies. Participate in small group discussion of these competencies
9. Peer teaching

*Evidence of completion:* Two page (typed, single-spaced) essay "The Ideal Middle School Teacher"

## ACTIVITY 2
### Begin to develop a mastery learning framework for your classroom.

One of the basic assumptions of mastery learning is that breaking down one's curriculum into smaller pieces will make successful learning experiences more likely. Each of the practitioners you read about in Activity 2 has done so and it should be particularly evident in Paul George's class description. Your first step toward implementing a mastery learning strategy requires this process. Section A of this activity gives another example of how this may be done; section B asks you to do it with a part of your curriculum.

**A.**   We'll use the example of Middle School Earth Science, without specifying any particular grade level or arguing about the appropriateness of the content for our sample curriculum. If you are in a relatively conventional situation, you probably have a textbook where instruction begins, so that's where we'll start here. We have taken an earth science textbook and proceeded to identify, from the chapters, all the smaller units and objectives which add up to the year's curriculum in earth science. Here's what we came up with:

### Year's Topic: Earth Science
### Unit Objectives for the Year

1. Size and shape of the earth
2. The earth's layered structure
3. Processes that change the land
4. Gravity
5. Minerals of the earth
6. Rocks of the earth
7. Methods of locating places on earth
8. Motions of the earth
9. Formation and initial development of the earth
10. The history of the earth written in rocks
11. Earth history from fossils
12. The sun: composition, structure, and action
13. The moon: Characteristics, features, and motions
14. Planets and orbits
15. All about earthquakes
16. Everything you ever wanted to know about igneous activity
17. Mountains
18. Continents
19. Running water
20. Glaciers
21. Oceans
22. The air above us
23. The basics of weather

Describing these smaller units of precise, educational objectives might look like the following. Your way of writing objectives may differ, of course, from the authors'. (If you are uncomfortable about your ability to write in an objective format, you may want to spend a little time reviewing some material on the subject. You might begin with Robert Mager's *Preparing Instructional Objectives* (Belmont, California: Fearon Publishers, 1962). The student will be able to:

1. Write a paragraph accurately describing the size and shape of the earth.
2. Identify the separate layers of the earth's surface.
3. List the major processes that change the shape of the land.
4. Define the term *gravity* and list three examples of the effect of this force.
5. Define the term *mineral* and identify five examples of the important minerals and their uses.
6. Define the term *rock* and name the three large classes of rocks, as to their origin.
7. Use a map to locate places on the earth and describe in writing the processes used for such tasks.
8. Write a paragraph describing the pattern of the revolution and the rotation of the earth.
9. Tell the story of the earth's history as geologists do, from the rock record.

10. Describe four different hypotheses as to the origin and evolution of the earth.
11. Tell how scientists use fossils to learn about earth history.
12. Write a one page story entitled "The Sun and What It Gives Us."
13. Write a one page essay entiteld "The Moon: Fact and Fantasy."
14. Name the planets in our solar system and draw a chart showing their relative size and relationship to the sun.
15. Describe the nature of earthquakes, their causes and results.
16. Define the terms "igneous," "magma," "volcano," "fissure," and "lava."
17. Describe the ways mountains are formed.
18. Repeat two theories of continental origin and drift.
19. Describe the nature and work of subsurface water, lakes, swamps, and rivers.
20. Write a paragraph describing the formation and movement of glaciers.
21. Draw charts illustrating a knowledge of the topography of ocean floors, and of the movement of ocean waters.
22. Draw a graph picturing the regions of the atmosphere and present a five minute explanation of the graph.
23. State five important facts about wind and its importance to human life.
24. Describe the main types of clouds and the major forms of precipitation.
25. Draw a diagram or a model illustrating major facts in the story of either weather or climate.

**B.** You should now be ready to try analyzing and sequencing a sample of your own curriculum or one you are familiar with. On a separate paper, list (1) the beginning year's theme, (2) the major units of this theme as we did in section A, and (3) the objectives which can be developed from these units (with at least one objective for each major unit). When you're finished, share your materials with a colleague or another teacher you are learning with. Ask for some feedback about the materials you have developed.

## ACTIVITY 3
### Read examples of learning activities.

The next step, implementing a mastery learning approach in your classroom, builds on Activity 2. Developing learning activities for your objectives is probably the most critically important step and the most time consuming part of the entire process. Activity 3 gives you some examples of activities developed by several teachers. Read these before you begin to develop activities for objectives of your own.

There are several things that need to be remembered when developing a list of learning activities. One is variety: students need several different types of learning activities from which to choose. Another is number: there should be, at the very least, five activities for every objective, with several additional activities for use as learning correctives. Finally, there ought to be enough differences in the levels of difficulty so that all learners are able to feel both successful and challenged.

With these criteria in mind, examine "Objectives and Activities Prepared by Middle School Teachers." These sample activities were actually designed and used by middle school teachers attempting to use a mastery learning approach. They are presented in no special order. You may also want to refer to "Mastery Learning in a College Classroom" as an illustration of planning varied activities for an objective.

## Objectives and Activities Prepared by Middle School Teachers

### SAMPLE UNIT ONE: ADJECTIVES

Objective: Students will recognize, know the functions of, and be able to demonstrate the proper use of adjectives.

*Activity 1:* Read the mimeographed sheet entitled "Adjectives and You." Do all of the exercises at the end.

*Activity 2:* Read the paragraph, "Ancient Greeks," on the board. There are twenty-five adjectives in the paragraph. Make a list of those you can identify in the space provided.

*Activity 3:* Here are twenty sentences your class has written this year. Underline the adjectives you find in these sentences.

*Activity 4:* Here are ten sentences with dull, boring adjectives. Please rewrite these sentences by supplying new and exciting adjectives in place of the old ones.

*Activity 5:* Listen to the cassette tape "Keeping Things Proper." If a sentence contains a proper noun, write it down; if it contains a proper adjective, copy both the adjective and the noun it modifies. Check your work with a friend.

*Activity 6:* Here is a list of twenty nouns. Write an appropriate adjective before each of the following nouns. Use as many proper adjectives as possible.

*Activity 7:* Look at the filmstrip "Adjectives in Comparisons." Do the exercises taped to the wall beside the projector.

*Activity 8:* Read the handout, "Degrees of Comparisons." Then use the following adjectives in comparisons by listing the word in all three forms: positive, comparative, superlative.

*Activity 9:* Get a copy of the newspaper or a magazine from the reading table. Choose an article, read it, and choose a way to illustrate the use of adjectives in the article.

Objective evaluation: Include all work in your folder, including corrections. Then ask the teacher for the adjective quiz.

### SAMPLE UNIT TWO: INVENTIONS

Objective: Students will be able to define *invention* and offer several significant examples.

*1. Read in *Human Adventure*, pp. 32-41, 44-45. Answer the questions on p. 54.

*2. Read in *Social Studies and Our World*, pp. 52-74. Answer the questions on p. 74.

*3. Ask five adults what the statement "necessity is the mother of invention" means to them, and write down what they say.

4. Early man invented many things to help him do his jobs more easily such as flints, tools, fire, and weapons. Invent a machine that helps you do a job that you don't like to do.
   a. Draw your machine.
   b. Write about how it works.
   c. What does it do?
   d. Talk about your invention to the class.
5. Read about a famous invention in the encyclopedia. Study the telephone, telegraph, or any one you like.
   a. Try to decide what were the necessities that caused this invention to be born.
   b. How was it invented?
6. Write a page in the imaginary diary of an early man you are familiar with. On your page discuss the things that you have trouble with and what inventions would make them easier.
7. Draw pictures of five inventions of early man. Beneath the picture write the necessities that led to the invention.
*8. Take the self-test posted on the board.

Final Objective Evaluation: When you have completed the self-test successfully, show it to the teacher and ask for the evaluation for this objective.

   * Required Activities.

## SAMPLE UNIT THREE: NOUNS AND PRONOUNS

Objective: The student will be able to identify and put into proper use the part of speech known as the possessive pronoun.

1. Read the handout entitled "Possessive Pronouns."
2. Here are twenty-five sentences. Underline the possessive pronouns in each one.
3. Read "The Actress." Above each underlined noun, write the appropriate possessive pronoun.
4. Choose an article that interests you from the newspaper. Circle all the possessive pronouns. Tape the article to tagboard and place it on the bulletin board.
5. View the filmstrip "Possessive Pronouns." Write a short paragraph in which you use possessive pronouns and the contractions that sound like them.
6. List all the personal pronouns that can be the subjects of a sentence, then write a sentence for each one. List all the personal pronouns that can be the objects of sentences and write a sentence using each one.
7. In the paragraph in Handout Seven, write the appropriate possessive pronouns in the spaces provided for them.
8. Rewrite the following ten sentences using possessive pronouns in place of the underlined words.

9. Underline all the pronouns in Handout Nine. Above each underlined word, indicate the kind of pronoun it is.

Objective evaluation: Include all work in your folder, including corrections. Then ask the teacher for the objective quiz.

## SAMPLE UNIT FOUR: INTRODUCING GEOMETRY

Objective: The student will identify and differentiate between equilateral, isosceles, and scalene triangles.

1. Using a dictionary or math book glossary, write the definition of each of the following terms: triangle, isosceles, equilateral, scalene.
2. View the filmstrip "Triangles." Answer the questions.
3. Rewrite each of the definitions from number one in your words.
4. Read pp. 160-162 in *Mathematics Structure and Skills;* do the exercises on those pages.
5. Read p. 74 in *Mathematics 7.* Write in your words the differences among the three types of triangles. Then write about the things they have in common.
6. Complete Worksheets 1, 2, and 3.
7. Draw three different sizes of isosceles trinagles. Using a protractor, measure all three angles in all three triangles. What generalization can you make from your findings about the angles in any isosceles triangle?
8. Repeat activity six for equilateral triangles.
9. Search the magazines on the table for examples of hidden triangles. Label each triangle accordingly.
10. Search the classroom for examples of hidden triangles. Point out two of them to the teacher. Record your responses also.

Objective evaluation: Complete the self-test successfully, then show it to the teacher and ask for the quiz for this objective.

## SAMPLE UNIT FIVE: THE SOLAR SYSTEM

Objective: The student will name the planets and draw a chart showing their relationship to the sun.

1. Read pp. 81-84 in *Middle School Earth Science.* Answer the questions at the end.
2. Read the handout entitled, "Our Solar Systems: The Planets." Answer the questions.
3. View the filmstrip, "Planets: Great and Small."
4. Examine the clay models of the planets on the Teacher's Table. Each one is numbered. Take a sheet of paper and write the names of each planet you can identify opposite its number on the paper.
5. Look up each planet in the class encyclopedia. Write at least two sentences describing each one.
6. Go to the models on the Teacher's Table. Arrange them in the order of

their distance from the sun. Record the order of their numbers on a separate sheet of paper.

7. Go to the game table. Play the concentration game by yourself or with one friend.

8. Take a copy of the "Outline Map of the Solar System." Label each planet accordingly. Color the paper if you wish.

9. Using crayons and colored pencils construct your own Solar System Map, showing the relationship of the planets and the sun.

Objective evaluation: Draw a chart of the planets with correct names and positions relative to the sun.

## ACTIVITY 4
### Develop learning activities to match your objectives.

1. You have now seen several examples of learning activities developed for specific objectives. To be sure that you understand how to do it yourself, select one of the objectives below, or substitute one of your own, and develop a list of learning activities for that objective. Give it to your instructor, a colleague, or someone you're learning with, and ask for feedback on the variety, quantity, and range of difficulty of the activities you submitted. List the activities on a separate page, share them, and rewrite the activities if necessary.

Choose from these objectives (or use your own objectives):

a. recognize and differentiate between complete and incomplete sentences
b. list all of the oceans of the world
c. use the protractor and the compass correctly and identify appropriate situations for the use of each in mathematics
d. identify and describe the contributions of five great women scientists

2. In section B of Activity 2 you wrote a set of objectives. Identify those objectives that you may be teaching and select six to eight of them for potential use in a pilot program. Now develop a list of activities for each of these objectives. Share them and have them critiqued in the same way you shared the first trial objective.

*Special note:* In none of the sample learning activities was the option of teacher lecture present. This is not meant to imply, however, that such an option should not be used. In fact, the Bloom version of mastery learning begins every objective with large group teacher presentations, then allows for the kind of activities listed. This may be appropriate for you as well. Whether you do or not depends, of course, on your own individual style and preference and analysis of student needs and learning styles.

## ACTIVITY 5
### Design formative and summative evaluations.

The materials you read earlier in this chapter referred to formative and summative evaluation, two different types of evaluation with two different purposes. In this model of mastery learning, formative evaluation occurs at the end of the work for each objective. It provides feedback to the learner on how well he or she is doing and feedback to the teacher on how effective the instruction has been to that point. Formative evaluation is like a progress check.

Most proponents of mastery learning suggest that formative evaluations be ungraded; or that they be graded "lack of mastery" or "mastery." Another strategy is to award points which indicate several levels of mastery while permitting students to recycle through some corrective learning activities and then retake the formative evaluation seeking to reach a higher level of mastery and a greater number of points. Whichever method is used, the learner should be able to adjust, restudy, and work on to greater mastery.

Summative evaluations, you remember, are final, in the sense of being given at the end of a unit. It sums up the learner's level of mastery. Ideally, the summative evaluation should be taken only when the student is ready. You will have to decide, based on the length of your reporting period and so on, whether students will be allowed to recycle through the objective(s).

In some of the samples you'll find both formative and summative evaluations contained within the same objective. The formative evaluation takes the shape of a self-test, self-administered by the student. If students do well, it is an indication that they are ready for the summative teacher-controlled test which records their achievement level on that objective. If they do poorly on the self-test, they recycle through learning correctives until they are able to complete the self-test at a mastery level. Only then do they proceed to the summative evaluation.

Your task in this activity is to design formative and summative evaluation processes for the objectives you've developed for your pilot mastery learning unit. When you've completed these evaluations, share them and revise them based on feedback you receive. Before you try to develop your own, go back and review the examples of formative evaluation in the samples. Remember, formative evaluation is a progress check along the way. It may be a quiz, an essay, a drawing, a self-test, or any of dozens of other methods of evaluating students work. The small quiz that comes at the completion of an objective is, for example, formative evaluation for the unit of which the objective is a part. Be sure to include all your work in your portfolio.

## ACTIVITY 6
### Think about your emerging design.

Prior to an attempt to try out and evaluate a mastery learning approach to instruction in Activity 7, you may find it helpful to have answers to a few practical questions. Below are nine questions and the authors' attempts at answers. If you have separate questions which are not dealt with here, consult your instructor, your colleagues, or some of the recommended readings. If you make notes, be sure to include them in your portfolio.

   Q. Should the units and objectives be arranged in a sequential order?
   A. Yes, if there is one. In areas such as mathematics, reading, etc., where one skill builds upon another, sequencing is very important. In other areas where sequence is less obvious, it may be less crucial to put the objectives in a required order for completion.

Q. Should formative evaluations be graded?

A. No. Unless students have the opportunity to recycle through the formative evaluations as well. The purpose of the formative test is to give students feedback on their progress, so that they can improve. There should be no penalty attached to this type of feedback.

Q. What level of mastery should I expect from my students?

A. This is something that only you can answer. Several mastery learning advocates suggest that your standard might be what you usually expect for a grade of "A" or "B."

Q. How many objectives should be contained in a year-long program?

A. One rule of thumb suggests that the average student in your class should be able to complete one objective per week (five class hours). This means a year-long program has thirty to forty objectives.

Q. If I have a series of 40 objectives in my year long curriculum, how will I know whether students are completing as many objectives as they should?

A. In the authors' experience, the fastest students will master all forty objectives and ask for more. The average students will complete between twenty and thirty objectives, while the slowest students in a typical middle school may complete from five to twenty objectives.

Q. How should these different levels of achievement be reported to parents?

A. Within the boundaries of whatever policy the school has adopted, your choice depends upon your preferences as a teacher. Some teachers use mastery learning contracts with students—those students who complete the contract receive an "A," regardless of the number of objectives required in the contracts. Other teachers give grades according to the number of objectives achieved during a particular grading period. Still others count points which have been assigned to each objective.

Q. Should I allow students to help each other?

A. Most certainly. If you are evaluating students on individual achievement rather than on some competitive scheme like a bell-shaped curve, there is no reason students shouldn't help each other learn. Peer teaching has proven benefits, both for the peer teacher and the learner.

Q. What's the best way to implement this strategy?

A. One way to begin is by talking it over with your students, sharing what you hope to accomplish and why, the procedures to be followed, etc. Be sure to tell them that they are participating in a pilot program, which means that after a short period everyone will have an opportunity to say whether or not they like it and want to continue. It is important not to overwhelm your students with too many objectives at once. If they have never had anything like this before, you may want to introduce one objective at a time, teach about it, then let students do as many additional learning activities as they need. Only when all students are deeply involved with the first objective and comfortable with the process should the next objective(s) be introduced.

Q. Does it make any difference what kind of objectives I write?

A. Memory objectives are the easiest to write and we all have a tendency to use them too much. Try to write objectives that encourage student thinking at the levels of interpretation, application, analysis, synthesis, and evaluation (a' la Bloom's Taxonomy).

## ACTIVITY 7
### Implement your pilot program.

**A.** *Preparation.*   You have planned a set of objectives, activities, and evaluation processes. Now is the time to try out these materials in a pilot mastery learning project, if you are asked to do so. You may be able to encourage a teacher friend to use them if you cannot. Prior to implementing the pilot, however, a few decisions need to be made:

1. What level of achievement, on each objective, will you consider mastery? (There are no hard and fast rules for defining mastery. Perhaps the standard(s) that you once used for "B" work will do. The important thing is that once you have defined mastery, this should be the only criterion for evaluation.)

2. How will unit grades be determined? Some teachers give grades according to the number of objectives mastered during the unit. Others contract individually with each student, according to ability and interest; if the student meets the terms of the contract, an "A" grade is given.

3. Will you pursue a totally individualistic approach or will you begin each objective with large group teacher presentations and use individualized activities as learning supplements and correctives?

4. Will students have all the time they need to master an objective or will all students working on a series of objectives begin and end the series on specific dates?

5. Will formative evaluations be graded? Whether you grade them or not, you need to examine all student products. Students quickly lose interest in their work if the teacher does not constantly demonstrate a high level of interest in what they produce. They reason, "If the teacher doesn't care enough about my work to read it, then I don't care either!" All efforts to individualize instruction at the middle school level still require constant teacher-student interaction to make them function effectively.

6. Do you have enough learning activities? Is there variety? Do the activities provide varying levels of difficulty?

7. Are the summative evaluations closely related to the activities and formative evaluations so that the formative evaluations are really helpful?

8. Does this unit contain some vital learning experience that simply cannot be measured in terms of behavioral objectives? If so, have you made some other provision to include them?

9. Have you planned a way of introducing the pilot mastery learning unit that will permit the students to adjust quickly to the new methods you're trying?

10. Have you devised a way of recording all student progress that is not excessively burdensome to you? For example, are you using self-evaluation, student monitors, individual and class folders, etc.?

11. Have you decided which classes will participate in the pilot and which will not?

12. Have you devised a way of gathering and using student feedback during the pilot?

After you have thought about these questions, get together with others who are attempting the same thing or who are familiar with mastery learning and can give you some helpful feedback. Explain what you plan to do and ask them to react. The idea is to be certain you have not left out anything crucial. Include your answers to these questions and the feedback in your portfolio.

**B.** *Proceed with the pilot program.* You should now be ready to implement the pilot program. Since the purposes of the program are to find out whether this type of learning fits your teaching style and whether the students like this version of mastery learning, the most important part of the pilot program is the evaluation, both formative and summative.

Here are some questions you and the students need to answer as a part of the evaluation process, both during and after the unit work:

1. What were the consequences of the mastery learning project in the area of achievement? Did students learn significantly more or less than they might have with your usual approach?

2. What were the consequences of the mastery learning project in the affective area? Did you notice any differences in motivation, on-task behaviors, attitudes toward the subject, attitudes toward you, toward themselves?

3. What problems arose during the pilot program? How did you resolve them? Were there any which remained unresolved?

4. What are your reactions to mastery learning now? For example, are you encouraged or discouraged regarding further implementation of mastery learning? What are its strengths and weaknesses, as you see them at this point?

These and other questions should be included in your evaluation of the pilot mastery learning effort. You may want to add student reactions in the form of a questionnaire to the evaluative data. Perhaps one of your colleagues who has been observing the mastery learning pilot could write up more observations. These and other materials (e.g., samples of handouts, student work, etc.) can now be assembled as evidence that you have achieved mastery in this chapter on mastery learning. Include all materials in your portfolio.

## ACTIVITY 8
### Evaluate what you have learned.

The materials you have produced as you moved through the processes outlined in this chapter should provide evidence of your personal experience in understanding and implementing mastery learning. These materials should also reflect the effectiveness of the chapter in helping you develop these skills.

If you have achieved mastery in this chapter, you should be able to share evidence that you can:

- analyze a year-long curriculum and break it down into smaller units.
- express these smaller units in terms of more precise objectives.
- develop learning activities which permit a heterogeneous group of learners to attain mastery of those objectives.
- design and administer formative as well as summative evaluations.
- put it all together in a way that permits greater numbers of students to achieve at higher levels of mastery.

## NEXT STEPS

1. If you want to learn more about mastery learning, the books cited earlier in the chapter will lead you in the right direction.
2. Being involved in any sort of change in instructional strategy requires a great deal of effort and an equal amount of support. You may want to form a temporary "support group" among those who are involved in mastery learning.
3. A great deal of research on effective teaching is now available in both book and periodical form. It deals with the type of structure in classrooms where high student achievement is found. Seek out and read some of the articles by the following researchers: Barak Rosenshine, Jere Brophy, Thomas Good, Nathan Gage, Carolyn Evertson, Herbert Walberg.

# CHAPTER 11

# PREPARING LEARNING ACTIVITY PACKS

The goal of this chapter is to help you inject variety into your classroom teaching through the use of learning activity packs, often called unipacs. The activities will acquaint you with the characteristics, organization and effective uses of unipacs. You will be involved in designing, implementing, and evaluating unipacs in conjunction with your own teaching.

It is important to note, prior to beginning the activities, that individualizing instruction means a great deal more than using teacher-designed booklets such as these. Because the unipac is a very popular teaching tool, it has sometimes been overused. To keep your teaching personalized and varied, you will want to have a variety of instructional methods, including the one described in this chapter.

The activities are written in language which fits teachers in service. If you are not teaching now, full utilization of this chapter will require that you find a teacher who will cooperate in trying out the unipac which you design.

## ACTIVITY 1
### Analyze and evaluate sample unipacs.

Turn to the first sample unipac, examine it carefully, then evaluate it, using the "Unipac Checklist" which follows. When you have done so, answer the following questions.

1.  Now that you have examined a unipac, what (in your own words) is it?

2.  Identify the main parts of a complete unipac, listing them in the order in which they are presented.

3.  Can you visualize using a unipac like this (in your teaching area) in your own classes? How? If not, why not?

4.  How would you modify this unipac to make it more effective for use with your students?

## Sample Unipac One
## Florida Government

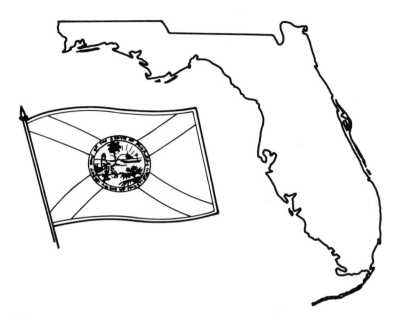

## INTRODUCTION

Did you ever think about how decisions on where and when to build state roads are made? How about the right of eighteen-year-olds to have the same rights and responsibilities as adults? Who levies state taxes? Who sets the standards for the school you attend? The processes that are required to do many of these things directly affect your life. This unipac is a part of your study of the state you live in—Florida. In any study about a state and its people, the way people govern themselves cannot be overlooked.

Your effectiveness as a citizen of this state depends, in part, on how well you understand the structure and function of Florida government. This unipac is designed to help you expand your knowledge of the state government and its relationship to local government and the federal government.

Upon completion of this unipac you should next take up the unipac entitled "Voting and Taxes," in order to get a clear idea of how people become state officials and how state government is financed.

To effectively use this packet you should:

1. Familiarize yourself with all parts of the unipac.
2. Take the pre-test. Use a sheet of notebook paper to write your answers. Check your test with the answer sheet located in the unipac. If you score 80 percent or better (according to the chart on the bottom of the answer

sheet), go on to the unipac on "Voting and Taxes." If you score below 80 percent on the pre-test, continue with the following steps.
3. Gather all materials needed:
   Pencil and notebook paper
   Cassette tape recorder/tape
   Filmstrip projector
   Drawing paper or newsprint
   Textbook: Fernald, *Florida, Its*
                    *Problems and Prospects.*
                    Chapter 8.
4. Work on the activities in order. You will note that there are activities in which you have a choice. Use your own judgment. *PLACE ALL PAPERS IN YOUR FOLDER.*
5. When you have completed all of the activities, take the post-test.

## GENERAL GOAL

It is desirable that middle school students will be knowledgeable about state government and its function.

## OBJECTIVES

Upon completion of this unipac each student will be able to describe in a paragraph the three branches of state government, and draw and label a diagram showing the shared responsibilities of local, state, and national governments.

## PRE-ASSESSMENT

This test is designed to determine how much you may already know about the government of Florida. When you have answered all of the questions, check your answers with the answer key for the pre-test. Write your answers on a separate sheet of paper. Good Luck!

1. Name the three branches of the state government.
   (a) _____
   (b) _____
   (c) _____

2. Which branch of government is the "chief law-administering and law-enforcement department" of the state?

   _____

3. Which one of the following departments is responsible to both the governor and the cabinet?
   _____ (a) Department of Air and Water Pollution
   _____ (b) Commissioner of Agriculture
   _____ (c) Department of Law Enforcement
   _____ (d) Department of Community Affairs

4. Name at least two special interest groups.

_____        _____

5. A person who represents some special interest and who works to influence political leaders is called a _____ .

6. How many members are in the state cabinet? _____

7. What is meant by "Bicameral Legislature"?

_____

8. The State Supreme Court is a part of the _____ branch of the government.
   (a) Executive
   (b) Judicial
   (c) Constitutional
   (d) Legislative

9. MATCHING:

| | |
|---|---|
| (a) Governor | _____ (1) Special interest group |
| (b) Attorney General | _____ (2) Heads of various agencies in the Executive department |
| (c) apportionment | |
| (d) Flordia Education | _____ (3) Keeps records of official acts |
| (e) Unicameral legislature | _____ (4) Insurance Commissioner; keeps funds and securities |
| (f) Treasurer | _____ (5) Not a member of the cabinet |
| (g) Lieutenant Governor | _____ (6) Legal advisor to Governor |
| (h) Little cabinet | _____ (7) Politically dividing the state into equal areas for representation |
| (i) Secretary of State | _____ (8) Chief Executive Officer of the state |
| | _____ (9) One house legislature |

## ANSWER KEY FOR PRE-TEST

1. (a) Executive (b) Legislative (c) Judicial
2. Executive Branch
3. (c) Department of Law Enforcement
4. If you listed two of the following—you're right. If you have one that is not listed here, check with teacher.
   Florida Education Association
   Florida Bar Association
   Florida Sheriffs' Association
   Florida Citrus Growers' Association
   Florida Cattlemen's Association
   Florida Civil Liberties Union

5. Lobbyist
6. Six (6)
7. Two-house legislature
8. Judicial
9. Matching:  (1) d  (2) h  (3) i  (4) f  (5) g  (6) b  (7) c  (8) a  (9) e

## SCORING:

Find the number you got correct on the top line. The box directly below that number is your percentage score.

| 1 | 2 | 3 | 4 | 5 | 6 | 7 | 8 | 9 | 10 | 11 | 12 | 13 | 14 | 15 | 16 | 17 | 18 | 19 | 20 |
|---|---|---|---|---|---|---|---|---|----|----|----|----|----|----|----|----|----|----|----|
| 5 | 10 | 15 | 20 | 25 | 30 | 35 | 40 | 45 | 50 | 55 | 60 | 65 | 70 | 75 | 80 | 85 | 90 | 95 | 100 |

If you scored better than 80 percent, you need to talk to the teacher. Otherwise, go right on with the rest of the unipac.

## ACTIVITIES

The activities listed here should be done in order, starting with number one and continuing until you have finished all of them. You will notice that there are some choice activities; you may do one or the other. Use your own judgment and do the one you think will best help you meet your objectives. You should place all completed exercises in your folder.

### ACTIVITY 1

Read pages 93 to 195 in the text (Fernald, *Florida, Its Problems and Prospects),* or listen to teacher-made cassette tape on the material. The purpose of this activity is to give you an overview of the material to be covered in this learning packet.

### ACTIVITY 2

Vocabulary. Use the dictionary and/or the text to write a definition for the following terms.

| | | |
|---|---|---|
| government | judicial | formal |
| public policy | cabinet | informal |
| special interest groups | vote | federal government |
| lobbyist | apportionment | local government |
| elite | bicameral | state government |
| executive | unicameral | |
| legislative | Supreme Court | |

ACTIVITY 3

Make a drawing of your own design that describes the relationship of powers and responsibilities of local, state, and national governments. Be sure to label your drawing. You may want to use the model shown on page 95 of the text.

ACTIVITIES 4 AND 5 (Choose one)

4. Study the models shown on pages 96 and 97 of the text. Then choose one of the hypotheses listed on page 98, and state in one or two sentences why you agree or disagree with it. Use a separate sheet of paper.

5. Collect four newspaper articles that show examples of state political policy or governmental action. Two articles should show initiation of political policy through requests of citizens and two should show initiation of political policy through the leadership of an official. Construct a folder to hold your articles. Use a separate sheet of paper.

ACTIVITY 6

Study the charts on pages 100 and 101 and the description of cabinet positions on page 102. Make a list of the cabinet offices, giving a brief description of what each does and the name of the individual currently holding that office. Use a separate sheet of paper.

ACTIVITIES 7 AND 8 (Choose one)

7. Go to the Learning Resource Center and select a filmstrip on state government. View the filmstrip and write a short report (one or two paragraphs) about it on a separate sheet of paper.

8. On a separate sheet of paper, draw a simple organizational diagram of the state government showing the three branches of government and their relationships to each other.

ACTIVITY 9

Draw a diagram of your city government and tell how it compares to the organization of the state government. Use a separate sheet of paper.

ACTIVITIES 10 AND 11 (Choose one)

10. Read a short story from the Learning Resource Center about Florida's government or about a person in the state government. Write the title, author, and the library call number on a piece of paper and place it in your folder.

11. Choose any activity you wish to do on state government such as stating your opinion on the eighteen-year-old vote, redesigning the state flag, or just stating what you like or don't like about the state government. Use a separate piece of paper.

QUEST ACTIVITY

Draw a sequence story picture showing one of the following:
>State law making
>The governor's day
>A day in the legislature
>What you would do if you were governor for a day
>Special session of the legislature

In order to do this you will need several pieces of drawing paper or a large piece of newsprint and some colors, either magic markers, crayons, or paints and a brush.

## POST-ASSESSMENT

This post-test is designed to determine how worthwhile the activities in this learning packet have been to you. Put your answers on a separate sheet of notebook paper. When you have finished, you may check it yourself or have it checked by the teacher or one of the designated assistants.

1. What is the difference between a bicameral and a unicameral legislature?

2. How many branches does the Florida state government contain?

3. Name the branches of state government.

4. Name two special interest groups.

5. How does a person get to be a member of the Florida supreme court?

6. What is the title of the head of the executive branch of the Florida state government?

7. Is it true that governments—national, state, and local—have overlapping power? In which of the below-listed areas is this overlap of governmental power NOT essential?
   (a) Interstate transportation
   (b) Ecology
   (c) Law enforcement
   (d) A house fire on 3rd Street.

8. Which of the following is NOT a member of the Florida cabinet?
   (a) Commissioner of education
   (b) Lieutenant governor
   (c) Secretary of state
   (d) Comptroller

9. The attorney general is the _____
   to the governor and other officers in the executive branch.

10. MATCHING:
   (a) lobbyist
   (b) governor
   (c) judicial branch
   (d) bicameral
       legislature
   (e) Florida Bar
       Association
   (f) treasurer
   (g) legislative
       branch
   (h) little cabinet
   (i) government
   (j) apportionment
   (k) special
       interest group

   _____ (1) made up of two houses, the
               Senate and the House
               of Representatives
   _____ (2) Special interest group
   _____ (3) Chief executive officer
               of the state
   _____ (4) made up of the heads of the
               various agencies in the
               executive department
   _____ (5) Two house legislature
   _____ (6) Insurance commissioner;
               keeps funds and securities
   _____ (7) System of courts
   _____ (8) Florida Education Association
   _____ (9) Formal and informal set of
               shared beliefs and practices
   _____ (10) Politically dividing the
                state into equal areas
                for representation
   _____ (11) represents special interest groups

11. Write a paragraph describing the three branches of state government.


## ANSWER KEY FOR POST-TEST

   1. Bicameral - two house legislature
      Unicameral - one house legislature
   2. three (3)
   3. Executive, Legislative, Judicial
   4. Florida Education Association
      Florida Bar Association
      Florida Sheriffs' Association
      Florida Citrus Growers' Association
      Florida Cattlemen's Association
      Florida Civil Liberties Union
      If you have one that is not listed here, check with the teacher.
   5. By being elected to the court
   6. Governor
   7. (d) A house fire on 3rd St. (local control)
   8. (b) Lieutenant governor
   9. legal advisor
   10. Matching:  (1) g   (2) e   (3) b   (4) h   (5) d   (6) f   (7) c   (8) k
       (9) i   (10) j   (11) a

11. The paragraph should mention (1) executive branch with the governor and cabinet; (2) the legislative branch made up of the Senate and House of Representatives; and (3) the judicial branch, which is a system of courts with the supreme court being the highest court in the state.

## SCORING:

After you have scored your paper and placed the number of correct answers on the top of the paper consult with the teacher.

## Unipac Checklist

Directions: Use this checklist to help complete a unipac or to evaluate one already done. For those items present in the unipac (answered "Yes"), place a checkmark in the space to the left of the item.

_____ 1.  Does the unipac begin with an attractive title page that will help attract and motivate students?

_____ 2.  Does the unipac follow with an introduction?

      _____ 2.1  Does the introduction contain some brief motivational rationale?

      _____ 2.2  Does it contain a brief description of how this unipac fits into the rest of the curriculum?

      _____ 2.3  Does it contain basic directions for completing the rest of the unipac?

      _____ 2.4  Does it provide a short overview, a "big picture" of the unipac?

      _____ 2.5  Does it list necessary materials and their location?

      _____ 2.6  Does it give directions to students who pass the pre-assessment and/or the post-assessment on what to do next?

_____ 3.  Is the introduction followed by a general goal statement?

_____ 4.  Is the goal statement followed by one or two more precise, specific objectives?

      _____ 4.1  Do the objectives relate to the general goal statement?

      _____ 4.2  Do the objectives state what the student is to be able to *do* as a result of this unipac?

      _____ 4.3  Is this performance (4.2) stated in clear, unambiguous, (behavioral) terms?

      _____ 4.4  Do the objectives state the conditions under which the performance will be carried out?

      _____ 4.5  Do the objectives state the criteria for acceptable performance? (How *well* it must be done.)

_____ 5.   Are the objectives followed by a method of pre-assessment?

        _____ 5.1  Does the pre-assessment relate to the objectives?

        _____ 5.2  Is it comprehensive without being lengthy or overwhelming?

        _____ 5.3  Can the student or an assistant score it, or identify learning needs by using it?

_____ 6.   Is the pre-assessment followed by learning activities?

        _____ 6.1  Do the activities relate clearly to the objectives?

        _____ 6.2  Are there several (4 or 5) learning activities for each objective?

        _____ 6.3  Do the learning activities involve a variety of mental operations: knowledge, comprehension, analysis, synthesis, evaluation?

        _____ 6.4  Are the activities relatively brief?

        _____ 6.5  Will completion of the set of activities require from one to five hours of effort from the average learner?

        _____ 6.6  Is there a variety of activities offered?

        _____ 6.7  Is there something here for everyone?

_____ 7.   Are the learning activities followed by a post-assessment?

        _____ 7.1  Does the post-assessment relate to the objective(s)?

        _____ 7.2  Can the student or an assistant score it?

        _____ 7.3  Does it cover all the objectives?

_____ 8.   Does the unipac end with quest activities?

        _____ 8.1  Are the quest activities likely to be enjoyable?

        _____ 8.2  Are the quest activities genuinely a quest, or more of the same?

        _____ 8.3  Is there something here for everyone?

_____ 9.   Does the unipac permit students to evaluate *it*?

## ACTIVITY 2
### Read and respond.

**A.**  Read the selection, "Using Unipacs in the Middle Grades."

**B.**  Complete the "Active Involvement Form." An activity like this one is much more appropriate for certain early adolescents than professional educators. It is included as an illustration of what can be used with your students, not as though it were appropriate otherwise.

## Using Unipacs in the Middle Grades

### GENERAL COMMENTS

The idea of the unipac or learning activity package was developed by the Kettering Foundation. The unipac is a self-contained, auto-instructional packet or booklet, usually teacher-made, which students can pick up and work through with a minimum of supervision or direction. The middle school unipac in the model we are sharing here has six basic components:

1. Introduction
2. Objective(s)
3. Pre-assessment
4. Learning activities
5. Post-assessment
6. Quest activities

The unipac, when well-written, is like a sentence or paragraph in that it should cover one complete thought or concept, one complete overall objective. Judging when one covers too much or too little must come from experience. Examples of appropriate topics for unipacs might include: writing paragraphs (language arts), long division (math), osmosis (science), or stereotyping (social studies).

A unipac is designed to cover from one day to one week's classwork for the average student. This means it should involve approximately five hours' work for the average student. Anything longer tends to drag; anything shorter requires too much work for the teacher. If this were the only teaching method you used (we hope it would not be), thirty to thirty-five unipacs could cover the entire school year.

One group of four middle school math teachers recently studied the math curriculum from second through ninth grades. They developed a continuum of over 700 objectives and have begun building unipacs for each objective! It will, naturally, take a long time to develop such a library of unipacs; but when they finish, there will be a huge and inexpensive source of materials for individualized instruction for the students of all these teachers to use.

### THE INTRODUCTION

The introduction should be brief, describing the major concept that is to be studied, the main thought, skill, or big idea that the student is expected to absorb during the use of a particular unipac. The student must be able to see the purpose or intent of the material.

The introduction should also tell the student why this particular concept or skill is important to learn. This process of having to justify the topic of the unipac is sometimes difficult and should suggest that some things we have been asking students to learn are probably of little value.

The introduction may also include a section for directions, although many of the directions will be found in the learning activities section. Remember how simple and straightforward such directions must be! If there are any prerequisites to this unipac (e.g., other unipacs to be done first), the student should be told about it here. If the unipac is part of a sequence, the introduction should tell the student how this unipac fits, how it relates to those that come before and after.

## THE OBJECTIVE(S)

The second essential element of the unipac is that objectives be stated in precise behavioral terms. Students, teachers, and parents must all understand exactly what the student is to be able to do as a result of the work in the unipac. Precise objectives help to eliminate confusion and guesswork about what is to be accomplished.

According to Robert Mager in *Preparing Instructional Objectives,* an adequate objective must contain three elements: performance, conditions, and extent. The objective should specify exactly what the student will be able to *do* when he has finished, in terms that are clear and communicative. A good objective should also explain the conditions or circumstances under which the student's behavior will be exhibited. Finally, it should state how well the performance needs to be done; in other words, the degree of accuracy.

Some examples of both traditional and behavioral objectives are listed below. See if you can tell them apart.

1. The student will understand and appreciate the value of individualized instruction.
2. Using a concept or skill that has been taught before, the teacher will construct a unipac, having the six essential parts, which two other teachers agree is complete.
3. Given a DC motor of ten horsepower or less that contains a single malfunction, and given a standard kit of tools and references, the learner must be able to repair the motor within a period of 45 minutes.
4. The teacher will grasp the significance of and believe in the use of precise objectives. °

The important thing about good objectives is, of course, that they communicate. While you may not value the extent to which behavioral objectives work toward this goal, precision is important. To be more precise, avoid using the following phrases in your objectives: to know, to understand, to really understand, to appreciate, to fully appreciate, to grasp the significance of, to enjoy, to believe, to have faith in, etc. Other words are open to fewer misinterpretations: to write, to recite, to identify, to differentiate, to solve, to construct, to list, to compare, to contrast, etc. Try to select those verbs which most accurately describe the behaviors you want demonstrated.

---

°If you did not immediately recognize that objectives 1 and 4 are traditional and that objectives 2 and 3 are behavioral, you could profit from practice in writing precise objectives. The recommended standard is Mager's *Preparing Instructional Objectives.* Palo Alto, CA: Fearon Publishers, Inc., 1962.

One final word about objectives—try to involve more modes of thinking than just pure memory or basic recall. Objectives can and should be stated for higher levels of cognitive learning—application, analysis, synthesis, and evaluation.

## THE PRE-ASSESSMENT

This assessment should be given to determine the amount of knowledge the student already possesses prior to studying a particular concept or other learning objective. A pre-test indicates the student's amount of knowledge in relation to the specific objectives listed in the unipac. If, for example, the student already knows the material in a particular unipac, that student may move on to the quest activities, the post-test, another unipac, or to some other learning activity.

You may eventually conclude that the pre-assessment is the least important element of a unipac, perhaps because you know your students so well. Don't be too sure! The pre-assessment also serves the purpose of alerting students to the fact that there is a lot in the packet that they don't know, as well as presenting a preview of sorts of the material to be covered. Keep in mind that the pre-assessment does not always need to be in the form of an objective quiz. It can call for a paragraph response, yes or no answers, or any of a variety of other possibilities.

## THE LEARNING ACTIVITIES

The learning activities make up the core of the unipac. These are the experiences which provide insights and knowledge that will help the learners attain the objectives. There are several principles to be followed when designing the activities:

1. Each objective should include several activities.
2. The activities should, ideally, be designed for the range of abilities of the students using the unipac. All students should be able to experience some success.
3. Because a unipac is brief and sharply focused, the variety of activities does not need to be as broad as that typically found in a learning center. The activities should be complete within the unipac, so that students can take the unipac to their desks and work on it there without the need to chase down resources in other areas of the classroom or school. It may involve reading from a text or another readily available resource, but not much more. Written activities will almost necessarily predominate. Be careful that the activities are brief, otherwise the demands for writing may become excessive. The purpose is to have the student move through the work quickly, experiencing successful closure after a relatively short period of time. In and out quickly and successfully is the standard for success.
4. The activities can and should go beyond pure memory. Even though the activities will be largely paper and pencil activites, they can involve the students in mental operations that require analysis, synthesis, evaluation, etc.

5. There can and should be a variety of activities, even though they are largely restricted to reading and writing; games, puzzles, maps, problem solving, and other possibilities should be included. They should be fun, whenever possible.

## POST-ASSESSMENT

The post-test, like the pre-test, is based on the unipac's objective. If the objective stated that the student would be given ten multiple choice questions, then the post-test would, of course, contain ten multiple choice questions. Generally, the questions on the pre-test and post-test are different.

Whenever feasible, the teacher should permit students to check their own or each other's tests. This not only reduces the burden on the teacher, but under the right circumstances it can help students become responsible for their own learning. Often student-scored quizzes or other mini-tests can be given along the way. The final post-test, however, should be scored by the teacher. This cuts down on teacher time spent correcting tests and also reduces the temptation to cheat on the student-scored quizzes prior to the post-assessment.

## QUEST ACTIVITIES

Quest activities should take the learner beyond what is required. They should be unusual, imaginative, enjoyable, more difficult, and exploratory in nature. They should be available primarily for the rapid learners, but activities that everyone will be able to do should also be included.

## SUGGESTIONS AND REMINDERS FOR CONSTRUCTING AND USING THE UNIPAC

1. Try using a different color paper for each part of the packet. All tests might be printed on green, for example, the rationale on blue, etc. Color-coding makes locating parts and referring to parts much easier for both students and teachers; it also increases the attractiveness of the package.
2. Keep consumable materials separate or have the students use their own paper for writing activities. This adds to the life of the unipac.
3. When writing a unipac for a heterogeneous class, design the vocabulary at a level that aims at the low average student. The unipac is designed to be a road map, and it must be clear to a large number of students in order to be useful. Aiming for the largest ability group may not be a perfect way, but it will be time-saving.
4. Students should receive orientation in the use of unipacs before they start working in them. They need an adjustment period. Plan to work very closely with them during the first unipac.
5. Unipacs work well in conjunction with the learning centers approach, lecturettes, and other instructional strategies. The extent to which you use

unipacs depends on your own style, but avoid using unipacs to the exclusion of other techniques. Learners need variety!

6. Give yourself some adjustment time before you make any judgments on the value of using unipacs in your classroom. Don't give up too soon. Any effective device needs fine tuning before it fits well in your unique situation.

7. Unipacs, like any teaching tool, are best used in combination with other tools. Frequently, a teacher or team of teachers can effectively use a combination of learning centers, unipacs, and a teacher-directed activity such as demonstration, lecturette, or discussion. An example of how such activities can be scheduled into a class is given below.

|  | Group A | Group B | Group C |
|---|---|---|---|
| Time Block 1 | Work in Learning Centers | Work in Unipacs | Lecturette and Discussion |
| Time Block 2 | Lecturette and Discussion | Work in Learning Centers | Work in Unipacs |
| Time Block 3 | Work in Unipacs | Lecturette and Discussion | Work in Learning Centers |

*Explanation:* Group A begins by working in the learning centers. In another part of the room or unit students in Group B are working in unipacs, while another group, Group C, is attending a lecturette and a related discussion. At a prearranged time, students move from one area to another. The time block is adjustable: 15 minutes, an hour, a day. This arrangement allows variety and change to occur regularly, but within a viable, orderly, and structured process. Following this model will avoid the appearance of chaos.

## Unipac Active Involvement Form

Try your best to fill in the blanks without turning back to "Using Unipacs in the Middle Grades" until it is time to check your work. Use the terms on the last page of this activity to help select the appropriate words.

The idea of the unipac or learning activity package was developed in Broward County, Florida, by the Kettering Foundation. The unipac is a _____, _____ packet or booklet, usually _____, which students can pick up and work through with a minimum of supervision or direction by the teacher. The unipac has _____ basic components:

1. Introduction: rationale, overview, directions
2. _____
3. Pre-assessment
4. Learning activities
5. _____: self-tests and teacher tests
6. Quest activities

The unipac, when well-written, is like a sentence or paragraph in that it should cover one complete thought or _____, one complete overall _____. Judging when one covers too much or too little must come from the _____ of using them with kids. Examples of appropriate topics for unipacs might include: writing paragraphs (language arts), long division (math), osmosis (science), or stereotyping (social studies).

It is designed to cover from one day to one _____ work for the average student. It should be approximately _____ hours work for the average student. Anything longer tends to drag; anything shorter requires too much work for the teacher.

One group of four middle school math teachers recently studied the math curriculum from second grade through ninth grade. They developed a _____ of over 700 objectives and have begun building _____ for each objective! It will, naturally, take a long time to develop such a library of unipacs; but when they finish, there will be a huge and inexpensive source of materials for _____ instruction for the students of all these teachers to use.

## THE INTRODUCTION

The introduction should describe the _____ _____ that is to be studied, the main thought, skill, or "big idea" that the students are expected to absorb during their use of a particular unipac. The student must be able to see the _____ or intent of the material.

The introduction should also tell the student _____ this particular concept or skill is important to learn. This process of having to justify the topic of the unipac is sometimes difficult and should suggest that some things we have been asking students to learn probably are of little _____.

The introduction may also include a place for _____, although many of the directions will be found in the _____ section. If there are any _____ (e.g., other unipacs to be done first) that the students must satisfy before this unipac, they should be told about it here. If the unipac is part of a _____, the introduction should tell the student how this unipac fits, how it is related to those that come before and after.

## THE OBJECTIVES

The second essential element of the unipac is that objectives be stated in precise, preferably _____ terms. Students and teachers must both understand exactly what the student is to be able to _____ as a result of the unipac. Precise _____ help to eliminate the _____ and guesswork about what is to be accomplished.

According to _____   _____ in *Preparing Instructional Objectives*, an adequate objective must have _____ elements: performance, _____, and extent. The objective should specify exactly what the student will be able to *do* when he has finished, in terms that are _____ and communicative. A good objective should also explain the conditions or circumstances under which the student's behavior will be exhibited. Finally, it should state how _____ the performance needs to be done.

Some examples of both _____ and behavioral objectives are listed below. See if you can tell them apart.

1. The student will understand and appreciate the value of individualized instruction.
2. Using a concept or skill that has been taught before, the teacher will contruct a unipac, having the six essential parts, which two other teachers agree is complete.
3. Given a DC motor of ten horsepower or less that contains a single malfunction, and given a standard kit of tools and references, the learner must be able to repair the motor within a period of 45 minutes.
4. The teacher will grasp the significance of and believe in the use of precise objectives.

The important thing about good objectives is, of course, that they _____. While you may not value the extent to which behavioral objectives go toward this end, _____ is important. To be more precise, try to _____ the following phrases in your objectives: to know, to understand, to really understand, to appreciate, to fully appreciate, to grasp the significance of, to enjoy, to believe, to have faith in, etc. Other words are open to fewer _____: to write, to recite, to identify, to differentiate, to solve, to construct, to list, to compare, to contrast, etc.

One final word about objectives—try to involve _____ modes of thinking than just pure memory or basic recall. Objectives can and should be stated for _____ levels of cognitive learning—application, analysis, synthesis, and evaluation.

## THE PRE-ASSESSMENT

This assessment should be given to determine how much knowledge the student already possesses _____ to studying a particular concept. A _____ indicates where students are in relation to the specific objectives listed in the unipac. If, for example, the student already knows what the particular unipac has to offer, he may _____ to another unipac or to some other learning activity.

## THE LEARNING ACTIVITIES

The _____ _____ are the core of the unipac. Their purpose is to lead the student through _____ that will help him attain the objectives. There are several _____ to be followed when designing the activities.

1. There should be at least two _____ for each _____ .
2. The activities should be staggered over a variety of _____ levels.
3. The activities should avoid being _____ . That is, it is crucial that the unipac avoid being merely a supervised correspondence course! Middle school students need all the _____ they can get, so be certain to include a number of different kinds of learning activities.
4. The activities can and should go beyond pure _____ .

## POST-ASSESSMENT

This post-test, like the pre-test, is based on the unipac's _____ . If the objective stated that the student would be given ten multiple choice questions, then the post-test would, of course, contain ten multiple choice questions. Generally, the questions on the pre-test and post-test would be different.

Whenever possible the teacher should permit students to try _____ their own or other's tests. This not only _____ the burden on the teacher; but under the right circumstances, it can help the students become _____ for their own learning.

## QUEST ACTIVITIES

Quest activities should take the learner beyond what is _____ . They should be unusual, imaginative, _____ , more difficult, and _____ in nature.

## SUGGESTIONS FOR USING THE UNIPAC

1. Try using a different _____ paper for each part of the packet. All tests could be printed on green, for example, the rationale on blue, etc. This makes locating parts and referring back much easier for both students and teachers, and it increases the _____ of the unipac.
2. Keep the _____ materials separate or have the students use their own _____ for writing activities. This adds to the life of the unipac.
3. Write the unipac at the _____ vocabulary level. The unipac is meant to be a _____ and it must be clear to a large number in order to be useful.

4. Students should receive _____ in the use of unipacs before they start working in them. An adjustment period is needed.
5. Unipacs work well in conjunction with the _____ _____ approach.
6. Give yourself some _____ time before you make any judgments on the value of using unipacs in your classroom. Don't give up too soon.

| | | | |
|---|---|---|---|
| ability | directions | misinterpretations | road map |
| activities | do | multimedia | Robert Mager |
| adjustment | enjoyable | objectives | self-contained |
| attractiveness | experiences | orientation | sequence |
| auto-instructional | exploratory | paper | six |
| avoid | five | post-assessment | teacher-made |
| behavioral | higher | precision | three |
| checking | individualized | prerequisites | traditional |
| clear | learning activities | pre-test | two |
| color | learning activities | principles | unimodel |
| communicate | learning centers | prior | unipacs |
| concept | low average | purpose | value |
| conditions | major concept | reduces | variety |
| confusion | memory | repetitious | week's |
| consumable | more | required | well |
| continuum | move on | responsible | why |

## ACTIVITY 3
### Analyze and complete a unipac.

Turn to the second sample unipac, a partially completed unipac on remedial mathematics. You should be able to deal with the required tasks easily, regardless of your own subject area expertise. Your task is to finish this unipac to the point that it could be used effectively with students. To do this, you will have to:

A. Design a cover page
B. Choose a title
C. Write a brief introduction
D. Redesign the objective and pre-assessment
E. Construct learning activities
F. Include a post-assessment and some quest activities.

When you finish, arrange for some feedback from your colleagues. They may include others who are working on this chapter, or a math teacher or two. You might even try it with some students. This is important; you need feedback before you go beyond the experimental stage.

## Sample Unipac Two

_____

_____

title

**Skill:**

Recognition of number words

**Objectives:**

Shown the number words, one, two, three, four, five, six, seven, eight, nine, ten, students will match all the words with their numerals.

**Pre-test**

Directions for the students. (To be taped or read by teacher.) Place the correct numeral beside the number word.

ten     _____

seven   _____

six     _____

four    _____

two     _____

one     _____

three   _____

five    _____

eight   _____

nine    _____

1    2    3    4    5    6    7    8    9    10

**ACTIVITIES**

## POST-ASSESSMENT

## QUEST ACTIVITIES

## ACTIVITY 4
**Observe the use of unipacs in a school.**

The unipac is a commonly used method of instruction, so there are likely to be several teachers in any school who use them. In your school, or in one with which you are familiar, find out who is using unipacs and arrange to visit their classes. Observe how unipacs are being used and discuss the process with the teacher or teachers involved. Find out:

**A.**   The ways in which the teacher uses unipacs.

**B.**   How other teaching techniques are involved.

**C.**   How the unipacs used by the teacher compare in structure to the design advocated in this chapter. Use the "Unipac Checklist" to help make the comparison. Be certain you use professional judgment, and remember not to criticize the teacher's material simply because it does not conform to someone else's model.

**D.**   What are the strengths and weaknesses of unipacs from this teacher's point of view?

You may also want to share the sample unipac you finished and get the teacher's feedback on how well suited it is for use in middle grades.

## ACTIVITY 5
**Plan, implement, and evaluate a unipac of your own.**

**A.**   Choose a topic that fits in with something you plan to teach about six weeks from now or whenever you are employed. The topic may be for extra credit, enrichment, or a regular part of the regular classroom activity for this unit. Construct a unipac for that topic which includes all the recommended parts. Remember, you should include all of the following: cover page, title, introduction, objective, pre-assessment, learning activities, post-assessment, and quest activities. When you finish, ask someone to critique your product.

When you have designed, implemented, and evaluated several unipacs, you will probably want to modify the recommended format to fit your own style and your students' abilities more closely. That will be fine. For now, however, please try to resist the temptation to omit or drastically change or rearrange any of the basic elements of the unipac as it has been presented.

Your trial unipac should be planned around one objective, intended to take the average student about three class hours to complete. It should be designed to be self-contained, with everything required to complete the work right there in the unipac.

**B.**   Introduce the unipac to your students. If you are not teaching, find a teacher who will use your product. Be sure to instruct the teacher on how it is to be used (e.g., not to be written in). You may wish students to turn in all their work at once when they have completed the unipac, or you may request the work section by section. Eventually you will want to try it both ways, to see which way works best in your situation. You may even be able to find a way to use student critiques of your unipac, perhaps saving the last page of the unipac for such comments.

**C.**   Observe the students closely as they work through the unipac. When the last student has finished, perhaps in about five days, analyze what occurred. Here are some questions which may help:

Did the students seem to understand what and why they were learning this way?

How long did it take the fastest student to finish the unipac correctly?

How long did it take the slowest student to finish correctly?

How long did the average student take to finish correctly?

Were the students able to move through the unipac without constantly asking you for directions about what to do next?

What could be changed to make this more likely, if it did not happen as you hoped?

Could you tell whether students read and understood the objective(s)? In either case, why was it so?

What was their reaction to the pre-assessment?

Did any students do sufficiently well on the pre-test so that they could go on to the post-test or the quest activities? More than you expected? Why was it so?

Which of the learning activities in the unipac seemed most successful? Why?

How well did the group perform on the post-test? Do you think the level of perform-ance is attributable to the learning activities, the post-test itself, or some other factor?

Were the quest activities used? Did students respond to them as you had expected? Elaborate on this if you can.

In general, how did the class respond to the unipac? What was it that made them respond this way?

Now that you've tried this one, what changes should you make when designing the next unipac?

## NEXT STEPS

Now that you have mastered the basic design and use of unipacs, here are some additional activities which may be appropriate:

1. Think of a unipac as, on the average, requiring approximately five hours of class time (or one week) to complete. There are, then, about 35 possible units in a year's work which could be approached through the use of unipacs. Naturally, you would want to do more than use unipacs for the whole year. Otherwise it would be just a supervised correspondence school.

    As one of a number of effective instructional strategies, however, unipacs are fine tools for learning. List a series of topics for unipacs that can be used as part of the coming year's program in one area or subject. You may even want to put the topics in objective form.

2. List at least five different ways you can use unipacs in combination with other instructional strategies.

3. You may be a member of a team that would like to develop a "bank" of unipacs, and exchange them.

4. With a colleague from your school, design and implement an inservice educa-tional program on unipacs for other interested teachers in your school or district.

5. Once your students have worked through a few unipacs, they may want to try designing one themselves. It may not work, but it's worth a try.

6. You may be aware that the chapters of this book are written in a modified unipac format. Send your critique of this or other chapters in the book to the author(s) at 2403 Norman Hall, University of Florida, Gainesville, FL 32611.

7. Write to Teacher's UNIPAC Exchange, 1653 Forest Hills Drive, Salt Lake City, Utah, for information on joining the process of swapping unipacs, if it still exists.

8. *Where to Look for More*

   Gilstrap, R. L. and W. R. Martin. "Performance-Based Learning Activity Package," in *Current Strategies for Teachers*. Glenview, Ill.: Scott, Foresman and Co., 1975.

   Hansen, John H. and A. C. Hearn. "Learning Activity Packages," in *The Middle School Program*. Chicago: Rand McNally & Co., 1971, pp. 109–120.

   Jones, Richard, "Learning Activity Packages: An Approach to Individualized Instruction," *Journal of Secondary Education* 43 (April 1968): 178–83.

   Kapfer, Philip G. "An Instructional Management Strategy for Individualized Learning," *Phi Delta Kappan* 49 (January, 1968): 260–263.

   Klingele, William C. *Teaching in Middle Schools*. Boston: Allyn and Bacon, Inc., 1979.

   Peterson, Penelope L. and Herbert J. Walbert, Eds. *Research on Teaching: Concepts, Findings and Implications*. Berkeley, Calif.: McCutchan Publishing Company, 1979.

   "Symposium-Learning Packages: Management Strategies, Instructional Strategies, Learning Strategies," *Journal of Secondary Education* 46 (May 1971): Entire issue, pp. 196–236.

   Talbert, Ray L. "A Learning Activity Package, What Is It?" *Educational Screen and Audiovisual Guide* 47 (January 1968): 20–21.

   Wolfe, A. B. and Q. E. Smith. "At Nova, Education Comes in Small Packages," *Nation's Schools* 81 (June 1968): 48–49.

9. Unipacs work well as a part of a mastery learning system. See if you can find a way to make them work together in your classroom.

# CHAPTER 12

# DESIGNING LEARNING CENTERS

Methods come and methods go, so much so that many teachers often feel as if someone has formed a "Method-of-the-Month-Club." What is it that determines whether a particular method becomes a permanent part of the repertoire of American teachers? What is it about a method that consigns it to pedagogical limbo after a brief flash through the schools?

The learning center fits with current ideas and directions in education theory. It is practical and relatively inexpensive, easily put to use in classrooms. Once a teacher is familiar with learning centers, they require little more work than what is traditionally required for good preparation, and they hold real potential for injecting more variety, student responsibility, and individualization into the classroom.

This chapter is designed to introduce you to the use of learning centers in your classroom. It describes a rationale for using learning centers; the components of a complete learning center; ways to use them; and how to design them. You will be invited to design, implement, and evaluate at least one learning center. The chapter includes some pointers on how to use learning centers in conjunction with other instruction strategies. If you wish, you may reverse the order of the first two activities, so that you can see some learning centers in use before reading about them.

## ACTIVITY 1
### Read about learning centers.

Read at least two of the following selections. All except the fourth one are included here:

1. "Introducing Learning Centers."
2. "Characteristics of a Learning Center."
3. "Personalizing Learning: One Way."
4. "Individualizing Instruction in Secondary Social Studies: The Learning Centers Approach," by Paul S. George in *American Secondary Education,* Volume 4 (September 1974) pp. 4–10.

As you read, make some notes that illustrate your grasp of the key ideas.

1. What is a learning center?
2. What are the ways I can use learning centers in my teaching?
3. Is there a way to use learning centers in team teaching?
4. What don't I understand about learning centers and their use?

If you feel the need to read more about learning centers before moving ahead, try and locate some of the following books. There have probably been several new books published on learning centers since this chapter was written. Include in your portfolio the notes you make on these books.

1. Kaplan, Sandra, and others. *Change for Children: Ideas and Activities for Individualizing Learning.* Glenview, Ill.: Scott, Foresman and Co., 1973.
2. Thomas, John I. *Learning Centers: Opening Up the Classroom.* Boston: Halbrook Press, Inc., 1975.
3. Voight, Ralph. *The Learning Centers' Handbook.* Washington, D.C.: Acropolis Books, 1973.
4. Davidson, Tom, and others. *The Learning Center Book.* Glenview, Ill.: Scott, Foresman and Co., 1976.

## Introducing Learning Centers

To say that there has been a revolution in the teaching strategies used in American school classrooms is, at the very least, an understatement. New methods of facilitating learning appear almost faster than they can be catalogued, certainly faster than individual classroom teachers can absorb their significance. Some methods disappear almost as rapidly as they appear.

The continued use of a particular teaching/learning method seems to depend in part on whether it is correlated with current ideas and directions in educational theory. Survival of a teaching method also depends on teachers being able to use it easily in their classrooms and achieve the desired results. The learning-centers approach seems to be one of the recent innovations destined to grow and to become a permanent part of the repertoire of a significant portion of American teachers.

As one of only a few successful strategies aimed largely at the popular and desirable goal of individualized instruction, the use of learning centers is spreading through elementary and middle schools across the nation. Because of this rapid spread, and because of the existence of other closely related and similarly named classroom strategies, some confusion exists as to the correct definition of the term "learning center." It is important, because of this confusion, to clarify the relationship of the learning center to other similar ideas and to distinguish their various uses. The first task is to define and describe a learning center.

### A DEFINITION OF LEARNING CENTERS

A learning center refers to an area for study and activity, in or near the classroom, that has been provided for the structured exploration of a particular subject, topic, skill, or interest. It is a place for using and storing materials that relate to a special interest or curriculum area. It may be in a corner, on a wall, next to a bookcase, or on a table; but it exists somewhere in the physical space of the classroom or school.

---

George, Paul S., and others. The Learning Centers Approach to Instruction, *Research Bulletin* 8 (4) (Fall 1973): 3–14. Gainesville, FL: Florida Educational Research and Development Council.

The learning center is not to be confused with Learning Resource Center, a term now used to describe a larger central area housing the combined contents of the school library, the media center, and other areas which previously served as repositories for learning materials shared by teachers and students on a school-wide basis. Nor should the learning center or station be confused with the term "learning laboratory" when that term is used to describe a larger area (usually a small room) devoted to the study of one particular subject. Language labs and math labs are good examples of the "learning laboratory" in its own room, containing a multitude of math or language games, films, tapes, problems, texts, and other materials. Typically, the laboratory is not organized for specific learner tasks or activities, serving usually only as a source of materials used, once again, by a number of teachers who may have had little or nothing to do with their construction.

Some teachers and writers in the field use the term "learning station" as a synonym or in the place of learning center. We have chosen to use the latter term in this paper only because it is the term more commonly used by teachers.

## CHARACTERISTICS OF A LEARNING CENTER

One important characteristic of a learning center is that it is *self-instructional*. That is, it does not, when properly designed, demand the direct and continuous presence of the teacher as an information-giver. Pupils, after consulting the teacher, may go directly to a learning center and begin work. Each center should have clear, easily-discovered objectives and plainly written directions for beginning and completing work.

Secondly, each center (or station, if you wish) can present ideas, materials, and activities on a *variety of levels of difficulty*. Individualization is the key, and each learning center should also allow the student some *choice in the direction* he wishes to go. Each center can present its tasks with different versions and different ability levels.

Third, at the learning center each student should be asked to achieve *specific objectives* which are clearly communicated. The directions must specify the nature of the task and exactly what exit behavior is required. When objectives, alternate pathways, and post-tests are clearly communicated, students are able to move through the center with a minimum of direct intervention from the teacher.

Fourth, each center must include a method of *recording the student's participation*. The teacher may provide an individual folder for each student or class. This folder can be stored with others in an area removed from the centers but convenient to both teacher and students. Students are able to make additions to their folder when needed and the teacher also has easy access to pupil records. When such progress-charting is done consistently, students may proceed from term to term, and even from one year to the next, with a minimum of disruption.

Experience with individualized strategies like learning centers has taught us that continued interaction with the teacher is still very necessary to the child's motivation and achievement. Teachers must continue to correct and comment on student written work often, daily if possible. Otherwise students assume their tasks are unimportant to the teacher and act accordingly.

Another characteristic of the effective learning center, related to record keeping is the inclusion of opportunities for *pupil assessment* in each center activity. Ideally, each center will have, for each activity, a pre-assessment and post-assessment which students can administer to themselves or each other without the presence of the teacher. Depending upon the teacher's preference, students may even check their own work or they can deposit the assessment records in their folders where the teacher will go to review them. A combination of student-scored and teacher-scored assessments seems to work best. If the teacher administers and scores the final assessment, students are less likely to be tempted to cheat on the interim assessments.

Each center involves the opportunity for *student decision-making* and steps toward independent learning. Optimally, students have the opportunity to choose from among a variety of objectives and in at least a small way help to determine their own goals. Contracting with teachers on the path to be followed can become an important aspect of this process. Ideally, a learning centers approach should enable students to help make the decisions on the following questions:

How and where should I learn?
How should I manage my time?
Which resources should I use?
What are my goals?
How do I know when I have learned?
Who will evaluate my work?

## HOW DO I USE LEARNING CENTERS?

### INTEREST CENTERS

A wide variety of uses for learning centers have now evolved. Teachers may use learning centers for one purpose or for a variety of tasks. One of the more traditional uses of the learning center has been in the sense of an "interest center" where students may go when their regularly assigned tasks are completed. Usually the experiences of the interest center are exploratory, outside the major instructional objectives. Using the learning center as a place where fast working students while away their time waiting for others to catch up is not the most desirable use of the learning center. It can be done, however, in a way that becomes quite profitable.

### ENRICHMENT CENTERS

Learning centers can be used as enrichment where students may go for additional work on a particular topic, skill, etc. This use of the learning center need not be restricted to only the brightest students in the class. It can serve as an excellent change of pace for students working at any ability level.

This use of learning centers is particularly adaptable to centers which remain up for the entire year. The topics within these centers change every three weeks or so, and students know they must work through such a center once a month. Subjects like current events, parts of speech, and many others can be taught well this way.

## REINFORCEMENT CENTER

A related use of the learning-centers approach is when it is employed as a "reinforcement center." This center usually operates as a supplement to small or large group teacher-led activities. Students may go to a reinforcement center in grammar, for example, after a small group lesson with the teacher. At the center students find a variety of games, problems, readings, etc., that strengthen the concepts introduced by the teacher in the larger group.

## MOTIVATION CENTER

Another part-time use of the learning center is as a "motivation station." Here teachers introduce new units of study, new topics for investigation, etc. The center may be used as a kick-off device for a new unit. Teachers, if they choose, may also use this learning center as a culminating activity for wrapup efforts, looking back at what has been accomplished and forward to new ideas and implications.

## REMEDIATION AND SELF-CORRECTION CENTER

The learning center may be used as a "remediation and self-correction center." Here students come when they need a booster shot in some subject or skill. They may come to the center on their own, at the teacher's direction, or be directed as the result of making particular choices at another learning center. They may, for example, choose an activity or experiment which demands certain skills as prerequisites. The direction of that particular activity should clearly specify the prerequisite skill and the source of remediation at the self-correction center.

The learning center may also be used for the development of those skills of continued learning which teachers rarely find time to deal with in the course of the regular day. A center may, for example, be used to teach the skills and responsibilities of independent learning and self-reliance. A complementary center may then be designed to provide short courses for independent learners.

## MAJOR INSTRUCTIONAL STRATEGY

Using learning centers as the central method in a unit is probably the most effective way to use them. Learning centers are particularly valuable as a short course which all students must complete. In a three week unit, for example, which has 10 objectives, a learning center might be used to accomplish three of them. A unit on astronomy, for example, might have a learning center which focuses on our solar system. Other methods, such as teacher lecture, would touch on this topic briefly.

## WHY SHOULD I TRY LEARNING CENTERS?

The learning center approach to class structure has as its major goal the increased personalization of instruction. There are several ways in which it works toward realization of this goal. First it provides instruction at a variety of ability levels, allowing students to choose the level most appropriate to them. In this way the teacher can "precipitate the student into just-manageable difficulty." The student, in other words, will be able to work at the level which demands as much as the student has to give but no more. In addition to exercising some choice in the direction of his work, the learning center also permits the student to work at his own pace. He does not need to wait for others or to go faster than the speed at which he works best.

The learning center takes an important step toward another related desirable goal, the development of self-initiating learners. We know that to live constructively, now and in the future, persons must be capable of recognizing the need for their own personal learning. They must, in addition, be predisposed to initiate that learning and possess the ability to do so.

This kind of active involvement in lifelong learning does not result from passive submission to total structure and direction from the teacher. The learning-centers approach permits at least some elements of this active role to develop, and it encourages the continued growth of the necessary skills.

A further advantage of the learning-centers approach derives from the ease with which it may be applied to instruction at virtually every grade and age level. With attention to the type of instructions and activities provided, the learning centers strategy may be employed from kindergarten through high school and, theoretically, beyond. As the ability of students to work independently grows, the complexity of the tasks and experiences presented at the learning center may be increased proportionately. In the earliest years children may go to the center for educational games, art and music activities, and other experiences which demand less skill in reading. As the age of pupils increases, directions and tasks may be made increasingly demanding.

One of the most attractive aspects of the learning-centers approach is the provision made for eliminating the need for uniform seat work, which teachers have been pressed to use as a group management technique. With a room full of students, teachers who needed to work with small groups have often had no alternative to such "holding work" as a method of keeping students quiet and in their seats. The focus of this kind of instruction was obviously control, rather than learning. The learning-centers approach makes it possible to avoid the worst abuses of these assignments.

The learning-centers approach is well adapted to the framework of team teaching. Teachers on a team may plan, construct, and implement centers together; or they may each be responsible for centers in a certain subject area or skill.

Interdisciplinary units initiated by a team of teachers are especially suited in the use of learning centers. A team of four teachers who represent language arts, social studies, science, and math might, for example, cooperatively design and implement a unit or topics such as Ecology or Latin America or the American Dream. Such a center would be available to all students taught by the team. At the end of this reading are diagrams and notes illustrating a variety of situations to which the learning-centers approach can be adapted.

In a related area, the learning-centers approach employs the services of paraprofessionals in a valuable way. Aides may be used in the construction of centers, as center facilitators, record keepers, question-askers, or any of a dozen other tasks.

Another advantage of the learning center is the relative ease with which it may be implemented. Centers can be implemented as the total instructional strategy or for any part of the school day. If the teacher chooses, it may be implemented in small steps as the teacher and students become familiar with the new process. This is particularly advantageous for teachers who have found other effective methods and have no desire to abandon them totally for an untried technique.

For teachers who are struggling for a realistic way to facilitate student thinking at higher levels, this strategy provides a way to apply the guides to those processes developed by Bloom, Taba, Hughes, and others. It also allows the teacher to plan questioning in advance, permitting an often striking improvement in the kinds of thinking asked of students in classrooms.

Centers allow students more physical freedom when used in either open space or traditional school facilities. And, since the teacher is free of the burden of holding the attention of the class on the front of the room, the movement is much less disturbing to learner and teacher. Students move from point to point, to and from teacher conferences, bathroom, etc., with little or no notice.

Centers facilitate more personalized instruction for every student. In addition to student decision-making and individualized pacing of study, the learning center builds toward more individual contact between student and teacher permitting the development of a personalized relationship with the teacher so difficult to obtain in today's schools. Teachers freed of the obligation of continual lecturing and other one-person techniques have more time for attention to individual needs and learning styles.

The learning center, therefore, makes the one-on-one relationship the basic organizing construct of the school. In a very real sense it permits increased multiple person contact for our students, a valuable thing in today's increasingly compartmentalized, impersonal society.

Perhaps most important of all, it allows what the teacher does to be based on the individual learner's learning needs. It makes what we know about children the primary source of curriculum and instruction. The nature of society and the nature of knowledge become secondary sources. It, therefore, enhances the quality of human interaction in the school by moving teachers toward being facilitators of learning and children toward being active deciders of their own direction.

Finally, the learning-centers approach provides opportunity for student self-evaluation. Each well-constructed center should contain an evaluation process which can be done by the student and checked later by the teacher or aide.

It is, perhaps, important to point out that the learning-centers approach is like other instructional strategies in that it does not guarantee the accomplishment of the advantages described here. The effectiveness depends on the quality of the planning. There is no guaranteed, fail-safe method of instruction, no method which can stand alone.

## HOW DO I GET STARTED?

The first step in creating learning centers for the classroom involves some decision-making by the teacher or teachers involved. Teachers must first decide what the role of the learning centers will be in their instructional programs. Will they be used for remediation, enrichment, motivation, short courses, or as the major instructional strategy? Will learning centers be used throughout the day or for a shorter portion of the day? Will they be used for all subjects, a few, or only in an interdisciplinary unit? There must be, in other words, some basic procedural decisions made prior to the first move toward construction of centers. The same detailed planning that must accompany any other method of instruction must also be present for learning centers to be successful.

The writers recommend that teachers interested in using learning centers begin by using this approach for only one subject area or for a few hours out of the day or week. In this way the teacher can slowly change the method of instruction with the least amount of disruption and confusion.

Once the teacher has determined the extent to which learning centers will be used, teacher and students may plan the identity of the centers. Such teacher-student planning is crucial to the use of learning centers, as in every method. It is very important that learning centers are appropriate for the intended population. Centers may focus on a subject area (e.g., long division), a problem or issue (e.g., censorship), a process such as cooperating, or a variety of other topics. The most important consideration, however, is that they be planned with the student's interests in mind.

While the scope of a particular learning center will vary greatly with topic and age level, a good rule of thumb is that from beginning to end the average student ought to be able to complete the activity in no less than three hours and no more than ten. When a center offers an activity of less than this time, creation of new centers becomes a pressing burden on the part of the teacher. When the activity demands much more time than the effort the average student might expend in a week when working at the center one hour a day, students tend to lose sight of the original objectives and to become less interested in completion of the task.

When constructing the learning centers, there are a number of other considerations to be weighed. Each center should, for example, contain activities at a variety of ability levels. Each center should provide alternative avenues for completing the activity whenever possible. Each center should provide activities which demand a variety of levels of student thinking, especially those levels of mental operations beyond pure memory.

Once the basic activity of the learning center is ready, the teacher should locate the part of the classroom where the center may be most appropriately located. Physical arrangements necessary for some activities need to be considered. Learning centers with activities calling for art work will need to be located near a sink while math activities might need to be located near a chalkboard. At this point the teacher will want to provide seating and writing space at each center. Except in very large classrooms, seating need not be rearranged for large group work. At the end of this reading are suggestions for setting up learning centers in various organizational arrangements and under various space conditions.

Whether there is one center or a dozen, the teacher must provide some plan for student movement and share it with the class. Classroom traffic may be determined entirely by pupil interest, by time span, or a combination of factors. For example, in a self-contained elementary classroom the teacher might want to provide centers for everything but certain reading activities which the teacher directs in a series of small groups. In this classroom each student might be identified with a particular reading group, letting personal interests or a teacher-student contract determine the direction and pace of each student's other learning experiences. Student movement from center to center in this classroom would be a function of reading group schedules.

Once the overall pattern of pupil movement has been determined, teachers and students are able to begin what must become a continuing process throughout the life of the learning center in the classroom. Together, the teacher and each pupil diagnose the pupil's needs and interests in various areas and develop appropriate plans for each day and week. Decisions are made concerning which centers will be visited, what tasks will be accomplished, when the student will join a small group meeting with the teacher, and when the next teacher-pupil conference will be held.

The students are now ready to choose centers and activities appropriate for them and to begin working at the centers in accordance with teacher directions and previously laid plans. The teacher becomes a facilitator of learning rather than the verbal funnel through which a stream of facts is poured into passive receptacles. Working with individuals and small groups, the teacher is able to make the individual contacts and interventions that are the ultimate test of personalized instruction.

With the first center, however, the teacher will want to be much more directive. Taking students through this center on a step-by-step basis may be a very good idea. Less and less of the teacher's time will have to be used this way, though, as students become more familiar with the centers.

When students complete work at a particular center, they submit a post-assessment from their file for the teacher to examine, or take the teacher's final test. They then proceed to a new task or center in line with the terms of their contracts. At the earliest opportunity the teacher evaluates the post-assessment and decides, perhaps in conference with individual students, where they go from there—a new center, small group instruction, back to the first center for remediation, etc.

When students are at work in learning centers, the teacher uses his/her time in several ways. One of these is, of course, to continue to be available for individual conferences, skill work, and introducing new concepts to small groups. In addition, the teacher continues to evaluate group progress and plans new centers or activities in anticipation of future student needs or interests.

A learning center is always in process. It is not intended to become something static and final or to be reproduced in exactly the same way every time it is used. The foregoing description of a center has been offered to spark thinking about possibilities for the design and use of centers for different purposes, and with different learners. The richness of the center approach to instruction is dependent primarily on the designer's imagination and ingenuity. The authors hope that the ideas, suggestions, and guidelines offered here will interest teachers in designing centers which tap and extend students' interests while promoting learning.

Learning centers are, of course, a valuable teaching tool. However, an over-reliance on this approach to instruction carries with it the same dangers as over-reliance on any major instructional strategy. The most obvious danger is that excessive use fails to offer students the necessary variety of classroom learning modes without which any school day may become an onerous chore.

The alternative of total class instruction is still a good way to complement the use of learning centers where the teacher recognizes an instructional need met more effectively in this way. When used as a change of pace, large group instruction becomes a more positive experience for teachers and students alike.

The students' learning styles must be the source of instructional techniques used in the classroom. While using this approach, however, the teacher has the opportunity to help the child develop the capacity to work effectively in other learning modes. The middle school student, for example, usually possesses the necessary skills for effective use of learning centers but can listen to verbal presentations for a limited length of time. Using the learning center as the major instructional strategy gives the teacher the chance to introduce other methods in steps small enough to allow students to cope instead of being defeated by them.

The learning centers approach to instruction, when correctly understood and well-planned, can be used from kindergarten to college. In every classroom where personalized instruction is a major objective, the learning center concept offers increased opportunities for individualization. As a result, it appears that in the years directly ahead the learning centers approach may be one of the small number of instructional innovations that attracts continued support rather than dust.


## PATTERNS OF CLASSROOM ORGANIZATION

Here are some ways to think about using learning centers in your school, whether self-contained, team teaching, or departmentalized. You'll want to adapt these designs to your situation, of course.

### LEARNING CENTERS FOR TEAMING IN A TRADITIONAL BUILDING

Team teaching in a traditional building is adaptable to the learning centers approach. It is quite possibly easier to accomplish if the learning center approach is used. Student movement and ease of access may be handicapped, but the virtues of silence and privacy may compensate. Teachers and students may rotate on the same basis as they do in the open classroom. In the following diagram, four teachers (or any number, really) can divide their responsibilities in a multitude of ways. Since mass movement of students can easily be eliminated by the proper use of the learning center, teachers may move from room to room or convene for brief planning sessions with ease.

A typical schedule for one student's day might look like this:

9:00   Finishes work in language arts center
9:05   Confers with teacher on the team

9:20   Moves to science center

9:45   Attends film in large group area

10:15   Returns to science center and continues work on science module; completes part one of new module

11:00   Goes to the reading center for recreational reading

11:30   Lunch

12:00   Meets in small group area with five other students who are also ready to complete social studies module by participating in an evaluative discussion.

12:45   Physical education

1:00   Unified arts

2:00   Independent study at an Interdisciplinary Center

3:00   Teacher conference

3:15   Dismissal

## Learning Centers for Teaming in a Traditional Building

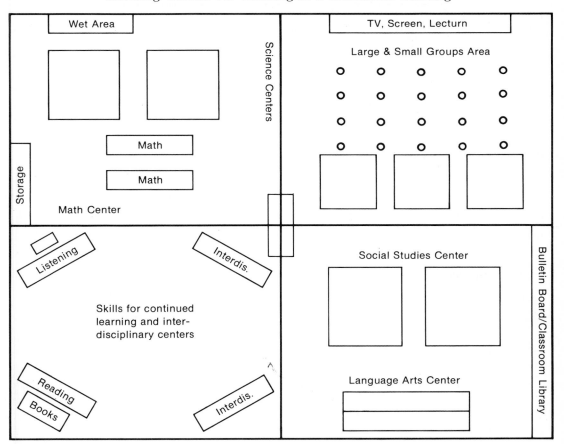

### Learning Center in a Disciplinary Classroom (Social Studies)

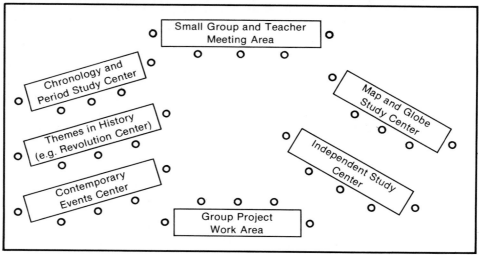

The configuration and movement patterns in the traditional subject-focused classrooms in middle school, junior or senior high, are not too different from the self-contained classroom. Students make contact with the teacher for individual work at the centers. Groups may gather in the appropriate area for cooperative project work. The teacher can plan conferences and small group work at the opposite end of the room. Large group instruction can utilize the whole room with students remaining where they are at the moment.

### Learning Centers in a Self-Contained Classroom

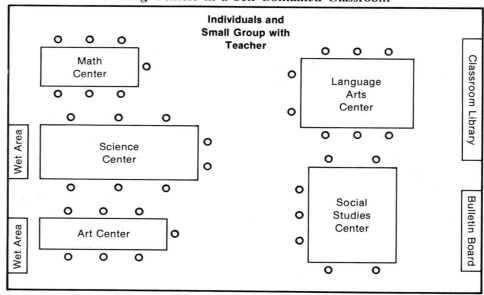

In the self-contained classroom students can move from center to center based on a predetermined scheme. The teacher works with individuals and small groups, and may move about the room making necessary interventions. Small groups may meet with the teacher for skill work, new concepts, etc., in the appropriate area.

Using learning centers in the open space physical facility with a teaching team can take a number of shapes. In many ways the open space team area is particularly well suited to the use of learning centers by all the team's teachers. Movement from one area or center to another is simplified and can be closely supervised.

In this situation the team may divide the responsibility for instruction in several ways. Teachers may work in the area of centers which fit their academic preparation. Following another strategy, they may rotate from area to area on the basis of their own interests. Or they may assign themselves to areas on the basis of which teacher has large or small group teaching tasks to complete at the time. There are probably as many ways of working team assignments as a team desires to use.

## Characteristics of a Learning Center
### Carol Hawkes, Lincoln Middle School, Gainesville, Florida

Teachers are very familiar with the traditional ways to *teach* students. They make use of lectures, textbooks, workbooks, assignments, and demonstrations. Learning centers vary the old teaching and learning processes according to the learning styles, interests, abilities, sociometrics, and achievement levels of the students. Teachers are concerned that students have not been reached by previous methods, and therefore they realize there is a need to change the structure of schooling. The learning center concept has grown out of this need. It focuses on the individual rather than the total class and can only be undertaken when the teacher focuses intently on each student. It is when all this is achieved, that the realization will come: children will be allowed to learn at different rates and by different means.

### LEARNING CENTERS—HOW ARE THEY DIFFERENT?

A learning center is not an assignment or a collection of worksheets. It is a self-contained unit of learning which organizes and directs learning, while allowing freedom of choice. It contains learning activities (which may or may not be manipulative), objectives, and an evaluation of some sort. It is further enhanced by a multimedia array of materials and information resources. The activities contained within are concrete and self-directing (auto-instructional), therefore the role of the teacher is altered to that of a facilitator, a nondirective influence.

Ms. Carol Hawkes, Learning Resources and Reading Teacher, Lincoln Middle School, Gainesville, Florida.

## LEARNING CENTERS—THE TEACHER'S ROLE

Teachers who elect the learning center method must be sensitive to student needs and wants. They must no longer limit themselves to a narrow conceptual scheme, but must be flexible enough to consider all variables when planning methodology. Their concern is with learning rather than with teaching. The role of teacher becomes less overt and more facilitative. Students utilize teachers as resource guides or counselors. Their time is spent in many ways: preparing, introducing, counseling, conferencing, encouraging. Essential to the establishment of good learning centers is that the teachers have the knowledge of many and varied materials for utilization in their centers. An awareness of the academic levels of the students is paramount when assessing these materials.

How then do the teachers assess the needs and the wants of their students? They may accomplish this in any of the following ways.

| | |
|---|---|
| standardized tests | cumulative folders |
| anecdotal records | interest inventories |
| conferences | questionnaires |
| personal dialogues | teacher-made tests |
| sociograms | observations |

All will allow for various means of grouping: ability, skill, sociometric, interest.

Once an assessment of the needs and the interests of the group has been accomplished, teachers must consider the learning environment in which they and the students must work. Is the physical situation suitable for learning centers? Does the room lend itself to an efficient traffic flow? Are there places for noisy work and quiet work? What about the furniture—is it arranged effectively, or can it be modified?

The task of converting to learning center methodology need not be a monumental one, if teachers make use of student assistance whenever possible. They may be involved in the groundwork by contributing ideas or by actually assembling the centers. Student input, with regard to deciding what evaluative procedures will be used or what will be the rules of behavior while using the centers, is extremely valuable and will surely ease the transition to this new mode of instruction. Reporting to parents is another component of learning centers in which the student can make worthwhile contributions.

## LEARNING CENTERS—SOME IMPORTANT CONCERNS

Of prime importance when undertaking any new teaching methodology is self-analysis. What style of teaching is most compatible with your behavioral makeup? This is accomplished by evaluating both your assets and limitations. Some important considerations for a learning-center oriented teacher should be: belief in students, creativity, curiosity, and energy.

After self-analysis the teacher should be aware of the following about learning centers.

A.  A learning center should be an attractive invitation to learn and explore. It should therefore arouse the students' curiosity.

B. It should be situated somewhere in the room: on a wall, shelf, large box, or it may be free-standing. The size of the center should be governed by the number of students who will use it.

C. A learning center must contribute to the purpose of the learner; whether they be to learn basic skills, solve a problem, or gain facts.

D. It should contribute to the interests of the learners and allow their creativity to be expanded; thus it must be open-ended.

E. A learning center must encourage self-selection by: offering a variety of choices; motivating the student to participate in the activities; and being self-directing with clear directions.

F. Record-keeping, both for the student and for the teacher, should be detailed enough but be quick and easy. The students should be able to check their own work and maintain a record of their own progress.

G. A learning center should meet specific objectives which are clear to the students upon the onset of their work. These objectives may be in the cognitive, affective, or psychomotor domain.

H. Centers should provide for a variety of learning styles, abilities, and modalities.

I. Learning centers should contain a multimedia array of materials.

J. Within a learning center provision must be made for some form of assessment and evaluation.

## LEARNING CENTERS—HOW ARE THEY USED WITH A GROUP?

A learning center does not aim to isolate individuals but rather to facilitate group learning situations. A teacher may use centers as supplements or adjuncts to an already existing program. A partial implementation allows a teacher to explore the possibilities for future learning centers as well as to note the reaction of students while using the existing ones. A total conversion to center methodology will require the teacher to group, identify, place, and decide on time allotments for the introduction and implementation of the centers to the students.

Learning centers may be used in the following ways with a large group:

A. A center may be designed around a unit or a theme.

B. A learning center may be used as a kickoff or motivational technique for a unit.

C. A learning center can help challenge high ability students, in that it allows a teacher to offer optional or additional topics.

D. A learning center may be designed by a student to emphasize a special interest.

E. A learning center can make learning fun by adding gimmicks to learning which ultimately make it more interesting.

F. A learning center may teach one skill or many skills.

G. A learning center may be built around a problem with many subproblems. Problems should be open-ended with multileveled activities.

H. A learning center may inventory or assess particular skills (diagnosis).

I. A learning center may be functional, whereby the students will use their newly acquired skills.

J.   A learning center can be used to foster group communication skills. Participants utilizing this type of center should be encouraged to work collectively toward a common goal, project, or joint action task.

## EVALUATION OF LEARNING CENTERS

The evaluation which takes place in learning centers should be a continuous task for both the teacher and the students. It should not be too complicated to get in the way of learning or teaching. Evaluation by students is accomplished when they receive immediate feedback as to how they have performed on a particular activity. They then keep records of what they have done. It is important, therefore, for the goals of the learning center to be clear and specific enough so that when the finished product is reached, the learner realizes it and can evaluate it. The teacher too can then assess the finished product. A teacher may evaluate the following:

A.  Basic understandings
B.  Use of materials
C.  Interest level
D.  Pride in self-motivation
E.  Accomplishing goals

Evaluation and feedback from the teacher to the student may be performed: orally during a conference; checked on a rating scale; graded by number or letter; written as an anecdotal report. These may be daily or weekly.

Evaluation usually has a threefold purpose: to inform the students of their performance; to allow the teacher to identify further needs and interests of the learners; to analyze pros and cons of the centers and make adjustments accordingly. A teacher may use the following to assess mastery of a center's skills.

| | |
|---|---|
| games | creative writing |
| projects | crossword puzzles |
| teacher-made tests | art projects |
| questions | logs |
| checklists | diaries |

## CLASSROOM ORGANIZATION

Learning centers run smoothly if the organizational problems are ironed out before the implementation of the centers.

A.  *Grouping:* In a learning center classroom, careful diagnosis of each student leads to some form of grouping procedure. Whether grouping is done by skill groups, by sociometrics, by interest, by student choice, by learning styles, or by teacher's choice, some decision must be made by the teacher before they begin. The number of students at a center will depend upon maturation and age level.

B. *Student Input:* Important to the program will, of course, be the students' input, so involvement during the organizational phase is vital and important. As stated previously, their interests and needs are the prime movers in your choice of a topic for a center. If the learning center is to prosper, the students involved must be self-initiated learners. Students understand the routine to be employed in the classroom, and therefore they must be trained in the mechanics of the operational flow as well as in the use of the centers. The goal is to ultimately develop autonomous learners.

C. *Learning Center Flow:* A format should be formulated to allow for the flow from center to center: checklists, prescriptions, modular scheduling, master sign-up strategies may be employed. These may be daily or long term. They may be kept by students or put on a wall chart so students know at all times where they are and where they are going.

D. *Availability of Teachers:* The availability of the teachers, once the centers are functioning, is paramount. Initially, they should be on call to ease students into the new format while helping with directions. As the program begins to take shape, the role as a facilitator, diagnostician, clinician becomes more apparent. During conferencing sessions with the students the teacher may:

1. Assess work
2. Give help
3. Collect data for reporting to parents
4. Decide future needs of a particular student
5. Decide what type of learning center suits a certain learner

Overall, by utilizing the learning-center format a teacher gets to know a student even more personally. In conferencing sessions the teacher may instruct one student in many or specific skill areas, introduce new concepts, reinforce old ones, or assemble students for discussion sessions. When a teacher performs the role of evaluator or assessor, he or she may assess the quality of work, quantity of work, or effort put forth by the students while performing their tasks. Information for this type of assessment is gleaned by observation or by perusal of the finished products of the center.

E. *Open Communication:* A plan should be devised in which students can communicate their needs for assistance from the teacher. Whether it be by hand-raising, note-writing, signing up, or placing a flag near their work areas, this is an important consideration and should not be left to chance.

F. *Replacement of Centers:* If a number of learning centers are functioning in a class, a calendar should be prepared for both center introduction and center replacement. This will ensure that all centers are not exhausted at the same time.

## A PLANNING SCHEME

How do we get all the elements of a learning center to synchronize? Where do we begin? In the following list a plan is advanced.

1. *Select a subject area or interest area* utilizing the aforementioned suggestions. Pick a topic with which you would be happy working.

2. *Determine your objectives.* What would you like students to be able to do or to get out of this center when they present their finished products? Will your purpose here be to teach, reinforce, or enrich? What skills or concepts will you incorporate?

3. *Decide the levels of the students to be involved with the center,* remembering your grouping suggestions and considering who you will be reaching.

4. *Assemble materials to be used:*
   
   library books               records
   film loops                  kits
   filmstrips                  transparencies
   hardware                    tangibles (real things,
   slides                          to touch and manipulate)
   games                       models

5. *Develop concepts or objectives into learning activities.* These activities should include many levels of thinking beyond simple, literal memory. The activities should also apply and extend concepts. The learning activities may involve:
   
   creative writing
   experimentation
   research
   listening
   art

6. *Establish time limits* based on maturation level and the sophistication of the student. (About one hour's worth of work is a good guideline.)

7. *Decide on management procedures.* Consider these questions:
   (a) Will the students rotate through all the centers?
       Will they have a choice of the centers they will do?
       Will the choice come within the activities?
   (b) When and where will the centers be utilized?
   (c) Will the centers be numbered or color-coded?

8. *Record-keeping is essential to center ideology.* It must develop a student's responsibility to follow-through. Records may be anecdotal or in checklist form—on the wall or personalized in the student's folder.

9. *Assessment procedures* may be based on effort, attitude, knowledge.

10. *Build your center* and make sure to use:
    
    bright colors
    pictures

strong paper
neat and orderly penmanship
many different audiovisual materials
  (give the center an eye-catching title,
  perhaps an open-ended question)

11. *Orientation*
    DIRECT: by introducing the centers to the students, giving directions, clarifying objectives, explaining activities, or
    INDIRECT: by simply leaving the center in the room and letting the curiosity of the students spark their interest.

If the whole class is involved in the center approach, then an important part of the orientation procedure should be an explanation of the flow. In other words, how will the class be managed?

## Personalizing Learning: One Way
### Nancy Doda, Lincoln Middle School, Gainesville, Florida

For some time I have been actively searching for more effective ways to teach transescent kids and, though my search has not ended, I'd like to stop and share my experiences and successes with those participating in this same search.

It was evident to me early in my experience with middle schoolers that they would be easier to love than to teach. Designing a learning program which attempts to meet the needs of these ever-changing learners is a challenging task. Since a primary concern for me has been in meeting their needs, I have listed those needs which seem to constantly seek satisfaction with middle school learners. They are:

1. To explore new areas of study, recognizing knowledge and skills as an integral part of life and living.
2. To see the self as a force directing learning and life.
3. To grapple with decisions, personal problems, and values/issues.
4. To be successful in learning.
5. To receive adult guidance, love, and support.

Although only a part of a longer list of needs, these have been outspoken and thus have been an activating force and essential concern to me in organizing my classroom.

Each day I teach six language arts classes with approximately 30 sixth, seventh, and eighth graders in each class. The students in a single class range from the ages of ten to fourteen and vary in learning ability and skills. The classes each meet with me for a forty-five minute period, during which time each student

Ms. Nancy Doda, language arts teacher, Lincoln Middle School, Gainesville, FL.

develops skills in language arts and reading. In a setting with such individual differences, it is difficult to justify or rationalize teaching all students the same thing, all of the time. Yet with limited time, materials, funds, and support, it is also impossible to provide a unique and individually prescribed, personalized learning program for each of 180 students. I have found some alternative ways of providing for the individual learner in this multi-age-grouped environment.

## GROUPS

With 180 students, 30 per class, I have had to rely on learning groups as an effective tool in meeting students' learning needs and interests. When beginning any unit of study, I establish student learning groups, usually three to four per class, based on either skills, deficiencies, interests, or social interaction. These groups are identified and even named to promote a sense of unity and cooperative effort.

## DIAGNOSES

In order to accurately identify learning groups for a particular set of skills or unit of study, I use a variety of diagnostic measures. For reading groups, I have experimented successfully with the Cloze-Test procedure, Stanford Diagnostic Reading Test results, informal reading inventories and other teacher-made tests. For skills apart from reading, I have found teacher-made tools easiest to administer and interpret. One tool which has proved very useful consists of selecting a set of skills, checking for deficiencies in students' work and charting deficiencies on a class roster sheet. From this chart, students that share weaknesses or strengths can be grouped together, and regrouped as deficiencies dissipate.

## GENERAL PROCEDURES

If grouping is to become a workable constant in a learning program, other procedural factors are crucial. Students at this age naturally tend to wait to be told where to go and what to do. With three to four groups per class, the teacher would consume valuable time orally directing each group. To avoid this, a chart with group names and daily and weekly schedules could be posted in the classroom. Not only does this avoid confusion, it encourages self-direction. To help students further organize their work and personalize their learning, each student in my classes has a folder. This folder is a place to collect work and chart progress on some dittoed checklist sheets which can be provided.

In addition to the chart and folders, the physical structure of the classroom is important. Chairs, tables, bookshelves can be arranged to set off sections of the room for particular learning groups. That way, students enter the room, check the chart for their daily schedule, then move quickly to their special area.

Having six different language arts classes, I found it helpful to have class boxes in which students from each class can place finished work. (I used Baskin-

Robbins Ice Cream containers, stacked.) At the end of a school day, I would take the papers from each box and put them in my single class folders for grading and recording.

All of these organizational factors make working with many different groups more manageable and smooth sailing.

## UNITS

In order to illustrate these general procedures in action, I would like to describe in as much detail as possible, several units of study which used learning groups for varying reasons. Moreover, these procedures when implemented in the classroom, show how grouping not only individualizes learning, but it facilitates self-directed, cooperative learning, more effective use of materials and resources, and superior use of teacher time and energy.

The units I will describe fall into three categories: They are (1) skill deficiency centered; (2) subject-centered; and (3) on-going component program.

In the early part of last year, for diagnostic reasons, I asked students to write a short composition. The papers showed that, while some students could write clearly and creatively, others could not write in complete sentences. The range in ability was great. For each class, I made a small chart listing the writing skills which needed attention. Each skill was given an abbreviated code and then the students' papers were coded. To create a class profile, I charted each student's weaknesses by using the code. Finally, students with common difficulties could be identified and learning groups established. Here's a chart to illustrate:

### Objectives to Observe

| Names | The student uses capital letters correctly. | The student knows parts of a business letter. | The student can write a business letter. | The student uses commas correctly. |
|---|---|---|---|---|
| Jay | W | W | W | M |
| Bobby | W | W | W | M |
| Mike | M | M | M | W |
| Scott | M | W | M | M |
| Jennie | M | M | M | M |
| Lesley | M | W | M | M |

M = mastered
W = weak

Since it would be impossible to teach all skills at once, I selected four groups of students with four skill areas to teach. Thus, I was ready to begin the instruction of a unit focused on skill deficiencies.

The classroom was divided into four sections with four centers of learning. Each group worked on skill objectives with different activities at different centers. I selected the skill objective; for example, the student will be able to use capital letters when necessary when writing sentences. Those students identified with weaknesses in this skill would go to this special center and work through the teacher-created activities. This same procedure was done for students working on other objectives.

This unit was successful because students were learning what they knew they needed to learn. Progress was evident and marked for most students.

One difficulty which arose was the element of time. Students were all finishing at different points so it was necessary to have additional quest activities for those whose progress was fast and furious.

In order to help students function effectively in groups for this unit, I posted signs near each center. In addition, the student had a record sheet in an individual folder where individual progress could be charted step by step. One inspirational item was a large wall chart with students' names, the four skills, and 'smiling faces' marked by those skills mastered. If a teacher found this approach comfortable, it could be used to work through all objectives in all skill areas.

Although this last approach met students' learning difficulties and needs, it failed to stimulate interest and it suggested in its design that capitalization, for example, had no relationship to other area knowledge or skills.

I then concluded that a subject-centered approach would be like a "spoonful of sugar," helping provide the needed and prescribed medicine to effectively reach the student.

To involve students, I listed seven different subjects on the board which were possibilities for units. Before discussing the options, I explained to the students the problem as I saw it and elaborated on what I hoped would be done. They were enthusiastic.

Out of the seven subjects, the majority selected Greek mythology. While the classes were completing their work in other areas, I collected materials to teach the unit. It was obvious to me that the subject lent itself to particular skills so I selected skills from our tentative curriculum which were reading, research, and writing oriented.

One reading skill I wanted all students to work on was comprehension. Every time a reading assignment of some kind was required, the activities focused on comprehension. In research and writing, I asked students to practice reading and summarizing material. This skill was reinforced continually.

This time I grouped my students on reading comprehension scores and the sophistication of writing skills. There were three groups of about ten students per group. Each group was color-coded, group A, red; group B, blue; and group C, green.

My next step was to design activities for learning centers which could accommodate all three levels.

The first center, called "The Gods," introduced the students to the gods of Mt. Olympus. All students were working with the same subject but performing different activities. At the center, the activities were also color-coded to direct students to their group activities.

The students in group A, for instance, would go to the center and would only be asked to complete the work colored red. One activity for all students was a reading describing the twelve Olympians. For this activity, group A read a simplified, teacher-written version of the facts and was asked to answer factual comprehension questions. Group B read from a text and answered questions which went beyond the factual and into the inferential. Group C also read the text account and answered questions which called for evaluative and synthesizing activities. All three worked through the same content, but with materials and activities geared to their levels. A second activity, a filmstrip-tape, was shared by all three groups, but the follow-up work was different for each group.

The second center had a total of eight activities, some required and some optional. For a period of five days, the students in one group worked at this center. While one group was busy in this area, another group, B for example, would be working at the next center, entitled "Independent Tic-Tac-Toe."

Physically, this was a large board with activities and directions written on nine large white squares. Each student could select three activities in any fashion as long as it was a Tic-Tac-Toe line across the board. This was an experimental center, not as controlled as the first. Amazingly enough, most students selected activities they could do, but almost always had one challenging project. Some of the activities were: (1) Preview one filmstrip from the mythology collection and choose *one* of the following to do: (a) write five questions on your filmstrip, (b) make a Seek n' Find puzzle of all new words you learned (it will be duplicated), (c) in writing, summarize your filmstrip; (2) read a myth from our collection and *choose* one of the following things to do: (a) illustrate a myth in drawings, (b) write five questions on the story, (c) using the same theme, write your own myth. These are just samples to illustrate the variety of activities that are possible.

Students had to work through three selected activities in five days and keep a log of their daily progress. The students were very involved in their projects at this center.

Third, and quite different from this last center, was the basically teacher-directed study of the *Odyssey*. In five days I worked with group C, for instance, introducing the *Odyssey* but working on reading for sequence and comprehension. Materials used were: short summaries of outstanding parts of the *Odyssey*, extensive two-part filmstrips, two large maps of Odysseus' journey, dittoed maps of his journey, dittoed questions on *all* levels about the story, direct readings from the real epic, discussions on larger questions pertaining to epics and heroes.

The unit then had three basic operations in action at once. It worked well. Students entered the room on the second day following a first day introduction, went directly to their designated center (noted by large signs) and began working with little or no help from me. Although I worked with one group for part of the time, I was free to help others for most of the class periods. I directed the *Odyssey* group, but I was not solely with that group.

After five days we had a "Show and Tell" day and then rotated again. This time, there was more enthusiasm than ever. With this approach, interest was at a maximum and skills were certainly being taught and reinforced.

One problem encountered was that I felt the need to establish time limits, yet philosphically this did not set with a mastery learning approach. I tried to allow for exceptions and in most cases, this was satisfactory.

As a language arts experience, the mythology unit was a plus for all involved. This year, kids still reminisce. This approach could be used often, but it is not good for all skills. Some skills are so basic, they are better taught by open admission of their existence and straightforward teaching.

A problem with the unit which remained unresolved was the final evaluation of student progress. The skill objectives were not going to be taught and checked off after this unit. They were ongoing skills and this unit was just one step along the way. If used with this condition acknowledged, this type of unit is valuable.

In an attempt to combine both approaches, I set up a four-part component program. This program was designed to be permanent, varying only the content when needed. The four parts were: skills; reading groups; independent study; and spelling and word development.

I grouped students for reading groups and then set up individualized work packets or activities with a pre-test and post-test system.

The student groups were called Avocados, Bananas, and Cantaloupes. Each group had a different daily and weekly schedule.

To envision this, here's a picture of the schedule.

| Monday | Tuesday | Wednesday | | Thursday | Friday |
|---|---|---|---|---|---|
| *Reading* | *Reading* | S | D | *Reading* | *Reading* |
| Avocados | Cantaloupes | P | E | Bananas | Avocados |
| | | E | V | | |
| *Skills* | *Skills* | L | E | *Skills* | *Skills* |
| Bananas | Avocados | L OR L | | Cantaloupes | Bananas |
| *Independent* | *Independent* | I | O | *Independent* | *Independent* |
| *Study* | *Study* | N | P | *Study* | *Study* |
| Cantaloupes | Bananas | G | M | Avocados | Cantaloupes |
| | | | E | | |
| | | | N | | |
| | | | T | | |

Here's a run-through of a student's week in this system:

(1) The student is an Avocado.

(2) He comes to class, gets his folder, goes to the wall chart to read his schedule, and gets his necessary materials.

(3) The student finds a seat near his materials and begins work. More specifically, the student, an Avocado, has reading on Monday, so he goes to his reading-group seat to begin work. With this component program, the reading groups were mostly teacher-directed. I introduced the reading to the group, distributed activity sheets, and later left the group to help others. I would return to

the group to do particular follow-up activities. Occasionally, work would be taken home to complete. On Tuesday, the student moves on to his skills activities. Everyone in his group may differ as to ability and knowledge of the skill studies, so the student takes a pre-test to see whether work on that skill is needed. For example, the skill may be writing a business letter correctly. If he needed work, Tuesday he would practice this skill; if not, other activities in writing letters would be available. Wednesday, all students work on spelling and word development. Although all students work in this area on the same day, it is individually structured.

Each student has a special notebook for word development. On Wednesdays students all have words they have misspelled in their week's work. They record correct spellings in their notebooks and any new words encountered during the week. Then, with a partner, they study their new words. Some with peculiar or extensive spelling difficulties work alone with a recorder. During this period students study, write, speak, and quiz with their own words. It's the best way I've found to teach spelling and vocabulary with some respect for individual differences. Students also work on vocabulary in reading.

Thursday, for our Avocado student, is a very personal day. For this one day he works on an independent project of his choice. Although he chooses the subject, the requirements and activities he is to do are determined by his ability to work independently. These project-plans are worked up to a five minute conference with the teacher. Knowledge of the student enables the teacher to guide the student in deciding what he will do on this special day, once a week.

A form such as the one drawn below is useful in administering such a plan.

## Independent Contract

Name _____

Group _____

Starting Date _____

Finishing Date _____

I. Topic _____

II. Objectives
 1.
 2.

III. Materials and Resources
 1.                            3.
 2.                            4.

IV. Activities
 1.                            3.
 2.                            4.

V. Evaluation
   1.
   2.

Contract Satisfied  _____  _____

There are many variations of this form which could be used to suit various student needs. I found that my younger, less mature, less self-directed students preferred and found success with a more prescriptive contract. This led me to formulate an idea for another learning system which, although demanding in terms of preparation, could be very vital for developing an entire language arts program.

The idea could be titled "Prescriptive Contracts." The teacher using curriculum objectives could develop contracts for every learning objective. The learning objectives and activities could be determined, but the topic student-selected. In any case, a file of these contracts with all activities written up and materials listed could be fantastic. It's something to work toward. I have developed a few and use them for students with special difficulties in specific areas.

In all of my experimenting I have found that students at this age need a delicate balance of structure and freedom. They need choice and options, but guidance in deciding what they need to learn. Even with the variety of learning styles and personalities among the students I teach, an organized, systematic, smooth-running, meaningful learning environment is critical to all. They take great pride and satisfaction in seeing grouping work effectively because they are so much a part of its success. They recognize its purpose and significance in terms of their own education.

What I have shared is only a part of my experience with middle school kids, but it represents several ways I've found to successfully meet the needs of many students with differing needs and interests.

I love middle school kids and these successes have made teaching them a joy!

## ACTIVITY 2
**Observe the use of learning centers.**

Learning centers are so popular that in the school you know best there is probably at least one teacher who uses them regularly. There may be more. Find out who they are and arrange to visit their classrooms. First, observe the classes in which learning centers are being used, then arrange to have a discussion with the teacher or teachers involved. Be certain you are clear about:

- How the teacher decided the way the learning centers would be used.
- How the learning centers were introduced to students.
- The plans which the teacher makes to ensure that the use of learning centers in the classroom achieves the desired results.
- How these uses of learning centers compare with the ideas in the readings in Activity 1. Use the "Learning Centers Checklist" on the next page to make your comparison.

## ACTIVITY 3
**Analyze and evaluate a learning center format.**

Using the "Learning Centers Checklist," analyze and evaluate the written description of the learning center on "Map-making." Make notes on the following questions.

- Does the learning center contain all of the parts as described in the readings in Activity 1? If not, do the parts which are missing seem to damage the effectiveness of the center by their absense?
- Do you think middle school students could complete these learning center activities successfully?
- Do you think you could design such a learning center or one similar to it?
- Could you find a way to integrate this center or one like it into your way of teaching?

## Learning Centers Checklist

*Directions:* Answer "yes" or "no" to each question.

### A. Backdrop
____ 1. Does the learning center look appealing from a distance? Is it inviting?
____ 2. Is it colorful and physically attractive?
____ 3. Is it neatly done? (With middle school students, the neater it is done, the more positively they will respond to it.)
____ 4. Is it well-spaced and balanced? Does it avoid the appearance of confusion or jumble?
____ 5. Are the printed words large and clear?

### B. Introduction
____ 1. Is there a simple description of the goal of the learning center?
____ 2. Does it present a brief overview of the purposes and activity of the learning center?
____ 3. Does it mention any prerequisites; things that must be done first?
____ 4. Are the directions for completing the learning center activities extremely clear and simple? (Sometimes even a flowchart is helpful.)

### C. Objectives
____ 1. Are there at least two but not more than five or six objectives?
____ 2. Are the objectives specific and precise, if not behavioral? (Do they avoid vague, unmeasurable words such as *appreciate* in favor of more precise verbs?)

### D. Pre-assessment
____ 1. Does it directly relate to the objectives?

_____ 2. Are there instructions for students who pass the pre-test? (e.g., are they told to go on to quest activities or the post-assessment?)

### E. Learning Activities

_____ 1. Are there at least three and preferably five activities to help students accomplish each objective?

_____ 2. Do the activities vary over a range of ability levels so that all students can achieve at least some measure of success?

_____ 3. Do the activities utilize a variety of instructional strategies: readings, filmstrips, tapes, writing, games, reports, small group tasks, etc.?

_____ 4. Are all of the resources necessary for successful completion of the activities located at or near the center?

_____ 5. Are the activities relatively brief? As a rule of thumb, could the average student finish at least one single activity within the space of one class period?

_____ 6. Will the activities for the entire center take the average student approximately five to ten hours to complete?

### F. Post-assessment

_____ 1. Have the students been provided with feedback on their work as they progressed, rather than waiting until they have finished the entire center?

_____ 2. Are there any choices at all for final assessment?

_____ 3. Does the assessment relate clearly to the objectives?

_____ 4. Do the results of the post-assessment suggest which parts of the learning center the students should return to, if they are partially unsuccessful?

### G. Quest Activities

_____ 1. Are they there?

_____ 2. Do they take the student beyond the requirements, perhaps in a different but related direction?

_____ 3. Are they more challenging?

_____ 4. Are they more fun?

_____ 5. Do they involve different kinds of learning activities?

_____ 6. Is there something for every learner, not just the brightest?

## Map Making: Description of a Learning Center

### INTRODUCTION

Do you know what the word *cartography* means? It is the art and science of drawing maps. People have been reading and drawing maps for hundreds of years. Remember the rough maps used by the pirates to hide their treasures on the lost island? Well, you may be drawing one of these maps. You may also draw more accurate maps.

## OBJECTIVES

Students will be able to:

1. Read and use an official state road map.
2. Recognize and use the basic symbols for map reading.
3. Draw a simple map using the five map symbols.

## PRE-ASSESSMENT

Take the test below to see how many of the skills you may already have. Don't worry about your score. It isn't important. If you score above 80, proceed to the quest activities. If you score below 80, try the unipacs titled "Map Reading" and "Map Drawing." Then proceed through any of the activities you decide to choose. When you have finished you will receive a map leading you to a treasure just for you!

### Activity 1

You are a pirate on the North Sea. You must hide your treasure on an island you have just discovered. Draw a map of this island with a key and directions to the treasure.

### Activity 2

Draw a map of the U.S. showing the average annual rainfall across the country. Be sure to include the key, scale, compass rose, one inch margin, and title.

### Activity 3

Draw a map of Great Britain using the following symbols to represent its resources. If you wish, you may make up your own symbols and add other resources.

Steel processing center

Coal Deposits

Iron Deposits

Petroleum refineries

(See *World Resources*)

### Activity 4

Choose a partner. Select one of the game sheets marked ACTIVITY 4. Play the game and have the winner pick up the prize from the teacher. This game is on reading the official Florida road map.

### Activity 5

You are a travel agent in the state of Florida. I have just entered your office to find out about a tour through the state. Using the official road map, list the special features, parts, and special attractions I could see if I travel from Panama City to Key West. Tell what highways I should use.

### Activity 6

Using the official road map, make a game of "Hide and Seek" for a friend. Start at Ocala. Tell what direction, which highways, and how many miles your friend must travel in order to find you. See if you can out-fox your friend.

### QUEST Activity 1

Find the game of "Jackpot" on the table. Select one or more of your friends to play the game with you. You will need about 30 minutes to play this game. If the cards are too easy, ask the teacher for more advanced cards.

### QUEST Activity 2

Have you ever made dough before? Well, you will need to in this exercise. You will find flour, salt, and food coloring on the table. With these materials make a relief map of the U.S. You can use the U.S. relief map from the Nystrom series as an aid.

### QUEST Activity 3

Use your imagination on this experience. Select any country you desire. With the crepe paper and glue on the table, make a relief map, a map of annual rainfall, or a vegetation map. If you run short of ideas, ask the teacher for help.

## POST-ASSESSMENT

Take the test below marked "Post-assessment" to see how many of the skills you have learned. If you score an 80 or above, ask the teacher for your "Treasure Hunt Map."

# ACTIVITY 4
### Plan, implement, and evaluate a learning center.

This is the real thing! Choose a topic for a learning center. As you think about an appropriate topic, try to select something (1) which is a part of a larger unit; (2) which will take the average student from three to ten hours to complete.

### Conceptualizing the Center

In preparing to design this center, answer the following questions. Record your answers on a separate sheet of paper.

1. What kind of center do I want to try first? Remedial? Enrichment? Short course?
2. What schedule will I design for its use? The whole period? The entire week? Some other way?
3. Who will use it? One class? Everyone? A pilot group?
4. Will it be optional or required?
5. How will it fit in with the other instructional strategies I use?
6. How long will it last?
7. How will students be evaluated for their work in the center?

## Planning the Center

When you begin to develop and implement the center, follow the steps listed below. If you are working with someone else, or in someone else's classroom, ask the person(s) to critique your written plans before you go further. If you are working alone, write all of these items down and find someone to react to them. Perhaps student reactions would be helpful. Be certain you get this critique before you go to all the trouble of physically constructing the center. Here are some suggested steps in planning:

1. Decide on the theme of the center and determine its role in your classroom. Record that information.

2. Identify two to five objectives that will comprise the learning goals for this center. Resist—repeat—resist the temptation to write these objectives *after* you have designed the activities. Write your objectives down now.

3. Create at least two learning activities through which each objective may be accomplished. Make certain the activities are of different types and levels of difficulty. Jot down your ideas for someone to react to.

4. Design the assessments. There should be a pre-assessment, if for no other reason than to show the students what they don't know. The post-assessment should probably be teacher-controlled, but there should be plenty of feedback to students along the way. How will you do it?

5. Now is the time to write the introduction. It should be brief and clear. Directions should be simple and complete. Record at least part of it for a colleague's reaction. Try it out on some students, too.

6. Once you've finished all of the above, match your plan against the Learning Center Checklist. Then ask some colleagues to react to your ideas perhaps in exchange for critiquing theirs.

7. Only when you can interpret the feedback you receive as a clear "go ahead" should you begin to construct any of the actual backdrop of the center. When doing so, try to use the most permanent materials possible. Laminating all your posterboard and tagboard is a great way to preserve it. Mounting this on a wall or heavy board or other surface will also help keep your materials from being "studied to pieces." The more colorful and attractive you can make the center, the better.

## Implementing the Center

It should be ready to go! If you have access to a classroom, here's one way to begin.

1. Get to school early on Monday (or stay late on Friday) and set up the center without any students around.
2. Prepare some written directions on how to use a center. When you're ready to orient the students, distribute the directions. Put a similar set on an overhead projector and talk your students through the directions.
3. Have them gather around the center while you point out all of the parts and explain what must be done there.
4. Have at least one student come to the center and tell you and the class how he or she would work through it.
5. Post and discuss a list of rules for behavior at the center.
6. For this first center only, you may even want to have everyone work through it together, step by step, discussing and explaining it as you go.
7. If possible, have a colleague visit your classroom while you introduce this first center. Talk with him/her afterwards about what you forgot to say.
8. As your students work through this center, make some notes on your progress. You should note students' reactions, problems you encounter with the use of the center, etc. Keep these items for later review and discussion.

## Evaluating the Center

1. When the introduction to the center is all over, conduct an evaluative session with the students. It doesn't have to be anything formal. Get some feedback from them on what they liked and what needs to be changed. What did they say? Make some notes and collect some samples of student work accomplished in the center.
2. You may want to compare the results of student achievement on the topic dealt with in the center to other occasions when you have taught the same topic but with other teaching methods.
3. What are your own reactions to this method of instruction? What went right? What went wrong? Strengths? Weaknesses? Include the notes in your portfolio, along with samples of student work and products of the center.

## NEXT STEPS

If you are now at the point where you have used at least one learning center with an acceptable level of success, you may want to try more. Some of the following activities may be appropriate:

1. If you are a member of a teaching team, during your next team unit planning session suggest that learning centers might be a good thing to include with other methods. One of you might take on the task of designing the centers,

with the same person or someone else assuming the responsibility for supervising and evaluating student work in the centers, while the unit is being taught.

2. If you are in your own classroom, you might try using two or three learning centers as a part of your next unit. Combine them with lecturettes, films, group projects, unipacs, and other instructional techniques.

3. Find out if other teachers in your school would like to try learning centers. You might organize a faculty workshop to instruct other interested faculty in the use of learning centers. Try doing it with learning centers!

4. Examine the research on instruction now widely available. Begin with N. L. Gage, *The Scientific Basis of the Art of Teaching* (New York: Teachers College Press, 1978), and with Penelope L. Peterson and Herbert J. Walbert, eds., *Research on Teaching: Concepts Findings and Implications* (Berkeley, Calif.: McCutchan Publishing Company, 1979). These two volumes extend our knowledge of the virtues of large group, whole class teacher-directed instruction and the need to use a balanced, varied approach to teaching middle school students.

5. Read Chapter Eight, "Instruction", in Alexander, William M. and George, Paul S. *The Exemplary Middle School* (New York: Holt, Rinehart and Winston, 1981).

# APPENDIX

# LEARNER-MANAGED PROFESSIONAL DEVELOPMENT

## INTRODUCTION

As suggested in the introduction to this book, we believe that the book is best used with a system of learner-management. We like the approach we call the "peer panel and portfolio procedure." Designed for teachers inservice, it has also been adapted for preservice teacher education. (It is described here as teachers inservice would use it, but preservice users can readily interpret the procedure for that setting.) A peer panel is a group of three to five teachers (or teacher candidates) who agree to help each other in developing and measuring teaching skills. Each chapter of the book includes skill objectives, activities for developing skills, procedures for measuring progress, and criteria for checking the quality of the outcomes. The chapters, in effect, provide all the structure a peer panel needs to guide its work, including most management functions typically performed by a supervisor (or an instructor). Working in the peer panel system, the panel members are co-producers rather than consumers of their professional development programs.

Those planning to use the book with the peer panel approach would typically follow this sequence:

1. Identify a compatible group of three to five persons. Compatibility, at the minimum, means a willingness to support each other in skill development, and individual time schedules that permit the members to meet as a group regularly, say, once a week for two hours. Meetings may be needed less frequently.
2. Select the chapter(s) to begin with. There are obvious advantages to having all panel members work on the same chapter at one time, but that is not essential for many of the chapters. Panel members can fill the roles necessary for the learning tasks without working on the same objectives themselves. They can begin with any of the chapters, but should first read and discuss the rest of this appendix. Before beginning, each peer panel should decide the first three or four chapters to be used. We recommend working through the activities of the appendix before finishing the second or third chapter. The activities here are designed to help strengthen the skills specifically needed for peer panel participation.
3. Begin work. Each chapter includes all the instructions and nearly all materials a peer panel will need. For example, if learning a new skill involves observing children's behavior, the chapter will include procedures for observation and perhaps a checklist for making a report. Whenever the chapter activities call for sharing with a colleague or involving a colleague in observation or other work, peer panel members call upon each other.

Panel members make records, report observations, and check each other's observations against given criteria, but they are not asked to evaluate work in the usual sense. Evaluation, which consists of making judgments about the worth of someone's work, is a task for an expert in that area. Peer panel members, who are fellow learners and are not yet experts, are called on to record, report, and check work rather than to judge it.

4. Begin to build individual portfolios. As a peer panel proceeds through a chapter, each member will produce various kinds of records of work: new lesson plans, materials for students, observation records, written analyses, etc., and will also have samples of student work—all of which represent accomplishments of the chapter goals. The peer panel, using procedures provided in the book, will give feedback to its members, and will endorse materials for inclusion in individual portfolios.

5. Each peer panel will work to build skills of giving and receiving feedback. This appendix contains a set of guidelines for the feedback process. We recommend that all panels use it in developing panel skills and rapport.

To sum up, users of the book will involve their peer panels in four ways: (1) as a sounding board for ideas and plans; (2) as observers to measure some skill or classroom situation; (3) to give feedback on things observed or work analyzed; and (4) to endorse for the portfolio the completion of some work.

The portfolio is a record of demonstrated competencies. In a teacher preparation program the instructor may accept it as evidence of completion for certain program requirements. In a school system, the portfolio may be part of a plan by which teachers can obtain extension of their teaching certificates or otherwise improve their professional status. We endorse this approach for both the preservice and inservice professional development programs. The portfolio can reflect a formal agreement between panel members and the instructor or supervisor.

## WHAT KIND OF PEER PANEL FITS YOUR SITUATION?

Different situations call for different compositions of the peer panel. If you are a teacher trainee, we recommend that your peer panel be composed of other trainees. Your cooperating teacher may be an important resource and a good person to observe you and give feedback, but your peer panel should consist of peers. If as an intern you are assigned to a teaching team, attend team coordinating meetings as an adjunct member. If the team meets as a peer panel periodically, attend those meetings as a guest if you are invited.

Teachers who are regular members of teaching teams generally use the existing team as their peer panel. Their team meetings then may have any of three kinds of agendas: the coordination of planning or teaching tasks, the support function of the peer panel (sharing problems, letting off steam, etc.), or the professional assistance activities of the peer panel (observing, giving feedback, etc.). If you are a member of a teaching team, we strongly recommend that your team find time to meet regularly to deal specifically with the peer panel agenda—support and assistance. We urge you to carve out some time just for professional conversation, apart from the daily responsibilities of planning and teaching.

Peer panel time is just as important for teachers who are not team members, perhaps more important. If your teaching situation does not include team teaching, give careful thought to the possibility of forming peer panels in your school. Perhaps your faculty and administrators can agree to a plan which designates an hour or more of each week as small-group time, in which everyone participates. Group membership can be decided in a number of ways. Faculty wishing to try the peer panel idea could be grouped together. Other faculty could use small-group time to discuss school improvements, write suggestions to the principal, or become involved in other activities as they choose.

The peer panel can be the heart of a general faculty development plan for your school. This book is intended to be a basic support for such a plan and, of course, it is designed to be used with peer panel management. If the time isn't right for the adoption of a general faculty development program, your peer panel can serve as a small support system for its members and at the same time provide a model for the rest of the faculty.

## NOTE TO INSTRUCTORS AND SUPERVISORS

Instructors and supervisors may differ in the way they treat data collected in portfolios. The data are evidence of demonstrated competencies, but you may want to supplement that evidence with personal observations of teaching activities or with other materials. You may want to apply quality standards not included in the book for peer panel use, and you may want to rate portfolio work. In such cases, those requirements can be part of the portfolio expectations that you design beyond those given in the book. For example, some instructors may choose to rate and assign grades to portfolio work and others may prefer to record this work as complete or incomplete according to specifications.

Whatever your preferences, we hope that our comments encourage you to use the peer panel and portfolio system and to give participants the support they will need as they learn the new roles involved. Participants can begin the peer panel process simply by reading this introduction, forming groups and starting one of the chapters. As they do so, you are likely to find that the peer panel process brings changes in the ways you use your time. Facilitating peer panel activities and checking off the portfolio work will be the major new roles. Finally, you do have the option of ignoring the peer panel format and using the book for conventional or other kinds of instruction. However you use it, we invite your reactions to the book and any information about ways you have used it.

## THE PURPOSE OF THIS APPENDIX

The skills of being an effective member of groups such as peer panels are skills that most of us must learn. We do not gain them without effort. The rest of this appendix describes procedures and skills needed in the peer panel approach to professional development. Included here are activities concerned with skills of:

- guiding the work of a peer panel;
- observing a fellow teacher and giving nonjudgmental feedback;
- careful listening and responding to peer panel members;
- analyzing and improving peer panel relationships.

If you are now considering whether to use the peer panel approach, we suggest that you read through the rest of the appendix. As for completing the activities here, panel members will need to complete them together.

## ACTIVITY 1
### Read about the rationale for peer panels.

Forming a peer panel involves finding people who wish to join you, arranging opportunities to meet, and making a commitment to try the process. During the first peer panel meeting, members can use the following section as a basis for discussing plans and next steps for your peer panel.

## A Peer Support System for Professional Development

No one doubts that people do better work when they feel supported. In organizations, however, support is easy to talk about and hard to achieve, and that fact is nowhere more evident than in schools. Most teachers we know feel harried and isolated, not supported. In our judgment, the support problem is neither superficial nor temporary, but deep and fundamental in the structure of the American school. This essay looks at one facet of the problem, the professional relationships among teachers, and it presents a peer support system that has good prospects as a means of managing staff development.

In brief, the system is based on small groups of teachers that have come to be called peer panels. Peer panels take on many of the managerial and supervisory functions of staff development: planning development activities; giving assistance to panel members; serving as a sounding-board for problems and ideas; analyzing teaching and giving feedback; and working as a curriculum development group. The key to the system's success, we believe, is that peer panels follow a set of norms and rules that emphasize nonjudgmental support.

### ORIGINS OF THE PEER PANEL

The peer panel idea emerged from the needs of teachers in Florida's middle schools in the early 1970s. Desegregation and other circumstances brought into

This material, in slightly different form, was first published as an article: Gordon Lawrence and Jan Branch, "Peer Support System as the Heart of Inservice Education." *Theory into Practice* 3 17 (*June 1978*): 245-247.

existence new middle schools, and many teachers who had not prepared themselves to teach ten- to fourteen-year-old students were placed in these schools. The teachers had some clear and immediate needs, including:

- getting accustomed to a different (sometimes radically different) teaching situation;
- developing new teaching competencies; and
- qualifying for a middle school teaching certificate.

As the teachers identified problems to be solved and teaching skills to be developed, they recognized that the existing supervisory personnel could not be stretched to cover all their needs. Workshops and college courses served some needs but often they were not flexible enough to coincide with a teacher's "teachable moment."

Recognizing the problem, the Florida Department of Education sponsored the development of inservice education materials that teachers could use as needed, with or without the assistance of supervisors.[1] All materials were designed so that supervisory functions could be performed by peer panels, and many teachers chose peer panels as a means of managing their inservice work.

## THE PEER PANEL PROCEDURE

What is a peer panel and how does it work? A peer panel is a group of three to five teachers who give each other assistance and support in a variety of ways, mainly to help each member improve in teaching ability. Successful peer panels have followed these support guidelines rather closely:

- Members freely choose each other.
- There are no superordinate-subordinate relationships in the peer panel.
- Matters that are discussed in the peer panel are private to its members except as agreed by all its members.
- Members avoid evaluating each other in the usual sense; instead they follow procedures for giving and receiving low-inference feedback, described below.
- A peer panel tries to work only with an agenda that is above the table.
- Empathy and mutual support are the tone for a peer panel, not detachment and inspection.

Working within these guidelines, what does a peer panel try to accomplish? It has two broad objectives: (1) to serve as an informal support group, for sharing, letting off steam, discussing problems, etc. and (2) to serve as a vehicle for the continuing professional development of its members. As peer panels work toward the second objective, the members *assist* each other, individually and collectively, in several ways:

- They act as a sounding board for one another's self-analysis of needs, and for ideas and plans for improvement.

---

1. State of Florida Department of Education, *Florida Modules on Generic Teaching Competencies*, 1972–1974 (available from PAEC, P.O. Drawer 190, Chipley, Florida 32428).

- They assist each other in analyzing teaching and curriculum, often by systematic observation in each other's classrooms—using low inference measures.
- They give one another low-inference feedback on behavior observed or work analyzed.
- They verify "for the record," if a record of competency development is needed, the member's attaining of an objective in his/her improvement plan.

## LOW-INFERENCE vs. HIGH-INFERENCE MEASUREMENT

Low-inference measurement and feedback are essential to the peer panel procedure. Low-inference observation means that the observer watches and records events according to some prearranged set of relatively objective categories; typically the teacher being observed asks that some particular events be recorded as to their frequency and timing (for example, students' "on-task" or distracted behavior, and the teacher's "smoothness" or "jerkiness" using Kounin's categories of classroom management.[2]) The observer then reports to the teacher the sensory data or facts observed and tries to include in the report little or no inference as to the meaning or value of the data. High-inference assessment, the way people often evaluate each other, is avoided because it interferes with the peer relationship. Peer panel members should not be obliged to pass judgment on each other. High-inference feedback (such as "You were firm and fair—you were not too casual") has some value when it comes from an expert, but expertise is not a prerequisite for being in a peer panel.

Here are some examples of low- and high-inference requests that a teacher may make. We hope the virtues of low-inference requests are obvious.

| Requests Implying High-Inference Judgments | Requests Implying Low-Inference Judgments |
|---|---|
| (a) "Watch my class and tell me what I can do about student motivation." | (a) "Follow these tally sheet instructions, watch the six students in that learning center, and record their on-task and off-task behaviors." |
| (b) "I'm trying to get vague and trite words out of my dialogue with students. Make a list of the bad ones you hear in the next ten minutes." | (b) "Here's a list of vague and trite words I'm trying to quit using. Give me a frequency count on any of them I use in the next ten minutes." |
| (c) "Would you please look over this unit plan and make suggestions for improvement?" | (c) "Do you see any objectives in this unit plan that I haven't covered with at least two activities our low readers can handle?" |

## APPLICATIONS OF THE PEER PANEL

As mentioned previously, the peer panel has been used as a supervisory system for many inservice teachers who were seeking to qualify for a new certification or to

2. J. S. Kounin. *Discipline and Group Management in Classrooms* (New York: Holt, Rinehart and Winston, 1970).

extend an existing one. It has also been used in a field-based college program for a masters degree. For administrative purposes of such programs, each teacher maintains a portfolio of materials that provide evidence of his or her professional growth, e.g., copies of new plans, new materials prepared for students, observation records, student products and other data from students, analyses and solutions, and appropriate feedback from other peer panel members. These materials are relatively low-inference records, many of which have a face-value meaning. The portfolio data are evaluated for quality and quantity by some prearranged process. The peer panel can apply preset criteria to the data or that task can be done by an administrator with whom the teacher has developed an improvement plan. If the work is part of a college-sponsored program, the instructor can evaluate the portfolio.

When schools begin to use the peer panel procedure, the initial process seems to go more smoothly if (a) administrators give the procedure visible and active support; (b) time is set aside during working hours for peer panels to meet; (c) teachers are given some help in understanding and using the process of low-inference measurement and feedback; and (d) peer panels have access to training materials that emphasize low-inference measurement and feedback. The support process, which involves trust relationships within the peer group, will develop gradually as the group works together, and each group should evaluate its own pace. Clearly, the peer support system depends upon the supervisor/administrator's trusting peer panels to work independently.

## RELATED RESEARCH

Research that indirectly bears on the peer panel procedure seems to give it very strong support. A recent comprehensive review of research on inservice education identified a number of patterns in effective inservice programs, including the following.

### Patterns of Effective Inservice Education

1. School-based programs in which teachers participate as helpers to each other and planners of inservice activities tend to have greater success in accomplishing their objectives than do programs which are conducted by college personnel or other outsiders without the assistance of teachers.

2. School-based inservice programs-that emphasize self-instruction by teachers have a strong record of effectiveness (seventeen studies, all reporting significant gains).

3. Inservice education programs that have differentiated training experiences for different teachers (that is, "individualized") are more likely to accomplish their objectives than are programs that have common activities for all participants.

4. Inservice education programs that emphasize demonstrations, supervised trials, and feedback sessions are more likely to accomplish their goals than are programs in which the teacher is expected to store up ideas and behavior prescriptions for future use.

5. Inservice education programs in which teachers share and provide mutual assistance to each other are more likely to accomplish their objectives than are programs in which each teacher works individually, or separately.

6. Teachers are more likely to benefit from inservice programs in which they can choose goals and activities for themselves as contrasted with programs in which the goals and activities are preplanned.[3]

For some of us, the findings are a pleasant surprise because they confirm what our experiences have shown us. The peer panel procedures include all of the six effective patterns described above. The formal and informal evidence surely warrant adoption and testing of the peer panel procedure on a wider scale.

## ACTIVITY 2
### Discuss and plan peer panel activities.

Before your panel continues with the other activities of the appendix, we suggest that your group select the chapter(s) you will use and begin. At the end of this appendix is a set of brief instructions for using each chapter with the peer panel process. Follow the instructions. After your panel has had the experience of working together on one or two chapters, continue with the activities here. Plan to answer these questions at a panel meeting.

### REACTIONS TO PEER PANEL ACTIVITIES

1. How clear was I about my role in the peer panel activities?
2. How readily did I share my ideas with the other members?
3. What were other members' reactions to my ideas—were they helpful, or did they make me defensive?
4. How did I react to other members' ideas—how did they receive my reactions?
5. How freely and clearly was I able to communicate my feelings, both positive and negative, when I was aware of them?
6. How clear was I about other members' feelings during the meeting?
7. To what extent did I feel the other members were my peers, neither senior nor junior, higher nor lower than I?
8. Was the tone of the meeting one of empathy and mutual support or one of impersonal inspection and reaction?
9. What is my evaluation of the accomplishments of the meeting?

Make notes on your personal reactions to the questions so that you will be prepared to communicate at the meeting.

At the same peer panel meeting, save time to examine each of the remaining activities in the appendix and decide how and when they will be carried out. The remaining activities involve practicing and analyzing the skills of peer panel membership. The process skills described below can be practiced only as you use them on tasks such as those in the

---

3. Gordon Lawrence and others. *Patterns of Effective Inservice Education*. Florida Department of Education, 1974 (available from PAEC, P.O. Drawer 190, Chipley, Florida 32428).

chapters. As you pursue the objectives of the chapters and assist each other in observing, analyzing, sharing ideas, and giving feedback, you will be practicing the skills described in this appendix. Your observation skills can be observed and analyzed, and you can receive feedback about them. You can receive feedback on your skills of giving feedback, and so on. Thus, you will alternate attention between the activities of the chapters and the appendix—first the content task, then the peer panel skills, then back to content, etc., until you are confident about your peer panel skills.

We recommend that each member keep notes of the meeting, including decisions made, calendar planned, and actions to be taken.

## ACTIVITY 3
### Take stock of relationships within the peer panel.

The quality of relationships among peer panel members is influenced by the quality of the members' communication skills (skills such as the ones dealt with in this activity and in Activities 4 and 5). To demonstrate the effects, we suggest that you respond to a short instrument, "Peer Panel Relationships." You can respond to it again at the end of these activities and then analyze changes that may appear. Give as accurate a response as you can. Then file it in your portfolio for later comparison.

## Peer Panel Relationships

*Directions:* Think about how peer panel members normally behave toward you. In the parentheses in each of the items below, place the number corresponding to your perceptions of the panel as a whole, using the following scale.

| | |
|---|---|
| 5 Always | 2 Sometimes |
| 4 Almost always | 1 Rarely |
| 3 Usually | 0 Never |

As a group, my peer panel members:

1. (_____) level with me.
2. (_____) get the drift of what I am trying to say.
3. (_____) are interested in me.
4. (_____) provide an atmosphere in which I can be myself.
5. (_____) are completely frank with me.
6. (_____) recognize readily when something is bothering me.
7. (_____) respect me as a person, apart from my skills or status.
8. (_____) accept me for what I am.
9. (_____) feel free to let me know when I "bug" them.
10. (_____) perceive what kind of person I really am.
11. (_____) include me in what's going on.

For the next five items, use this key with reversed numbers:

| | |
|---|---|
| 0 Always | 3 Sometimes |
| 1 Almost always | 4 Rarely |
| 2 Usually | 5 Never |

As a group, my peer panel members:

12. (_____) act "judgmental" with me.
13. (_____) keep things to themselves to spare my feelings.
14. (_____) misconstrue things I say or do.
15. (_____) interrupt me or ignore my comments.
16. (_____) ridicule me or disapprove if I show my peculiarities.

## ACTIVITY 4
### Read about nonjudgmental feedback.

**A.** The reading below offers a rationale and some guidelines for giving and receiving feedback, a process essential to peer panels.

## Nonjudgmental Feedback

It is not surprising that most teachers are uneasy about having another adult examine their work. Examine, analyze, critique, inspect, review ... evaluate. All of the words carry the same undertone: I'm going to be judged. Good or bad, worthy or unworthy. In the shadows of the mind looms the dark-robed judge or the stern parent about to pronounce a judgment ... What did I do wrong this time?

The problem with that kind of judgment is that it makes the receiver feel less in control, less able. An evaluation process that places the teacher in a child role in relation to the big-parent evaluator is not the best process for improving instruction.

The peer panel can make an end-run around that specter of inspection and criticism. Peer panel members are partners in an effort to improve teaching. They never try to play a role of judge, above and outside the improvement process. A judge is never a partner with the one being judged. In the peer panel, evaluation is replaced by feedback. Feedback always implies partnership or collaboration, while evaluation does not. The pilot and the flight controller in the tower, for example, are collaborators, even when strangers to each other. The flight controller gives the pilot feedback as the pilot makes course adjustments. The purpose of feedback to pilots is not to evaluate or rate their performance, but to help them adjust their performance so they can reach the objective. The collaboration requires trust, a common language, an agreed-upon objective, and a system of feedback that both understand. All of these conditions apply to the peer panel.

Peer panels are not likely to start out with widespread trust among the members. Trust builds gradually as a byproduct of successful collaboration or partnership. So at the outset peer panels should focus on the following.

1. An intent to form a partnership
2. An agreed-upon agenda
3. A common language, that is, clear ways of talking about peer panel activities
4. A system of feedback understood by all
5. An avoidance of evaluation, passing judgment on each other

The peer panel activities in this book call for nonjudgmental (nonevaluative) feedback. They offer a pattern for you to follow when you ask for feedback beyond the book's activities. Below is a set of guidelines for giving and receiving feedback. This is the process we had in mind as we designed the activities. Read it carefully. These guidelines have been used extensively. They work. But they are guidelines, not rules. Your peer panel may well find variations or exceptions that work better for you. Duplicate as many copies as you need for the feedback practice sessions described in the next activity.

## GUIDELINES FOR GIVING AND RECEIVING FEEDBACK[4]

When you are a *giver* of feedback, you:

_____ 1. Check the readiness of the receiver, find out what sort of feedback is expected.

_____ 2. Describe and don't interpret what you observed. Like a camera, you report what you see without elaboration.

_____ 3. Report recent events, fresh in memory.

_____ 4. Check timing, give feedback at suitable times.

_____ 5. Offer feedback specifically about things that *can be changed*.

_____ 6. Avoid requesting or urging a change in the receiver.

_____ 7. Avoid giving an overload of messages.

_____ 8. Really offer help rather than just unload feelings or biases. ("Help" that isn't perceived as help, isn't help.)

_____ 9. Share something of your own concerns; avoid lecturing and "one-upmanship."

_____ 10. Offer personal reactions *only after* being asked for them.

When you are a *receiver* of feedback, you:

_____ 1. Before the feedback is given, state specifically what you want feedback about.

---

4. Adapted from C. Jung and others, *Interpersonal Communications*. Portland, Oregon: Northwest Regional Educational Laboratory, 1972, pages 112–113.

_____ 2. Check to be sure you understand what the giver is trying to say.

_____ 3. Share your reactions to the feedback. Your reactions help the giver to improve feedback skills and to tune in to your feelings.

**B.** When peer panels are new, and members are just developing feedback skills, we strongly recommend that you try to keep feedback messages at a *low-inference* level. Low-inference feedback is the least likely to be judgmental. The activities of the book generally provide a way for panel members to give low-inference feedback. We suggest you reread the section "Low Inference vs. High Inference," in the first activity of the appendix. Then read the section below, "Low-Inference Measurement." Practice low-inference requests when you use the feedback skills. We believe this is the fastest route to development of greater trust within the peer panel.

## Low-Inference Measurement[5]

Tools for measuring behavior range along a continuum from high to low inference. High inference means that the tool or technique requires its user to infer one thing from another, to make a value judgment. For example, a rating sheet that asks an observer to score a teacher somewhere on a scale from "friendly" to "aloof" calls for quite a high inference. The observer must accumulate a number of bits of sensory data and make a judgment, placing a single mark on the scale. Because no criteria are given with the scale, another observer might be sensitive to quite different data and give a different rating.

Low inference means that the measurer is asked to *report* sensory data and include little or no inferring as to the meaning or value of the data. A well-known measure of teacher behavior, Flanders' Interaction Analysis System, has an observer tally, among other things, the number of teacher statements of praise and criticism that occur in a specific time period. That is a relatively low-inference measure. The outcome of that measurement, added to other measures, might make possible a judgment about "friendliness" and "aloofness." However, that judgment is not for the observer to make. Moreover, "praise" and "criticism" are categories of behavior that a teacher can do something about; "friendliness" and "aloofness" are categories that offer little guidance as to what behaviors the teacher might change if he or she wanted to.

To sum up, a low-inference measure requires the measurer to report data and not make judgments (or make only low-order judgments). It should be added that low-inference data have a more constant meaning than do high-inference reports. A "C" in mathematics on a student report card, or a score of 82, are examples of high-inference data that mean different things to different people. A file of a student's mathematics work sends a lower-inference message.

_____

5. From Gordon Lawrence and Charles Branch, *Guidelines for Developing a Competency Based Inservice Teacher Education Program.* State of Florida, Department of Education, 1974, p. 20.

## ACTIVITY 5
### Practice feedback skills.

Feedback skills simply do not develop without practice. To practice feedback skills, your peer panel needs to plan a round-robin schedule in which one member asks for feedback, one gives it, and one or more observe the process. If your peer panel has three members, you will each cycle through the three roles. If there are four or five members, the fourth and fifth members are also observers in the first cycle. The instructions for the process assume five members, but may be altered to suit a smaller number.

Select a task that calls for each member to practice a skill and receive feedback from another member. For example, Activity 6 in Chapter Three, "Intellectual Development: Ten to Fourteen," calls for an observer to record the pacing of a question-answer dialogue in the classroom of a peer panel member. When the observed teacher (A) and the observer (B) discuss the observation results, they can use the feedback skills of this activity. As A and B talk and try to use feedback skills, other peer panel members (C, D, and E) listen and then give reactions to A and B. The chart on page 350 offers a sequence for feedback practice sessions. It can be used for any kind of feedback practice: observation, analysis of a lesson plan or a teacher-made test, reaction to the handling of a student's problem, etc.

1. At a peer panel meeting, agree on who will undertake development of what skills and who will observe or analyze. Assign names to the chart.
2. The member who needs feedback will arrange with other members to have the needed help provided. Work through one or more of the feedback cycles. Do not rush the process. Remember that the overall objective of the process is to give help and support to each other. The receiver of feedback will be sure that each member has a copy of the "Guidelines for Giving and Receiving Feedback."
3. The receiver of feedback begins the conversation, reviewing the purposes of the feedback. The receiver and giver then carry their dialogue to completion, following the guidelines.
4. During the dialogue, the observers take notes on what they see and hear as illustrations of the guidelines being used or not used in the dialogue.
5. When the dialogue is completed, the observers report their observations as specifically and objectively as they can. Observers follow the same guidelines for giving feedback, with particular attention to guidelines 2, 8, 9, and 10.
6. When each observer has finished reporting, the other members share their reactions to the reports. They should also comment on whether the reporting process followed the feedback guidelines.
7. When discussion of the first cycle process is finished, the second cycle can begin. The second cycle follows the same pattern but with each person taking a different role.
8. Each member keeps notes and a short description of the process to be filed in the portfolio.

The feedback analysis cycles may not need to be continued beyond one complete round, but we recommend that the guidelines sheet be used regularly as a simple check list whenever members are giving and receiving feedback. Following the guidelines and using low-inference judgment helps people avoid some of the risks and traps that weaken the value of observation and feedback. Some of these traps include:

- Prejudgments—having a mind-set of what one will see before actually observing
- Snap judgments—deciding too quickly on first impressions
- Projection—the risk of attributing to the observed person one's own motives and faults
- Distractibility—attending to unrelated matters or being preoccupied with other thoughts

Used correctly, the feedback process is surprisingly powerful. Its use, of course, is not limited to professional development purposes. The principles are valid in all aspects of personal and public life.

|  | PERSON A | PERSON B | PERSON C | PERSON D | PERSON E |
|---|---|---|---|---|---|
| Cycle 1 | Ask for observation or anlaysis; ask for feedback | Observe or analyze A's work; give feedback | Observer 1. of feedback process | Observer 2. of feedback process | Observer 3. of feedback process |
| Cycle 2 | Observer 3. of feedback process | Ask for observation or analysis; ask for feedback | Observe or analyze B's work; give feedback | Observer 1. of feedback process | Observer 2. of feedback process |
| Cycle 3 | Observer 2. of feedback process | Observer 3. of feedback process | Ask for observation or analysis; ask for feedback | Observe or analyze C's work; give feedback | Observer 1. of feedback process |
| Cycle 4 | Observer 1. of feedback process | Observer 2. of feedback process | Observer 3. of feedback process | Ask for observation or analysis; ask for feedback | Observe or analyze D's work; give feedback |
| Cycle 5 | Observe or analyze E's work; give feedback | Observer 1. of feedback process | Observer 2. of feedback process | Observer 3. of feedback process | Ask for observation or analysis; ask for feedback |

*Explanation of the chart:* During the first cycle, A and B are the receiver and the giver of feedback. A arranges with B to observe in A's classroom or to analyze some of A's plans or other work. At the appropriate time, B gives feedback, with C, D, and E observing the feedback dialogue. All will have copies of the "Guidelines for Giving and Receiving Feedback." C (Observer 1) will watch the *giver* of feedback, using guidelines 1 through 5. D (Observer 2) will also watch the *giver*, but will use only guidelines 6 through 10. E (Observer 3) will watch the *receiver*, using the three receiver guidelines. If your peer panel has four members, one observer will watch the giver of feedback, using all ten guidelines, and one will watch the receiver. If your peer panel has three members, the work of Observer 1, 2, and 3 are all done by one person.

## ACTIVITY 6
**Read "Guidelines for Classroom Observation."**

## Guidelines for Classroom Observation

When one is applying the idea of low-inference feedback to observation in another teacher's classroom, it helps to have more specific guidelines than the thirteen general ones you have already used. Robert Goldhammer,[6] Morris Cogan[7] and others have carefully developed observation guidelines for supervisors that can be adapted to the peer panel situation. The total sequence has five stages: a preobservation conference; the observation; postobservation analysis and conference preparation; postobservation conference; and feedback to the observer (the feedback giver).

### STAGE ONE: PREOBSERVATION CONFERENCE

The teacher who will be observed and will receive feedback (the receiver) arranges the meeting. This person's initiatives, thought patterns, perceptions, vocabulary, and ways of defining problems become the framework within which the whole observation and feedback process occurs. The person who will observe and give feedback (the giver) uses this conference to learn the receiver's framework and to get a clear idea of what the observation task is. If either person has anxieties about the observing, this "getting acquainted" dialogue should help to relieve them. A third member, a process observer, attends the meeting, but does not observe in the classroom. This person monitors the dialogue of giver and receiver and works to assist the dialogue.

A. The receiver describes the students, the curriculum, and the classroom environment (that is, if the giver is not already familiar with them).

B. The receiver describes the purpose of the observation, the problem or the giver's observation task. If the receiver's task is one specified by this book, then the giver's task should be easy to determine. If the receiver's request is not stated in low-inference terms, the giver's questions should try to get the task restated in low-inference terms. Usually the receiver's framework becomes clear by this time.

C. The receiver presents a written plan of what will happen in the classroom, including objective(s), materials, groupings, procedures, etc.

D. The logistics of the observation visit are discussed, including where the visitor will sit.

---

6. R. Goldhammer, *Clinical Supervision* (New York: Holt, Rinehart & Winston, 1969).

7. M. Cogan, *Clinical Supervision* (Boston: Houghton Mifflin Co., 1973).

E. The discussion may result in some revisions to the lesson plan, but the giver does not offer criticisms or suggestions outside the receiver's framework.

## STAGE TWO: OBSERVATION

A. Besides recording classroom events according to the prearranged plan, the visitor (giver) takes notes, as time permits, about the context of what is being recorded; e.g., the activity that takes place, the way that it is introduced, the number of students involved, the time of day, and the physical setting. The notes also include anecdotes and verbatim dialogue that will illustrate the events.
B. Recorded data should be as factual and as low inference as possible.
C. Some way of recording the timing and sequence of events is often useful.
D. The visitor should be as unobtrusive as possible and not interfere in classroom events except by explicit agreement with the teacher (receiver).

## STAGE THREE: POSTOBSERVATION ANALYSIS AND CONFERENCE PREPARATION

Generally, the giver will need to organize the notes before sharing them with the receiver. Stage Three entails the giver working alone to prepare the feedback data.

A. The observation data are put in a form that the receiver can keep and clearly understand when referring to them at some future time.
B. The giver looks for patterns in the data, such as sequences of behavior or patterns that relate to the observation task agreed upon.
C. The giver reviews the guidelines for giving feedback so as to plan what to say in the conference with the receiver.

## STAGE FOUR: POSTOBSERVATION CONFERENCE

A. The conference occurs as soon after the observation as can be arranged— on the same day if possible. The process observer is also present to observe the feedback process and to report those observations.
B. The giver begins by reviewing his or her understanding of the agreed upon observation task. When the receiver agrees with the giver's definition of the task, the giver offers the feedback in the manner planned in Stage Three.
C. The giver-receiver dialogue continues as long as needed. The members should feel free to use the feedback guidelines as a reminder.
D. The giver does not offer opinions or suggestions or carry the dialogue outside the receiver's framework until specifically requested by the receiver.

## STAGE FIVE: FEEDBACK TO THE GIVER

A. When the feedback dialogue has ended, the process observer reports whether or not the guidelines were followed out and, if asked, comments on other aspects of pre- and post-conferences.
B. The receiver also has the opportunity to offer reactions to the feedback.

## ACTIVITY 7
### Practice skills of classroom observation.

The objective is to follow the "Guidelines for Classroom Observation" in giving and receiving help. We recommend that you and two other panel members form a helping trio, each in turn being a receiver of help, a giver of help, and a process observer.

1. The receiver in the first cycle arranges a preobservation conference, attended by the other two members. The process observer helps the other two follow the guidelines. All three keep their own notes.
2. A classroom observation is arranged. Only the giver of feedback visits the classroom, not the third member. The giver follows the guidelines through the observation and postobservation strategy stage.
3. The postobservation conference is arranged by the giver of feedback, but all three attend. The process observer makes notes and reports specific ways the giver and receiver did or did not follow the guidelines. The process observer, of course, follows the guidelines for giving low-inference feedback. All three then share their reactions to the process. The next cycle, with each member shifting roles, can be planned before the meeting ends. Make notes covering each cycle and file them in your portfolio.

## ACTIVITY 8
### Consider gains you have made in peer panel relationships.

Since you began these activities you have worked on several skills of group membership and have met several times with members of your peer panel. Have your relationships in the peer panel improved as your skills have increased? You can get one indication of growth by responding to the instrument, "Peer Panel Relationships—Form 2." Use the instrument without referring to your first responses (Activity 3). Tally your sub-scores as indicated on the instrument and then compare the "before" and "after" scores.

Convene the peer panel, after each member has responded to the instrument. Include the instrument results on your agenda as well as any other aspects of the appendix activities that members suggest.

To discuss the instrument results, the members need not tell their scores to the others. We suggest that one member prepare four slips of paper to pass out to each person. Each person will receive a slip with *genuineness* written on it. Each person will write the genuineness "before" and "after" score, for example, before, 9; after, 15. The process will be repeated for scores on *understanding, valuing,* and *appreciation.* Discuss each set of scores when they are collected. Each person may take a turn describing an aspect of group relationships that has improved and an aspect that needs further development. Allow enough time for each member to comment about each of the four categories of the instrument.

Each of the chapters of the book is concluded with a suggestion of Next Steps to pursue. The next steps in the development of teamwork and support relationships should begin with this peer panel meeting.

From your analysis of the results from the Peer Panel Relationships instrument, consider what aspects of your group relationships need further development. Re-examine the resources you used in this appendix and decide whether additional work is needed with some of those.

## Peer Panel Relationships—Form 2

*Directions:* Think about how peer panel members normally behave toward you. In the parentheses in front of the items below, place the number corresponding to your perceptions of the panel as a whole, using the following scale.

5 Always          2 Sometimes
4 Almost always   1 Rarely
3 Usually         0 Never

As a group, my peer panel members:

1. (_____) level with me.
2. (_____) get the drift of what I am trying to say.
3. (_____) are interested in me.
4. (_____) provide an atomsphere in which I can be myself.
5. (_____) are completely frank with me.
6. (_____) recognize readily when something is bothering me.
7. (_____) respect me as a person, apart from my skills or status.
8. (_____) accept me for what I am.
9. (_____) feel free to let me know when I "bug" them.
10. (_____) perceive what kind of person I really am.
11. (_____) include me in what's going on.

For the next five items, use this key with reversed numbers:

0 Always          3 Sometimes
1 Almost always   4 Rarely
2 Usually         5 Never

As a group, my peer panel members:

12. (_____) act "judgmental" with me.
13. (_____) keep things to themselves to spare my feelings.
14. (_____) misconstrue things I say or do.
15. (_____) interrupt me or ignore my comments.
16. (_____) ridicule me or disapprove if I show my peculiarities.

## SCORING THE INSTRUMENT

Items 1, 5, 9, and 13 indicate *genuineness* in relationships. Add the *genuineness* scores and record your totals below. Items 2, 6, 10, and 14 indicate *understanding* in relationships. Add your *understanding* scores and record them. Items 3, 7, 11, and 15 indicate *valuing* in relationships. Add your *valuing* scores and record them. Finally, items 4, 8, 12, and 16 indicate *acceptance* in relationships. Add your *acceptance* scores and record them.

|  | Genuineness | Understanding | Valuing | Acceptance |
|---|---|---|---|---|
| Before | _____ | _____ | _____ | _____ |
| After | _____ | _____ | _____ | _____ |

## Suggested Agendas for Peer Panel Meetings for Each Chapter

### CHAPTER ONE Childhood into Adolescence

**A.** If your peer panel members are using Chapter One at the same time as you, hold the meeting after each member has completed Activity 4. If you are the only member using this chapter, explain its activities to them before you share your results with them.

**B.** Each member shares reactions and reflections on Activities 1 and 2.

**C.** Each member who did Activity 3 relates his or her analysis and interpretation of, and feelings about, the students' autobiographical sketches. Did the students' responses change in some ways your perceptions of them? Read aloud any portions of your autobiographical sketch you wish to share.

**D.** Each member shares his or her analysis of the school as prepared in Activity 4. Two possible ways of sharing analyses are to pass sheets around the group and then discuss each of them or to read aloud in sequence the responses to number one and discuss them, then number two, and so on. Discuss the value of the twelve needs statements.

**E.** Make notes of the peer panel meeting and put them in your portfolio— along with samples of students' papers (A Thirteen-Year-Old Looks Back) and your other notes and analyses.

### CHAPTER TWO Physical Development: Ten to Fourteen

The agenda of the meeting should include:

A. Sharing each member's observation results and conclusions from Activities 1 and 2.

B. Comparing and discussing each other's lists of what students need in the school setting to accommodate their physical development (from Activity 3).

C. Receiving feedback on specific changes implemented in Activity 4.

D. Receiving suggestions for further changes and for additional ways of measuring the effects of changes made.

E. Holding a wrap-up discussion to compare results, to share insights, and to consider possibilities for future changes.

## CHAPTER THREE Intellectual Development: Ten to Fourteen

Your peer panel meeting will have a large agenda, covering all the activities of the chapter. Schedule time accordingly. Take to the meeting the following materials:

- Cards containing student responses to the question, "Why should people generally do everything they can to keep from breaking the law?" Include your own analysis and reactions (Activity 1).
- Notes and self-quiz on "Mental Development Processes in Transescence" (Activity 2). Decide what aspects of this material you want to discuss in the meeting.
- Notes on your interviews with four (or six) students (Activity 3).
- Your written analysis of a textbook or other instructional material (Activity 4).
- Your lesson plan(s) for leading students from concrete experience into abstract reasoning, and notes on its implementation (Activity 5).
- The record of your efforts to improve wait time and related improvements in the quality of student thinking (Activity 6).
- Samples of students' questions and comments that show a shift from pat-answer to reflective thinking (Activity 7).

Your panel can use this list as an agenda. We suggest that members take turns leading off on agenda items.

## CHAPTER FOUR Social and Emotional Development: Ten to Fourteen

The agenda for the meeting will cover all the activities you selected and undertook in this chapter. Take to the meeting any of the following materials that you have:

- Reaction notes on the reading, "Social Development: Myths and Facts" (Activity 1).
- Report of two goals, classroom plans, written reactions of colleagues, and a record of outcomes you obtained in Activity 2.
- Notes and observations to identify students' social maturity (Activity 3A).
- Log of the shadow study (Activity 3B).
- Notes on students' journals and perhaps some sample journals that students are willing to have someone else read (Activity 3C).
- Tabulation of responses to student questionnaire and your analysis of the responses (Activity 3D).
- Notes on students' "Who Am I?" collages, and sample collages that students are willing to share (Activity 3E).
- Samples of students' activity logs from students who are willing to have the logs shared (Activity 3F).

- Lists and analysis notes of students' colloquial expressions (Activity 3G).
- Observation records and analysis notes from observations of boys and girls outside and inside school (Activity 4A).
- Notes from interviews with teachers about students' social behavior (Activity 4B).
- Lists that show your analysis of ways that school structure helps or impedes social development (Activity 4C).
- "Before" and "after" records and your notes of an experiment in changing your teaching behavior (Activity 4D).

This is a fairly long agenda. Plan to have materials prepared in a way that they can be shared and discussed with an efficient use of time. Your peer panel may prefer to divide the agenda into two meetings so that members' outcomes and insights can be fully discussed.

**CHAPTER FIVE Understanding the Middle School Concept**

We suggest that the final meeting for this chapter center upon your results from Activities 1, 4, 5, and 6; and a final writing activity described below. Bring to the meeting and discuss:

- Notes from your visit to a school (Activity 1).
- Your analysis of a school's program (Activity 4).
- Your reactions to and questions about three school schedules (Activity 5).
- Notes of consensus on school priorities (Activity 6).

Finally, complete either A or B and bring your written results to the meeting. This can serve as a way to check the level of attainment you have reached:

A. Write a one or two page statement entitled "The Emerging Middle School: Who, What, Why?" Summarize the essentials of the rationale of the middle-school movement and the basic elements of a fully functioning middle school.
B. Assume you are involved in a discussion with a parent who knows little about the middle school concept. The parent asks you several of the following questions which you want to answer well. Write out your answers to these questions.
   1. "Why do we need to go to all the trouble of reorganizing the intermediate grades? Why is a middle school better?"
   2. "Can you tell me, in a few words, just what a middle school is?"
   3. "Can the middle school emphasize personal development and exploration without cutting down on attention to the basics?"
C. Exchange your statements from part A or B with your peers and compare ideas. Discuss the differences. Insert the written material into your portfolio.

**CHAPTER SIX Team Planning and Support Skills**

Chapter Six has no culminating meeting because the team meets as a peer panel as part of the activities of the chapter.

## CHAPTER SEVEN Exploration in the Curriculum

If you have completed this chapter successfully, you can report and share information and materials on:

A. Your analysis of a school's exploratory curriculum (Activity 1)
B. A rationale for an exploratory curriculum in middle grades (Activity 2, reading notes)
C. Examples of an exploratory emphasis and of specific exploratory programs (Bring your reactions to the three exploratory programs described in Activity 3.)
D. Ways to modify a school schedule to accommodate a greater emphasis on exploration (Activity 5)
E. Your own plan for designing, implementing, and evaluating a special exploratory program (Activity 7)
F. Your version of an exploratory minicourse (Activity 8)

## CHAPTER EIGHT The Teacher as Advisor

Plan to share and discuss all your work related to the chapter. The meeting agenda can be based on these materials:

A. Your answers to questions about affective education (Activity 1)
B. Your summary description and analysis of an affective education program (Activity 1)
C. Information you have found and names of additional printed sources about affective education (Activity 2)
D. Your file of "Ideas for Affective Education" (Activity 3)
E. Your notes on nonprint sources for affective education (Activity 4)
F. Your reactions to participating in affective education activities (Activity 5)
G. Your outline for a year-long affective education program (Activity 6)
H. Your responses to the "What if . . . ?" questions (Activity 7)

## CHAPTER NINE The Other Side of Discipline: Helping Students Take Responsibility

This is a long chapter with many outcomes to share. Depending upon how many members are involved with these activities, you may need several meetings. For example, you may be ready for a meeting after Activity 5 is completed (agenda items A through G below); a meeting after Activity 8 (to cover items H, I, and J); and the last meeting for items K and L.

A. Results of student survey and discussion on feeling responsible (Activity 1)
B. Analysis of school structure: features that discourage responsibility-taking (Activity 2)
C. Diagrams of each person's most typical lesson patterns (Activity 3)
D. Diagrams and descriptions of new lesson patterns devised, and descriptions of results with students (Activity 3)
E. Results of student session on school and classroom rules (Activity 4)

  F. Reactions to "The Ideal *vs* The Real Teacher" (Activity 5)

  G. Analysis of sanctioning scores and reactions to the research on teacher approval and disapproval (Activity 6)

  H. From Activity 7, discuss:
    — the list of your own most-used sanctioning phrases and your reaction notes
    — your goals for change in your uses of sanctioning
    — fifteen nonjudgmental responses you converted from sanctioning responses
    — analysis of observations made to show your changes in the use of sanctioning

  I. From Activity 8, discuss:
    — the list of your controlling statements (from a tape)
    — your estimate of control-time/content-time
    — your analysis of ways to reduce controlling time
    — your plan for change (uses of control) and your log of progress
    — list of converted commands
    — student responsibility lists and your analysis of them

  J. From Activity 9, discuss:
    — tally and notes from student survey on responsibility climate of the classroom
    — notes on discussion about fear of failure

  K. From Activity 10, discuss:
    — your paper on ways to bring students into the school and classroom planning processes
    — your self-rating on classroom management

  L. From Activity 11, discuss:
    — tally of student survey on classroom management and/or observer's report on your management behaviors
    — your plan of changes, and changes accomplished

  M. From Activity 12, discuss:
    — comparison of "before" and "after" samples of student responsible/dependent talk; your plan of changes; and changes accomplished

  N. From Activity 13, discuss your written plan for student independent study

## CHAPTER 10 Mastery Learning

We suggest six agenda items, one for each activity in the chapter:

  A. Your answers to questions about master learning concepts (Activity 1)

  B. Your analysis of a year-long curriculum, broken into smaller units (Activity 2)

  C. Precise objectives to match the small curriculum units (Activity 3)

  D. Learning activities designed for mastery learning of selected objectives (Activity 4)

    E.  Samples of formative and summative evaluations of the selected objectives (Activity 5)

    F.  Your record of implementing a pilot mastery learning program—the rationale, design, and your evaluation of outcomes (Activity 6)

## CHAPTER ELEVEN Preparing Learning Activity Packs

When you have wrapped up the evaluation of your first unipac, share what happened with your colleagues during the next peer panel session. Bring in samples of what you did. Talk about what happened: what went right, or wrong; advantages and disadvantages of unipacs as you now see it; other ways to use them, etc. Find out what others working in this chapter have done. Include notes from the meeting in your portfolio, along with the materials you produced as a part of this chapter.

## CHAPTER TWELVE Designing Learning Centers

To conclude the work of this chapter, bring to a peer panel meeting samples of activities and materials from your center. If you can, display the whole center. Talk about: What went right or wrong; what changes you may make; advantages and disadvantages of learning centers; other ways to use them. You may even want to find out how your colleagues designed the following: orientation, student movement, evaluation, and record keeping. Include the notes from the meeting in your portfolio.